FOURTH EDITION

THE STRENGTHS PERSPECTIVE IN SOCIAL WORK PRACTICE

Edited by

DENNIS SALEEBEY, PROFESSOR EMERITUS

University of Kansas

PEARSON

and

Boston ▪ New York ▪ San Francisco
Mexico City ▪ Montreal ▪ Toronto ▪ London ▪ Madrid ▪ Munich ▪ Paris
Hong Kong ▪ Singapore ▪ Tokyo ▪ Cape Town ▪ Sydney

Series Editor: Patricia Quinlin
Series Editorial Assistant: Sara Holliday
Marketing Manager: Laura Lee Manley
Editorial-Production Service: Whitney Acres Editorial
Manufacturing Buyer: JoAnne Sweeney
Electronic Composition: Omegatype Typography, Inc.
Cover Administrator: Joel Gendron

For related titles and support materials, visit our online catalog at www.ablongman.com.

Between the time website information is gathered and then published, it is not unusual for some sites to have closed. Also, the transcription of URLs can result in typographical errors. The publisher would appreciate notification where these occur.

Library of Congress Cataloging-in-Publication Data

The strengths perspective in social work practice / edited by Dennis Saleebey.—4th ed.
     p. cm.
   Includes bibliographical references and index.
   ISBN 0-205-40817-6 (paper)
    1. Social service—Psychological aspects.   I. Saleebey, Dennis.

  HV41.S827   2005
  361.3'2'0973—dc22

                                            2005043121

To my family:
My mother and father, June Hoff and Ted Saleebey, the seeds of my
strength; my children, Jennifer, David, John, and Meghan, whose growth is
the definition of possibility; and Ann, my wife, whose wisdom I count on,
and whose shoulder I lean on.

In Memoriam

June Celestine Hoff
Bette A. Saleebey
Liane V. Davis
Howard Goldstein

Their strengths are found yet in the lives of others.

Nothing worth doing is completed in our lifetime; therefore we must be saved by hope. Nothing true or beautiful or good makes complete sense in the immediate context of history; therefore we must be saved by faith. Nothing we do, however virtuous, can be accomplished alone; therefore we are saved by love.

—Reinhold Niebuhr (*The Irony of History*)

We confide in our strength, without boasting of it;
We respect that of others, without fearing it.

—Thomas Jefferson (Letter to William Carmichael and William Short)

CONTENTS

v

PART THREE   STRENGTHS-BASED ASSESSMENT AND APPROACHES TO PRACTICE

CHAPTER FIVE

The Strengths Approach to Practice   77

Dennis Saleebey

CHAPTER SIX

Assessing Strengths: The Political Context of Individual, Family, and Community Empowerment   93

Charles D. Cowger, Kim M. Anderson, and Carol A. Snively

CHAPTER SEVEN

Solving Problems from a Strengths Perspective   116

Ann Weick, James Kreider, and Ronna Chamberlain

CHAPTER EIGHT

Strengths-Based Case Management: Enhancing Treatment for Persons with Substance Abuse Problems   128

Richard C. Rapp

CHAPTER NINE

The Strengths Model with Older Adults: Critical Practice Components   148

Holly Nelson-Becker, Rosemary Chapin, and Becky Fast

CHAPTER TEN

The Opportunities and Challenges of Strengths-Based, Person-Centered Practice: Purpose, Principles, and Applications in a Climate of Systems' Integration   171

Walter E. Kisthardt

CHAPTER ELEVEN

Using Strengths-Based Practice to Tap the Resilience of Families   197

Bonnie Benard

PART FOUR   STRENGTHS IN CONTEXT

CHAPTER TWELVE

"That History Becomes You": Slave Narratives and Today's Movement to End Poverty   221

Willie Baptist, Mary Bricker-Jenkins, Sarah Gentry, Marsha Johnson, and Corrine Novak

---

CHAPTER THIRTEEN

Community Development, Neighborhood Empowerment, and Individual Resilience   241

Dennis Saleebey

FOREWORD

The strengths perspective will not go away. Despite the continued dominance of deficit and disease orientations in the social and behavioral sciences, the voice of the strength perspective persists, unobtrusively making inroads into the collective consciousness of social judgments.

Since the publication of the first edition of this book in 1992, the strengths perspective has become a staple of social work education programs across the United States and in other parts of the world. It has influenced thinking and practice not only in social work, but in psychology (where it has appeared in somewhat different guise as "positive psychology") and various sub-fields of the social sciences. The chapters in this book (as in the previous editions) attest to its ongoing development and its application in an increasing number of contexts. The publication of a fourth edition also suggests continued interest among practitioners and educators.

Because the strengths perspective is neither prescriptive nor tied to specific techniques, its influence on everyday practice may elude both the casual observer and those who measure the minutia of social intercourse. Rather, its influence tends to be contextual, observers are repositioned in a way that allow them to "see" new possibilities. Through its lens, people, organizations, and communities are understood from a different standpoint. This understanding may require finding new words or ways of using words (for example, "at promise" instead of "at risk"), suspending belief in the taken-for-granted, and thinking counter to "the evidence." It requires becoming "naive," a term used by the organizational psychologist Karl Weick to mean "reject[ing] received wisdom that something is a problem," "start[ing] with fewer preconceptions," and "favor[ing] optimism." It is not easy to shift perception or unlearn past truths. Doing so also carries risks. These are not easy tasks. Inventing new expressions risks obfuscation, questioning the self-evident or the "scientifically documented" risks charges of irreverence or extremism.

The field of aging provides an illustrative example. Understanding aging as a process of decline characterized by diminished capacities and infirmities is deeply ingrained in our culture. Such a process seems to reflect "the way things are." Support for this impression can be found in gerontological research journals replete with reports "documenting" the various declines associated with aging. Recently, however, other voices have surfaced that question these "facts." For example, Ken Gergen and Mary Gergen in their *Positive Aging Newsletter* (2004), identified various limitations of the gerontological research literature (using the research on cognitive decline as an example) including: searching for deficits rather than positive characteristics, ignoring the influence of contextual demands, reporting trivial differences and capacities, attributing cause to aging rather than other plausible factors, and overgeneralizing findings to (and underestimating variability among) elders as a group. Given these limitations, other more positive interpretations may be equally likely.

It seems to me that these limitations also apply, in varying degrees, to research in other areas. The point is not that one interpretation is right and the other wrong, but that the complexity of social life enables us to construe people and situations in multiple ways. Given the dominance of the deficit model, the strengths perspective provides an important, alternative way of interpreting human life in which unassailable truths and inevitable processes may be neither. This realization invites new stories of hope and refocuses our attention toward heretofore unrecognized resources. Dennis Saleebey and his colleagues tell such stories and remind us that the limits on someone's potential may be more cultural than existential.

Given that it has been more than a decade since the first edition of this book appeared, readers might wonder why this approach has remained merely a "perspective." If progress has really been made, why is there not a strengths theory? In response, I want to suggest that there are good reasons for maintaining perspective (pun intended). Theory, in the formal sense, while potentially useful implies an esoteric type of knowledge that is not easy to understand and to which only "experts" have access. In contrast, "perspective" is a word of everyday language. In common usage, according to my dictionary, it has several meanings: 1.) a way of viewing a subject or situation, such as a historical or philosophical perspective; 2.) a particular point-of-view, as in a feminist perspective or a client's perspective; 3.) a reasoned or complete understanding of a situation, as in "laughter helped me put my problems in perspective"; and 4.) the way objects appear relative to each other and to their distance from the viewer.

The term "strengths perspective" suggests all of these definitions. It certainly is a way of viewing people and situations (definition one) although as an intellectual framework it is more integrative than distinct. Second, the strengths perspective may be considered to promote a particular point-of-view, one that privileges accomplishments over failure, health over disease, and resources over deficits. Nevertheless, this is not a perspective of naive optimism or superficial wish-fulfillment. Life's brutalities and pain are accorded due respect and soothing balms are applied where possible. Such adverse experiences are not, however, given "master status," taken as the entirety or even the most significant aspects of a person's life. Rather, and here we come to the third definition, the strengths perspective fills in the gaps of theories that reify diagnoses or emphasize defects, providing balance and relation to the various dimensions of lives. Finally, consistent with the fourth definition, the strengths perspective reminds us that the way something appears is relative to where you are, not only physically, but culturally, historically, geographically, emotionally, and spiritually.

There is no "non-perspective" position. We all have multiple perspectives influenced by, among others, our location in the world, nationality, social class, gender, education, and experiences. These perspectives can also change in light of new information or experience; for example, "I gained a new perspective on poverty after living in a public housing project." The strengths perspective reminds us that there is nothing obligatory or sacrosanct about any particular perspective. Why some choices seem to make sense or are dominant may have more to do with historical and cultural factors than with the degree of correspondence between a position and "reality." So there is choice. Adopting the strengths perspective is to enter this melange of possibilities, not asserting the truth, but rather proposing that our attempts to help others may be enhanced. And as experienced practitioners know, in the process of trying to change others, we ourselves change. Thus it is not uncommon for those who diligently apply the strengths perspective to report after some time that they experience the world differently. There's nothing magical about this. The social world is highly variegated and complex. It "offers itself up to [our] imagination" according to the poet, Mary Oliver. This book invites us to imagine a world in which all people are treated with respect and dignity. A world where even the most downtrodden and debilitated can harbor and pursue a dream of a better life. Where no limits are placed on the individual potential. And where our natural inclinations toward health and well-being are identified and nurtured. For those new to the strengths perspective, I hope that reading this book will be a doorway to this world and that it will enrich your relationships, professional and personal, with others.

Stanley Witkin, Ph.D.,
Professor, University of Vermont

REFERENCES

Gergen, K., & Gergen, M. (2003). Questioning Cognitive Decline in Aging. *The Positive Aging Newsletter,* No. 22, http://www.healthandage.com

Oliver, M. (1986). Wild geese. *Dream Work.* Boston: Atlantic Monthly Press.

Weick, K. (2001). *Making Sense of the Organization.* (pp. 438–9). NY: Oxford, UK: Basil Blackwell.

PREFACE

The interest in and work on the development of a strengths-based approach to case management, practice with individuals and groups, and community development continues not only at the School of Social Welfare, University of Kansas but around the country and even internationally. Much remains to be done, of course, with respect to inquiry and the further development of concepts and principles as well as techniques. But it is gratifying to witness, from the views of practitioners, and their clients, students, and faculty how poignant the strengths perspective has been in their pedagogy and practice. It may be, too, that the strengths perspective will remain just that: a perspective, a way of thinking about and orienting yourself to your work and obligating yourself to your clients and their families and communities.

The responses to the first three editions of *The Strengths Perspective in Social Work Practice* have been gratifying. The authors are truly grateful for those reactions as well as the critiques that have been forwarded. In this edition, we kept some of the elements that have provoked positive responses, added some new ones that were thought to be essential, and responded to some of the criticism with revisions. You will find new chapters by Robert Blundo, Mary Bricker-Jenkins and her colleagues, Bonnie Benard, Margaret Waller, Ann Weick, and her colleagues Jim Kreider, and Ronna Chamberlain, Richard Rapp, and Pat Sullivan and Charlie Rapp. All the other chapters have substantial revisions, making this edition a stronger, more inviting one, I believe. And, for the most part, the other chapters have significant revisions. We have tried to be attentive to concerns about working with oppressed groups and remembering our professional commitment to social and economic justice. Spirituality is defined in this edition as a strength, and we have provided some new examples as well as some fresh ideas about practice.

We hope, of course, that this book will assist you in developing in your own professional work and pedagogy, a genuine strengths perspective. I have been privileged to travel around the country and, to a limited extent, abroad and consult with groups and organizations attempting to incorporate this perspective into their work or curriculum. Believe me, there are people doing some amazing things. But I also see that it is easy to think that one is using a strengths perspective when, in some ways, that isn't the case. The problem is that it requires a dedication and depth of commitment that, on the surface, does not seem warranted. Nonetheless, the authors of these chapters—who, by the way, are not of one mind about this perspective—hope that you see the enormity of the undertaking but also the joys that come from the use of a strengths approach.

PLAN OF THE BOOK

The first part of the book, "The Philosophy, Principles, and Language of the Strengths Perspective" introduces you to the basic assumptions, the values, the guiding principles, and the lexicon of the strengths perspective. In Chapter 1, Dennis Saleebey lays out some of the assumptions and principles and contrasts them with the more dominant problem-based and medical models. In chapter two Robert Blundo develops the idea of the strengths perspective as a very different kind of frame and contrasts it with other frames that have dominated social work theory and practice over the past century.

Part two, "The Remarkable Strengths of Indigenous People(s)," begins with Margeret Waller's dramatic account of how the stark reality of oppression in the lives of Indigenous Peoples has promoted not just anguish and destruction, but a variety of cultural, tribal, and individual capacities and virtues that have helped people withstand the withering effects of genocide. In Chapter 4, Edward Canda details a qualitative study of how spirituality has sustained people confronting a serious chronic illness, cystic fibrosis. The struggle to come to terms with their illness led many people to form a bulwark of transcendent meaning and religion, a strength in the face of uncertainty and pain.

Part three, "Strengths-Based Assessment and Approaches to Practice," begins with Dennis Saleebey's overview of a strengths-based approach to practice as well as some ideas about how to discover and use strengths in practice. Charles Cowger, Kim Anderson, and Carol Snively lay out in great detail, a way of conducting an assessment that honors strengths and is not an instrument of political and professional domination. In Chapter 7, Ann Weick, Jim Kreider, and Ronna Chamberlain develop a novel conceptualization of problems and a strategy for minimizing their influence on practice, allowing strengths and solutions to come to the fore. Richard Rapp brings an update on his strengths-based case management model with people with substance abuse problems, a program that has been successful and ongoing at Wright State University for several years. Holly Nelson-Becker, Rosemary Chapin, and Becky Fast employ a strengths perspective in understanding the struggles that older citizens face. They present some very useful practice guidelines, attending to culture and spirituality as important components of helping. In Chapter 10, Walter Kisthardt updates and expands his well-researched and well-received strengths-based case management principles and practices with people. In the following chapter, Bonnie Benard reports on the enormous array of research documenting the resilience and strength of all kinds of families and she develops from that her own framework for practice that capitalizes upon those strengths.

Part four, "Strengths in Context," is intended to move the interests of the strengths perspective to the environment. In Chapter 12 Mary Bricker-Jenkins and colleagues discuss their work to end poverty and detail the elements of that work that are based on the wisdom, work, narratives, and sacrifice of people who are poor and oppressed. In the following chapter, Dennis Saleebey discusses how a strengths perspective plays out in community building with three examples of extraordinarily successful community-building programs. There are also some blueprints derived from the literature on what makes for a successful community-building effort. In Chapter 14, Patrick Sullivan and Charles Rapp, two of the foremost thinkers and developers of the strengths-based approach to case management, lay out the principles of the "match game" in strengths-based work: how important it is to understand, marshal, and employ the resources that exist in the natural, social, and built environments and how to match those with the needs and strengths of individuals, groups, and communities.

In the final part, "Conclusion," Dennis Saleebey examines the consequences of taking on a strengths approach, answers some of the most commonly asked questions about it, and discusses its future as well as converging lines of thought and practice that seem consonant with the assumptions and outlook of the strengths perspective.

ACKNOWLEDGMENTS

The authors who have contributed to this edition of the book have my deepest appreciation and gratitude. They are all very busy practitioners and scholars, but they are also committed to the strengths perspective. This, for them, was a labor of love—as you can tell from reading their work. I have derived great benefit and insight from reading their words, and I am sure you will too. These individuals do not just preach the sermon, they do the good work as well.

I would also like to thank the contributors to the first three editions: John Poertner, John Ronnau, Eloise Rathbone-McCuan, Julian Rappaport, Gary Holmes, Michael Yellow Bird, Jennifer C. Jones, and James Taylor. Their work on and dedication to the strengths approach continues. We would like to thank the reviewers for their suggestions: Robert Blundo, University of North Carolina, Wilmington; Brenda Bryson, Barry University; Debra Gohagan, Minnesota State University, Mankato; and Cecilia L. Thomas, University of North Texas.

The editors at Longman, then Allyn and Bacon, have been extraordinarily supportive and patient. They have believed in this project from the inception of the first edition to this one. In particular, thanks to Janice Wiggins, Judith Fifer, and Karen Hanson. For this edition, the guiding hands of Patricia Quinlin and Sara Holliday have been most helpful. Without their encouragement, I am not at all sure that I would have attempted another edition of this book.

Finally, a word about two special people. Howard Goldstein died in 2000. He was one of the most intellectually audacious and bold scholars I have ever known. He also was a sensitive and skilled practitioner, and his concern for others always shone through. But his moral and intellectual vision for social work was unsurpassed in its clarity and reach. He had wondrous qualities of his mind and heart. We will miss him. The profession will miss him.

My wife, Ann Weick, is an exquisite partner in life and work. She is remarkable in the steadfastness of her belief in the strengths of others, her vision for this profession, and her love for those who have come to rely on her wisdom and caring.

CONTRIBUTORS

Kim M. Anderson, Ph.D., is an assistant professor of social work at the University of Missouri, Columbia. She is a licensed clinical social worker. For the past 15 years, Dr. Anderson has specialized in the area of psychological trauma due to family violence. Presently, she is involved in designing and evaluating outcomes for the Boone County Mental Health Court in Columbia, Missouri. Her research interests include assessment of risk and resiliency in trauma populations, and implementation of strengths-based mental health practice.

Bonnie Benard has brought the concept of resilience to the attention of national and international audiences for more than 20 years. She writes widely, leads professional development, and makes presentations in the field of prevention and resilience/youth development theory, policy, and practice. Her 1991 WestEd publication, *Fostering Resiliency in Kids: Protective Factors in the Family, School, and Community,* is credited with introducing resiliency theory and application to the fields of prevention and education. Her most recent publication, *Resiliency: What We Have Learned* (2004), synthesizes a decade and more of resiliency research and describes what application of the research looks like in our most successful efforts to support young people.

Robert Blundo, Ph.D., LCSW, is an associate professor in the Department of Social Work at the University of North Carolina at Wilmington. He has 25 years of clinical practice experience and is presently engaged in his second career as a teacher of social work. He has helped develop a strengths based and solution-focused practice curriculum for both the BSW and the new MSW program. He is very active with local agencies in training in the strengths and solution-focused approach. His favorite time of the year is the summer when his rural social work service-learning course takes students to Appalachia to learn from and work with local communities.

Edward R. Canda, Ph.D., is professor and director of the Ph.D. Program at the University of Kansas School of Social Welfare. He has published numerous books and articles on the topic of spirituality and social work. His website includes extensive resources related to connections between spiritual diversity, health, and social work: www.socwel.ku.edu/canda.

Rosemary Chapin is an award winning teacher and researcher. She has extensive teaching, research, policy and program development experience in the long-term care arena. After receiving her Ph.D., she worked for the Minnesota Department of Human Services as a research/policy analyst where she was involved in crafting numerous long-term care reform initiatives. In 1989, she joined the faculty at the University of Kansas, where she established and now directs the Office of Aging and Long Term Care (OALTC). The office was created to improve social service practice and policy for older adults, particularly low-income elders. A variety of research and strengths-based training initiatives have been completed by faculty, students and staff that are part of the office. Research reports can be downloaded at www.oaltc.ku.edu. She has recently completed a social policy text which integrates the strengths perspective into policy practice with an expected publication date of 2005.

Charles D. Cowger, Ph.D., is a professor emeritus of the School of Social Work at the University of Missouri, Columbia. Formerly, he was the director of the School of Social Work at the University of Missouri, Columbia, and was on faculty at the University of Illinois School of Social Work where he served in various administrative capacities. Other interests include woodworking, canoe backpacking, and pottery.

Walter Kisthardt is currently an assistant professor at the University of Missouri Kansas City School of Social Work. His research has focused upon evaluating strengths-based, person-centered practice as indicated by social outcomes as well ethnographically from the perspective of service participants. Dr. Kisthardt has provided training in strengths-based practice in 42 states, in England and New Zealand. He incorporates his own gifts and talents through his original poetry and music which captures the essence of interpersonal helping in a humorous and often poignant manner.

James W. Kreider, MSW, LSCSW, is an instructor at the School of Social Welfare, University of Kansas, and owner of Kreider Consulting, LLC, where he provides clinical services, training, consultation, and supervision. He has worked extensively using solution-focused therapy with various challenging populations, and is the author of *Solution-Focused Ideas for Briefer Therapy with Longer-Term Clients* in *The Handbook of Constructive Therapies*.

Holly Nelson-Becker is an assistant professor at the School of Social Welfare at the University of Kansas. She is also a Hartford Faculty Scholar, Cohort III. She received a dissertation research award at the University of Chicago for her research with an African American and European American older adult sample on the use of religion and spirituality to manage life challenges. Dr. Nelson-Becker's research interests continue to focus on perceptions of religion and spirituality as resources in fostering resilience; mental health needs of older adults with a focus on depression, life satisfaction, and quality of life; international gerontological programs; and productive aging in retirement. As a Hartford Faculty Scholar, Dr. Nelson-Becker has been examining the strengths perspective through the spiritual and nonspiritual coping mechanisms of individuals who are terminally ill and under hospice care.

Charles A. Rapp is professor at the University of Kansas School of Social Welfare and Director of the Office of Mental Health Research and Training. He holds a

Ph.D. and MSW from the University of Illinois and a BS from Millikin University. He is the co-developer of strengths model of case management and the client-centered performance model of social administration. His book, *The Strengths Model: Case Management with People Suffering from Severe and Persistent Mental Illness*, was published by Oxford Press in August, 1998.

Richard C. Rapp, MSW, ACSW, is an assistant professor in the Wright State University School of Medicine (WSUSOM) and clinical services developer and researcher with the Center for Interventions, Treatment, and Addictions Research (CITAR). He is currently co-principal investigator for the Reducing Barriers Project, a National Institute on Drug Abuse funded project. The Reducing Barriers Project is testing two brief interventions—strengths-based case management and motivational interviewing—for their effectiveness in facilitating treatment linkage among adult substance abusers.

Carol A. Snively, Ph.D., is an assistant professor of Social Work at the University of Missouri, Columbia. Her research areas include youth and community development, effective helping strategies for sexual minority youth and the use of art making as a tool in community organization. Dr. Snively's most recent community practice and research projects have focused on understanding how economically disadvantaged and sexual minority teens experience their communities and participate in community betterment activities. Prior to academia, she practiced for 15 years as a registered/board certified art therapist and licensed clinical social worker with youth and their families in mental health and addiction treatment.

Patrick Sullivan is a professor at the Indiana University School of Social Work and former State Director of Mental Health and Addictions. A graduate of the University of Kansas, he was a member of the first pilot project using the strengths model in case management services in mental health in the early 1980s, and he was among the first to apply the model in substance abuse services. He has contributed to each edition of *The Strengths Perspective in Social Work Practice*.

Margaret Waller is an associate professor at the School of Social Work, Arizona State University. Her research and teaching center on individual, family, and community resilience and inter-cultural understanding with particular emphasis on Indigenous Peoples of the Southwest. She has also been a family therapist since 1982.

Ann Weick is dean and professor at the University of Kansas School of Social Welfare. She received an MSW from University of California, Berkeley, a Ph.D. from Brandeis University, and has been a member of the University of Kansas faculty since 1976. Her publications have focused on a variety of topics related to social work theory and practice, including articles on human development theory, women's issues, health and healing, the development of the strengths perspective, and philosophical issues related to the scientific paradigm.

CHAPTER ONE

INTRODUCTION
Power in the People[1]

DENNIS SALEEBEY

In the lore of professional social work, the idea of building on people's strengths has become axiomatic. Authors of textbooks, educators, and practitioners all regularly acknowledge the importance of this principle. Many of these calls to attend to the capacities and competencies of clients are little more than professional cant. So let us be clear: The strengths perspective is a dramatic departure from conventional social work practice. Practicing from a strengths orientation means this—*everything* you do as a social worker will be predicated, in some way, on helping to discover and embellish, explore and exploit clients' strengths and resources in the service of assisting them to achieve their goals, realize their dreams, and shed the irons of their own inhibitions and misgivings, and society's domination. This is a versatile practice approach, relying heavily on the ingenuity and creativity, the courage and common sense, of both clients and their social workers. It is a collaborative process depending on clients and workers to be purposeful agents and not mere functionaries. It is an approach honoring the innate wisdom of the human spirit, the inherent capacity for transformation of even the most humbled and abused. When you adopt the strengths approach to practice, you can expect exciting changes in the character of your work and in the tenor of your relationships with your clients.

Many of us believe (or have at one time believed) that we are building on client strengths. But sometimes we fall short. To really practice from a strengths perspective demands a different way of seeing clients, their environments, and their current situation. Rather than focusing exclusively or dominantly on problems, your eye turns toward possibility. In the thicket of trauma, pain, and trouble you can see blooms of hope and transformation. The formula is simple: Mobilize clients' strengths (talents, knowledge, capacities, resources) in the service of achieving their goals and visions and the clients will have a better quality of life on their terms. Though the recipe is uncomplicated, as you will see, the work is hard. In the chapters that follow, you will encounter descriptions of the strengths

---

[1]Part of this chapter is based on D. Saleebey, The strengths perspective in social work: Extensions and cautions. *Social Work, 41*(3), 1996, 295–305. With permission of the National Association of Social Workers.

approach used with a variety of populations, in a variety of circumstances. You will be exposed to schemes of assessment, methods of employment, examples of application, and discussions of issues related to moving from a concentration on problems to a fascination with strengths.

In the past few years, there has been an increasing interest in developing strengths-based approaches to practice, case management in particular, with a variety of client groups—the elderly, youth in trouble, people with addictions, people with chronic mental illness, communities and schools (Benard, 1994; Clark, 1997; Kretzmann & McKnight, 1993; Miller & Berg, 1995; Mills, 1995; Parsons & Cox, 1994; Rapp, 1998; Benard, 2004; Pransky, 1998). In addition, rapidly developing literature, inquiry, and practice methods in a variety of fields bear a striking similarity to the strengths perspective—developmental resilience, healing and wellness, positive psychology, solution-focused therapy, assets-based community development, and narrative and story to name a few.

THE FASCINATION WITH PROBLEMS
AND PATHOLOGY

The impetus for these elaborations comes from many sources, but of singular importance is a reaction to our culture's continued obsession and fascination with psychopathology, victimization, abnormality, and moral and interpersonal aberrations. A swelling conglomerate of businesses and professions, institutions and agencies, from medicine to pharmaceuticals, from the insurance industry to the mass media, turn handsome profits by assuring us that we are in the clutch (or soon will be) of any number of emotional, physical, or behavioral maladies. Each of us, it seems, is a reservoir of vulnerabilities and weaknesses usually born of toxic experiences in early life. The *Diagnostic and Statistical Manual* of The American Psychiatric Association (APA) has become the primary handbook for the diagnosing of mental disorders. Not only is it widely used, insurance companies typically require, for reimbursement purposes, a diagnosis made from the DSM lexicon. While DSMs I and II were modest documents having less than 100 pages each of description of mental disorders (causality was also a focus), and were written by a handful of psychiatrists in predominantly psychodynamic language, DSM III was a sea change in this psychiatric glossary. Fueled by a group who wanted to emulate the descriptive precision and clarity of the early psychiatrist, Emil Kraepelin (who over time wrote 11 increasingly large editions of his psychiatric diagnostic manual), DSM III had hundreds of pages of descriptions of various categories of mental illness. It also was intended to be descriptive, not analytic. Many more disorders were included between its pages. Since that time, the APA has put the DSM on a 12 year cycle (by the way, it and its attendant manuals, and guides are highly successful and, for professional books, runaway best-sellers). For example, DSM IV, out in 1994, was followed by DSM IV TR (Text Revision) in 2000. DSM V will probably be out in 2006, followed by V TR in 2012. And each addition will surely have new disorders (look at the back of DSM IV TR under the heading Criteria Sets and Axes Provided for Further Study and you will see a list of disorders-in-wait-ing). All of this is to say that we are in a relentless march toward hemming in each aspect of the human condition, even human nature itself, as reflective of some behavioral, emotional, and/or cognitive ills.

Not only are we mesmerized by disease and disorder, many of us have been designated as casualties by the ever growing phalanx of mental health profession-als, turning mental health into a thriving and handsomely rewarding business. Prodded by a variety of gurus, swamis, ministers, and therapists, some of us are in hot pursuit of our wounded inner children and find ourselves dripping with the residue of the poisons of our family background. If you listen carefully, you can hear the echoes of evangelism in some of these current cultural fixations. And these are cultural preoccupations as well. The Jerry Springer show is no anomaly, except perhaps in regard to the level of schtick and tastelessness it exudes. Ken-neth Gergen (1994) sees the result of this symbiosis between mental health pro-fessions and culture, as a rapidly accelerating "cycle of progressive infirmity" (p. 155). He wryly observes,

> How may I fault thee? Let me count the ways: impulsive personality, malingering, reactive depression, anorexia, mania, attention deficit disorder, psychopathia, external control orientation, low self-esteem . . . (p. 148)

To make these observations is not to callously disregard the real pains and struggles of individuals, families, and communities; neither is it to casually avert our glance from the realities of abuse of all kinds inflicted on children; nor is it to deny the tenacious grip and beguiling thrall of addictions. It is, however, to foreswear the ascendancy of psychopathology as society's principal civic, moral, and medical categorical imperative. It is to denounce the idea that most people who experience hurt, trauma, and neglect inevitably suffer wounds and become less than they might be. It is to return a semblance of balance to the equation of understanding and helping those who are hurting. The balance is hard to come by because the language of strength and resilience is nascent and just developing and, therefore, scant. Sybil and Steve Wolin (1997) say this about the two paradigms (risk and resiliency):

> As a result, the resiliency paradigm is no match for the risk paradigm, Talking about the human capacity to repair from harm, inner strengths, and protective factors, professionals feel that they have entered alien territory. They grope for words and fear sounding unschooled and naïve when they replace pathology terminology with the more mundane vocabulary of resourcefulness, hope, creativity, compe-tence, and the like . . . . We believe that the struggle can be tipped in the other direction by offering a systematic, developmental vocabulary of strengths that can stand up to pathology terminology that is standard in our field. (p. 27)

Social work, like other helping professions, has not been immune to the con-tagion of disease- and disorder-based thinking. Social work has constructed much of its theory and practice around the supposition that clients become clients because they have deficits, problems, pathologies, and diseases; that they are, in some essential way, flawed or weak. This orientation leaps from a past in which the certitude of conception about the moral defects of the poor, the despised, and the deviant captivated us. More sophisticated terminology prevails today, but the metaphors and narratives that guide our thinking and acting, often papered over with more salutary language, are sometimes negative constructions that are fateful for the future of those we help. The diction and symbolism of weakness, failure, and deficit shape how others regard clients, how clients regard themselves, and how resources are allocated to groups of clients. In the extreme, such designations may even invoke punitive sanctions.

The lexicon of pathology gives voice to a number of assumptions and these in turn have painted pictures of clients in vivid but not very flattering tones. Some of these assumptions and their consequences are summarized below.

The person is the problem or pathology named. Diagnostic labels of all kinds tend to become "master statuses" (Becker, 1963), designations and roles that subsume all others under their mantle. A person suffering from schizophrenia *becomes* a schizophrenic, a convention so common that we hardly give it a thought. Once labeled a schizophrenic, other elements of a person's character, experiences, knowledge, aspirations, slowly recede into the background, replaced by the language of symptom and syndrome. Inevitably, conversation about the person becomes dominated by the imagery of disease, and relationships with the ailing person re-form around such representations. To the extent that these labels take hold, the individual, through a process of surrender and increasing dependence, becomes the once alien identification (Gergen, 1994; Goffman, 1961; Scheff, 1984). These are not value neutral terms, either. They serve to separate those who suffer these "ailments" from those who do not; a distinction that if not physical (as in hospitalization) is at least moral. Those who are labeled, in ways both subtle and brutish, are degraded—certainly in terms of social regard and status. However, these labels provide a measure of relief for some suffering individuals and their families—knowing, finally, what the matter is. In addition labels are certainly better than being thought of as possessed by demons. Nonetheless they do create a situation for far too many individuals of self-enfeeblement—moral, psychological, and civil (Gergen, 1994, p. 150).

The language of pessimism and doubt: Professional cynicism. Accentuating the problems of clients creates a wave of pessimistic expectations of, and predictions about, the client, the client's environment, and the client's capacity to cope with that environment. Furthermore, these labels have the insidious potential, repeated over time, to alter how individuals see themselves and how others see them. In the long run, these changes seep into the individual's identity. Paulo Freire (1996) maintained for many years that the views and expectations of oppressors have an uncanny and implacable impact on the oppressed. Under the weight of these once-foreign views, the oppressed begin to subjugate their own knowledge and understanding to those of their tormentors.

The focus on what is wrong often reveals an egregious doubt about the ability of individuals to cope with life's challenges or to rehabilitate themselves. Andrew Weil (1995) laments the profound pessimism and negativity in his own profession, medicine, about the body's innate inclination to transform, regenerate, and heal itself.

> I cannot help feeling embarrassed by my profession when I hear the myriad ways in which doctors convey their pessimism to patients. I . . . am working to require instruction in medical school about the power of words and the need for physicians to use extreme care in choosing the words they speak to patients. A larger subject is the problem of making doctors more conscious of the power projected on them by patients and the possibilities for reflecting that power back in ways that influence health for better rather than worse, that stimulate rather than retard spontaneous healing. (p. 64)

The situation is so bad that Weil refers to it as medical *hexing*—dire medical predictions and inimical attributions by physicians powerful enough to create anxiety, fear, depression, and resignation in patients. This is a common consequence of the biomedical model—a model that has profoundly influenced some fields of social work practice. The biomedical model and its more widely influential kin in the human service professions, the "Technical/Rationalist" model (Schön, 1983), are despairing of natural healing and people's capacity to know what is right. Extraordinarily materialistic, these models disregard the functional wholeness and fitness of anything under their scrutiny—including human beings. Social work's continuing emphasis on problems and disorders and the profession's increasing commerce with theories that focus on deficits and pathologies tend to promote the portrayal of individuals as sites of specific problems and as medleys of singular deficiencies. Such an attitude takes the social work profession away from its avowed and historical interest in the person-in-context, the understanding of the web of institutional and interpersonal relationships in which any person is enmeshed, and the possibility for rebirth and renewal even under dire circumstances.

Distance, power inequality, control, and manipulation mark the relationship between helper and helped. The idea that we have empirically grounded or theoretically potent techniques to apply is beguiling. But in some way it may create distance between clients and helpers. Distance itself, whether the distance of class, privileged knowledge, institutionalized role, or normative position, may imply a power inequality between helper and helped. In the end, the client's view may become fugitive or irrelevant. In discussing "resistant" clients, Miller and colleagues (1997) say this:

> If a therapist . . . suggests or implies that the client's point of view is wrong, somehow invalidates, or upstages the client, 'resistance' may appear. After all, even if not already demoralized, who wants to be reminded of failure, criticized, and judged, or made to feel that you have to follow orders? What we come to call resistance may sometimes reflect the client's attempt to salvage a small portion of self-respect. As such, some cases become impossible simply because the treatment allows the client no way of 'saving face' or upholding dignity. (p. 12)

The surest route to detachment and a kind of depersonalization is the building of a case—assembling a portfolio on the client created from the identity-stripping descriptions of, for example, DSM IV TR or the juvenile justice code. Furthermore, the legal and political mandates of many agencies, the elements of social control embodied in both the institution and ethos of the agency, may strike a further blow to the possibility of partnership and collaboration between client and helper.

Context-stripping. Problem-based assessments encourage individualistic rather than ecological accounts of clients. When we transform persons into cases, we often see only them and how well they fit into a category. In this way, we miss important elements of the client's life—cultural, social, political, ethnic, spiritual, and economic—and how they contribute to, sustain, and shape a person's misery or struggles or mistakes. The irony here is that, in making a case we really do not individualize. Rather, we are in the act of finding an appropriate diagnostic niche for the individual, thus making the client one among many and not truly unique. All individuals suffering from bipolar disorder hence become more like each other and less distinctive. In doing this, we selectively destroy or at least ignore contextual information that, although not salient to our assessment scheme, might well reveal the abiding distinctiveness of the individual in this particular milieu. It might also indicate important resources for help and transformation as well as problem-solving.

The supposition of disease assumes a cause for the disorder and, thus, a solution. Naming the poison leads to an antidote. But in the world of human relationships and experiences, the idea of a regression line between cause, disease, and cure ignores the steamy morass of uncertainty and complexity that is the human condition. It also happens to take out of the hands of the person, family and friends, the neighborhood—the daily lifeworld of all involved—the capacity and resources for change. There are many cultural and spiritual avenues for transformation and healing. They, rightly enough, also suppose linkages between the nature of the problem (is it natural or unnatural? spiritual or mundane?) and its relief. But to bury these tools under the weight of a medico-scientific model is to inter a variety of familial and cultural media for change.

Remedies in the lifeworld usually begin with reinterpretations of the problem that come out of continuing dialogue with the situation and with clients. These renderings are mutually crafted constructs that may only be good for this client, at this time, under these conditions. Though they may have the power to transform clients' understandings, choices, and actions, these expositions are tentative and provisional. The capacity to devise such interpretations depends not on a strict relationship between problem and solution but on intuition, tacit knowing, hunches, and conceptual risk taking (Saleebey, 1989). Schön (1983) has characterized the tension between the usual conception of professional knowing and doing and this more reflective one as that between rigor and relevance. Relevance asks these questions of us: To what extent are clients consulted about matters pertinent to them? What do they want? What do they need? How do they think they can get it? How do they see their situation—problems as well as possibilities? What values do they want to maximize? How have they managed to survive thus far? These and similar questions, as answers draw near, move us a step toward a deeper appreciation of all clients' distinctive attributes, abilities, and competencies, and the world of their experience. They require of the social worker and the client a degree of reflection, the interest in making meaning and making sense. Iris Murdoch said that when we return home and share our day

> We are artfully shaping material into story form. So in a way as word-users we all exist in a literary atmosphere, we live and breathe literature, we are all literary artists, we are constantly employing language to make interesting forms out of experience which perhaps originally seemed dull or incoherent. (cited in Mattingly, 1991, p. 237)

Finding the words that shout the reality of the lived experience of people, and perhaps finding other words that reflect genuine possibility and hope is, in a modest and unscientific sense, finding cause for celebration—of promise.

THE STRENGTHS PERSPECTIVE: PHILOSOPHY, CONCEPTS, AND PRINCIPLES

I want to discuss two major philosophical principles as a way of staking out the claims of the strengths perspective, but in the context of the sometimes numbing and usually complex realities of daily life.

Liberation and Empowerment: Heroism and Hope

Liberation is founded on the idea of possibility: the opportunities for choice, commitment, and action whether pursued in relative tranquility or in grievous circumstance. We have fabulous powers and potentials. Some are muted, unrealized, and immanent. Others glimmer brilliantly about us. All around are people and policies, circumstances and conventions, contingencies and conceptions that may nurture and emancipate these powers or that may crush and degrade them. Somewhere within, and we may call it by different names, lies the longing for the heroic: to transcend circumstances, to develop one's own powers, to face adversity down, to stand up and be counted. All too often social institutions, oppressors, other people, some even with good intentions, tamp out this yearning or distort it so that it serves the interests and purposes of others. Nonetheless, however muted, this precious craving abides. It is incumbent on the healer, the humane leader, the shaman, the teacher, and, yes, the social worker to find ways for this penchant for the possible and unimaginable to survive and find expression in life-affirming ways. Of course, things go more smoothly if people simply play their roles, pay their taxes, and stifle their opinions. Liberation exerts tremendous pressure on the repressive inclinations of institutions and individuals. Collectively, liberation unleashes human energy and spirit, critical thinking, the questioning of authority, challenges to the conventional wisdom, and new ways of being and doing. But liberation may also be modest and unassuming. We may try out new behaviors, forge new relationships, or make a new commitment. Hope and the belief in the possible is central to liberation. Before his death, the great pedagogue of liberation, Paulo Freire, wrote in his last book, *Pedagogy of Hope* (1996), that he had previously underestimated the power of hope.

But the attempt to do without hope, in the struggle to improve the world, as if that struggle could be reduced to calculated acts alone, or a purely scientific approach, is a frivolous illusion. To attempt to do without hope, which is based on the need for truth as an ethical quality of the struggle, is tantamount to denying that struggler as one of its mainstays . . . [H]ope, as an ontological need, demands an anchoring in practice. . . . Without a minimum of hope, we cannot so much as start the struggle. (pp. 8–9)

I would go so far as to say that the central dynamic of the strengths perspective is precisely the rousing of hope, of tapping into the visions and the promise of that individual, family, or community. Circumstances, bad luck, unfortunate decisions, the harshness of life lived on the edge of need and vulnerability, of course, may smother these. Nonetheless, it is the flicker of possibility that can ignite the fire of hope.

The heroism of everyday life is all around us. People carrying on in the midst of mind-searing stress; people coming to the fore when the needs around them require someone to act and to act out of the ordinary; people whose moral imagination allows them to see, even in distant and unfamiliar places, the utter humanity of those who suffer (Glover, 2000). 9/11 is an instructive example. Fire and police personnel, rescue teams, the people who risked their lives and faced serious harm in helping to clear away the hellish debris (Langewiesche, 2003), social workers who met with survivors and witnesses to help ease the psychological and interpersonal wreckage of the trauma; people trapped in the inferno, facing certain death, who called their loved ones to tell them goodbye and to express their love: many of these pushed the boundaries of the heroic outward and upward. Clearly, the destruction wrought on that day was a deliberate, heinous, and murderous crime. But even on the other side, given their point of view, the terrorists thought themselves to be heroic. In a letter to his wife, speaking of his certain death, one of them wrote, ". . . Know that my death is a martyrdom, my imprisonment hermitage, my exile tourism in God's land. I would like to meet you in heaven, so please help me by waking up at night to pray, fasting during the day, and staying away from temptation." (Cullison, 2004, p. 66) Obviously, we are required here to make a moral judgment about the lethal and vicious acts they committed against us, but we must also look through their eyes to understand more fully the meaning of heroism for the human condition.

Alienation and Oppression: Anxiety and Evil

The circumstances around us will not let us deny the existence of harsh and tyrannical institutions, relationships, circumstances, and regimes. Bigotry, hatred, war, slaughter, repression, and, more quietly but no less devastating, setting people aside, treating them as the despised other, and acting as though they are not fully human, are all daily reminders of the existence of evil, brutality, and despotism. But why is the capacity for evil the seeming companion to the urge to the heroic?

How often do we stand, agape, horrified at what we see or hear about or read about? Vicious acts of cruelty, violence born of intolerance and hate—how can they happen, we cry? Yet, aren't there times when we have been propelled to act or been a party to actions that have inflicted emotional or physical pain on others, often those who are different from us? Why?

We are small, and vulnerable. The cosmos is enormous. We tremble at the insignificance and frailty of our being when cast against the magnitude of time and the vastness of space. At times, our fear and trembling is best handled by taking matters into our own hands, individually or collectively, and dealing the instrumentalities of fear and loathing onto others. Thus we subdue our own uncertainties and obscure our cosmic smallness. It may even be that some of these acts of violence or marginalizing are "immortality projects" designed to blind us to the reality of our own organismic vulnerability and eventual demise (Becker, 1973; Fromm, 1973; Rank, 1941).

But from the ashes of destruction, mayhem, and oppression may emerge the human spirit, the capacity for the heroic. So we can never dismiss the possibility of redemption, resurrection, and regeneration. However, the sweep of history, the grandeur of wholesale creation and destruction eventually find their way into the nooks and crannies of our lives. These sweeping generalities occur in the small confines of daily life as well. You see a single mother and her 10-year-old daughter. They have come to the family service agency you work for. The mother is worried. Her daughter, once sweet and compliant, a joy to be around, is becoming morose, uncommunicative, anxious, and weepy. The quality of her work at school is plummeting, and friends seem unimportant to her. Father left the family suddenly and left them in dire financial straits. It had been a marriage of youthful misjudgments the mother allows, but, she says, in spite of the financial hardships maybe it is better that he has gone. The mother wonders if her daughter's current woes aren't related to his leaving about 6 months ago. You spend considerable time over the next weeks exploring the situation with the mother and daughter. Eventually you discover that for a period of almost 2 years the young girl had experienced physical and sexual depredation and brutality at the hands of her father. She had vowed to herself never to tell anyone! Never to let him know how much he had hurt her. Never! And she maintained her vow until he left. Now she was falling apart, grieving, experiencing rage, and feeling the wounds of violation. But in the ashes of devastation, this young girl's spirit, against all odds, flourished. Now the mother and the social worker must make an alliance with this tiny, amazing soul.

We have seen that the preoccupation with problems and pathologies, while producing an impressive lode of technical and theoretical writing, may be less fruitful when it comes to actually helping clients grow, develop, change directions, realize their visions, or revise their personal meanings and narratives. What follows is a brief glossary of terms supporting an orientation to strengths as well as a statement of the principles of practice central to a strengths perspective. These are meant to give you a vital sense of what a frame of mind devoted to the strengths of individuals and groups requires.

THE LEXICON OF STRENGTHS

"We can act," wrote William James (1902) in reflecting upon Immanuel Kant's notions about conceptions, "as *if* there were a God; feel as *if* we were free; consider nature as *if* she were full of special designs; lay plans as *if* we were to be immortal; and we find then that these words **do** [emphasis added] make a genuine difference in our moral life" (p. 55). Language and words have power. They can elevate and inspire or demoralize and destroy. If words are a part of the nutriment that feeds one's sense of self, then we are compelled to examine our dictionary of helping to see what our words portend for clients. Any approach to practice speaks a language that, in the end, may have a pronounced effect on the way that clients think of themselves and how they act. Not only that, our professional diction has a profound effect on the way that *we* regard clients, their world, and their troubles. In the strengths approach to practice, some words are essential and direct us to an appreciation of the assets of individuals, families, and communities.

A simple device for framing and remembering the essentials of the strengths perspective can be found in Figure 1.1.

These words capture, I think, the core values of the strengths lexicon. The central dynamic of strength discovery and articulation lies in hope and possibility; the vision of a better future or quality of life.

Plasticity (and the placebo effect).   It is a miracle of the brain that it "never loses the power to transform itself on the basis of experience and that the transformation can occur over short intervals. . . . your brain is different today than it

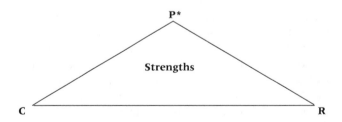

Where C stands for:

Competence, capacities, courage

And P symbolizes:

Promise, possibility, positive expectations

And R signifies:

Resilience, reserves, resources

FIGURE 1.1

*Thanks to my daughter Meghan for suggesting this.

was yesterday. " (Restak, 2003, p. 8) It was once thought that after adolescence the brain is pretty much structural monolith, hardly changing. But now, thanks to sophisticated imaging techniques, it is clear that the brain, in ways minute and substantial, continually undergoes change. Most of these changes take place at the synapse (the place where neurons communicate with each other), and are the result of experience and learning or simply one's current state of mind (LeDoux, 2002). These relationships are, at one site or another, in flux and are the basis of plasticity. Therefore, we have a marvelous capacity to alter, extend, and reshape behavior, feeling, and cognition. Of course, much of what happens here is beyond our conscious recognition.

The placebo effect has been long noted (even before modern medicine although it was not called that). In contemporary usage it refers to a phenomenon in the clinical trials of various medical procedures and medications. Typically, one group is given the actual drug and another is given an inert substance (although now it is becoming more common to give a placebo that does provoke side effects so that people are less likely to guess they are being given the placebo). Neither the administrators of the drugs and placebos nor the "patients" know which is which. A drug's power is thought to be measured in the extent to which it is superior to the placebo in promoting the appropriate effects. In many clinical trials of psychoactive drugs it is not uncommon for 40–60% of the placebo group to experience the therapeutic outcome provided by the drug. And we do not really know how many of the people who get the actual drug experienced a placebo rather than a drug effect (or some combination of the two). Recently, four physicians, using the Freedom of Information Act, were able to get the results of clinical trials done over the last 15 years from the Food and Drug Administration (FDA) for six of the most popular antidepressant drugs. Pharmaceutical companies conduct clinical trials and then send the results to the FDA. Up until now no one has had access to the results of these trials, so we have to take the drug company's word that its drug is effective. These researchers conducted meta-analyses of the clinical trials and found, no matter how generous or conservative their statistical analysis, that there were no clinically significant differences between the placebos and the drugs (Kirsch et al., 2003). Whatever else this means, it does, I think, bespeak the power of hope, positive expectations, and belief in the healing ministration. It seems odd that we would not have made more of the placebo effect (even if it is only a short-term one).

Empowerment.   Although rapidly becoming hackneyed, empowerment indicates the intent to, and the processes of, assisting individuals, groups, families, and communities to discover and expend the resources and tools within and around them. Stephen Rose (2000) says this about empowerment practice as he came to understand it:

> Central to this [empowerment] practice was understanding the notion as a relational expression, not a technique or instrument. In empowering relationships, meaning was restored to each person; earned trust was built into the explicit acknowledgement of the purpose of the practice; interactions were explored for their links to social structures and their interests; and clients' lives were envisioned

simultaneously as unique in terms of meaning, but collective or population-based in terms of patterns of domination and system barriers to validity. (p. 412)

To discover the power within people and communities, we must subvert and abjure pejorative labels; provide opportunities for connections to family, institutional, and communal resources; assail the victim mind-set; foreswear paternalism; trust people's intuitions, accounts, perspectives, and energies; and believe in people's dreams. Barbara Levy Simon (1994) builds the concept of empowerment with five necessary ideas: collaborative partnerships with clients and constituents; an emphasis on the expansion of client strengths and capacities; a focus on both the individual or family and the environment; assuming that clients are active subjects and agents; and directing one's energies to the historically disenfranchised and oppressed. Pursuing the empowerment agenda requires a deep conviction about the necessity of democracy. It requires us to address the tensions and conflicts, the institutions and people that subdue and limit those we help, and compels us to help people free themselves from these restraints (Pinderhughes, 1994). Too often, helping professions (although social work has been very wary of falling into this trap) have thwarted this imperative by assuming a paternalistic posture, informing people about what is good for them, and exhorting people to do the right thing. The strengths approach imposes a different attitude and commitment. The strengths of individuals and communities are renewable and expandable resources. Furthermore, the assets of individuals almost always lie embedded in a community of interest and involvement. Thus, the ideas of community and membership are central to the strengths approach.

Membership.   To be without membership, writes Michael Walzer, is to be in a "condition of infinite danger" (1983, p. 32). To be without membership is to be alienated, to be at risk for marginalization and oppression. People need to be citizens, responsible and valued members of a community. To sever people from the roots of their "place" subverts, for all, civic and moral vigor. The strengths orientation proceeds from the recognition that all of those whom we serve are, like ourselves, members of a species, entitled to the dignity, respect, and responsibility that comes with such membership. But, too often, people we help have either no place to be (or to be comfortable) or no sense of belonging. The sigh of relief from those who come to be members and citizens and bask in the attendant rights and responsibilities, assurances and securities, is the first breath of empowerment. There is another meaning of membership and that is that people must often band together to make their voices heard, get their needs met, to redress inequities, and to reach their dreams. Jonathon Kozol writes eloquently about the lived experience of people, especially children, who are poor and struggle with the ignorance, hostility, lack of regard, and destructive policies of the outside world. He describes places of refuge, resurrection, and membership. St. Ann's Church and School in the South Bronx is one such place. Here, Mother Martha, the pastor, invites the membership of children and adults. The reality of segregation and separation from the mainstream is never very far from the halls of St. Ann's.

Despite the isolation and betrayal that may be suggested by these governing realities, St. Ann's is not a place of sorrow, but at least during the hours when children
fill its corridors and classrooms with their voices and their questions and their
paperpads and their notebooks and their games, it is a place of irresistible vitality
and energy and sometimes complicated hope, and now and then uncomplicated
joy. For grown-ups in the neighborhood, it is an energizing place as well, although
the burdens that they bring with them when they come here in times of crisis to
seek out the priest can often seem at first overwhelming. (2000, p. 33)

The same kind of trustful energy is poured into community-building and
neighborhood development projects all over this country. In her investigation of
programs that work Lisbeth Schorr (1997) says this about successful community
building programs:

Community building . . . is more an orientation than a technique, more a mission
than a program, more an outlook than an activity. It catalyzes a process of change
grounded in local life and priorities. Community building addresses the developmental needs of individuals, families, and organizations within the neighborhood.
It changes the nature of the relationship between the neighborhood and the systems outside its boundaries. A community's own strengths—whether they are
found in churches, block clubs, local leadership, or its problem-solving abilities—
are seen as central. (pp. 361–362)

You can see that the ingredients of the strengths perspective abound in this
definition of community building—empowerment, membership, and, certainly,
indigenous resilience.

Resilience.   A growing body of inquiry and practice makes it clear that the rule,
not the exception, in human affairs is that people do rebound from serious trouble, that individuals and communities do surmount and overcome serious and
troubling adversity.

At best or worst, depending on one's perspective, only about a third [of children
who face dramatic stress] generally succumb; approximately two thirds do not. The
purpose of resilience research is to learn how and why [this two thirds] beat the
odds. (Wolin & Wolin, 1996, p. 246)

Much of this literature documents and demonstrates that particularly
demanding and stressful experiences, even ongoing ones, *do not lead inevitably to
vulnerability, failure to adapt, and psychopathology* (Benard, 2004; Katz, 1997; Werner
& Smith, 1992; Wolin & Wolin, 1996). Resilience is not the cheerful disregard of
one's difficult and traumatic life experiences; neither is it the naive discounting of
life's pains. It is, rather, the ability to bear up in spite of these ordeals. Damage has
been done. Emotional and physical scars bear witness to that. In spite of the
wounds, however, for many the trials have been instructive and propitious.
Resilience is a process—the continuing growth and articulation of capacities,

knowledge, insight, and virtues derived through meeting the demands and challenges of one's world, however chastening.

Healing and Wholeness.   Healing implies both wholeness and the inborn facility of the body and the mind to regenerate and resist when faced with disorder, disease, and disruption. Healing also requires a beneficent relationship between the individual and the larger social and physical environment. The natural state of affairs for human beings, evolved over eons of time and at every level of organization from cell to self-image, is the repair of one's mind and body. Just as the resilience literature assures us that individuals have naturally occurring self-righting tendencies, even though they can be compromised (Werner & Smith, 1992), it seems also the case that all human organisms have the inclination for healing. This evolutionary legacy, of course, can be compromised by trauma, by environmental toxins, by bodily disorganization, and, not the least, by some of our professional intervention philosophies and systems. But, the bottom line is this: If spontaneous healing occurs miraculously in one human being, you can expect it to occur in another and another. Such organismic ingenuity only makes common sense. Otherwise, how could we have survived as a species for hundreds of thousands of years without hospitals, HMOs, physicians, psychiatrists, pharmacists, or talk show hosts? Healing occurs when the healer or the individual makes an alliance with, or instigates the power of, the organism to restore itself (Cousins, 1989; Pelletier, 2000; Weil, 1995). So healing and self-regeneration are intrinsic life support systems, always working and, for most of us, most of the time, on call. Such a reality has dramatic implications, not just for medicine but for all the helping professions. At the least, it challenges the assumption of the disease model that only experts know what is best for their clients and that curing, healing, or transformation comes exclusively from outside sources.

Dialogue and Collaboration.   Humans can only come into being through a creative and emergent relationship with others. Without such transactions, there can be no discovery and testing of one's powers, no knowledge, no heightening of one's awareness and internal strengths. In dialogue, we confirm the importance of others and begin to heal the rift between self, other, and institution.

Dialogue requires empathy, identification with, and the inclusion of other people. Paulo Freire (1973) was convinced, based on his years of work with oppressed peoples, that only humble and loving dialogue can surmount the barrier of mistrust built from years of paternalism and the rampant subjugation of the knowledge and wisdom of the oppressed. "Founding itself upon love, humility, and faith, dialogue becomes a horizontal relationship of which mutual trust between the dialoguers is the logical consequence" (pp. 79–80). A caring community is a community that confirms otherness, in part by giving each person and group a ground of their own, and affirming this ground through encounters that are egalitarian and dedicated to healing and empowerment.

The idea of collaboration has a more specific focus. When we work together with clients we become their agents, their consultants, stakeholders with them in mutually crafted projects. This requires us to be open to negotiation and to appreciate the authenticity of the views and aspirations of those with whom we collaborate. Our voices may have to be quieted so that we can give voice to our clients. Comfortably ensconced in the expert role, sometimes we may have great difficulty assuming such a conjoint posture.

Suspension of Disbelief.   It would be hard to exaggerate the extent of disbelief of clients' words and stories in the culture of professionalism. While social work because of its enduring values may fancy itself less culpable in this regard than other professions, a little circumspection is warranted. As just one example (and probably somewhat unfair because this is a brief excerpt from a text on social work practice that generally assumes a positive view of clients), Hepworth and Larsen (1990) wrote:

> Though it is the primary source of information, verbal report is vulnerable to error because of possible faulty recall, distorted perceptions, biases, and limited self-awareness on the part of clients. It is thus vital to avoid the tendency to accept clients' views, descriptions, and reports as valid representations of reality. Similarly, it is important to recognize that feelings expressed by clients may emanate from faulty perceptions or may be altogether irrational. (p. 197)

Two observations: First, the idea that there are valid representations of reality is questionable. That is, there are many representations of the real world. Is, say, a Lakota understanding of fever any less relevant in context than a Manhattan internist's? Second, to begin work with clients in this frame of mind would seem to subvert the idea that clients often do know exactly what they are talking about and that they are experts on their own lives. And, are social workers own interpretations less subject to faulty recall, or their own interpretive forestructures less likely to be slathered over clients' own understanding? Perhaps, the suspension of belief in clients' accounts comes from the radiation of scientific thinking throughout our culture and into the professions. The ideal of the scientific investigator as objective and dispassionate observer has been transfigured into a certain incredulity about, and distancing from, clients. If the rise of the professions (and the ideology of professionalism) was part of the extension and reinforcement of the institutions of socialization and social control during the Victorian era, then a certain detachment and restraint in accepting clients and their stories made sense (Bledstein, 1978).
   Professionals have contained the affirmation of clients in a number of ways:

- by imposing their own theories over the theories and accounts of clients
- by using assessment in an interrogative style designed to ascertain certain diagnostic and largely preemptive hypotheses that, in the end, confirm suspicions about the client
- by engaging in self-protective maneuvers (like skepticism) designed to prevent the ultimate embarrassment for a professional—being fooled by or lied to by a cunning client

The frequent talk about manipulative and resistant clients in many social agencies may stem from the fear of being made the fool. To protect self-esteem, nonnormative lifestyles, self-interests, or benefits, clients may have a vested interest in not telling the truth. But we must consider the possibility that avoiding the truth may be a function of the manner in which the professional pursues and/or asserts the truth. The professional's knowledge, information, and perspective are privileged and carry institutional and legal weight. The client's do not.

In summary, the lexicon of strengths provides us with a vocabulary of appreciation and not aspersion about those with whom we work. In essence, the effort is to move away from defining professional work as the articulation of the power of expert knowledge toward collaboration with the power within the individual or community toward a life that is palpably better—and better on the clients' own terms.

PRINCIPLES OF THE STRENGTHS PERSPECTIVE

What exactly is a perspective? It is not a theory. Theories seek to explain some phenomena, or at least describe them analytically. It is not a model. Models are meant to represent, logically and graphically, some aspect of the world. A perspective is somewhat harder to define. At the least it is a standpoint, a way of viewing and understanding certain aspects of experience. It is a lens through which we choose to perceive and appreciate. It provides us with a slant on the world, built of words and principles. We have already reviewed some of the words. What follows now are some of the principles.

The principles that follow are the guiding assumptions and regulating understandings of the strengths perspective. They are tentative, still evolving, and subject to revision. They do, however, give a flavor of what practicing from a strengths appreciation involves.

Every Individual, Group, Family, and Community Has Strengths.   While it may be hard at times to invoke, it is essential to remind oneself that the person or family in front of you and the community around you possess assets, resources, wisdom, and knowledge that, at the outset, you probably know nothing about. First *and* foremost, the strengths perspective is about discerning those resources, and respecting them and the potential they may have for reversing misfortune, countering illness, easing pain, and reaching goals. To detect strengths, however, the social work practitioner must be genuinely interested in, and respectful of, clients' stories, narratives, and accounts—the interpretive angles they take on their own experiences. These are important "theories" that can guide practice. The unearthing of clients' identities and realities does not come only from a ritual litany of troubles, embarrassments, snares, foibles, and barriers. Rather, clients come into view when you assume that they know something, have learned lessons from experience, have hopes, have interests, and can do some things masterfully. These may be obscured by the stresses of the moment, submerged under the weight of crisis, oppression, or illness but, nonetheless, they abide.

In the end, clients want to know that you actually care about them, that how they fare makes a difference to you, that you will listen to them, that you will respect them no matter what their history, and that you believe that they can build something of value with the resources within and around them. But most of all, clients want to know that you believe they can surmount adversity and begin the climb toward transformation and growth.

Trauma and Abuse, Illness and Struggle May Be Injurious but They May also Be Sources of Challenge and Opportunity.   The Wolins (1997) point out that the "damage model" of development so prevalent in today's thinking only leads to discouragement, pessimism, and the victim mind-set. It also foretells a continuing future of psychopathology and troubled relationships. Individuals exposed to a variety of abuses, especially in childhood, are thought always to be victims or to be damaged in ways that obscure or override any strengths or possibilities for rebound. In the Wolins' "challenge model," children are not seen as merely passive recipients of parental unpredictability, abuse, disappointment, or violence. Rather, children are seen as active and developing individuals who, through these trials, learn skills and develop personal attributes that stand them in good stead in adulthood. Not that they do not suffer. They do. Not that they do not bear scars. They do. But they also may acquire traits and capacities that are preservative and life affirming. There is dignity to be drawn from having prevailed over obstacles to one's growth and maturing. The Wolins (1993) refer to this as "survivor's pride." It is a deep-dwelling sense of accomplishment in having met life's challenges and walked away, not without fear, even terror, and certainly not without wounds. Often this pride is buried under embarrassment, confusion, distraction, or self-doubt. But when it exists and is lit, it can ignite the engine of change.

Individuals, groups, and communities are more likely to continue development and growth when they are funded by the currency of their capacities, knowledge, and skills (Delgado, 2000; Kretzmann & McKnight, 1993). While the strengths perspective is powered by a similar belief, the observation of many who practice using a strengths approach is that many people who struggle to find their daily bread, a job, or shelter are already resilient, resourceful, and, though in pain, motivated for achievement on their terms. Kaplan and Girard (1994) put it this way:

> People are more motivated to change when their strengths are supported. Instead of asking family members what their problems are, a worker can ask what strengths they bring to the family and what they think are the strengths of other family members. Through this process the worker helps the family discover its capabilities and formulate a new way to think about themselves. . . . The worker creates a language of strength, hope, and movement. . . . (p. 53)

Assume That You Do Not Know the Upper Limits of the Capacity to Grow and Change and Take Individual, Group, and Community Aspirations Seriously.   Too often, professionals assume that a diagnosis, an assessment, or a profile sets the parameters of possibility for their clients. In our personal lives, looking back, we sometimes marvel at the road we traveled—a road that we, at the outset, might not have even considered taking—and the distance that we have come. For our clients, too often, we cannot imagine the prospect of similar dizzying and unanticipated destinations. The diagnosis or the assessment becomes a verdict and a sentence. Our clients will be better served when we make an overt pact with their promise and possibility. This means that we must hold high our expectations of clients and make allegiance with their hopes, visions, and values.

It is becoming increasingly clear that emotions have a profound effect on wellness and health. Emotions experienced as positive can activate the inner pharmacoepia, those chemicals that relax, help fight infection, and restore. This is undoubtedly part of our evolutionary success; our ability to adapt to situations, even highly toxic ones, that were not foretold in our genome (Damasio, 1994). When people believe that they can recover, that they have prospects, that their hopes are palpable, their bodies often respond optimally. That does not mean that people do not get sick. It does mean that when people are sick, healers can make an alliance with the body's regenerative powers and augment them with real but nonetheless fortifying and uplifting expectations (Weil, 1995). Roger Mills's (1995) health realization/community empowerment projects (detailed in Chapter 13) are based on similar principles. Mills's idea is that everyone has innate wisdom, intelligence, and motivating emotions and that these, even if muted by circumstance, are accessible through education, support, and encouragement. The goals of his projects are to "reconnect people to the [physical and mental] health in themselves and then direct them in ways to bring forth the health of others in their community. The result is a change in people and communities which builds up from within rather than [being] imposed from without" (Mills, 1993, cited in Benard, 1994, p. 22). So it is that individuals and communities have the capacity for restoration and rebound.

We Best Serve Clients by Collaborating with Them.   The role of expert or professional may not provide the best vantage point from which to appreciate clients' strengths and assets. A helper may best be defined as a collaborator or consultant: an individual clearly presumed, because of specialized education and experience, to know some things and to have some tools at the ready but definitely not the only one in the situation to have relevant, even esoteric, knowledge and understanding. Ms. Johnson knows more about thriving in a public housing project than anyone I can think of. Over the course of 35 years, she successfully raised 11 children. She maintained a demeanor of poise, and she demonstrated intelligence and vigor, even as her community underwent dramatic, often frightening changes. Her contributions to the community are, simply put, amazing. She has much to teach us and other residents of her community. I certainly would not presume to work *on* Ms. Johnson but would be privileged to work *with* her.

We make a serious error when we subjugate clients' wisdom and knowledge to official views. There is something liberating, for all parties involved, in connecting to clients' stories and narratives, their hopes and fears, their wherewithal and resources rather than trying to stuff them into the narrow confines of a diagnostic category or treatment protocol. Ultimately a collaborative stance may make us less vulnerable to some of the more political elements of helping: paternalism, victim-blaming (or, more currently, victim-creating), and preemption of client views. It is likewise important to get the stories and views of clients out to those who need to hear them—schools, agencies, employers, local governments, churches, and businesses. This is part of the role of advocacy. The policies and regulations that affect many of our clients are crafted in the halls of Congress and are often far removed from their daily reality. Furthermore, these policies rarely take advantage of the wisdom and resources of their intended beneficiaries and recipients.

Every Environment Is Full of Resources.   (See Chapters 11, 12, 13, and 14.) In communities that seem to amplify individual and group resilience, there is awareness, recognition, and use of the assets of most members of the community (Kretzmann & McKnight, 1993). Informal systems and associations of individuals, families, and groups, social circuits of peers, and intergenerational mentoring work to assist, support, instruct, and include all members of a community (Schorr, 1997). In inclusive communities, there are many opportunities for involvement, to make contributions to the moral and civic life of the whole; to become, in other words, a citizen in place. No matter how harsh an environment, how it may test the mettle of its inhabitants, it can also be understood as a potentially lush topography of resources and possibilities. In every environment, there are individuals, associations, groups, and institutions who have something to give, something that others may desperately need: knowledge, succor, an actual resource or talent, or simply time and place. Such resources usually exist outside the usual matrix of social and human service agencies. And, for the most part, they are unsolicited and untapped. Melvin Delgado (2000), in his articulation of the capacity-enhancement approach to urban social work practice, describes the five critical assumptions of that approach: " (1) The community has the will and the resources to help itself; (2) it knows what is best for itself; (3) ownership of the strategy rests within, rather than outside, the community; (4) partnerships involving organizations and communities are the preferred route for initiatives; and (5) the use of strengths in one area will translate into strengths in other areas . . . a ripple effect" (p. 28).

Such a view of the environment, while seeming to comfort those who believe that people(s) should pull themselves up by their collective and individual bootstraps, *does not* abrogate the responsibility for working for social and economic justice. It does, however, recognize that while we await political transformation, there are reservoirs of energy, ideas, talents, and tools out there on which to draw. To regard the environment as only inimical or toxic moves us to disregard these resources or mistakenly judge them as disreputable. When it comes, the community that is aware of and employing its human and social capital to the degree possible is in a much better position to drink the cooling waters of social justice.

Caring, Caretaking, and Context.   The idea that care is essential to human well-being does not sit well in a society beset by two centuries of rugged individualism. Deborah Stone (2000) says that we have three rights to care. First, all families must be permitted and assisted in caring for their members. Second, all those paid caregivers need to be able give the support and quality care that is commensurate with the highest ideals of care without subverting their own well-being. Finally, a right to care boils down to this: that all people (and there may be 38 million children under the age of 10 who clearly need care and anywhere between 30 and 50 million adults who need some degree of care) who need care get it. We do have a horror of dependence. But, as Stone says,

> Caring for each other is the most basic form of civic participation. We learn to care in families, and we enlarge our communities of concern as we mature. Caring is the essential democratic act, the prerequisite to voting, joining associations, attending meetings, holding office, and all the other ways we sustain democracy. (p. 15)

In one sense, social work is about care and caretaking. Ann Weick (2000) makes the case that social caretaking as an activity is the profession's hidden (and first) voice; hidden because it is also woman's voice. Caretaking is, in a diffuse sense, also the work of the strengths perspective.

> Recognizing the capacity for toughness and tenderness, for clear reason and fluid intuition, for radical hope and dry-eyed reality brings us back to the challenges of caretaking. But rather than discounting its demands and possibilities, the lesson of our first voice tells us to pay attention to every dimension it encompasses. Social work is social caretaking. . . . We need to turn our attention to the humblest activities of social caretaking and offer our boldest ideas about strengthening the social web connecting us all. (p. 401)

Like social caretaking, and social work, the strengths perspective is about the revolutionary possibility of hope; hope realized through the strengthened sinew of social relationships in family, neighborhood, community, culture, and country. That contextual sinew is fortified by the expression of the individual and communal capacities of all.

SOME PRELIMINARY THOUGHTS

Social work has had something of a dissociative history with regard to building on client strengths. From its inception as a profession, the field has been exhorted to respect and energize client capacities. Bertha Capen Reynolds(1951) looked at the issue in terms of workers' obligations:

> The real choice before us as social workers is whether *we* are to be passive or active. . . . Shall we be content to give with one hand and withhold with the other, to build up or tear down at the same time the strength of a person's life? Or shall we become conscious of our own part in making a profession which will stand forthrightly for human well-being, *including the right to be an active citizen?* (p. 175, emphasis added)

The historical and continuing tension between the desire to become more professional, more technically adept, to focus on "function" rather than "cause" (Lee, 1929), to elevate social work to a new level of respect and comparability among the professions, and, on the other hand, to retain the interest in social action and the redress of social inequities seems to have been resolved recently in favor of the former. The writing, lexicon, and perspective of, say, clinical social work and those of social action or community development are quite different, maybe even at odds. While there is no implacable conflict between the interests of social work practice and social action, the infusion of psychodynamic thinking, the rise of private practice and vendorship, the mass appeal of DSM IV TR among other factors have driven social work toward a model of practice that is more heavily aligned with psychological thinking and psychopathology theories (Specht & Courtney, 1993). The theories that define such an alignment are typically oriented toward family and individual dysfunctions and disorders. While we must respect the impact of problems on the quality of life for our clients, we must also exercise extraordinary diligence to assure that the resources and positive attributes of clients draw our attention and define our efforts.

It does seem to be the case that group work has a long history of attention to the strengths and resources of group members and their neighborhoods. Andrew Malekoff (2001) puts it this way:

> There is so much talk today about strengths and wellness. This is hardly a new or revolutionary concept. But it has been neglected for too long. However, good group work practice has been paying attention to people's strengths since the days of the original settlement houses over 100 years ago, mostly without fanfare. (p. 247)

Although today's social work practice texts typically nod in the direction of client strengths but provide little guidance to the student or worker about how to make an accounting of strengths and how to employ them in helping, we are currently seeing movement away from the problem or pathology perspective. The solution-focused approach is one example. In essence, it regards clients in the light of what they have done well, those times that the problem has not been apparent, or those times when exceptions to difficulty have occurred. Furthermore, client goals and visions are the centerpiece of the work to be done. It is not unusual for solution-focused practitioners to ask how things would be positively different if a miracle occurred overnight and the problem no longer held (de Jong & Berg, 2001). The literature on resilience, discussed briefly earlier in this chapter, also provides conceptual and clinical ground for employing client strengths as a central part of the helping process. In the words of Benard (1994; see also Chapter 12), "Using resilience as the knowledge base for practice creates a *sense of optimism and hope*. It allows anyone working with troubled youth to, as poet Emily Dickinson urges, "dwell in possibility," to have confidence in their futures and, therefore, to convey this positive expectation to them" (p. 4).

Finally, the research on the effectiveness of a strengths approach, although very preliminary, suggests that it may be an effective and economical framework for practice or case management (Rapp, 1998). Related research on power of mind/health realization; resilience-based practice; solution-focused therapy; community-building; and the research done on the critical factors in successful therapy provide some associated support for the elements of a strengths perspective that make a difference. Research actually done from the vantage point of a strengths approach includes the views and concerns of the stakeholders (subjects and clients) from the outset. The results of the research are to be used to achieve stated objectives of the stakeholders and/or to aid in the solving of identified problems.

In Chapter 15, I will discuss in more detail some of the converging lines of research and practice that are reinforcing the strengths perspective. I will also address some of the persistent and significant criticisms of it.

CONCLUSION

This edition of the book continues the effort to expand the conceptual, clinical, and practical elements of the strengths perspective. At its philosophical core, this perspective merely affirms or, rather, re-affirms, our dedication to understanding and revering the resources and resourcefulness that individuals, families, and communities bring to us when they seek our help. The central proposition of social work practice, as I see it, is to exploit the best in all of us; to work together to surmount adversity and trouble; to confront the appalling with all the tools available within us and around us; to wrestle distress and disillusionment to the ground with determination and grit; to grab the hands of others and march unwaveringly, even heroically, in the direction of hopes, dreams, and possibilities.

Let it be said once again. *The strengths perspective is not about ignoring trauma, problems, illness, and adversity.* While practitioners of the perspective disagree about the role of problems in the work that they do, all believe that this approach, at the very least, is about restoring some balance to our efforts—a balance that requires that we appreciate the struggles of an individual, family, or community but that more importantly we look at those struggles for hints and intimations, or solid evidence of strengths, capacities, and competencies. The emphasis on problems and pathologies, no matter what we claim as a profession, surely is careening out of control. The medical/psychiatric/pharmaceutical/insurance cartel (and I use the term advisedly) has a tightening grip on the ways that we see and consider human nature and the human condition. It is de rigueur in popular culture, in the media, in clinics and agencies, even in personal relationships to allow what is problematic to seize our perceptions and interest. As social workers we are obligated to resist the siren call of the medical model in our work together with clients.

Duncan and Miller (2000) put it well:

> If therapists are to resist the pull to steer clients automatically toward diagnosis and medication, the belief in client capacity to conquer even extreme (and often dangerous) personal circumstances must go deep. Clients can use an ally in overcoming often dramatic obstacles to personal recovery. When professionals use their inevitable positions of power to hand power back to the clients rather than block client capacities, clients can even more readily reach their goals. (p. 216)

DISCUSSION QUESTIONS

1. What are the most significant contrasts between a strengths approach and a problem-focused one?

2. If you were to employ the strengths perspective in your practice, what would your first steps in working with a client be?

3. What are the barriers you have found in approaching your practice with individuals, families, groups or communities from a strengths vantage point?

4. What do you consider to be your strengths? How do they shape or affect your practice? How do they shape your personal life?

5. Think of a client you have worked with. Did you ever account for some of the client's (whether an individual, family, or community) capacities and assets? Did you use them in practice? How?

REFERENCES

American Psychiatric Association. (2000). *Diagnostic and statistical manual of mental disorders IV TR.* Washington, DC: American Psychiatric Association.

Becker, E. (1973). *The denial of death.* New York: Free Press.

Becker, H. (1963). *Outsiders: Studies in the sociology of deviance.* New York: Free Press.

Benard, B. (1991). *Fostering resiliency in kids: Protective factors in the family, school, and community.* San Francisco: Western Regional Center.

Benard, B. (1994). *Applications of resilience.* Paper presented at a conference on the Role of Resilience in Drug Abuse, Alcohol Abuse, and Mental Illness. Dec. 5–6. Washington, DC.

Benard, B. (2004). *Resiliency: What we have learned.* San Francisco: WestEd.

Bledstein, B. (1978). *The culture of professionalism.* New York: Norton.

Clark, M.D. (1997, April). Strengths-based practice: The new paradigm. *Corrections Today, 165,* 110–111.

Cousins, N. (1989). *Head first: The biology of hope.* New York: Dutton.

Cullison A. (September, 2004). Inside Al-Qaeda's hard drive. *The Atlantic, 294,* 55–70.

Damasio, A. R. (1994). *Descartes' error: Emotion, reason, and the human brain.* New York: Grosset/Dunlap Books.

DeJong, P. & Berg, I. K. (2001). *Interviewing for solutions.* 2nd ed. Belmont, CA: Wadsworth.

Delgado, M. (2000). *Community social work practice in an urban context: The potential of a capacity-enhancement perspective.* New York: Oxford University Press.

Duncan, B. L. & Miller, S. D. (2000). *The heroic client: Doing client-directed, outcome-informed therapy.* San Francisco: Jossey-Bass.

Freire, P. (1973). *Pedagogy of the oppressed.* New York: Seabury.

Freire, P. (1996). *Pedagogy of hope: Reliving pedagogy of the oppressed.* New York: Continuum.

Fromm, E. (1973). *The anatomy of human destructiveness.* New York: Holt, Rinehart & Winston.

Gergen, K. J. (1994). *Realities and relationships: Soundings in social construction.* Cambridge: Harvard University Press.

Glover, J. (2000). *Humanity: A moral history of the twentieth century.* New Haven, CT: Yale University Press.

Goffman, E. (1961). *Asylums: Essays on the situation of mental patients and other inmates.* Garden City, NY: Anchor/Doubleday.

Hepworth, D. H., & Larsen, J. (1990). *Direct social work practice: Theory and skills* (3rd ed.). Chicago: Dorsey Press.

James, W. (1902). *The varieties of religious experience.* New York: Modern Library.

Kaplan, L., & Girard, J. (1994). *Strengthening high-risk families.* New York: Lexington Books.

Katz, M. (1997). *On playing a poor hand well: Insights from the lives of those who have overcome childhood risks and adversities.* New York: Norton.

Kirsch, I., Moore, T. J., Scoboria, A., & Nicholls, S. (2003). The emperor's new drugs: An analysis of antidepressant medication data submitted to the U.S. Food and Drug Administration. *Prevention & Treatment, 5,* 5–23. It is an online journal: http://journals.apa.org/prevention/volume5/pre0050023a.html.

Kozol, J. (2000). *Ordinary resurrections: Children in the years of hope.* New York: Crowne Publishers.

Kretzmann, J. P., & McKnight, J. L. (1993). *Building communities from the inside out: Toward finding and mobilizing a community's assets.* Evanston, IL: Northwestern University, Center for Urban Affairs and Policy Research.

Langewiesche, W. (2003). *American Ground: Unbuilding the world trade center.* New York: North Point Press.

LeDoux, J. (2002). *Synaptic self: How our brains become who we are.* New York: Viking.

Lee, P. R. (1929). Social work: Cause and function. *Proceedings of the National Conference of Social Work, 3–20.*

Malekoff, A. (2001). The power of group work with kids: A practitioner's reflection on strengths-based practice. *Families in Society, 82,* 243–250.

Mattingly, C. (1991). Narrative reflections on practical actions: Two experiments in reflective story-telling. In D. A. Schön (Ed.), *The reflective turn: Case studies in and on educational practice.* New York: Teacher's College Press.

Mills, R. (1995). *Realizing mental health: Toward a new psychology of resiliency.* New York: Sulzburger & Graham.

Parsons, R. J., & Cox, E. O. (1994). *Empowerment-oriented social work practice with the elderly.* Newbury Park, CA: Sage.

Pelletier, K. R. (2000). *The best alternative medicine: What works? What does not?* New York: Simon & Schuster.

Pinderhughes, E. (1994). Empowerment as intervention goals: Early ideas. In L. Gutierrez & P. Nurius (Eds.), *Education and research for empowerment practice.* Seattle, WA: University of Washington School of Social Work, Center for Policy and Practice Research.

Pransky, J. (1998). *Modello: A story of hope for the inner city and beyond.* Burlington, VT: NorthEast Health Realization Publications.

Rank, O. (1941). *Beyond psychology.* New York: Dover Books.

Rapp, C. A. (1998). *The strengths model: Case management with people suffering from severe and persistent mental illness.* New York: Oxford University Press.

Restak, R. (2003). *The new brain: How the modern age is rewiring your mind.* New York: St. Martin's Press.

Reynolds, B. C. (1951). *Social work and social living: Explorations in philosophy and practice.* Silver Spring, MD: National Association of Social Workers.

Rose, S. M. (2000). Reflections on empowerment-based practice. *Social Work, 45,* 401–412.

Saleebey, D. (1989). Professions in crisis: The estrangement of knowing and doing. *Social Casework, 70,* 556–563.

Scheff, T. J. (1984). *Being mentally ill: A sociological theory* (3rd ed.). New York: Aldine.

Schön, D. A. (1983). *The reflective practitioner.* New York: Basic Books.

Schorr, L. B. (1997). *Common purpose: rebuilding families and neighborhoods to rebuild America.* New York: Anchor/Doubleday.

Simon, B. L. (1994). *The empowerment tradition in social work: A history.* New York: Columbia University Press.

Specht, H., & Courtney, M. (1993). *Unfaithful angels: How social work has abandoned its mission.* New York: Free Press.

Stone, D. (2000). Why we need a care movement. *The Nation, 270,* 13–15.

Walzer, M. (1983). *Spheres of justice.* New York: Basic Books.

Weick, A. (2000). Hidden voices. *Social Work, 45,* 395–402.

Weil, A. (1995). *Spontaneous healing.* New York: Knopf.

Werner, E., & Smith, R. S. (1992). *Overcoming the odds.* Ithaca, NY: Cornell University Press.

Wolin, S. J., & Wolin, S. (1993). *The resilient self: How survivors of troubled families rise above adversity.* New York: Villard.

Wolin, S., & Wolin, S. J. (1996). The challenge model: Working with strengths in children of substance abusing parents. *Adolescent Substance Abuse and Dual Disorders, 5,* 243–256.

Wolin, S., & Wolin, S. J. (1997). Shifting paradigms: Talking a paradoxical approach. *Resiliency in Action, 2,* 23–28.

CHAPTER TWO

SHIFTING OUR HABITS OF MIND: LEARNING TO PRACTICE FROM A STRENGTHS PERSPECTIVE[1]

ROBERT BLUNDO

Assumptions can be like blinkers on a horse—they keep us from straying from the road, but they block our view of other routes and possibilities along the roadside.
—Armand Eisen

You have been assigned a new case at your agency. The individual is a college student starting the third year at the local university where classes just began a little more than a week ago. Please read the following process recording and note your thoughts as you take in the information being presented. That is, please note the "data" or specific information that appears most important or significant to your beginning understanding. Now, even though you may want more information, think of what immediately comes to mind in terms of how you would go about starting to work with this person? What questions do you want to ask? What do you focus on as important information? How do you define the issue being presented? Do you think of a diagnosis?

Sorry, I am a little late, had to give some notes to a friend. I called last week to make this appointment because I just felt that I was not going to make it. I felt so anxious and stressed at school the other day, I had to leave and did not attend my first class session. Actually, it was my first day back in school since taking a break last year. I had pushed myself too hard with work, school, and trying to keep the gay/lesbian/bi alliance

[1]This chapter is based on an article by the author published in May/June 2001 in *Families in Society 82*, 296–304 entitled *Learning strengths-based practice: Challenging our personal and professional frames.*

going, I just couldn't do it anymore. My drinking was getting worse and I was yelling at my partner so much I was always leaving to get away to calm down. My dad would hit my mother and he drank a lot. Maybe I am just too much like him . . . "

So, what do you think? What comes to mind when you think of what you have just been told? What gender is this young person? Do you need more information? What type of information or data do you think you would need? What thoughts do you have about treatment? If your social work background is similar to mine, you might be thinking about the multiple problems or maybe even a dual-diagnosis to start. Maybe you considered an evaluation of the drinking problem, obtaining more information about sexual orientation, family history of possible abuse, maybe an evaluation of suicide potential, possibly using the anxiety and/or depression scales, so definitely treatment is needed, possibly couples work later on.

The information here is very limited but for most of us social workers just a few pieces of information can get us started thinking and concluding, even though it is just preliminary at this point. What we usually see as most provocative are the "problems" apparent in the story being told. We look for what is going wrong, symptoms, what might be failings, underlying pathologies, and the history of the problems to substantiate these early assumptions that are being constructed into a mental picture of our client. It is the client's faults and weaknesses that we key in on as most significant in our listening. In many ways, we are rewriting or translating the story told by the client into our own professional language, a language largely made up of concepts having to do with problems, pathology, deficits, and failings to which we will apply some form of intervention. By the way, the young person is a woman

Now for a moment try a second look at what was revealed in her story. Were you at all surprised that the young person was a woman? If so, what does that say about how "natural" our assumptions appear without awareness? Let's take a further look. It has been at least a week since the "incident" of anxiety at school and no reports of anxiety since then. In fact, it appears as if she is doing her work and has friends with whom she shares notes. Even though it is not clear, the vignette reveals that she missed the "first class session" on the first day back and appears to have made it to the other classes that day and the remaining classes during the week prior to seeing you. The comment about the drinking referred to a time last year while she was under stress. At least in this presentation there is no mention of a drinking problem at present or evidence of what she meant by "drinking too much." The individual demonstrated awareness of her provocative behavior with her partner and, importantly, addressed the issue by leaving so as not to provoke any further distress on the relationship that we only assume may have included threats of physical acts. Note, though, that physical acts were not actually mentioned at that point, except with regard to her father. The client handled her own previous stress by choosing to take time off from school to take care of her self and possibly her relationship. She also reports taking on a responsible effort with her gay/lesbian/bisexual organization on campus. She made an effort to help her self by calling for an appointment and has kept that appointment even though the anxiety level appears to have lessened. Finally, she shows a willingness to be open and to talk about her self with you.

If your experience was similar to mine at first reading, you too must have been struck by the contrast between the two interpretations or versions of the client's story. It is this contrast that is at the heart of shifting one's perspective from a traditional pathology based medical model of practice to a strengths-based understanding of practice. Making this shift in practice is a considerable challenge for social workers like myself who have been educated and tutored in the basic tenets of the profession's knowledge base and practice methods. It is additionally difficult for students just learning practice skills. Students often come with a bias toward seeing problems and then trying to fix them by making suggestions to the client.

Unlike shifts in techniques, models, skills, and intervention protocols that many social workers are familiar with, such as adding onto one's repertoire a set of cognitive-behavioral intervention skills, taking on the challenge of learning strengths-based practice requires a more fundamental shift in how we think and view the world. The strengths perspective requires a significant alteration in how we actually understand and think about those with whom we work, how we think about ourselves as professionals, and the nature of the knowledge base for our practice, as well as the process of social work practice itself. It is the fundamental nature of this shift that is the challenge to practitioners and students just learning the profession. This is a significant shift for social work practitioners, students, and educators if social work is to truly embrace this egalitarian, collaborative working relationship that builds upon the strengths and resilience of individuals, families, and communities.

This chapter will examine this challenge in terms of the learning process of students new to the profession as well as practitioners who have been comfortably settled into the familiar world of pathology and deficit assessment and intervention. A brief review of the background and entrenchment of the medical/pathology/expert model of practice taught and practiced today will set the context of the challenges found in shifting perspectives. This will be followed by an exploration of some of the specific challenges that emerge when learning this new paradigm. Two specific issues—overcoming our natural predisposition to help by introducing our ideas and our trained biases such as professional knowledge/expertise and professional practice traditions— will be explored by contrasting the traditional deficit based assessment and problem focused, expert directed practice with the strengths based assessment and a solution-focused, collaborative based practice.

THE DEFICIT/PATHOLOGY KNOWLEDGE BASE
BECOMES SYNONYMOUS WITH SOCIAL WORK

The preoccupation with problems, human deficits, with what is broken, gone wrong or failed, has dominated the attention of social work since its early development and exists today in the form of the taken for granted "problem focused" practice models. Underlying this simple and innocuous looking model, found in most of social work texts and demonstrated in our practice, generally is an entrenched foundation of assumptions about the human condition, models of helping, and a philosophy of science. (Lubove, 1965; Specht & Courtney, 1994; Reid, 1995; Goldstein, 1997; Rapp, 1998;).

By the early 1900s, the work of organizations like Charitable Organization Society (COS) and case workers such as Mary Richmond were moving the friendly visitor away from seeing poverty and human difficulties as merely moral failings in need of moral uplifting to one that viewed human suffering as something that could be rationally understood. The application of a "scientific" or supposedly subjective free or rational study and analysis of problems and social conditions could result in finding causes and applying treatments to amend the problem. Even though many early social work efforts had directed energies to changing the social conditions that resulted in human misery, the professionalization of social work, in particular social casework, began to purposely shift its focus toward intervention at the level of the individual and family. Five important elements coalesced and helped contribute to this shift. They were: 1) the growing professionalization and training of the "friendly visitor"; 2) the growing fear of Bolshevism, the "Red Scare," following the Russian Revolution [1917–1918]; 3) the integration of the medical model of practice into social casework; 4) the embracing of Freudian psychoanalytic theory and practice; and 5) the strong faith in reason and the "scientific" paradigm.

Professionalism and Education

As the 20th century started, there was a growing "white collar" and professional middle class that included many new occupations including social casework which was made up of mostly college educated women and men. Following the developments in medicine and engineering, "professionalization was a major social trend during this era" (Popple & Reid, 1999, p. 12). Charity Organization Societies started to organize in-service training classes with a focus on the "techniques" of social work. As the first schools of social work emerged in New York, Boston, and Chicago, the movement was away from content on social issues, social reform, and social/economic inequalities and toward the practice techniques to be used with families and individuals. Although some educators such as Edward Devine of the New School of Social Work did not support such a shift in emphasis, the movement grew. Abraham Flexner's speech at the National Conference of Charities and Corrections in 1915 sealed the direction when he proclaimed that social work was not a profession because it did not possess a standard method of practice that could be taught by means of a specific social work knowledge base. This reinforced the impetus toward education and training. Leaders in social work education encouraged the growth of training programs in university settings with an increasing focus on common techniques and methods of practice.

Bolshevism and Rising Fears

As social work moved away from addressing social inequities and social conditions, the national political agenda turned away from social reforms and issues of inequality. Fear of "foreigners" and fears of conflict created by obvious social class differences took center stage. Jane Addams (1930) described the reaction to this growing fear of social reform within social work itself: "Social workers exhibited many symptoms of this panic [Red Scare] and with a kind of protective instinct carefully avoided any identification with the phraseology of social reform" (p. 155). The national fears of collectivism and of social class conflict further supported the movement away from addressing poverty and social conditions. Not only were social reforms neglected, social workers focused more on treating the pathologies of the families, and individuals, without providing financial or social assistance.

The Medical Model and the Diagnostic School

Mary Richmond's practice text, "Social Diagnosis," published in 1917, represented this shift of emphasis in rationality being directed toward the individual and away from social action and social reform. It represented the movement toward professionalism in terms of a transferable knowledge base and a model of practice that could be applied to a range of clients and situations. Importantly, it formalized the insinuation of concepts of medical practice into a model of social work practice.

Mary Richmond specifically formulated the start of much of our present day social work language and thinking, greatly influenced by the developments and innovations in community medical practice efforts being made by Dr. Adolf Meyer at Johns Hopkins University Hospital in Baltimore, Maryland, and the work of Dr. Richard Cabot at Massachusetts General Hospital. The use of the "study, diagnosis and treatment" model used in the emerging science of medicine was adapted to the practice of social work. Mary Richmond (1917) called the process "social diagnosis" and described the developing social work perspective in this manner:

> Social diagnosis is the attempt to arrive at as *exact a definition* as possible of the social situation and *personality of a given client*. The *gathering of evidence, or investigation,* begins the process, the *critical examination* and *comparison of evidence* follows, and last come its *interpretation and the definition* of the social difficulty. Where one word must describe the whole process, *diagnosis* is a better word than *investigation,* though in strict use the former belongs to the end of the process (emphases added) (p. 62).

These fundamental "medical" constructs became the basis of social work practice within the developing schools of social work over the next decades and became the benchmark of good practice taught in the classroom and in social work practice texts. Thus began the diligence accorded lengthy process recordings and intake summaries focused on obtaining a broad spectrum of information believed necessary in constructing the diagnosis of the problem in a manner similar to that of diagnosing a physical illness.

Freudian Psychoanalytic Theory

Mary Richmond's (1917, 1922) efforts represented the start of a knowledge base for practice in terms of a model for gathering information, making an assessment and a social diagnosis. What was needed now was a theory or model of causality that would explain why individuals or families did what they did. In 1909, Sigmund

Freud had been invited to give a series of lectures at Clark University and by 1915 *Good Housekeeping* magazine had published a series of stories popularizing psychoanalytic ideas (Heller & Rudnick, 1991). Psychoanalytic theory and practice methods were quickly adopted by some influential American psychiatrists as a "scientific" theory for understanding and treating a wide range of conditions.

Given the emphasis of the medical model on discovering the cause of illness and then prescribing a means to intervene in the cause and thus to cure the disease, social work was open to a means of understanding the cause of human suffering on an individual or psychological level. Psychoanalysis was embraced by many caseworkers working with children, the courts, medicine, and psychiatry as the knowledge base for understanding and intervention. Mary Jarrett (1918) commented "We see case work about to pass into a psychological phase . . . It is becoming evident that personality will become the leading interest in the future" (p. 287). A year later, Mary Jarrett (1919) proclaimed that it is the internal mental life of clients that would be at the heart of social casework (cited in Robinson, 1930). Social work was developing as a profession with a specific common method or practice to be called "social casework" and a body of knowledge and practice principles to support that work. The internal mental life of clients emerged as the focus of professional knowing and doing for future generations of social workers.

So it was that during the early years of the profession's development, social work practitioners and scholars embraced psychiatry as well as the emerging scientific inquiry into the nature of personality development. Early schools of social work integrated psychoanalytic theory into the curriculum along with human development, psychopathology and, in particular, psychoanalytic thinking and practices. This institutionalized emphasis on assessment and diagnosis came to be termed the "Diagnostic School" of social work practice. But for a brief time in the 1930s through the 1950s, another group of social workers developed an alternative theory and method of practice from a different perspective. They called it the "Functionalist School" approach to practice and they challenged some of the basic constructs of the medical or pathology model. Jessie Taft (1944), a leader in this group, noted that the use of diagnosis and treatment as construed within medicine, psychiatry, and social work were "fundamentally antagonistic" to the principles of social work. The Functional School believed that the "client is not a sick person whose illness must be classified, but a human being, like the worker" and called for embracing the psychology of "growth" rather than "disease" (Taft, 1944, pp. 7–8.). The further developments within psychiatry, psychology, and the emerging practice of psychotherapy following World War II, saw the end of this effort to redirect the basically "psychoanalytically" oriented theories of human development and intervention principles incorporated into the foundation of social work education and practice

Faith in Science or Scientism

Scientism refers to the "exaggerated trust in the efficacy of a method" of inquiry that assumes objectivity or the ability to see the world independent of human thought, social context, or perspective (Merriam Webster's Collegiate Dictionary,

1994). This is reflective of a "modernist" approach to knowledge that assumes that what we think as being "reality" is singular, stable, linear, and knowable by observation. This is in contrast to a "postmodernist" approach that assumes "multiple realities conditioned by individual, social, and temporal factors" that places people within ever-changing persons-in-context and expresses the uniqueness of human beings and social circumstances (Neimeyer & Raskin, 2000, p. 5).

The early "scientific" developments such as widespread utilization of electricity, the telegraph and the telephone, the prodigious feats in engineering (bridges, skyscrapers, etc.), all had a profound effect on a growing faith in science to provide answers to human problems and possibilities. Freud was considered a scientist (as you may recall, he began his career as a neuroscientist) even though his observations about human nature and the human condition were not conducted as formal experiments. The medical community that welcomed Freud's theories considered themselves to be scientific and believed that their new field was built on a rational and objective understanding of human life. Science brought with it a sense of authority in that claims in its name were thought to be discoveries of a basic truth of nature.

This was a simplistic view of science and reflected an assumption that with diligence and careful observation, and analysis one could understand, predict and treat any condition. Social casework came into being during this scientific age and incorporated the attitudes and beliefs of this time. The theories and methods of social casework practice reflected this faith in science and with it, scientific authority for its methods of practice. In the summer of 1918, Smith College hosted an eight-week training for social workers. One of the instructors noted that the "training of social case-work [is to] be based on scientific method rather than on philanthropic technique . . . serious social work must . . . lift its eyes from the routine of simple fact-getting to . . . a more scientific method" (Chapin, 1918, pp. 591–592). The assumption was that a basic truth about human motivation and behavior had been or could be "discovered" and that the methods of "assessing, diagnosing and treating" these conditions had also been "discovered" as if a natural condition.

Reiteration and Entrenchment of Practice Principles

An early text by Margaret Bristol (1936) noted that although case records were needed for a wide range of necessary agency and educational functions, the most significant remained the creation of the diagnosis. She believed that the very process of creating a case record and diagnosis required "critical thinking and careful organization of material" and "compelled [the worker] to think through the situation and to make a diagnosis of the problem" (Bristol, 1936, p. 6). Gordon Hamilton (1946) referred to the social worker as a "trained diagnostician" who has the ability to "pluck from an unending web of social experience that thread of probable significance" (p.134). Felix Biestek (1957) saw the diagnosis as central. It was developed as the "caseworker begins at once to formulate some notion of the *real nature* of the problem" (p. 45). We still see this assumed need reflected in the enormous amount of information social workers are encouraged to gather today with the ultimate goal of making an accurate diagnosis or assessment of the problem. The majority of our present day social work practice texts used in schools of social work contain pages of assessment forms, inventories, and grids created to assist the social worker in gathering abundant amounts of information. Mary Richmond's (1917; 1922) translation of the medical pathology model of practice in medicine is the primary process still used and taught today even though the language might be somewhat different. This orientation is at the heart of how most social workers think of practice today—focusing on the problem or what underlies the problem, looking for the cause of the problem by gathering evidence or data, assessing the data, reformulating the problem into a diagnosis—cause and effect—and developing a plan or intervention to address the "diagnosis" or problem as *understood by the social worker.*

The "scientifically" based psychoanalytic constructs had become synonymous with the profession itself. It is hard to conceive of social work today without assuming the standards and knowledge base set down nearly 80 years ago. First, social work adopted as its foundation the medical/scientific method of data collection, analysis, and diagnosis and continued to evolve this in terms of its own mission. This prescribed a focus on the problem or underlying causes to be discovered by means of "objective" observation and inquiry. It demanded the incorporation and reliance upon theories of behavior, thinking, and emotion to provide the means for understanding the client's problem. It was this "scientific" knowledge possessed by the social worker "expert" that was needed to decipher what had gone wrong or failed in order to address the client's problems. Secondly, social work had embraced practice principles derived from the psychoanalytic model. Social work was now focused upon the inner life (psychology) of the client and personality development or, more to the point, defective intrapsychic and interpersonal development. The need for historical data concerning early childhood development assumed to underlie current conflicts, the significance of emotions and catharsis, unconscious motivations and defenses, constructs such as transference and resistance, and ideas of professional distance became part of our everyday social work practice language. While the present translations of these concepts are not always expressed in the exact same ways, the underlying assumptions have been integrated within much of traditional social work practice today. This developing model of practice and the attendant theories of behavior and emotion were to guide the social worker's relationship with the client, the social worker's understanding of the client and his or her circumstances, as well as the nature of the intervention process itself. These concepts have become, even to this day, ingrained in the mind of the profession as so fundamental to the practice of social work that it is nearly impossible to consider a practice that does not include most of these essential principles in some form or another.

The Tenacity of Our Traditional Paradigm

The depth of the attachment to the ideas perpetuated by this knowledge base were reflected in the criticism Helen Harris Perlman's (1957) book, "Social Casework: A Problem-solving Process," received from some of her colleagues. They were critical of an approach that placed the ego capacities in such a prominent position in relation to that of the unconscious and the instinctual drives. Florence Hollis (1964) reiterated this attitude in her highly influential casework text, "Casework: A Psychosocial Therapy." She insisted, "case work will drastically impoverish itself if it follows the lead of Horney and Sullivan in trying to explain human behavior primarily in interpersonal terms, omitting those *key intrapsychic phenomena* that from the start influence the child's perception of and reaction to his interpersonal experiences" (p. 11).

MAINTAINING OUR SENSE OF WHAT IS "RIGHT"

It is the tenaciousness with which we humans attach ourselves to or create meanings about our world that is at the center of the challenge of learning the strengths perspective. Our professional training and practices have been for the most part a set of traditions handed down and reified. Focusing on the problems and potential or underlying causes, making a diagnosis, and attempting to decrease the symptoms represents constructs that prevent us from conceptualizing our work in any other way. These traditions are like lenses or blinders that keep us focused on a particular path but keep us from seeing other possibilities. Erving Goffman's (1974) concept of "frames" captures this ongoing process within each of us as individuals and as we come together to create a "profession." The notion of living within a "frame" refers to the constructed meanings or definitions we share with others that provide us with "models" of daily interactions and practices. For example when we enter a restaurant, we have little to think about other than what we might want to order. Unless we have never been in, read about, or heard about a restaurant, most of the activity will seem very natural and seemingly without thought about the process itself. Everyone participating in the "restaurant" experience knows what they are expected to do. There are numerous rules and roles to be played out in getting a quick bite. It is only when someone does not follow the script that we are aware of the "frame" or process. Once ensconced within the world of constructed meaning shared by others in the profession, doing things differently is met with attempts to maintain the predominant frame. To suggest changing the frame is very difficult, as the examples of Helen Harris Perlman and Florence Hollis demonstrate. It is like being asked to change "reality" as we live it out day to day in our professional relationships.

A consequence of constructed realities is that each of us selectively attends to that which matches our worldview. We therefore see a world as we have imagined it and in a way that our theories and actions reinforce the sense of its existence out there in the world. This frame or constructed reality being shared by others with whom we work and live, shared and reinforced by our profession in terms of its teachings and socialization processes, is comfortable and "real" as if a natural phenomena. So real it is often hard to become even aware of the existence of our frames and constructed meanings. It is only when something unexpected or unimagined shakes up the process that we became aware of being engaged in a set of expectations, rules of action, and modes of thought. Even under these contradictions or evidence that our frames might not be the whole story we are very persistent in maintaining our perspectives and beliefs. The "primacy effect" and "belief perseverance" among other concepts in the study of human inference demonstrate that people are very resistant to changing or altering their initial beliefs (Nisbett & Ross, 1980; Lord, Ross, and Lepper, 1979; Kirshner & Witson, 1997). Importantly, once this belief or theory is in place, individuals are very resistant to any conflicting evidence. In the face of alternative evidence, individuals selectively choose that evidence that substantiates their original idea or theory.

Professional Literature Maintaining Traditional Frames

Shifting frames is not easy. It is disturbing and uncomfortable to contemplate. It is easier to attach small asides to existing frames, even though incongruent with aspects of the dominant frame within which we live day to day. This is what takes place most often within social work practice literature. Authors incorporate new ideas but often as attachments to older frames without altering the basic structures of practice. In some sense they "talk the talk" but don't "walk the walk." This is particularly true as the concepts of empowerment, strengths, self-determination, and diversity start to emerge within the profession's language. But it usually stays just that, language without substance in terms of shifting the basic frames of thinking and action. For example, authors such as Jeffrey Kottler (2000), Naomi Brill (1998), and Bradford Sheafor and colleagues (2000) talk about client strengths, self-determination, and empowerment without integrating these ideas into a practice reflective of the deepest meaning these new frames or perspectives would provide practitioners. Therefore, the possibilities of these new perspectives become diluted and overshadowed by the familiar social work paradigm. Students and practitioners assume that because they "think about" strength, add strengths questions to their assessment battery, or use the words that they have understood the significance these ideas might bring to their practice and to the profession.

Jeffrey Kottler's (2000) book, "The Nuts and Bolts of Helping," is a good example of the discussion of what might be considered standard practice skills within several human service domains, including social work. The focus of the text is on instructing the beginning practitioner as the significant player in the helping process—not of course the client. This is as it should be if we are seeing the world from the perspective of the traditional model of social work. In fact, this observation might even sound absurdly obvious, unworthy of being discussed here at all. Yet, it is just this assumption that reflects the significance of our traditional frame: that is the expertise of the social worker, the mastering of theories, the development of practice skills, and the accumulation of professional experience that will make the difference in the client's life as we have all learned and accepted this traditional frame.

For example, Kottler (2000) places the work being done as centered on the expertise of the worker. He states that to understand what a particular client needs as they sit in front of you crying and in despair, you must have a theory to help you "explain" what is going on in terms of causing this problem and what "you believe should be the focus of treatment" (p.30). Similarly, Naomi Brill (1998) notes that it is the *worker's* appraisal of the situation and the people involved that is at the heart of the process. The *worker* must gather the data and facts, evaluate this information, and come to some definition of the problem. She argues that "we can fully understand the present only in light of what has happened in the past" and without understanding underlying causes we cannot sustain a cure, promote a solution, or prevent recurrence (Brill, 1998, p.116).

The premise of these practice attitudes and procedures comes out of the traditional medical/pathology frame. It is the incapacity of the client that is being addressed, not only in terms of the underlying cause of the problem but in the person's inability to create any change. Brill's (1998) traditional professional stance exemplifies the fundamental importance of the worker's expertise in the traditional model of practice and the *incapacity* of the client. She states that the "worker who does not possess more and better knowledge about how to deal with the concerns of their clients than do either the clients or the general public have no right to intervene in people's lives" (Brill, 1998, p.102). She is not talking about the process skills of working *with* another person. She is asserting authoritative knowledge *about* another person's own life and how it is being lived out. In support of this position, Brill quotes a client who says " I know what's wrong—I need her to tell me what to do and how to do it" (Brill, 1998, p. 102). This is classic medical model practice training. It is the trained "expert" who is central to any change that is to take place.

Not much has really changed in the last 80 years. Although we sound more sophisticated and "eclectic" in our thinking, the basic model of the "professional expert" using "scientifically" based knowledge of human development and pathology is replicated every day. We engage in an assessment, at which time "available information is organized and studied to make sense of the client's situation and lay the foundation for a plan of action. When the assessment is completed, the social worker [is] able to describe the problem or the situation accurately and identify what needs to be changed to improve the client's situation" (Sheafor, Horejsi, & Horejsi, 2000, p. 301). Then the appropriate "approach" can be employed to address the problem *as understood by the worker.* How can concepts such as empowerment, strengths, and self-determination be assumed inside a frame such as this?

Recent social work educators have started to expand the use of concepts such as empowerment, strengths, and self-determination in more recent texts. For example, found in the new fifth edition of the Sheaffor, Horejsi, and Horejsi (2000) text "Techniques and Guidelines for Social Work Practice," is a section on practice frameworks for social workers dedicated to presenting strengths concept. One can read statements scattered throughout the text that reflect an appreciation of strengths and empowerment. As a matter of fact, "strengths" appears as one of five other perspectives presented to the student and is followed by fifteen "selected practice theories and models" (pp. 96–113). Yet, the strengths perspective exists in stark contrast to an overriding traditional medical/pathology frame. In the text, students are presented with criteria to consider when evaluating the validity and usefulness of a practice perspective, the authors include rules such that the perspective: 1.) should help the *worker analyze* and understand highly complex and often chaotic situations, 2.) provide *guidance and direction* during various phases of the change process, and 3.) it should rest on *empirical* foundations. The worker is warned not to be attached to any one perspective. The approach assumes a level of expertise on the part of the student to select after careful and critical appraisal the appropriate perspective for the particular client at the particular time. Of course, this expert choice is based upon professionally wrought, "empirically based" knowledge. Once again, the social worker is the key to change and change is based upon the social worker's understanding and ability to select the appropriate approach to a particular client and a particular problem—of course after the worker makes appropriate assessments. It is only by having at hand a multiple arsenal of "paradigms" or perspectives, as well as practice theories and techniques that are the interchangeable armaments of the social worker, that change can take place for the client. The authors even suggest that "expertness—or at least the appearance of expertness—can have a positive impact on the initial phases of the helping process. Such things as certificates and diplomas on the wall, a large office, proper use of language, and professional dress can increase the client's respect for the helper and the result in the client being more open to influence" (p. 142). Such a practice does not represent an understanding of the fundamental implications of a strengths perspective and empowerment on the social work process itself. But it does reflect what Leslie Margolin (1997) describes as "social workers inserting themselves into client's lives, initiating actions, judging outcomes, controlling technologies and meanings" (p. 119). Traditional social work practice can be *disempowering* as workers use technical skills such as confrontation, overcoming resistance, and managing the manipulative client while at the same time manipulating the relationship to enhance compliance with professional decisions. For example, Hepworth (1993) alerts the worker to the manipulative client "gaining varying degrees of control of the helping relationship [and therefore] constrain[ing] the maneuverability of the social worker, thereby undermining the helping relationship" (p. 682). In contrast, from a strengths perspective, the "manipulative" client is understood as using considerable skill and thought for a purpose that is meaningful to that person. It is resistance only when these actions are perceived by the worker as the client challenging what the worker wants to take place.

What is most problematic with the inclusion of strengths talk in social work conversations is that the insertion of the strengths and empowerment lexicon into a traditional frame or perspective gives a false sense of understanding to those learning and engaging in practice. Social workers have thus managed to use the language of strengths and empowerment while maintaining the "prerogative to plan and strategize, direct and control" the process while convincing themselves that they have "empowered" the client (Margolin, 1997, p.122). Margolin (1997) has referred to this as the "central paradox" of mainstream social work practice conceptualizations of strengths and empowerment. That is, "to become who one truly is, and to do what one truly wants, one has to absorb [the social worker's] definitions, interpretations, and prescriptions" (Margolin, 1997, p. 124). Therefore, to learn the strengths perspective one must seriously challenge the basic foundations of practice knowledge, the 80 years of variations on a basic theme of disease and expertise as it is taught and practiced today. Anything less is a distortion of the meanings employed in a practice from a strengths/empowerment perspective.

SHIFTING THE FUNDAMENTAL
FRAME OF PRACTICE

In contrast to the continuing adherence to traditional constructs identified with the profession, the strengths perspective offers the profession an opportunity to change frames and learn to collaborate with individuals, families, and communities in a more egalitarian working relationship based upon the strengths and resilience of individuals, families, and communities. The client as well as the client's support system or environment would move into a central role in the entire social work process. In a frame challenging, mind-bending example of family practice, a social worker enters a family residence and the first question she asks is "What is working well that you want to see continue?" (Miley, O'Melia, & DuBois, 1998, p. 4). Needless to say, the family members who were very familiar with professional techniques and attitudes [professional clients] were taken aback as will be those professionals reading this for the first time. The social worker's intervention did not and could not eliminate the inherent inequality of the relationship but did challenge the preeminence of the worker as sole determiner of what should be going on and how this family should be living its life. In many ways the social worker's effort was reflective of the latest research on psychotherapy and counseling that is seriously challenging the traditional practice relationship, as well as the processes.

There is growing evidence that it is actually the client who is responsible for the changes that take place. It is what the client brings in terms of strengths, resilience, and social supports that are responsible for most of what is going to change and how it is going to change. The evidence is clear about the fact that psychotherapy and professional "helping" is effective across the board, whatever the model or techniques used (Bergin & Lambert, 1978; Lambert & Bergin, 1994). But surprisingly there is strong evidence that our techniques or interventions are responsible for only about 15% of the outcome, in contrast to the notion of "evidence based" or "empirically supported treatments" (EST) that suggests a specific treatment or technique for a specific diagnostic group (Lambert, 1992). The factor most responsible for the outcome (40%) is what Lambert (1992) has called "extratherapeutic change." That is, those factors or qualities that are part of the client and the client's environment such as social support, individual and social resources and assets, and fortuitous, contingent events. The practitioner does play a significant part in terms of the relationship that accounts for about 30% of the change. Here it is the experience felt by the client and not the worker that is at play. That is, it is the *client's perceptions* of the worker that creates the quality of the relationship. This plays a part *if the client* experiences the worker as warm, understanding, accepting, and encouraging, not if the worker thinks of his or her self in this way. Another key factor in client change is what Lambert (1992) refers to as "expectancy or placebo effects" which complete the remaining 15% of the change influences. Jerome Frank (1973) noted this same factor in "Persuasion and Healing." It is the belief that something can be done or an inherent hopefulness that is expressed in the very act of seeking help. These findings leave a great deal of room for social work education and training but suggest a different emphasis, a different frame or perspective from the traditional perspective and the emerging belief in "scientific evidence" that a specific treatment or technique is better with a particular diagnostic group. The center of attention would move to understanding how clients make changes and how practitioners can support that unique and individualized process in the most productive ways. The focus would shift to the client's abilities even in the face of "overwhelming evidence" to the contrary.

How do we challenge our lived theories of practice, beliefs, and sense of being a "professional" in the traditional social work sense? It often takes the form of a shift to some place outside the frame, similar in some ways to Helen Harris Perlman's (1957) efforts, one that offers an alternative variation to the standard frame or offers an entirely new alternative. This variation or alternative is often seen as misinformed, lacking understanding, not reflecting training or experience, and maybe just a "nut." Harold Werner's (1965) publication of "A Rational Approach to Social Casework" presented a very practical cognitive approach to casework that received scathing reviews. Bernice Simon (1966) stated that the theory and practice presented appeared "simplistic and shallow as an explanation of human behavior or basis of professional practice [and concluded that it was] a dreary, shallow, narrow approach to human problems" (pp.117–118). Gaining insight into our own "groupthink" is like opening the door to uncertainty and uneasiness and this is the challenge, to truly exploring the strengths frame and seeing what it can offer.

Shifting Frames to a Strengths Perspective

The strengths perspective is a significant alteration of thinking for traditional social workers as well as students just learning social work practice. Dennis Saleebey (1997) strongly emphasizes that "everything you do as a social worker will be predicated, in some way, on helping to discover and embellish, explore and exploit client's strengths and resources in the service of assisting them to achieve their goals . . ." (p. 3). The emphasis shifts from problems and deficits defined by the worker to possibilities and strengths identified in egalitarian, collaborative relationships with clients. Saleebey (1997) describes the frame of the strengths perspective as reflected in three basic principles:

- Given the difficulties they have, and the known resources available to them, people are often doing amazingly well—the best they can at the time.
- People have survived to this point—certainly not without pain and struggle—through employing their will, their vision, their skills, and, as they have grappled with life, what they have learned about themselves and their world. We must understand these capacities and make alliance with this knowledge in order to help.
- Change can only come when you collaborate with client's aspirations, perceptions, and strengths, and when you *firmly believe* in them. (p. 49).

But these inspiring words are not an easy task to undertake as my initial example hopefully demonstrated. To make them more than words, to translate them into practice is a significant challenge.

One of the most important steps in meeting this challenge is what Saleebey (1997) has referred to as "suspending disbelief" in the client's understandings and explanations, and desired outcomes. Unlike the advice of Hepworth and Larsen

[handwritten: "... Embrace the world-view of the client ..."]

(1993) who caution the worker to "avoid the tendency to accept client's views, descriptions, and reports as valid representations of reality," the strengths perspective embraces the world view of the client (p.197). It is truly "starting where the client is" rather than "starting where the theory is." Duncan, Hubble, and Miller (1997) describe it this way:

> We have learned to listen more, turn off the intervention spigot, stay still, and direct our attention to them [the client]—recalling, as Ram Dass once said, 'The quieter you become the more you will hear.' The greater success we have experienced in doing this, the more room clients have had to be themselves, use their own resources, discover possibilities, attribute self-enhancing meanings to their actions, and take responsibility. (p. 207)

De-Centering: Turning "Facts" into Hypotheses

But how do you shift such habits that seem part of our social understandings as well as the traditional doctrine of social work professionalism? I am speaking of a real shift in orientation or basic viewpoint rather than merely adding on a component as I have mentioned above. This shift is similar to altering what Aaron Beck (1972) refers to as "automatic thoughts" in that our professional habits of the mind or frames occur without recognition on our part. Yet, these frames are the "lens" through which we see and we interact with clients. It is this accustomed or habitual professional thinking that guides our perceptions, thinking, and understanding that must be "de-centered" as the cognitive therapist would say or "externalized" in terms of its dominate traditional social work narrative as White and Epston (1990) refer to a similar process in narrative therapy.

Following the mode of cognitive therapy, each of us would need to "distance" ourselves from the automatic thoughts. That is, in order to shift perspectives from our traditional medical model to a strengths perspective, it would be necessary to first recognize the frame and then to view our professional conceptualizations as "hypothesis" rather than "fact." This would permit dissociating oneself from the constructs we operate from and to examine them from a different point of view. We each would suspend our traditional professional constructs and look at the client from the perspective of strength and resilience.

De-centering and Shifting Frames: Some Examples

Working with students just entering into social work training, has been very helpful in my own de-centering process. The students come with a "natural" affinity or bias for looking at what is wrong or broken and quickly set about to offer suggestions or answers for the "client" to follow. The students and I have explored the strengths perspective from within solution based conversations held during class. In doing so, both the students and I have been confronted by our own assumptions or frames. The "clients" [actually students who are being interviewed in class and talking about real issues or challenges such as a roommate problem that they are dealing with at the time] reveal that they have actually been successful in addressing their issues in ways none of the members of the class or myself would have guessed or suspected. Being confronted with awareness of our own "automatic" perceptions and assumptions, mine being professional training and theirs the natural desire to do something, holds us back from listening to the issues as described by the client and brings a sense of uneasiness to all of us in the classroom. For all of us to develop trust in the experiences, students and I began to purposely eliminate any questions about background or about the problem. In its place, we went straight to the type of question often used by solution-focused practitioners such as Insoo Kim Berg (1994): If six months from now you were to believe strongly that our work together was successful or it had a made a difference, what would be different then that would let you know that our work here was successful? With some clarification and checking out our assumptions about the answers, a clearer and specific goal often emerged that was something much different than anyone in the class would have suggested. These goals were inclusive of support systems, cultural values and reflected reasonable expectations and outcomes on the part of the "client." What steps could be taken to make the goal more likely were likewise straightforward and specific as described by the "client." As a matter of fact, many times the "client" had actually accomplished the goals in the recent past. Strengths and solution oriented helpers think of these as "exceptions," similar to White and Epston's (1990) narrative notion of "unique outcomes" or lived experiences that are outside the dominant story, not part of the problem saturated talk. These are the alternative stories or outcomes that represent possibilities or strengths from which goals and changes are possible. The results of our experiment usually left the students, the "client" and myself energized, hopeful, and surprised by what had happened time and time again. In one moving story, a student revealed that she had had a life of considerable turmoil and pain [she did not share the details in class]. From a strengths perspective, it was obvious that she had somehow made it to this point, obviously not without pain and scars, but was with us in class and working on her degree. As we asked a strengths-based question about how she had managed to do this, she revealed that a family with whom she was a friend had taken her into their home to live [without the involvement of social services]. Thinking from a strengths perspective, it was recognized that she must have done something to create such caring on the part of this family. That is, there was recognition that she must have had certain qualities that had lead to such a meaningful relationship. The student had never considered her own qualities. As a matter of fact, she generally had very negative opinions about herself. Subsequently, the student reported how meaningful this awareness had been for her and how she had used it to help herself during some rough times during the semester.

It is often the simplest comment that goes unnoticed by my students and myself as we strain to "hear strengths" over the noise of "problems" being searched out by our minds. In one case, a student reported that he had been driving a friend who had serious drug problems when the friend revealed that he had just "shot up" for the first time in several weeks. The student who had considerable experience working in traditional drug treatment facilities, was ready to challenge his friend's actions and thought of making him get out of the car. Then, the student considered what we had been talking about in class. He said "what the heck" and asked a strengths-based question: How did you stay clean for so many weeks? The student could not remember such a long conversation with his friend about what he was doing to stop and how he had been successful for such a length of time. The student learned a great deal more about his friend's struggles and his successes.

In another example of hearing strengths through the noise of problem drenched talk, my students and I watched a video demonstrating Insoo Kim Berg's (1995) work with a couple. The man did not really want to be in counseling and the woman had already gone to see a lawyer about a divorce. My students are always caught up with the fact that the husband is not wearing a wedding ring. They always want to ask "why?" and declare "How the wife must feel!" Of course, the easy deduction that he must be "having an affair." They are so caught up in "problem saturated" thinking that they often miss the work that Kim Berg and the couple are doing together. The students are asked to speculate as to the outcome of the first interview. They have a hard time imagining anything productive happening. Some have strong beliefs that the issue of the ring needed to be addressed, some wanted to hear more about feelings and past histories. When the second interview is shown, Kim Berg herself is surprised by the turn of events when the couple returns two weeks later for the second interview. They have engaged in changes in their lives that neither Kim Berg nor my students could have conceived or suggested. The students had missed the strengths, resilience, and unique outcomes possible when clients direct their own lives. It was those "extratherapeutic" factors, combined with Insoo's asking for directions in terms of what *they wanted* different, that played out in the significant shift that emerged. It was the choices made by the couple together outside of the sessions that had resulted in the shifts they made. The problem as presented initially by the couple did little to predict the outcome. The fundamental point for the students was the challenge this process presented to their assumptions of something being broken and needing fixing by the expert. The same easily holds true for professionals and habitual ways of working where the theory and technique direct the work.

CONCLUSION

The strengths perspective is an attitude and frame from which to engage those with whom we are working. The strengths perspective shifts our orientation from a worker-directed effort to a client-directed effort in collaboration with the professional. Professional knowledge is about how to be available in a different way. That is, in a way that exploits the strengths and resilience of the client.

For a professional practitioner to fully appreciate the implications of the strengths perspective, it is necessary to engage in a personal analysis just as if attempting to shift "automatic thoughts" or to engage "unique outcomes" as alternative narratives to the dominant professional perspective. It is only in the de-centering or recognition of the traditional frame that any shift can be made. For my students and myself, de-centering comes in the form of surprise and uneasiness. When the "client" is made the center of practice in a true sense, uncertainty and "not knowing" take center stage. A truly mutual/collaborative dialogue takes place resulting in unique outcomes unanticipated by the clever professional or the eager student. But, what always follows is a mistrust of our own experiences. It is the uncertainty, the not knowing, and maybe the unfamiliarity of relying on the client to take the lead, in giving direction to the work to be done, that is so uncomfortable.

Isn't it the job of the social worker to "treat" the client with an intervention based upon empirically grounded expert knowledge about how lives are to be lived? What about the unconscious motivations and defenses that must be understood and overcome? These expectations on the part of the professional's habit and the student's eagerness to help need to be challenged again and again until an actual shift in frame takes place and becomes an active part of a strengths-based practice. Once the frame is shifted, it is easier to then integrate the necessary and appropriate process demanded by agencies and funding sources and, more importantly, that will enhance the collaborative effort toward client directed change.

The strengths perspective challenges our professional conventions, our habits of the mind. Thinking in terms of strengths and resilience confronts our Western European cultural tradition that assumes that "truth" is discovered only by looking at assumed underlying and often hidden meanings, making causal links in some sequential order leading to the "cause" of it all. Duncan, Hubble, and Miller (1997) note, "traditions are important in all human pursuits, but they can also have inhibiting and damaging consequences. The source of [social work practice] traditions are mainly grounded in theory, not fact, and yet they often assume the status of fact" (p. 7). Adherence to pathological models of human development and practice imposes an agenda onto those with whom we work. It can blind us to seeing the possibilities, resilience, and strengths of people caught up in often difficult and complex issues. Challenging this cultural and linguistic tradition as well as a process that has become synonymous with the social work profession is a serious task that needs to be undertaken if social work is to embrace a belief in human resilience, possibilities and strengths.

One last example: Joanne, a 16-year-old female, has been hospitalized several times for threatening suicide, running away, and self-harming behavior. She has several diagnoses, among them borderline personality disorder and attachment disorder. She has spent the past several years living in residential settings away from her mother and older sister. One of my students volunteered to work at the residential setting and met Joanne. The student, Jessica, was initially "scared" about the "problems and suicide" and was unsure about how to talk with the young girl. She decided to try to get to know Joanne while trying to "think from a strengths perspective" and started to have regular conversations with Joanne. She discovered that Joanne was a very good writer and artist. Jessica recognized that the writing and artwork she saw were more than just being good at art or writing. Joanne wanted to be an artist and a writer and had thought a good deal about going to art school some day. In one conversation, Jessica asked Joanne what she thought the staff thought about her. Joanne quickly said that they thought she was "crazy . . . mentally ill, I am not those things." In further conversations, Joanne revealed that when a bunch of things go wrong and she is upset, she writes or draws to help herself get through it. She feels much better when she does this. When the issues pile up and conflicts start getting out of hand, that is when she tries to run away or threatens suicide.

All the residents are on a point system. Daily, their behavior is monitored and they are given points for any infraction of the rules. This easily cycles into a spiral with more restrictions and then resistance followed by further restrictions and limitations on what the resident can do and for greater lengths of time. It is during these cycles that Joanne is more likely to be threatened and to run away or to cut herself. The "treatment" is based upon counseling sessions to address the pathology and a point system to manage her behavior. Jessica reported that none of her discoveries about Joanne (writing and drawing, self-calming work, goals) were in her very large file at the agency.

When a serious episode of conflict occurred between Joanne and the evening staff, Joanne asked to see Jessica, who was coming onto the shift. They spent several hours together. Joanne asked permission to sleep in the common room so that she could be close to Jessica, she "felt safer" with her close by. My student had been helping Joanne work toward a possible part-time job at a local art gallery by finding ways to not get points. Joanne had managed to have only a couple of points for two weeks. She had asked to have a staff meeting about her request to interview for the part-time job but had been turned down. The staff believed that she was just manipulating them. They did not believe her and felt that she had been trying to use Jessica too. It was after this that the incident occurred. The incident became the evidence for their beliefs about Joanne and justification for seeing her as manipulative.

This is not a success story from our traditional perspective. Joanne had not been compliant nor had she demonstrated adequate culpability. But, it was in many ways for Joanne and Jessica. It opened up a number of questions about how our traditional focus on pathology, seeing people as their diagnosis, making control a central theme, and trying to get rid of the problem or pathological behaviors is problematic in many ways. In this case it contributed to not seeing the full potential and possibilities of this person. It resulted in thwarting the possibilities for this young woman. Jessica, the student, was awakened to what "might have been" if the strengths and potential of Joanne had been listened to and supported. She recognized that her openness and ability to listen and hear Joanne's strengths, desires, goals, and her possibilities lead to a real relationship built on trust and understanding. It led to a broader understanding of her strengths and resiliency. How do you build attachments when there is very little trust or recognition of human potential and strengths? Milbrey McLaughlin (Poertner, 1993) has one response and that is "if adults were to stop viewing young people as something to be fixed and controlled and, instead, helped enable their development, there would be 'phenomenal change' in their lives and in society" (p. 4).

For my students and myself as learners, it is not easy to give up the idea of helping by taking charge or intervening under some form of professionally disguised control. Yet, as we make our way, we are amazed at what we can learn to hear as we collaborate with those with whom we work. When we believe in their possibilities and potentials and work together with people to make a life moving toward their dreams and goals, the human capacity for thriving stands out even in the most painful and difficult circumstances.

My students and I found three statements, one by Ludwig Wittgenstein, another by Shunryu Suzuki, and the third by Howard Goldstein that seemed to speak to each of us in learning to "listen" for the possibilities in people's lives and to attend to strengths and potentials as starting points:

> Those who keep on asking 'why' are like tourists who read the guidebook while standing in front of the monument: They are so busy reading about the monument's history, origins, etc., etc., that they don't even take time to look at it. [to experience it, feel it, explore it].
>
> —Ludwig Wittgenstein

> In the beginner's mind there are many possibilities, but in the expert's there are few.
>
> —Shunryu Suzuki

> We are at our best as helpers when we can cast off the pretentious role of expert or technician and join with our clients as colleagues and companions in the pursuit of all that is of consequence for a more reasonable life.
>
> —Howard Goldstein

DISCUSSION QUESTIONS

1. Even though Jessica's work with Joanne was not a success from the conventional perspective, why does the author (Blundo) see it as a success? What is your view?

2. How would you go about challenging the traditional or conventional problem, and deficit-dominated discourse in your agency?

3. What exactly is a "frame" and how does it affect the way we act and respond in the world around us?

4. What are two of the historical circumstances that help entrench the exclusive problem based perspective in social work?

5. How does the strengths perspective free us from the problem frame?

REFERENCES

Addams, J. (1930). *The second twenty years at Hull-House*. New York: The Macmillan Company.

Beck, A. T. (1972). *Depression: Causes and treatment*. Philadelphia: University of Pennsylvania Press.

Berg, I. K. (1994). *Family based services: A solution-focused approach*. New York: W. W. Norton & Company.

Bergin, A. E., & Lambert, M. J. (1978). The evaluation of therapeutic outcomes. In S. L. Garfield & A. E. Bergin (Eds.), *Handbook of psychotherapy and behavior change* (2nd ed., pp. 139–190). New York: Wiley.

Biertek, F. P., Jr. (1957). *The Casework relationship*. Chicago, IL: Loyola University Press.

Brill, N. I. (1998). *Working with people*, (6th ed.). New York: Longman.

Bristol, M. C. (1936). *Handbook on social case recording*. Chicago, IL: University of Chicago Press.

Chapin, F. S. (1918). A scientific basis for training social workers. *Mental Hygiene, 2* (3), 590–592.

Duncan, B. L., Hubble, M., & Miller, S. D. (1997). *Psychotherapy with Impossible Cases: The Efficient Treatment of Therapy Veterans*. NY: Norton.

Frank, J. (1973). *Persuasion and Healing* (2nd ed.). Baltimore, MD: The Johns Hopkins University Press.

Goffman, I. (1974). *Frame analysis*. Cambridge, MA: Harvard University Press.

Goldstein, H. (1997). Victors or Victims? In D. Saleebey (Ed.), *The strengths perspective in social work practice*, (2nd ed., pp. 21–35). New York: Longman.

Hamilton, G. (1946). *Principles of social case recordings*. New York: Columbia University Press.

Heller, A. F., & Rudnick, L. (1991). *1915, the cultural moment*. New Brunswick, NJ: Rutgers University Press.

Hepworth, D. H. (1993). Managing manipulative behavior in the helping relationship. *Social Work, 38,* 674–682.

Hepworth, D. H., & Larson, J. A. (1993). *Direct Social Work Practice* (4th ed.). Pacific Grove, CA: Brooks/Cole.

Hollis, F. (1964). *Casework: A psychosocial therapy.* New York: Random House.

Hubble, M. A., Duncan, B. L., & Miller, S. D. (1999). *The heart and soul of change: What works in therapy.* Washington, DC: American Psychological Association.

Jarrett, M. C. (1918). Psychiatric social work. *Mental Hygiene, 2* (2), 283–290.

Kottler, J. A. (2000). *The Nuts and Bolts of Helping.* Boston: Allyn & Bacon.

Lambert, M. J. (1992). Psychotherapy outcome research. In J. C. Norcross & M. R. Goldfried (Eds.), *Handbook of psychotherapy integration* (pp. 94–129). New York: Basic Books.

Lambert, M. J., & Bergin, A. E. (1994). The effectiveness of psychotherapy. In A. E. Bergin & S. L. Garfield (Eds.), *Handbook of psychotherapy and behavior change* (4th ed., pp.143–189). New York: Wiley.

Lord, C., Ross, L., & Lepper, M. R. (1979). Biased assimilation and attitude polarization: The effects of prior theories on subsequently considered evidence. *Journal of Personality and Social Psychology, 37,* pp. 2098–2109.

Lubove, R. (1965). *The professional altruist: The emergence of social work as a career.* Cambridge, MA: Harvard University Press.

Margolin, L. (1997). *Under the cover of kindness: The invention of social work.* Charlottesville, VA: University Press of Virginia.

Merriam-Webster's Collegiate Dictionary (10th ed.). Springfield, MA: Merriam-Webster.

Miley, K. K., O'Melia, M., & DuBois, B. (1998). *Generalist social work practice: An empowerment approach* (3rd ed.). Boston: Allyn and Bacon

Neimeyer, R. A., & Raskin, J. D. (2000). On practicing postmodern therapy in modern times. In R. A. Neimeyer, & J. D. Raskin (Eds.), *Constructions of disorder: Meaning-making framework for psychotherapy.* Washington, DC: American Psychological Association.

Nisbett, R. Ross, L. (1980). *Human inference: Strategies and shortcomings of social judgment.* Englewood Cliffs, NJ: Prentice-Hall.

Perlman, H. H. (1957). *Social casework: A problem-solving process.* Chicago, IL: The University of Chicago Press.

Popple, P., & Reid, P. N. (1999). A profession for the poor? A history of social work in the United States. In G. R. Lowe, & P. N. Reid (Eds.), *The professionalization of poverty* (pp. 9–28). New York: Aldine De Gruyter.

Poertner, J. (1993, April 6). The search for elusive 'sanctuaries' for urban youths. [Electronic version]. Education Week, pp-1–8. Retrieved June 1, 2004, from http://www.edweek.org/ew/ew-printstory.cfm?slug+28milb.h13.

Rapp, C. A. (1998*). The strengths model: Case management with people suffering from severe and persistent mental illness.* New York: Oxford Press.

Reid, P. N. (1995). American social welfare history. In R. L. Edwards (Ed.-in-Chief). *Encyclopedia of social work* (19th ed.-Vol.3, pp. 2206–2225). Washington, DC: NASW Press.

Richmond, M. E. (1917). *Social diagnosis.* New York: Russell Sage Foundation.

Richmond, M. E. (1922). *What is social casework? An introductory description.* New York: Russell Sage Foundation.

Robinson, V. A. (1930). *A changing psychology in social casework.* Chapel Hill, NC: The University of North Carolina Press.

Saleebey, D. (1997). The strengths approach to practice. In D. Saleebey, (Ed.), *The strengths perspective in social work practice* (2nd ed.). New York: Longman.

Sheafor, B. W., Horejsi, C. R., & Horejsi, G. A. (2000). *Techniques and guidelines for social work practice,* (5th ed.). Boston: Allyn and Bacon.

Simon, B. (1966). Review of the book A rational approach to social casework. *Social Work,* July, 117–118.

Specht, H., & Courtney, M. (1994). *Unfaithful angels: How social work has abandoned its mission.* New York: Free Press.

Taft, J. (1944). Introduction. In J. Taft (Ed.), *A functional approach to family case work.* Philadelphia: University of Pennsylvania Press.

Werner, H. (1965). *A rational approach to casework.* New York: Associated Press.

White, M., & Epston, D. (1990). *Narrative means to therapeutic ends.* New York: W. W. Norton & Company.

CHAPTER THREE

STRENGTHS OF INDIGENOUS PEOPLES

MARGARET WALLER

Creation stories of many North American tribes teach that Native Peoples[1] have been in North and South America since the beginning of time. One researcher's estimate is 75,000 years (Josephy, 1991). When European colonizers crossed the Atlantic beginning in the late 15th century, they found themselves in a land more vast than they could imagine, populated by 30 million people from hundreds of distinct cultures (Marger, 1994).

European colonists interpreted Indigenous Peoples' unfamiliar physical appearances, beliefs, and practices as signs of biological, intellectual, cultural, and moral inferiority. To the Europeans, this supposed inferiority justified exploitation and attempted genocide. They claimed that Manifest Destiny, e.g., "God's will," entitled them to Native Lands and natural resources (Marger, 1994; Thornton, 1987).

The Europeans' genocidal mission was nearly successful. Between 1500 and 1900, slavery, disease, introduction of alcohol, warfare, and forced removal from traditional lands destroyed between 95 and 99 percent of the Indigenous population (Stiffarm & Lane, 1992). To this day, Indigenous Peoples contend with the continuing sequelae of colonialism,[2] including social problems related to income, education, occupation, employment, health care, mortality, and housing, more severe than those of any other population group in the United States (Marger, 1994).

However, contrary to the widespread notion of the "Vanishing Indian," Native Peoples have refused to vanish (Nichols, 2004). Today, Indigenous Peoples are among the fastest growing and youngest population groups in the United States (Locke, 1992). As of 2000 (U.S. Census), 2.5 million people in the United States

[1]The generic term Indigenous Peoples, First Nations Peoples, or Native Peoples are used interchangeably here in reference to 660 distinct cultural groups. Individuals often self-identify according to the term in their native language for their particular Nation, but may prefer any of a variety of terms connoting ethnic identity.

[2]Colonialism refers to a form of domination in which one ethnic group within a country imposes its political, economic, social, and cultural institutions on an indigenous people (Ferrante & Brown, 2001).

self-identified as Native American with another 450,000 identifying as predominantly Native American (150,000) or part Native American (300,000). This is double the Native population in 1990, and eight times the 1960 population (Marger, 1994). The average age of Indigenous People is 16. There are 840 Indigenous Nations in the United States, including 562 federally recognized tribes, 33 tribes recognized by States, and 245 tribes still struggling with government agencies to gain federal recognition (Wright, Lopez, & Zumwalt, 1997). Native People in the United States are nearly evenly split between those who live on reservations and those living in metropolitan areas. However, the balance is shifting as an increasing number of Native People move to the city (Riding In, 1996; Snipp, 1996).

In Canada, Indigenous People are also a rapidly growing and youthful population group. In 2001, there were nearly one million Indigenous People, from 630 First Nations communities (Assembly of First Nations, 2001), one third of whom were age 14 or younger. As in the U.S., Native People in Canada are about equally split between those who live on reservations and those who live in metropolitan areas (2001 Canada Census).

HISTORICAL DISTORTION OF STRENGTHS

As Standing Rock Sioux scholar Vine Deloria (2004) points out, much of the professional and popular literature about Native Peoples is a tangled web of distortions suffused by the influence of colonialism. For example, most social science research related to Indigenous Peoples focuses on social problems (Riding In, 1996). This is true even in social work, a profession purportedly committed to the strengths perspective (Hepworth & Larsen, 1982; Towle, 1945; Waller, Risley-Curtiss, Murphy, Medell, & Moore, 1998). With professional helpers whose model is a conglomeration of negative stereotypes, who needs enemies?

WHAT ARE THE STRENGTHS OF INDIGENOUS PEOPLES?

Although the hundreds of Indigenous Nations have distinct languages, beliefs, and customs, a constellation of strengths are widely shared. This chapter presents a sampling of these shared strengths.

Resistance to Assimilation

Native People have consistently frustrated colonial attempts to force their assimilation into the American mainstream. A striking example is the boarding school "experiment." Between 1879 and 1970, federal agents forcibly removed grade school children from their families and transported them to boarding schools. In collusion with missionaries, Richard Henry Pratt, a former military officer, designed the original boarding-school program that became the model for many others. The formula was to isolate a generation of young children from their families for several years, indoctrinate them in the Christian European worldview, and train them in trades. The objective was the eventual extinction of Native cultures, as indicated in Pratt's motto, "Kill the Indian and save the man" (Child, 1996).

With missionary zeal, teachers cut the children's hair, dressed them in European clothes, and punished them severely for speaking their own languages or "acting Indian." Emotional, physical, and sexual abuse were commonplace—if children died as a result of their punishments, their deaths were recorded as accidents or suicides (Anderson, Putnam, Sinclair-Daisy, & Squetimkin-Anquoe, 1999). Essentially, the federal government, in collusion with missionaries, waged psychological and cultural warfare on 20,000 Native children (Davis, 2001; Tinker, 1996).

Native children and their families found ingenious ways to resist the boarding school "experiment" and preserve their personal, family, and cultural integrity (Reyner & Eder, 2004; Wright & Tierney, 2000). Groups of children created surrogate families bound by ties of friendship and loyalty. Some used subversive strategies such as insulting nicknames for teachers, or secretly telling familiar stories and playing traditional games. Others overtly resisted by fighting, running away, or setting school buildings on fire.

Steadfast parents visited their children as often as possible and learned strategies to convince administrators to send their children home for the summer. When their children visited, parents immersed them in their Native languages and cultures. Some families found ways to evade the federal agents altogether. A Diné social worker related the following story (personal communication, C. Endischee, July 31, 1999).

> My grandmother lived in the mountains in the traditional way. I loved visiting my grandmother but it was hard for me to help out with the sheep and chores, since I had grown up in the city. I felt ignorant next to the "rez" kids who seemed to know how to do everything. Sometimes my grandmother would see me getting discouraged and she would stop her work, sit me down, and tell me a story. One afternoon, she called me over and handed me a small ball of dried adobe. "Go ahead, break it open and look inside," she said. I cracked open the ball and found fresh bread inside. "Go ahead and eat it," she said. I made a face. This bread with dried mud on it didn't look very appetizing to a city girl. Seeing my disgust, my grandmother told me this story. "When I was a child, the federal agents would come to everyone's house, trying to steal our children and send them off to boarding schools. Sometimes, after years of abuse, our children would return home forever changed. Sometimes they never came home at all. So we escaped to the mountains to hide, but they kept coming after us, taking our children. It wasn't safe to stay in one camp too long because they would see the smoke from our fires and find us. So we learned to make a fresh dough, cover it with wet adobe, and bury it under the coals from the fire. Then, at daybreak we left and hid somewhere else. Pretty soon, the white men would see the smoke and find our camp, but we would be gone, so they would leave. After a while, we would circle back around and there our bread was, already baked and ready to eat. That's how we outsmarted them." The grandmother blessed the bread and she and her granddaughter ate it together.

Resistance was so effective that the boarding school "experiment" failed and was ultimately abandoned.

Sovereignty

Unlike any other ethnic or racial group in the United States, First Nations Peoples are a political entity. The U.S. government recognizes Indigenous Peoples as having a special, legal "government-to-government" relationship with the United States (Norgren, 2004; Pevar, 1992). By law, they are "distinct, independent political communities possessing and exercising the power of self government" (Worcester v. Georgia, 1831). As a consequence of sovereignty, individuals who belong to recognized tribes have dual citizenship—both Indigenous and U.S. and by trust agreement, are eligible to receive federally funded health care, social services, and education.

Sovereign Indigenous Nations have inherent powers of self-government. They have the right to make, pass, and enforce laws, implement taxation, create tribal constitutional codes, license social workers, declare war, and seek remedy in international courts of law. They also possess aboriginal territories (lands) that are protected under trust agreement with the United States.

Social workers working in Indigenous communities must abide by local laws. For example, any issues related to the welfare and protection if Indigenous children fall under the province of Indigenous nations.

Governmental Reform

The federal government has imposed bureaucratic structures on Native communities, and, in the case of agencies like the IHS (Indian Health Services) and the OIEP (Office of Indian Education Programs), controls them from afar, while chronically underfunding services. Reformers argue that these hierarchical European models are out of sync with traditional community values of harmonious coexistence between people with shared power, they lack local legitimacy (Wakeling, Jorgensen, Michaelson, & Begay, 2001), and undermine sovereignty (Taiaiake, 1999). In recent decades, Native communities have been rejecting current structures in favor of self-governance more consonant with cultural values. Many communities have established locally controlled governments, schools, social service agencies, courts, and police departments.

For example, Lemont (2001–2002), describes reforms in the Cherokee, Hualapai, Navajo, and Northern Cheyenne Nations, "Creating representative and independent tribal institutions to manage reform processes and investing in civic education can help launch reform processes, achieve effective citizen participation, resolve conflict, and incorporate aspects of traditional government into new governing frameworks" (p. 21).

In the Navajo Nation, since 1991, the traditional Navajo Peacemaker Court has offered an alternative to the adversarial Justice Court. Depending on the issue, citizens may choose to have their cases diverted to the Peacemaker Court where their disputes will be resolved by respected community leaders rather than litigation. The objective of the traditional Peacemaker is restorative justice, in which the perpetrator makes amends and is restored to full membership in the community.

Another reform is the shift to community policing in which departments are locally controlled and reflect local norms and values. For example, a local elder might accompany a police officer on a call. Depending on the situation, either the officer or the elder might be in charge, with the other in the supporting role (Wakeling, et.al, 2001).

The common elements in educational and governmental reforms taking place in many Indigenous communities are tribal control and reintegration of traditional values. Wakeling et. al (2001) note, "Only those tribes that have acquired meaningful control over their governing institutions have experienced improvements in the local economic and social conditions. The research has not found a single case of sustained economic development where the tribe is not in the driver's seat" (p. viii).

Advocacy and Political Activism

Contemporary Native communities are increasingly savvy about the need to use political and legal means to protect their lands and natural resources from outside profiteers. Hundreds of Native communities are involved in ongoing legal battles with federal, state, and local governments as well as private entities.

Political activism has contributed greatly to the preservation of Indigenous culture, language, religious freedom, traditional healing practices, self-determination, repatriation of sacred objects, and reclamation of sacred sites (Deloria & Lytle, 1998; Morris, 1992). The National Congress of American Indians (NCAI), founded in 1944, in Denver, Colorado was the first national organization representing First Nations Peoples. The NCAI uses strategies similar to those of the NAACP and continues to play an important role in protecting the rights of Native People.

The 1960s and 1970s were marked by political organizing and increasingly militant protests by First Nations Peoples. The American Indian Movement (AIM), founded in 1968, is known for its use of confrontational tactics to challenge inequities perpetrated by the BIA and law enforcement agencies. In the late 1960s, the National Congress of American Indians began an effort to eliminate racist stereotypes of Native Peoples, such as cartoon-like sports team names, logos, and mascots (e.g., "The Savages," "The Chieftans," and "The Redskins") that dehumanize Native People and trivialize their concerns. Many individuals and organizations have joined the battle, and have had some success, yet hundreds of sports teams and manufacturers persist in this racist practice, claiming that it does no harm, or that it even is a sign of respect (King & Springwood, 2001; Spindel, 2001). The Alaskan Federation of Natives (AFN) organized in 1967 to stop the state of Alaska from illegally appropriating oil-rich Native land. As a result of the efforts of the AFN, legislation granted control and ownership of 44 million acres to Alaska's native Intuits, Aleuts, and other peoples, and gave them a cash settlement of nearly $1 billion (Schaefer, 1998).

Another legislative milestone, resulting from political activism was the Indian Child Welfare Act of 1978. Prior to this legislation, government agencies and religious groups removed nearly 35 percent of all Indigenous children from their homes and placed them in non-Native foster care or adoptive placements, or in institutional care. As a result of this legislation, placement of Native children is at the direction of tribal social service and court systems and, to the extent possible, placement is with Indigenous families who can foster the development of a strong, positive, cultural identity (Goodluck, 1993).

Education

Although Native People eventually subverted the boarding school experiment, the legacy of trauma continues to inform peoples' perceptions of mainstream educational institutions and is reflected in current educational statistics (Hurtado, 1992). For example, in 2000, if 100 Native students entered the ninth grade, only 60 graduated from high school. Of these graduates, only 20 entered a mainstream college, and only ten received a four-year degree (Aguirre & Baker, 2000, p. 97).

Over the past 30 years, Indigenous communities have established tribal colleges—usually two-year community colleges—that offer culturally relevant curricula emphasizing tribal history, Native languages, and that foster a strong, positive cultural identity (Harjo, 1993). The Navajo Community College, established in 1968, was the first tribal college. By 1999, there were 28 tribal colleges nationwide (American Indian Higher Education Corsortium, 1999), serving nearly 25,000 students. Marjane Ambler (2003), editor of *Tribal College Journal* views tribal colleges as powerful engines for community healing and positive social change. In a recent survey of the American Indian Higher Education Consortium (2000), 91% of graduates from Tribal colleges were either employed (52%) or attending college (17%), or both (39%).

There is also growing awareness among Native People that university education provides access to necessary economic and political resources. Native Studies departments offer opportunities to learn about colonization and its continuing effects that have touched every Native person's life in one way or another— including systematic oppression, within-group violence, historical trauma, and self-destructiveness. Naming social problems, reading about them, discussing them, writing about them, and learning their sociohistorical context, engenders strong, positive cultural identity and strengthens students in their efforts to fulfill their potential (Taiaiake, 1999).

Separation and Identity

The most resilient Indigenous cultures have recognized the importance of maintaining physical, social, psychological, and spiritual distance between themselves and the rest of the United States (Weaver, 1999). Protected tribal lands make that separation possible (Elsass, 1992; Wilkinson, 1987).

In the Taos Pueblo, for example, while tourism is an important part of the economy, contact with the dominant culture is strictly regulated. Outsiders are allowed to visit public areas during certain hours and may observe some seasonal dances, however, most of the Pueblo land and the most sacred ceremonies are closed to the public.

Another powerful strategy preserving Taos culture is the period of months in which Taos boys reside in the Kiva and are steeped in Taos language, beliefs, and practices. During this time the boys wear traditional clothing, speak only Tewa, and eat only traditional foods provided for them by family members. They receive daily instruction from tribal elders, preparing them to fulfill traditional roles in their families and clans. During the Kiva time, a boy has contact only with Taos people and culture. No contact with outsiders is permitted. At the end of a boy's time in the Kiva, he is fluent in his native language, knowledgeable about traditional beliefs and practices, and ready to take his place as a man in the Taos community.

For Native People who were born elsewhere or who have moved away, protected tribal lands nevertheless provide spiritual and psychological homes. Maintaining relationship ties and participating in tribal traditions reinforces a strong, positive ethnic identity and contributes to resiliency (Oetting & Beauvais, 1991; Waller & McAllen-Walker, 2001).

Esther grew up in the Taos Pueblo community, participating in traditional lifeways. Because of economic necessity, for the past 30 years, she has lived, worked, and raised her children in Albuquerque, three hours away from her home community. Esther maintains her cultural identity by returning regularly to her home community to spend time with family and friends and participate in seasonal dances and feast days. Though she lives in Albuquerque, she considers Taos Pueblo to be her home.

Kinship and Mutual Assistance

In Indigenous societies, human beings are interconnected through a complex web of relationships, including relatives by blood, clan, tribe, and adoption. Generosity and mutual assistance are held in high regard. A family's wealth and status are measured not in terms of what family members possess, but by their generosity to others. The Kiowa Gourd Dance, for example, includes a "giveaway," in which families honor a particular member by distributing food, clothing, linens, and other household items to other families.

Among the Diné, mutual dependence and cooperation are givens, and individual standing in the community is largely related to the extent to which a person is helpful to others. Those who are able, but refuse to help, or think of themselves before others are not held in high esteem (Nofz, 1988). To be Diné is to fulfill one's responsibility to one's relations. This is why one of the harshest forms of retribution is to be told, "You act as if you have no relatives" (Austin, 1993). In many Indigenous cultures, individuals are expected to fulfill prescribed relationship roles. Among the Diné, the maternal uncle is expected to be a father figure.

Roland is the first in his extended family to complete college. He has a law degree as well and is currently a college professor in an urban area several hours from his home community. As soon as Roland became professionally settled, he bought a home large enough to accommodate the next generation of college students in his family. He provided housing, food, tuition, books, and many other necessities for his three nieces throughout their college education. Kinship relations and expectations in Roland's family promote a sense of belonging and security. No one is expected to stand alone.

Social workers who are outsiders must adapt their thinking and approaches when working with Native families. Professional helpers are not the first line of defense in many communities and, in fact, may not ever have been used. For example, of 100 helping episodes described by members of one Diné community, none involved a professional helper (Waller & Patterson, 2000). In communities such as this one, in which people rely on informal helping systems, the social worker should identify and collaborate with natural helping systems.

According to traditional values, children are claimed and cared for, not only by their parents, but by all of their relations. In many Indigenous languages, for example, there is no term for "cousin," "niece," or "nephew." A child is addressed by the entire clan as brother, sister, son, or daughter—terms generally reserved for immediate family in the dominant culture (Cross, 1986; Red Horse, 1980). Relations are expected to rally and give what they can when a member is in need. This may be why many languages have no term for "orphan." Similarly, young mothers are not stigmatized, and their children are embraced by their relations. Elders are treasured, cared for, and respected. If one member is estranged or rejected, it is a blight on the whole relationship system. While each family is unique and subject to myriad influences, the legacy of these traditional values is embedded in the collective consciousness of Native Peoples.

Intertribal Celebrations

Over the past hundred years, intertribal celebrations such as powwows and gourd dances have evolved into regular gatherings in which tribes from over 1,000 locations across the U.S. participate. These celebrations not only demonstrate the power and richness of contemporary Native cultures, they also strengthen intertribal bonds and solidarity and facilitate political activism. Collectively, Nations amplify their "voices" and more effectively advocate for solutions to common concerns (Parfit, 1994). People reconnect with friends, pray together, and share crafts and artwork, traditional dances, songs, competitions, giveaways, and news. Ironically, intertribal connections and gatherings, and a sense of pan-Indian identity are largely a result of relationships forged between children in the boarding schools that were designed to eradicate Native cultures.

Traditional Spirituality and Healing Practices

Indigenous Peoples continue to practice many sacred and secular rituals rooted in diverse ontological beliefs and cosmologies. Beliefs and practices are often deeply connected to the lands that people occupy or have come from and may feature sacred mountains, waters, forests, stories, songs, plants (medicines), dances, and symbols. Beliefs and ceremonial practices have great importance in many people's lives and are an important source of comfort, strength, meaning, self-renewal, and connectedness. Spirituality is ubiquitous, infusing experience so completely that in many languages there is no term for "religion." Osage scholar George Tinker (1996) notes, "Most adherents to traditional American Indian ways characteristically deny that their people ever engaged in any religion at all. Rather, these spokespeople insist, their whole culture and social structure was and still is infused with a spirituality that cannot be separated from the rest of the community's life at any point" (p. 2).

Generations of repression and the forceful imposition of Christianity have led some people to reject their ancient traditions and replace them with Christian beliefs and practices. Others combine Christianity with traditional beliefs and practices. As a result of intertribal connections, some groups have borrowed ceremonies from other groups in an effort to help their own people. Examples are the use of the Sundance and the Sweat Lodge, both of which are thought to have originated with the plains tribes, but are now widely practiced. Similarly, the Native American Church, organized in 1918, began in the Southwest, but now has members from many tribes across the U.S.

Following generations of religious and legal repression of Indigenous beliefs and practices, the 1978 American Indian Religious Freedom Act declared the U.S. government's commitment to "protect and preserve the inherent right of American Indians to believe, express, and practice their traditional religions" (Schaefer, 1998). Drawing on this legislation, Native Peoples are seeking to reclaim sacred areas and are gaining protection for conducting traditional ceremonies on and off reservations and for military personnel and individuals confined to treatment centers and prisons. For many Native People, traditional beliefs and ceremonies have provided a sustaining sense of coherence, safety, and sustenance.

Stories and Storytelling

Storytelling among First Nations Peoples has a long and rich tradition and is an important source of strength. From generation to generation, Indigenous Peoples have used storytelling to pass down traditional teachings and guidance, strengthen relationships, and provide enjoyment. Storytelling is a primary means of transmitting oral tradition and history across generations, and, as such, sustains cultures.

Laguna poet and professor, Leslie Marmon Silko, describes having often returned to Laguna Pueblo, seeking respite from the challenges and pressures of life in the American mainstream. Her elder relatives would listen to her descriptions of situations and events and wrap her experiences in ancient stories or humorous anecdotes that invariably comforted her and gave her a sense of shared experience, perspective, and direction.

Tribal and personal narratives also serve to convey important messages about how to conduct oneself in the world and are a principle means of teaching, correcting, and guiding children. For example, among the Sahnish, storytelling includes myths of ancient times, legends of supernatural power bestowed on selected individuals, historical accounts, anecdotes of mysterious incidents, and fictional tales (Parks, 1991). Tribal narratives depict situations, places, persons, or events that enable Sahnish individuals to understand who they are, how they should behave, what they should know and value, and where they come from (Yellow Bird, 1995). Among the Diné, stories " . . . are not only the basis of the complex ceremonials, they are also the history of the people, much as the Old Testament is both the Judaic religious base and the history of the ancient Jews" (Locke, 1992, p. 55).

Storytelling also nurtures cultural pride and can be a form of resistance. For example, there are many humorous stories that give encounters with Custer, Columbus, and the Pilgrims a new twist. While the storytelling of Indigenous Peoples is often done in the context of enjoyment and entertainment, it is far from being a frivolous event. Among many nations, there is a strict protocol about who can tell which stories and when, where, and how these stories can be shared.

Skepticism

Skepticism about the intentions of outsiders is adaptive and often a necessary survival strategy (Schaefer, 1998; Weaver, 1999). Consider, for example, the persistent stereotypes about Native Peoples: the bloodthirsty savage, the noble savage, the vanishing Indian, the medicine man, the Indian maiden, the silent Indian, the dumb Indian, the drunk Indian, the spiritual Indian, and so on. Many outsiders relate to these objectifying caricatures, never noticing the actual person before them. As Modoc novelist Michael Dorris (1987) puts it,

> The Indian mystique was designed for mass consumption by a European audience . . . it is little wonder then, that many non-Indians literally would not know a real Native American if they fell over one, for they have been prepared for a well-defined, carefully honed legend . . . For most people the myth has become a real and a preferred substitute for reality (p. 99).

"The Indian Mystique" is dehumanizing. It is also dangerous, in that it rationalizes exploitation or violence—physical, psychological, and spiritual—and mutes guilt. Anyone who believes that the violence of colonization is a thing of the past, need only observe the way that "new age" colonists distort, appropriate, and capitalize on Native spirituality. A typical example in a metropolitan newspaper, the *Omega Directory* (April, 2004) is a photograph of a dozen or so naked white people standing, holding hands around a Maypole. The advertisement read, " . . . skyclad (unclothed) ritual celebrating the return of fertility of the season. There will be a Maypole ritual and fire rituals with body painting, drumming, dancing, a pot-luck feasting, hot-tubbing and a sweat lodge . . . a five dollar admission is requested . . . (p. 7)."

This form of colonialism is particularly insidious because appropriation of spirituality is an attack on a person's inner most sanctum of meaning—the ultimate invasion. Having exploited Native lands and resources, and having attempted to eradicate hundreds of cultures and forcing people to think and act white, the colonizers are now invading and exploiting Native spirituality. Tinker (1996) describes the corrosive effect this has on the traditions that sustain Native Peoples:

> It seems now, at the end of the 20th century, deeply held Indian traditions and beliefs have been politicized—on the one hand by academic experts, and on the other by New Age aficionados who have mistakenly seen Indian spirituality as a new trade commodity . . . [T]he modern Euro-American appropriation of native traditions is introducing a mutation that is now shaping those traditions in the image of European individualism.

Distrust poses a special challenge for professional helpers, both Native and non-Native. Clients may wonder if Native helpers can be truly empathic or whether they have "sold out" and become "apples," a colloquial term for a person who is "red" on the outside but "white" on the inside. Similarly, it is reasonable for a Native client to assume that a non-Native worker is guilty until proven innocent, as regards harboring stereotypes—negative or positive. This sort of skepticism is not a problem; it is a healthy coping mechanism.

Humor

Humor is cherished and cultivated in many Indigenous cultures, and permeates peoples' spiritual, social, and political lives. For example, sacred clowns are key players in many ceremonies. They delight young and old with their oratorical talents and use humorous stories to convey important cultural knowledge. No one is exempt from the exaggerated acts and mimicking behavior of the sacred clowns— including tribal officials; and the clown's disregard for authority provides added enjoyment (Shutiva, 1997). At powwows, emcees are chosen, in part, because they speak knowledgeably about tradition and charm the gathering with humorous stories, jokes, and puns (Giago, 1990).

Relatives and friends share reservoirs of jokes and funny stories that predictably surface at every get-together. No one escapes playful teasing. These exchanges transport members of the group to a common place that lifts spirits. Oft repeated stories are comforting in their familiarity. Imagine the confusion of an outsider who expects to hear the same story from the same person only once!

The Navajo language is full of subtle meaning and words that may be slightly modified for humorous effect. Since traditional Diné culture possesses no system of social stratification, anyone can engage in playful humor. "A respected elder can act the fool without losing dignity. Too, children can tease their parents or even their grandparents unmercifully and to a degree that would never be accepted in white society" (Locke, 1992, p. 28).

Humor can also be used as a means of socialization and social control, for example, to correct inappropriate behavior in children or adults in a way that gets the point across without shaming or embarrassing the person who is out of step. In one Diné family, a beloved uncle living away in the city would occasionally break with the family protocol and be out of touch for weeks at a time. When family members began playfully referring to him as "Hides A Lot, " he started calling home and visiting more often.

Jokes can also be a strategy for coping with intrusive outsiders. Here is one widely circulated example[3]:

White man: It's time to reclaim America from illegal immigrants!

Native man: I'll help you pack.

And another:

TOP 10 THINGS YOU CAN SAY TO A WHITE PERSON UPON FIRST MEETING:
10. How much white are you?

---

[3]These jokes are anonymous.

9. I'm part white myself, you know.
8. I learned all your people's ways in the Boy Scouts.
7. My great-great-grandmother was a full-blooded white-English princess.
6. Funny, you don't look white.
5. Where's your powdered wig and knickers?
4. Do you live in a covered wagon?
3. What's the meaning behind the square dance?
2. What's your feeling about river-boat casinos? Do they really help your people, or are they just a short-term fix?
1. Oh wow, I really love your hair! Can I touch it?

A favorite pastime is to poke fun at one's own people as in this joke (in abbreviated form):

> Why Did the Chicken Cross the Road? *Sovereign Indian:* This is the Chicken's inherent right as he is indigenous to this land!!! *Colonized Indian:* We must have roads. We must cross the roads that the white man built for us. We have to be thankful to the white man for this. I don't know why you Indians are always complaining. You embarrass us. Roads are good for us. *BIA Indian:* It crossed it because CFR 49, Section 11299, article 5C, line 12 grants it the authority to do so. It wrote a grant and we funded them. We are very proud of that chicken!

Cultural Resilience

This sampling of strengths and the many others contribute to "cultural resilience," that constellation of culture-related characteristics that has sustained and protected Indigenous Peoples even as colonization has sought to destroy them (Angell, 2000; Heavy Runner and Marshall, 2003).

Sudan Shown Harjo (1993), Cheyenne and Hidalgo Muskogee president of the Morning Star Institute, captures the essence of cultural resilience:

> "At this time, under new laws that we have crafted, our relatives and sacred objects are returning home from museums and educational institutions nationwide. We have the privilege of settling the spirits. For many of our ancestors of the not-so-distant past, commemorating and mourning ceremonies were a luxury of life on the run. We today are mourning for them and for ourselves, learning the mighty power of grief, using ceremonies that honor the dead and revitalize the living.
>
> We today are celebrating the recovery of much of our history. We are greeting sacred, living beings who have been "museum pieces" during all our lifetimes, honored in our memories and customs, but never seen in their context by anyone living. With their return to the Native Peoples who have the collective knowledge and wisdom to feed and care for them properly comes information about yesterday and tomorrow—how to reconcile the past, prepare for the future, avoid the voices of distraction.
>
> This is the spiritual and tangible equivalent of the buffalo coming back.
>
> They bring strength over a long journey, confidence in the longer one ahead. They fill the heart with joy and give assurance as real as a healthy birth. We are so fortunate to be the ones here at this place and moment.
>
> This is a good day to live."

DISCUSSION QUESTIONS

1. How many of the strengths of Indigenous Peoples does your ethnic/racial group have?

2. What is the importance of the names we ascribe to other peoples?

3. What is the "Indian Mystique?" What role has it played in the subjugation of Indigenous Peoples?

4. Why is this "a good day to live?"

REFERENCES

Aguirre, A., & Baker, D. V. (2000). *Structured inequality in the United States: Critical discussions and the continuing significance of race, ethnicity, and gender.* Upper Saddle River, NJ: Prentice Hall.

Akwesasne Notes (1972). Columbus a trader in Indian slaves. 4 (Early Autumn), p. 22. In R. T. Schaefer (1998). *Racial and ethnic groups.* 7th ed. New York: Longman.

Ambler, M. (Summer, 2003). Putting a name to cultural resilience. *The tribal college journal, 14*(4).

American Indian Higher Education Corsortium, The Institute for Higher Education Policy. (2000). *Creating role models for change: A survey of tribal college graduates.* Author.

American Indian Higher Education Corsortium, The Institute for Higher Education Policy. (1999). *Tribal Colleges: An introduction.* Alexandria, VA.

Anderson, L., Putnam, J., Sinclair-Daisy, F., & Squetimkin-Anquoe, A. (1999). American Indian and Alaskan Native Single Parents. In C. L. Schmitz & S. S. Tebb (Eds.), *Diversity in single-parent families: Working from strength* (pp. 33–68). Milwaukee, WI: Families International, Inc.

Angell, G. B. (2000). Cultural resilience in North American Indian First Nations: The story of Little Turtle. *Critical Social Work, 1*(1), electronic journal.

Assembly of First Nations (2001). *Description of First Nations.* Ottawa, Ontario, Canada. Online: http://www.afn.ca/Assembly_of_First_Nations.htm.

Austin, R. (1993, Spring). Freedom, responsibility and duty: ADR and the Navajo Peacemaker Court. *The Judges Journal, 32*(2), 8–11; 47–48.

Canada Census (2001). *Young, fast growing native population seeking hope for future.* On line: http://www.canada.com/national/features/census/story.html?id=C2FAF7DD-B689-4F50-9899-2A36B9C35914.

Child, B. J. (1996). Reservations. In *Encyclopedia of North American Indians.* F. E. Hoxie (Ed.). New York: Houghton Mifflin. On line: http://college.hmco.com/history/readerscomp/naind/html/na_004500_boardingscho.htm.

Cross, T. L. (1986). Drawing on cultural tradition in Indian child welfare. *Social Casework, 67,* 283–289.

Davis, J. (Winter, 2001). American Indian Boarding School Experiences: Recent Studies from Native Perspectives. *Organization of American Historians Magazine of History, 15.* Bloomington, IN: Organization of American Historians.

Deloria, V. (2004). *Red earth, white lies: Native Americans and the myth of scientific fact.* Golden, CO: Fulkrum Publishing.

Deloria, V., Jr., & Lytle, C. (1998). *The nations within: The past and future of American Indian Sovereignty.* New York: Pantheon Books.

Dorris, M. (1987). Indians on the shelf. In C. Martin (Ed.), *The American Indian and the problem of history* (pp. 98–113). New York: Oxford University Press.

Dunn, S. (February, 2004). Rituals of healing—Native intelligence—Native American sweat lodges and spiritual healing. *Natural Health.*

Elsass, P. (1992). *Strategies for survival: The psychology of cultural resilience in ethnic minorities.* New York: New York University Press.

Ferrante, J., & Brown, P. (2001). *The social construction of race and ethnicity in the United States* (2nd ed.). Upper Saddle River, NJ: Prentice Hall.

Giago, T., Jr. (1990). My Laughter. *Native Peoples: The Arts and Lifeways, 3*(3), 52–56.

Goodluck, C. (1993). Social services with Native Americans: Current status of the Indian Child Welfare Act. In H. P. McAdoo (Ed.), *Family ethnicity: Strength in diversity* (pp. 217–226). Newbury Park, CA: Sage Publications.

Harjo, S. S. (1993, Winter). This is a good day to live. *Native People's Magazine.* Reprinted in R. T. Schaefer. *Racial and ethnic groups.* (7th ed.; pp. 167–168). New York: Longman.

Heavy Runner, I., & Marshall, K. (2003). Miracle Survivors: Promoting resilience in Indian students. *The Tribal College Journal 14*(4), 14–19.

Hepworth, D., & Larsen, J. (1982). *Direct social work practice.* Homewood, IL: Dorsey Press.

Hosmer, B. C. (1999). *American Indians in the marketplace: Persistence and innovation among the Menominees and Metlakatlans, 1870–1920.* Lawrence, KS: University Press of Kansas.

Hurtado, S. (1992). The campus racial climate: Contexts for conflict. *The Journal of Higher Education, 63*(5), 539–569.

Indian Country (May 5, 2004). Pueblos struggle to protect petroglyphs: Developers press for highway.

Indian Country (May 4, 2004). Navajo win another court round.

Jennings, F. (1996). Historians and Indians. In *Encyclopedia of North American Indians.* F. E. Hoxie (Ed.). New York: Houghton Mifflin. On line: http://college.hmco.com/history/readerscomp/naind/html/na_041400_urbanindians.htm.

Josephy, A. (1991). *The Indian heritage of America.* New York: Houghton Mifflin.

King, C. J., & Springwood, C. F. (Eds.). (2001). *Team spirits. The Native American mascots controversy.* Lincoln, NE: University of Nebraska Press.

Lemont, E. (2001–2002). Developing Effective Processes of American Indian Constitutional and Governmental Reform: Lessons from the Cherokee Nation of Oklahoma, Hualapai Nation, Navajo Nation and Northern Cheyenne Tribe. *American Indian Law Review, 26*(2).

Locke, R. F. (1992). *The book of the Navajo.* (5th ed.). Los Angeles, CA: Mankind Publishing Company.

Marger, M. N. (1994). *Race and ethnic relations: American and global perspectives (3rd ed.).* Belmont, CA: Wadsworth Publishing Company.

Meyer, R. W. (1977). *The Village Indians of the Upper Missouri.* Lincoln, NE: University of Nebraska Press.

Morris, G. T. (1992). International law and politics: Toward a right to self-determination for indigenous peoples. In M. A. Jaimes (Ed.), *The state of Native America: Genocide, colonization, and resistance* (pp. 55–86). Boston: South End Press.

Murg, W. (2003). Interview with Native filmmaker Stacey Fox. *Indian Country,* December 4.

Nichols, R. L. (2004). *American Indians in U.S. History.* Norman, OK: The University of Oklahoma Press.

Nofz, M. P. (1988, February). Alcohol abuse and culturally marginal American Indians. *Social Casework: The Journal of Contemporary Social Work, 69*(2), 67–73.

Norgren, J. (2004). *The Cherokee cases: Two landmark federal decisions in the fight for sovereignty.* Norman, OK: The University of Oklahoma Press.

Oetting, E. R., & Beauvais, F. (1991). Orthogonal cultural identification theory: The cultural identification of minority adolescents. *International Journal of Addictions, 25,* 655–685.

The *Omega Directory* (April, 2004). Mountain Temple scheduling Beltain [Mayday] Celebration. p. 7.

Parfit, M. (1994). Powwows. *National Geographic, 185* (June), 85–113.

Parks, D. (1991). *Traditional narratives of the Arikara Indians.* (vol. 3). Lincoln, NE: University of Nebraska Press.

Pevar, S. (1992). *The Rights of Indians and Tribes: The Basic ACLU Guide to Indian and Tribal Rights.* (2nd ed.). Carbondale and Edwardsville, IL: Southern Illinois University Press.

Red Horse, J. G. (1980). American Indian elders: Unifiers of Indian families. *Social Casework, 61,* 490–493.

Riding In, J. (1996). Reservations. In *Encyclopedia of North American Indians.* F. E. Hoxie (Ed.). New York: Houghton Mifflin. On line: http://college.hmco.com/history/readerscomp/naind/html/na_033000_reservations.htm.

Reyner, J., & Eder, J. (2004). *American Indian education: A history.* Norman, OK: The University of Oklahoma Press.

Schaefer, R. T. (1998). *Racial and ethnic groups.* 7th ed. New York: Longman.

Shutiva, C. (1997). Native American culture and communication through humor. In A. Gonzalez, M. Houston, & V. Chen (Eds.), *Our voices: Essays in culture, ethnicity, and communication* (pp. 113–118). Los Angeles, CA: Roxbury Publishing Company.

Snipp, C. M. (1996). Urban Indians. In *Encyclopedia of North American Indians.* F. E. Hoxie (Ed.). New York: Houghton Mifflin. On line: http://college.hmco.com/history/readerscomp/naind/html/na_041400_urbanindians.htm

Spindel, C. (2001). *Dancing at half time: Sports and the controversy over American Indian mascots.* New York: New York University Press.

Statistical Reference Centre (National Capitol Region). *Canada's ethnocultural portrait: The changing mosaic.* Online report. (2001). Ottawa, Ontario. http://142.206.72.67/02/02a/02a_009_e.htm

Stiffarm, L. A. & Lane, P. Jr. (1992). The demography of native North America: A question of American Indian survival. In M. A. Jaimes (Ed.), *The state of Native America: Genocide, colonization, and resistance* (pp. 23–53). Boston: South End Press.

Taiaiake A. (1999). *Peace, Power, Righteousness: An Indigenous Manifesto.* New York: Oxford University Press.

Tinker, G. E. (1996). Missions and missionaries. In *Encyclopedia of North American Indians.* F. E. Hoxie (Ed.). New York: Houghton Mifflin. On line: http://college.hmco.com/history/readerscomp/naind/html/na_004500_boardingscho.htm

Thornton, R. (1987). *American Indian holocaust and survival: A population history since 1492.* Norman, OK: University of Oklahoma Press.

Towle, C. (1945). A social work approach to courses in growth and behavior. *Social Service Review, 34,* 402–414.

U.S. Census Bureau (2000). United States Census 2000. Retrieved January 26, 2005 from http://www.census.gov.

Wakeling, S., Jorgensen, M., Michaelson, S., & Begay, M. (July, 2001).Policing on American Indian Reservations: A report to the National Institute of Justice. July, 2001, NCJ 188095. Aguirre, A. & Baker, D. V. (2000), *Structured inequality in the United States: Critical discussions and the continuing significance of race, ethnicity, and gender.* Upper Saddle River, NJ: Prentice Hall.

Waller, M., & McAllen-Walker, R. (2001). One man's story of being gay and Diné: A study in resiliency. In *Queer Families, Queer Politics: Challenging culture and the state,* (pp. 87–103). New York: Columbia University Press.

Waller, M., & Patterson, S. (2000). *Natural helping and resilience in a Diné community.* Manuscript submitted for publication.

Waller, M., Risley-Curtiss, Murphy, S., Medill, A., & Moore, G. (1998). Harnessing the positive power of language: American Indian women, a case example. *Journal of Poverty, 2* (4), 63–81.

Weaver, H. (1999). Indigenous People in a multicultural society. In P. L. Ewalt, E. M. Freeman, A. E. Fortune, D. L. Poole, & S. L. Witkin (Eds.), *Multicultural issues in social work: Practice and research.* Washington, DC: NASW Press.

Wilkinson, C. F. (1987). *American Indians, time and the law.* New Haven, CT: Yale University Press.

Worcester v. Georgia., 31 U.S., [6 Pet.] 515 (1831).

Wright, B., & Tierney, W. G. (2000). American Indians in higher education: A history of cultural conflict. In A. Aguirre Jr. & D. Baker, *Structured inequality in the United States: Critical discussions on the continuing significance of race, ethnicity, and gender.* Upper Saddle River, NJ: Prentice Hall.

Wright, J., Lopez, M. & Zumwalt, L. (1997). That's what they say: The implications of American gay and lesbian literature for social service workers. In L. Brown (Ed.), *Two-Spirit People* (pp. 67–82). New York: Haworth.

Wood, N. (1974). *Many winters.* New York: Doubleday.

Yellow Bird, M. J. (1995). Spirituality in First Nations Story Telling: A Sahnish-Hidatsa Approach to Narrative. *Reflections: Narratives of Professional Helping 1,* (4), pp. 65–72.

CHAPTER FOUR

THE SIGNIFICANCE OF SPIRITUALITY FOR RESILIENT RESPONSE TO CHRONIC ILLNESS[1]

A Qualitative Study of Adults with Cystic Fibrosis

EDWARD R. CANDA

This chapter is dedicated to the late Lisa McDonough, who was a consultant to this study. She inspired and encouraged me. She graced many by her wonderful spirit.

Spirituality is not escapism. It is who we are. It is our daily life. It's everything rolled into one.

—Doug (study participant)

Interest in spirituality as a source of strength for people facing serious life challenges is growing rapidly among social workers. This interest connects four types of theoretical and empirical studies: formulations of definitions of spirituality (e.g., Canda & Furman, 1999; Carroll, 2001; Ellor, Netting, & Thibault, 1999); research

[1]The author wishes to thank the following people: Robert C. Stern, M.D., and Carl F. Doershuk, M.D., of the Department of Pediatrics, Case Western Reserve University and Rainbow Babies and Childrens Hospital, Cleveland, Ohio, for significant assistance throughout the study; and Paula K. Duke, M.A., for going well beyond the call of duty as research assistant. The research was supported in part by a Graduate Research Fund Faculty Development Grant from the University of Kansas School of Social Welfare.

on sources of people's strengths and resiliency (e.g., Palmer, 1999; Saleebey, 2002); studies on the role of religion and spirituality in supporting health (e.g., Hawks, Hull, Thalman, & Richins, 1995; Koenig, McCullough, & Larson, 2001; Van Hook, Hugen, & Aguilar, 2001); and studies of people's growth through crisis and illness (e.g., Dunbar, Mueller, Medina, & Wolf, 1998; Sidell, 1997; Smith, 1995; Young & McNicoll, 1998). However, previous studies of the impact of spirituality on people experiencing crisis, illness, and disability were guided mainly by assumptions formed by scholars and professional helpers, rather than the views of service consumers.

Accordingly, this qualitative study had three purposes: to identify the views of adults with cystic fibrosis (CF), which is a genetic, chronic, and usually terminal illness, concerning their usage and definitions of spirituality and related terms; to describe their accounts of the contributions of spirituality to their resilient response to having CF; and to convey their recommendations for social workers and health care professionals. The situation of people with CF serves as an especially strong example of how spirituality can be a source of strength in adverse circumstances, since the illness is presently incurable.

METHODOLOGY

To develop interview questions, the author first reviewed transcripts from 1 year of discussion on the Cystic-L on-line internet group, 5 years' material from the mutual support newsletter *CF Roundtable*, and books about the lives of people with CF (Deford, 1983; Lab & Lab, 1990; Staunton, 1991; Woodson, 1991). The author then identified 16 adult respondents from the patient population of a national CF medical treatment center. A previous quantitative survey there of all 402 patients revealed use of spiritually oriented health support activities among approximately 60% of patients, but did not give details of the performance, meaning, and impact of these practices (Stern, Canda, & Doershuk, 1992). The most commonly reported of these were group prayer, faith healing using religious healing objects (such as a religious medal), meditation, and pilgrimage. Most patients or their adult representatives reported self-perceived benefits from all practices, including amelioration of symptoms and providing a sense of care and comfort for patient and loved ones. No injury or significant costs were incurred.

To explore these people's views in more detail, the author used a purposive sampling strategy to select adult respondents who demonstrated a high level of interest in spirituality as a source of strength in the previous survey and whose status reflected a variety of characteristics, including health status (mild symptoms to lung transplant candidates and lung transplant recipient), gender (8 male; 8 female), age (range 22–45), ethnicity (2 African American, 14 European American), religious affiliation (6 mainline Protestant, 6 evangelical Protestant, 2 Catholic, 1 Catholic/Buddhist; 1 agnostic), and other variations of educational level, marital status, geographic residency, occupation, and employment. In accord with empowerment-oriented research, people with CF were involved in all phases of the study from the very beginning and findings are being used to contribute to service improvements on their behalf (Chamberlain, Stephens, & Lyons, 1997; Fetterman, 2001; Lincoln, 1992, 1995; Rapp, Shera, & Kisthardt, 1993). This research approach recognizes that the insights of participants, gleaned from their long perseverance, soul searching, and personal growth, are important assets for their own resilience and for sharing with others.

Respondents received a list of topics prior to the interview so they could prepare responses. Topics included the meaning of spirituality and related terms, impact of illness on daily living, use of spiritual activities and supports to deal with CF, and advice for professional helpers. Telephone interviews (1½–2 hours) were transcribed verbatim and coded, sorted, and analyzed by the constant comparative method to identify patterns of themes and variations within themes with the assistance of a word processing program (MS Word) (Berg, 1997; Lincoln & Guba, 1985).

In accordance with empowerment, ethnographic, and phenomenological approaches to research, the researcher (who has CF) included himself as a participant/observer in the study, while bracketing his own assumptions so that they did not distort the first 15 interviews nor the analysis of their transcripts (Agar, 1996; Braud & Anderson, 1998). The researcher used his personal experience and professional study of this topic to enhance empathic interviewing, to support realism in portrayal of CF, and to deepen nuances in analysis and interpretation of data. The researcher trained an assistant to interview him according to the same interview guide as was used for the first 15 interviews. The resulting transcript was set aside until all other transcripts were analyzed. Then, the researcher analyzed his transcript and compared it with those of the other 15 interviewees. This was helpful in checking the tentatively derived patterns of themes, because the researcher had a significantly different vantage point from most of the other participants by virtue of his role as researcher as well as unusual features of his spiritual perspective and health status. The themes that emerged from analysis of the first 15 participants were supported through this comparison.

To check the credibility of conclusions with participants, a draft of this manuscript was sent to all participants to give an opportunity for response. Of the 14 respondents who could be reached, none expressed objection to the content. Four wrote to emphasize support for it.

To seek confirmation of the relevancy of observations to other adults with CF (i.e., transferability) and to caution against researcher bias, findings were shared in detail with a consultant with CF, Ms. Lisa McDonough (2002), who was a nationally known columnist on spirituality. She had no involvement with the design of the study or prior contact with the researcher. Feedback from this consultant supported the broad relevance of themes and implications for people with CF and professional helpers. Further, the findings from this sample of the 402 participants in the original survey are consistent with the themes identified for those 60% who used spiritually oriented healing, though much more detailed. In addition, the consensus statement (in the following section) was distributed, with a request for response, to hundreds of people with CF, including all readers of *CF Roundtable* and subscribers to two internet discussion groups for people with CF (CYSTIC-L@HOME.EASE.LSOFT.COM and cysticfibrosis@conncoll.edu). No one expressed objection to the content; all responders supported it.

Finally, to support the dependability of procedures and to confirm accurate inferences from data analysis, periodic self audits of a detailed methodological audit trail and checks with medical and social work colleagues were performed.

In the following presentation of findings, words in quotation marks represent exact quotes or close paraphrases from respondents' interview transcripts. First, patterns of similarity and difference among the participants as a group will be presented. Then, to illustrate the distinct voices of participants, two contrasting participants' stories will be summarized, mostly in their own words.

SUMMARY OF FINDINGS

Understandings of Faith, Religion, and Spirituality

None of the preestablished demographic or personal characteristics appeared to influence major variations on the themes. Although religious affiliation itself was not a distinguishing feature, differences of spiritual propensity (Canda & Furman, 1999) were important in relation to metaphors and key terms used to describe the process of dealing with CF. Participants could be divided into two groups: those who were evangelical, exclusively committed Christians (n = 6) and those with an ecumenical viewpoint, that is, inclusive of multiple spiritual perspectives. The ecumenical group included Christians (n = 9) and an agnostic (n = 1). All of the members of the evangelical group affiliated with Protestant non-mainline denominations and small local church groups. They described themselves by expressions such as "Bible-based," "born-again," "nondenominational," and "accepting Jesus as Lord and Savior." If they referred to other religions, they indicated the belief that everyone should accept Jesus as their Lord. This was stated in the context of wishing to share the benefits of faith that they receive with other people who have CF and their professional helpers.

Most members of the ecumenical group affiliated with mainline Protestant (e.g., Lutheran or Methodist) and Catholic denominations; one agnostic developed a personally tailored humanistic spiritual perspective. The ecumenical Christians emphasized the importance of their faith in Christ and their membership in Christian communities, as did the evangelical Christians. However, when referring to other religions, they said that there are many ways of approaching spiritual life that can be valuable. Some of the ecumenical Christians participated in other religions, including a Catholic who practiced Zen Buddhist meditation and a Protestant who shared worship services with his Catholic wife. The ecumenical agnostic described herself as a former Catholic who attends a Protestant church according to her husband's preference. She is open to the possibility of God's existence, but focuses on expressing spirituality through a sense of "brotherhood with all people" and "oneness with the universe."

All respondents distinguished spirituality and faith from religion. They described religion to be associated with institutionalized formal patterns of beliefs, rituals, and symbols related to faith and spirituality. Participants commonly described religion by terms such as "ritualistic, organized, institutional, relating to membership in a group, based on rules and regulations." All evangelical Christian respondents and the ecumenical agnostic respondent used the term religion with some ambivalence and negative connotations, reflecting the idea that institutionalized "man-made" religions can become overly rigid, conformist, or authoritarian, thus distracting from the core experiences of faith and spirituality. The ecumenical Christian respondents recognized that religions can sometimes divert attention from spirituality, but they referred to the positive contributions of religion without ambivalence. On all other matters, the ecumenical agnostic and the ecumenical Christians were more similar in their views in contrast to the evangelical Christians.

All respondents described spirituality as a way of life involving a search for meaning oriented toward a sacred realm (e.g., supernatural powers such as God, Jesus, angels, and heaven, or, for the agnostic, nature and the oneness of the universe) as well as primary motivating values (such as love, compassion, and service). The participants conceived of spirituality as an integration of core personal beliefs, values, and religious activities together with experience of the sacred within daily life, social relationships, and strategies for dealing with CF.

All participants, except the agnostic, frequently used the term *faith*. Faith referred to personal relationship and experience with divinity and the associated contents of beliefs in God. Faith was occasionally used in the sense of trust and confidence, especially in God and the promise of "eternal life with Jesus." For the evangelical Christian participants, faith was given greatest importance and was closely associated with spirituality. For the ecumenical Christians, all three terms (*faith, religion,* and *spirituality*) were closely interconnected. The agnostic respondent did not view faith as important to her, because she defined it in Christian terms that did not fit her belief system. Overall, 75 percent of respondents rated faith and spirituality as much more important and fundamental to them than formalized religion.

Beyond the differences between the two groups (evangelical and ecumenical) in theological language, both shared the conviction that faith and spirituality (and religious participation as a secondary expression of them) are sources of great strength. They are important for practical management of symptoms of CF, for achieving a sense of personal and social well-being, and for discovering meaning that infuses and transcends confrontation with physical limitations and death. All participants also reported various kinds of transpersonal experiences, such as feeling the presence of God, that gave deep significance to their spiritual beliefs and practices and that supported them in their use of conventional medical and spiritually based healing (Canda, 2001). As the implications section will discuss, most current social work literature uses the term *spirituality* to include matters of faith and religious and nonreligious spiritual perspectives. In this sense, participants' shared strategy of using spirituality to deal with CF created a commonality of outlook that was stronger than differences of spiritual propensity and demographic characteristics.

Ideas about Impacts of CF on Participants

Since CF is presently an incurable illness, it is not surprising that all participants identified severely negative physical impacts but no directly beneficial physical impacts. These included manifestations of lung disease and pancreatic dysfunction (enzymatic insufficiency), general decline in stamina, and toxic or distressing side effects of medications, extended hospitalizations, and other medical treatments. This was the aspect of life that was seen to have been affected in the most negative way by CF. Yet two people mentioned indirect physical benefits of having CF. One of them explained that "God used CF" to warn him to change from a self-destructive pattern of behavior. Another said that health care requirements challenged him to live in a balanced manner, thus enhancing overall well-being and physical health.

Fourteen people described the mental (i.e., intellectual and emotional) impact of having CF. Most participants (n = 13) identified this impact as negative, specifically they described negative feelings triggered by the struggle with CF, such as sadness (e.g., "discouragement, depression, grief"), and anxiousness (e.g., "fear, sense of danger, worry, distress"). Three people described feelings of anger or bitterness about having CF. Six people also mentioned troublesome thoughts related to low self-esteem, blaming oneself for sickness, pessimism, occasional suicidal ideas, or inability to set long-term goals. However, four participants identified ways that they improved mentally by responding to the challenges of having CF. They said they became stronger persons, more intellectual and self-reflective, more self-accepting, or more appreciative of life.

All participants described the effects on social relationships of having CF. This was an area in which there were both strong negative and positive impacts. Eleven respondents referred to negative impacts, such as difficulty performing tasks at workplace, school, and home and the distress of loved ones in response to the participant's having CF. Eleven people mentioned positive social impacts. Of these, six people mentioned that dealing with CF together with loved ones enhances feelings of mutual caring and love. Five people emphasized that they have witnessed other people being inspired and encouraged through their example of coping well with CF. Two participants said that their experience of CF has heightened their sensitivity to others' needs.

Thirteen respondents described ways that having CF directly affects their spirituality and these were mostly positive. Only four described negative spiritual consequences, such as "a difficult test of faith" during times of health crisis or unsuccessful faith healing cures. Thirteen participants explained that dealing with CF enhanced their spiritual lives by yielding deep insights into the meaning and purpose of life, helping them draw closer to God, witnessing to the benefits of faith to others, and stimulating overall personal growth and well-being.

Spirituality offered participants a way of living with and transcending through limits and discomforts imposed by CF. This is reflected in the contrast between the impacts of CF described for the physical aspect of life (primarily negative) and those for the spiritual aspect of life (primarily positive). Overall, benefits accrued from dealing with CF in each of the life domains were attributed to the importance of faith, spirituality, and religion. That is, according to participants, when CF and related challenges and disabilities are put in a spiritual context, it is possible to learn and to grow as a person in all realms of one's life. Spirituality is a strength that integrates and edifies the whole person.

Metaphors for the Challenges of CF

Overall, 16 people used negatively toned metaphors to describe dealing with CF and 11 used positively toned metaphors. This reemphasizes that having CF is undesirable but "not all bad" for the participants. It poses grave challenges and surprising opportunities.

Everyone used negative medical or physical metaphors, such as "disease, genetic illness, terminal illness, or handicap," and "my body is falling apart," "things are slipping away," or "I feel like I am descending into illness." There were no positive metaphors used for the physical aspect of the illness.

However, spirituality enabled people to find meaning within and beyond this physical aspect of illness. Thirteen participants used explicit religious or nonreligious spiritual metaphors to describe their coping with CF. Some of these were negative. For example, evangelical Christian respondents used metaphors relating to a battle between personified forces of good (Jesus, God, and angels) and evil (Satan, the devil). On the positive side, in response to these "trials and tribulations," they had a sense of divine protection and ultimate "Victory through Christ" (even in death) over the illness.

Ecumenical Christian respondents did not use metaphors involving battle with evil. However, some described negative metaphors such as "Dealing with CF, I feel like the survivors of the holocaust," and "CF really plays mind games with you." On the positive side, they shared the evangelical Christians' descriptions of divine protection, nurturance, and support. Some also said, "I offer up my suffering with Christ to benefit others" and "CF is a very stern teacher about life."

Challenges Associated with Spirituality

In general, participants emphasized that spirituality, faith, and religion have been of great importance in their resiliency. However, most (n = 12) reported some difficulties that arose regarding the use of spirituality in coping with illness. Ten people mentioned obstacles arising from their own religious communities. Although participants' religious communities were usually described as very supportive, some members of congregations were described as generating conflicts or tensions for the person with CF. Five of these 10 respondents said that sometimes other religious people attribute the cause of CF or the lack of successful prayer-based healing to some moral fault of the person with CF. Some have advised the person to rely only on prayer-based healing to the neglect of medical intervention. Four respondents said that certain religious teachings are too strict, rigid, or socially unjust. One explained that it is difficult to find a satisfactory minister.

Five people described skeptical, patronizing, and disparaging attitudes and comments regarding their spirituality from physicians, psychiatrists, or social workers. Four people mentioned tensions arising from differences of spiritual beliefs with significant others including family, coworkers, and friends. One person indicated that the pervasive dichotomy between medicine and spirituality in society generally inhibits patients' access to holistic, spiritually oriented health care.

Seven people described spiritual difficulties that arise from within themselves. Three of them mentioned that they sometimes have counterproductive personal qualities, such as insufficient effort in spiritual practice, being overly rational, and feeling stuck in an inner struggle over faith matters. Three mentioned that they developed self-doubts about the strength of their faith when prayers for the healing of symptoms were unsuccessful. One said that the challenges of CF keep the pressure on for constant self-reflection.

However, it is important to clarify that all these difficulties were described in the context of a predominantly positive experience of faith, spirituality, and religion. Both the interpersonal and intrapersonal difficulties were seen as challenges to overcome in the process of personal growth. For example, working through moralistic blaming from others or self-doubts led to a stronger sense of faith and clarity of spiritual perspective for participants. The ability to recognize these spiritual difficulties as challenges and opportunities for growth was another source of strength and resilience for them.

A CONSENSUS STATEMENT ON SPIRITUALITY AS A SOURCE OF STRENGTH BY ADULTS WITH CF

To convey a more detailed and comprehensive impression of the views shared by the participants, the researcher constructed the following consensus statement about the role of spirituality as a strength that supports health and well-being. This statement represents a synthesis of commonly shared views among all participants and, as previously explained, was supported by checks with hundreds of other people with CF.

As adults with CF, we have experienced many years of health challenges, including the daily grind of numerous medications and respiratory clearance treatments, as well as times of life threatening physical crises and prolonged hospitalizations. Most of us have had to deal with symptoms of CF since childhood. Although there are many variations of onset, course, and severity of illness for people with CF, we are all acutely aware that without a lung transplant, we may die from complications of cystic fibrosis. But the very fact that we have had this challenge for so long means that we have had a powerful opportunity to learn from our experience. We have gleaned a sense of the meaning, purpose, and importance of life. And we have learned how spirituality and faith can help people with health challenges to be resilient. Since everyone must confront sickness and death eventually, we hope that what we have learned might be of some benefit to others.

The physical, mental, social, and spiritual challenges of CF give us a clear choice: We can give up and give in, or, we can learn and grow from the experience. We have found that if we approach CF as a challenge and opportunity for learning, our well-being can actually be enhanced, even if our physical condition wavers and declines. This is not easy. Sometimes we feel worn out and lose a sense of life direction. But in the long run it is much better to face the challenge than to give in to despair. The ability to find meaning through illness and to transcend the limitations of the body comes through our spirituality, including our faith in a Sacred

Source of strength, our use of spiritually based healing practices to augment conventional medicine, and our sharing of a spiritual way of life with loved ones and community members.

For many of us, faith in a Sacred Source of strength means that we experience God as an active presence who helps us through the difficult times and guides us in our daily lives. Some of us feel the supportive presence of angels or the nurturing energy of nature and communion with the universe. When we share our spirituality with other members of our spiritual support community, we can help each other in our spiritual growth. At times when we are feeling down, members of the community help us; and we return the favor when we are needed. Our faith traditions also provide us with practices of individual and group prayer, reading of scripture and other inspirational texts, symbols of grace and salvation, rituals of worship, and occasions for fellowship and mutual support. All these spiritually based activities help to increase our sense of support by loved ones, friends, and sacred powers. They encourage us to be diligent in our medical care and to stay well balanced in our personal life styles. And they assist our physical health by relieving stress and providing relief for some of our symptoms of illness.

Spirituality also helps us to deal with the so-called end stage of CF and the anticipation of death. Most of us believe that death is not a terminal condition because there is a spiritual life beyond the trials and tribulations of this physical existence. And all of us recognize that approaching life and death as opportunities for insight and growth gives a sense of integrity, worth, and significance to life. So not even death can defeat us.

We have learned that it is important not to be discouraged or confused by some religious people who blame us for having CF, or who cast doubt on our faith when a miracle cure is not forthcoming, because of their own misunderstanding. And even when health care professionals ignore or depreciate our spirituality, we have learned that it is important to make our own spiritual commitments and practices clear and consistent in our own lives.

The challenges of CF remind us to set our priorities firmly according to the guidance of our Sacred Source of strength, to treasure every moment of life, to cherish our loved ones, and to use our own situation as a means to help and inspire others. Paradoxically, when we approach life and death this way, even if our physical condition worsens, our overall sense of well-being can improve.

The following two stories illustrate individual variations within this consensus view. Names and details were changed to protect confidentiality.

Gary's Story: Trying to Figure It All Out

At the time of his interview, Gary described himself as a Protestant who shares participation in his Catholic wife's religious services. For him, spirituality and faith guide all aspects of life, infuse formal religious practice with significance, and help him answer the "Why are we here?" existential questions. Persevering in the search, even when there are no clear answers, characterized Gary's resilient response to having a chronic illness.

I try to live according to the beliefs of the Christian church every day—not, of course, always successfully. And with some recent changes in my health, I feel it is even more imperative to me to really start to understand exactly what life is all about. And it's a little frustrating that I can't quite figure it all out. I'm at the point where I'm starting to feel a time pressure to try to figure it out before something drastic happens.

At church on Sundays I always pray for my health to be maintained, and if not, for the strength to deal with it, for me and my wife. I also try to pray every day for my health and the health of my wife. I guess I've given up praying for miracles. I think somewhere in the back of my mind I always figured something big would happen and that somehow I would find my way out of CF. But that doesn't seem to be in the cards.

Although I've given up on miracles, my prayer and religious activities affect my health by giving me the strength to continue with all the medical care that I've done. They give me motivation and a sense that there is a purpose out there that I've just got to figure out. And when other people pray for me, maybe the prayers are answered and it makes me feel better mentally and physically to know that other people care enough about me to pray for me.

The difficulty I have with CF is that it is a progressive disease; it only goes in one direction, and that is very difficult to deal with mentally. You have to invest so much time and effort in CF. It takes away from other things you could be doing in life. And I find that whole combination of factors to be very difficult mentally and exhausting and the inevitability of the disease is disheartening.

Having CF makes you question your faith. I'm sure you've heard it a million times. But I think it is important for all of us to figure it out. Why does God allow CF to happen? Why doesn't He cure me? You look around and see an awful lot of suffering . . . why is all this allowed to happen? Am I supposed to pray to get well? Am I supposed to pray just for the strength to deal with this? Or, is this a God who just lets things happen, and even though He loves us all, suffering is inevitable? I keep trying to evolve into a stronger faith by asking these questions. I use my faith to improve my sense of well-being, to help me deal with what's coming. And maybe sometimes there just isn't any purpose. Sometimes things just happen. And if you accept that, and I am beginning to accept that, then you have to reexamine the whole belief of what God chooses to do and not do.

I am still scared to death of death. I don't want to try it anytime in the near future. I'm having a pretty good time here. My wife and I are very happy and I like my life. And in terms of the inevitable outcome though, I'm kind of surprised at how convinced I am that when I do die, and when my wife dies, we will be reunited somewhere in heaven. And that's a comfort.

I feel if there is a purpose to life, I've got to do my best and take care of myself to stick around and figure it out. It also shows my appreciation for having this life in the first place. It makes me feel that every little bit of life is a gift and I'll stick around a little bit longer to enjoy it.

Teresa's Story: I Am Already Healed

Teresa, an African American member of a theologically conservative denomination, tells a story of certainty that contrasts with Gary's constant questioning. She described herself as a "born-again Christian." Hers is a story of confident faith and strong church community giving strength in the face of illness and death.

Spirituality and faith relate to my belief in God, a Higher Power. Faith is believing in something you can't see and the evidence of things hoped for. I put them at a 10 on a scale of 1–10. Religion (going to church every Sunday) is high up there if it is in the context of faith.

I pray daily by myself and, especially in the evening, with my daughter and husband. I also have a devotional period where I read scripture and a little daily prayer book. I may pray about my day at work. I may have prayer requests from someone. I pray for my family and their physical well-being. Being a born-again Christian, I believe that I'm already healed, it just hasn't been manifested in the natural world yet. But I just continue to pray that God continues to heal my body and make me feel better at that particular moment. All my family members pray for me and sometimes, if I am not feeling well, they come over to my house. And my sisters believe in the laying on of hands. Sometimes they place their hands right over my chest, just lay them anywhere on my body, and they'll say a prayer of healing and faith. They may anoint with oil on my forehead and pray. And sometimes I get together with a couple coworkers and we may share ideas and prayers. At church we also have a Wednesday night prayer and praise service. We share testimonies about what the Lord has done for us this week and then we'll pray for specific needs in our church or our community, pray for our school district.

These activities affect my physical health a lot. It always makes me feel better to pray and have a group of believers around who really believe that prayers are answered. My health comes and goes, but I have a belief that no matter what, I'm going to be with the Lord. And the groups from my church and my family, they just always back up that belief whenever I get depressed. I've always got that support there. And when people pray for me there's changes in my physical health, because if my mind is up and healthy and thinking the right way, I feel my body is okay.

I also know that if something ever does happen to me, I am not alone. There's community and family there that are going to step in and be with my family, my husband and daughter. Sometimes I don't even have to say anything. They can just sense that I'm not having a good day and come in with an encouraging word, or say a prayer, or I may not even need anything but a hug.

In the Bible it says that by Jesus Christ we are healed. And I believe that literally. And he said, "No weapons formed against me shall prosper." And I believe that CF is like a weapon trying to come against me; and the Bible says it won't prosper. I keep that belief and then I just wait for the natural manifestation in my body. I am pretty healthy compared to most people with CF.

Sometimes I ask myself "What is my purpose?" I've been told by others that I am an inspiration to them by how I never give up. I was always told I'll never be able to go to college and hold down a job, but I've done all that. I've had an opportunity to counsel people with chronic diseases. If my only purpose to be here is to be an example or an inspiration to somebody else, that's good enough for me. I guess my purpose is to live a positive life and try to bring somebody to Christ by example.

The most important thing I've learned is never to give up on faith. No matter how bleak it may seem. Always keep striving, keep going. And just realize that I have victory because I have a prosperous life and I know in the end I will be with the Lord Jesus Christ. That means that one day I'll be in heaven, a place where there is no sickness and no death and no sorrow. That's victorious for me. I won't have to be in this shell with pain and suffering. I'll be able to see my loved ones again one day.

IMPLICATIONS FOR SOCIAL WORK

The general themes revealed in this study are most likely to be shared by other adults with CF for whom faith, spirituality, and religion are important. In addition, considering the numerous other related studies on adversity and spirituality, as identified in the introduction, it is clear that spirituality can be a tremendous resource for resilience and meaning in many situations. The stories of Gary and Teresa illustrate that common themes take on distinctive form in particular lives and contexts. This distinctness is just as precious as the commonality. Indeed, no broadly stated theme is really a strength for anybody. A person's strength is always what is specific to her or him at a particular place, time, and situation. For example, Gary channeled his tendency to doubt and question everything into an existential quest. His sense of mystery and the preciousness of life was keen. His commitment to persevere and to make the most of life was strong. In contrast, Teresa felt very sure of her beliefs and had a strong network of social support through her faith community. Teresa found comforting beliefs, healing practices, and meaning for life within her solid faith.

Participants strongly encouraged practitioners to explore the possible roles of spiritual beliefs and practices in promoting people's resilient response to chronic illness and disability. Ten of the 16 participants said that they had little or no contact with social workers, despite significant involvement with health care systems. Eleven people indicated that social workers never brought up the subject of spirituality, but rather limited themselves to practical aspects of discharge planning (exclusive of coordinating with spiritual support systems). A national survey of direct practitioner members of the National Association of Social Workers (NASW) showed that most practitioners recognize the appropriateness of assessing and utilizing religious and nonreligious spiritual supports with interested clients, but that they feel unprepared by education or training for how to do so (Canda & Furman, 1999). Perhaps that helps account for social workers' lack of attention to this topic in the experience of these participants. It is especially relevant to this study that a significant majority of survey respondents believed that it is appropriate to raise the topics of religion and spirituality with clients regarding issues of terminal illness and bereavement, and in helping clients reflect on their beliefs about what happens after death (see also Canda, Nakashima, & Furman, 2004). These observations support Aguilar's (1997) call for a holistic, spiritually attuned approach to social work in health care.

To utilize spirituality as a strength in practice, social workers need to consider carefully how we use related concepts and terminology with clients. The prevailing definitions of spirituality in the social work literature provide general conceptualizations as common ground for communication among social workers regarding all religious and nonreligious spiritual perspectives (Canda & Furman, 1999). These definitions usually present spirituality as the striving of the person for a sense of meaning, purpose, and morality in relation with the world and ultimate reality, however that is conceived. In contrast, religion refers to institutionalized patterns of spiritual beliefs, values, and practices shared by a community.

Spirituality may be expressed within or outside of religious contexts. The Canda and Furman (1999) survey of NASW members demonstrated that this distinction may be common among practitioners in the field as well. Spirituality is also sometimes understood as a holistic quality of the person in relationship with self, world, and the ground of being. This quality infuses and integrates all the particular bio-psycho-social and spiritual aspects of the person. As indicated by the nuances of the terms spirituality, religion, and faith found in this study, practitioners need to tailor understandings and language about spirituality based on a careful assessment of clients' own perspectives.

Study participants made a distinction between institutional religion and the spiritual aspect of human experience; they also portrayed spirituality as a holistic quality infusing all aspects of life. The similarity to social work usage suggests that professional definitions may provide a good starting point for discussion with them. However, most participants used terms, meanings, and symbols that were particular to their spiritual beliefs and experiences with health challenges. For example, most participants placed strong importance on faith, described in Christian terms, due to their religious affiliations. The prevalence of Christian affiliation among participants was probably influenced by the genetic basis of CF, since most people with CF are non-Jewish European descendents. There is a small percentage of African Americans with CF, but most European and African descendents in the United States have a Christian affiliation. Various Christian terminologies connected to faith and theology, and metaphors relating to health and illness, such as occurred in this study, are not commonly employed in social work outside of Christian religious settings (Hodge, 2002). Further, each individual's story involved distinctive spiritual healing practices, religious attitudes, and imagery. This reminds us of the importance of demonstrating relevant knowledge, respect, and skill for relating to clients' religious or nonreligious spiritual perspectives, Christian or otherwise, that are unique to particular people, cultures, religions, places, times, and situations.

This study highlights the need to address spirituality as a strength in situations that are distinct to people with physical disabilities and health challenges. For example, alternative and complementary healing practices employed by clients could be coordinated with conventional medical and psychosocial care to maximize the benefits and minimize the risks of spiritual practices and support systems. This study, and the original survey of all 402 patients at the CF treatment center, revealed no medical harm from any of these practices. However, several participants described stress related to blaming or condescending messages from some members of their religious groups and health care professionals as well as personal doubts and confusions of faith. Given the evidence of benefits of spirituality for resilience, clients might be well served with assistance in addressing these challenges through self-reflection, therapeutic dialogue, and collaboration with relevant clergy or other spiritual friends and mentors.

Participants' stories of spiritual growth through adversity raise a serious caution about using conventional psychosocial and cognitive stage theories of human development in assessing clients with chronic illness. These theories have been criticized for assuming that spiritual issues of life's meaning and mortality do not emerge until middle age (Robbins, Chatterjee, & Canda, 1998). This study indicates that chronic health challenges can provoke precocious and life-long spiritual searching and growth for some people. Participants often mentioned this as one of their personal strengths. Participants did not reduce themselves to an illness, but rather expanded themselves toward wellness. Participants' use of spirituality to enhance well-being in the midst of all aspects of living and dying illuminates the human condition. While we all share mortality, we also share capacity for meaning and thriving, both within and beyond physical limitations. Issues of illness, disability, and resilience should not be limited to a special topics section of the curriculum or to specialized practice in health and hospice settings. Rather, social workers can be prepared to examine these whenever and wherever relevant to clients.

The stories of participants in this study also provide vivid realism to the strengths perspective. For them, utilizing spirituality as strength did not mean lapsing into denial of physical illness and life challenges. Rather, spiritual beliefs, experiences, and social supports provided resources for managing suffering, persevering in health care, appreciating life and loved ones, and looking into and beyond the nitty-gritty physicality of mortality.

POSTSCRIPT

One of the tenets of strengths-oriented empowerment research is that researchers should conduct studies that let people speak for themselves. As I explained in the methodology section, I included myself in this study. The consensus statement reflects that this chapter is not about *they*. Also it is not just about *me*. It is really about *we*. The doing of this study has been one of the most powerfully self-transforming (and often befuddling) research projects of my career. This is because my own quandaries, challenges, insights, and stories about having CF have been inwardly recalled, questioned, stretched, and inspired as I talked with participants, analyzed their transcripts, and tried to find a realistic way of presenting them.

I became more appreciative of spiritual styles and languages very different from my own as I recognized our common themes and the inherent worth for people of their own distinctive ways. I have come to be a bit more outspoken advocate for people with disabilities and for people with cystic fibrosis. I made the choice to be public about my own disability in order to tell our stories and to advocate for us and for others. And in the process, I have achieved a little more congruity between private and professional aspects of my life. I also extended my connections and friendships in the community of people with CF. I have become stronger by doing strengths-oriented research! The process of doing this research has been a spiritual journey for me. This is how I reflected on the process during my own interview for this study:

> Deciding to do this study is part of my personal working through of issues pertaining to having CF. I can get more comfortable about the issues that participants bring

up. One good thing about listening to them has been seeing how we are all in this boat together. How do they deal with it? And seeing some similarities and differences and learning from that. I don't want to tell them much about my situation (until after the interviews) because I don't want to interfere with their stories; but hearing them has helped me overcome a sense of being alone about having CF.

And the idea of being of service. All right, I have CF. I am learning something from it. How can I use that as a means of helping other people? So doing a professional research project on this has been what I could do. Well, I am not just going to become detached and pretend I'm an objective observer floating off someplace, looking down at these participants, and analyzing them like bugs under a microscope. They're fellows. Just like everybody. We're all in it together, and in particular we share having this illness and I want to learn from them. I want to help distribute what they've learned to help other people. And I want to bring myself into that process, so other people can learn from my experience. And by interconnecting the participants' perspectives and mine, I'm going to learn from that too. Just having to think this through and articulate it, and when I do the analysis of the transcripts, it's going to be a lot of soul searching and reflection for me.

Dear reader, I can honestly convey the sentiments of all of the participants in this study, including myself: If this chapter contributes in some small way to your own soul searching, and to finding more strength within yourself, we will be very glad to have shared our stories.

DISCUSSION QUESTIONS

1. What is spirituality? How would you define your own sense of spirituality? Has it helped you through some of the inevitable turns and troubles of life?

2. In what sense is Teresa healed even though she has a terminal illness?

3. Can you use your understanding of and struggles with your own frailties and difficulties as something that can be valuable for others as they confront adversity? How would you do it?

4. How can it be that people can improve their quality of life, expand toward wellness even though they are seriously or even terminally ill? How can you assist in that effort?

REFERENCES

Agar, M. H. (1996). *The professional stranger* (2nd ed.). San Diego: Academic Press.

Aguilar, M. A. (1997). Re-engineering social work's approach to holistic healing. *Health and Social Work, 22*(2), 83–84.

Berg, B. L. (1997). *Qualitative methods for the social sciences* (3rd ed.). Boston: Allyn and Bacon.

Braud, W., & Anderson, R. (1998). *Transpersonal research methods for the social sciences.* Thousand Oaks, CA: Sage.

Canda, E. R. (2001). Transcending through disability and death: Transpersonal themes in living with cystic fibrosis. In E. R. Canda & E. D. Smith (Eds.), *Transpersonal perspectives on spirituality in social work* (pp. 109–134). Binghamton, NY: Haworth Press.

Canda, E. R., & Furman, L. D. (1999). *Spirituality diversity in social work practice: The heart of helping.* New York: Free Press.

Canda, E. R., Nakashima, M., & Furman, L. D. (2004). Ethical considerations about spirituality in social work: Insights from a national qualitative survey. *Families in Society, 85*(1), 27–35.

Carroll, M. M. (2001). Conceptual models of spirituality. In E. R. Canda & E. D. Smith (Eds.), *Transpersonal perspectives on spirituality in social work* (pp. 5–21). Binghamton, NY: Haworth Press.

Chamberlain, K., Stephens, C., & Lyons, A. C. (1997). Encompassing experience: Meanings and methods in health psychology. *Psychology and Health, 12,* 691–709.

Deford, F. (1983). *Alex: The life of a child.* Baltimore, MD: Cystic Fibrosis Foundation.

Dunbar, H. T., Mueller, C., W., Medina, C., & Wolf, T. (1998). Psychological and spiritual growth in women living with HIV. *Social Work, 43*(2), 144–154.

Ellor, J. W., Netting, F. E., & Thibault, J. M. (1999). *Religious and spiritual aspects of human service practice.* Charleston, SC: University of South Carolina.

Fetterman, D. M. (2001). *Foundations of empowerment evaluation.* Thousand Oaks, CA: Sage.

Hawks, S. R., Hull, M. L., Thalman, R. L., & Richins, P. M. (1995). Review of spiritual health: Definition, role, and intervention strategies in health promotion. *American Journal of Health Promotion, 9*(5), 371–378.

Hodge, D. R. (2002). Conceptualizing spirituality in social work: How the metaphysical beliefs of social workers may foster bias toward theistic consumers. *Social Thought, 21*(1), 39–61.

Koenig, H. G., McCullough, M. E., & Larson, D. B. (2001). *Handbook of religion and health.* New York: Oxford University Press.

Lab, D., & Lab, O. K. (1990). *My life in my hands: Living with cystic fibrosis.* Thousand Palms, CA: LabPro Press.

Lincoln, Y. S. (1992). Sympathetic connections between qualitative methods and health research. *Qualitative Health Research, 2*(4), 375–391.

Lincoln, Y. S. (1995). Emerging criteria for quality in qualitative and interpretive research. *Qualitative Inquiry, 1*(3), 275–289.

Lincoln, Y. S., & Guba, E. (1985). *Naturalistic inquiry.* Beverly Hills, CA: Sage.

McDonough, L. M. (2002). *Lisa, The brief life of a writer.* www.Xlibris.com.

Palmer, N. (1999). Fostering resiliency in children: Lessons learned in transcending adversity. *Social Thought, 19*(2), 69–87.

Rapp, C., Shera, W., & Kisthardt, W. (1993). Research strategies for consumer empowerment of people with severe mental illness. *Social Work, 38*(6), 727–735.

Robbins, S. P., Chatterjee, P., & Canda, E. R. (1998). *Contemporary human behavior theory: A critical perspective for social work.* Boston: Allyn and Bacon.

Saleebey, D. (Ed.). (2002). *The strengths perspective in social work practice* (3rd ed.). New York: Longman.

Sidell, N. L. (1997). Adult adjustment to chronic illness: A review of the literature. *Health and Social Work, 22*(1), 5–11.

Smith, E. (1995). Addressing the psychospiritual distress of death as reality: A transpersonal approach. *Social Work, 40,* 402–413.

Staunton, V. (1991). *Gillian: A second chance.* Dublin, Ireland: Blackwater Press.

Stern, R. C., Canda, E. R., & Doershuk, C. F. (1992). Use of nonmedical treatment by cystic fibrosis patients. *Journal of Adolescent Health, 13,* 612–615.

Van Hook, M., Hugen, B., & Aguilar, M. (Eds.). (2001). *Spirituality within religious traditions in social work practice.* Pacific Grove, CA: Brooks/Cole.

Woodson, M. (1991). *Turn it into glory.* Minneapolis, MN: Bethany House Publishers.

Young, J. M., & McNicoll, P. (1998). Against all odds: Positive life experiences of people with advanced amylotrophic lateral sclerosis. *Health and Social Work, 23*(1), 35–43.

CHAPTER FIVE

THE STRENGTHS APPROACH TO PRACTICE

DENNIS SALEEBEY

In Part Two, we saw the strengths and capacities of people with physical and developmental disabilities, and of people from different and unappreciated cultures. The chapters in Parts Three and Four describe and discuss strengths-based practice with a number of different populations, including people with chronic mental illness, people with addictions, elders in long-term care, youth at risk, residents of economically distressed communities, and families and children. While you will perceive differences among these approaches, you will see throughout the chapters a vital and unmistakable belief in the capabilities of individuals, groups, families, and communities. It comes across in many ways, but the following ideas are resoundingly clear from beginning to end:

■ People who confront stress almost always develop some ideas, capacities, traits, and motivations that may subsequently be of use to them in the search for a better life. We have been much too energetic in looking for the impediments and injuries, the deficits and desolation rather than people's compensating and transformative responses to challenges.

■ Even in the most demanding, tough, lean, and mean environments there is a bounty of natural resources—individuals, families, associations, institutions— available. While some communities are clearly more abundant than others, all neighborhoods have assets.

■ Even though individuals may have labored for years under the blame and disapproving opinions of others, or self-criticism, habitual pessimism, or unfortunate life decisions, at some level, they almost always know what is right for them.

■ As a species we surely have—or we would not have survived thus far—an innate capacity for self-righting and health.

■ Healing, transformation, regeneration, and problem solving almost always occur within the confines of a personal, friendly, supportive, and dialogical relationship (Edward Sampson (1993) calls it "a celebration of the other"). Whether friend, intimate partner, physician, social worker, shaman, or teacher, the more we entreat the power of a caring, egalitarian relationship with those we assist, the better for them and us.

■ Everybody has knowledge and talents, skills and resources that can be used for pressing forward toward a life defined in their own terms—toward their hopes and dreams, the solution of their problems, the meeting of their needs, and the invigoration of the quality of their lives—individually and collectively.

■ It is far more important to set one's gaze toward a better future, to traffic in possibility, than it is to obsess about the disappointments and injuries of a dank, dark past.

■ Even when people do injurious things to themselves and others, they are often trying to meet needs that all of us have—for respect, control, security, love, and connection.

To recognize the strengths in people and their situation implies that we give credence to the way clients experience and construct their social realities. We cannot impose from without our own versions (or those of the agency or other social institutions) of the world. This appreciation of context and construction is an acknowledgment of the special and distinctive social circumstances of each client or group (Saleebey, 1994). To hear the stories and narratives in a family or a community is one way to discover not only their preoccupations and challenges, but also to unearth their particular assets and abilities. Learning the language, the symbols, the images, and the perspectives that move clients—for good or ill—is to encounter their challenges and triumphs, over time. In discussing the recovery from chemical dependency from a transpersonal perspective, Moxley and Washington (2001) say:

> The person's journey in recovery [may] best be expressed as a personal narrative. Helping each person to express his or her story may be a potent way to help an individual understand a career of chemical dependency and to make sense of the social forces that shaped it. The construction of a personal narrative may be the most influential pathway to reveal the shadow and to illuminate the person's accommodation (pp. 258–259).

You will see in the chapters that follow the high level of commitment and resolve that is required to get you into the client's life-world authentically and respectfully. Other themes that abound in the following chapters include the importance of genuine dialogue; forming positive expectations of clients; helping clients participate more fully in their world of people, institutions, and communities; identifying natural resources in the clients' world; and learning from clients. One thing becomes clear in reading these chapters: Operating from a strengths perspective is good, basic social work practice. There is nothing here that is not coincidental with the core of values that energizes and drives the profession. All that we can do in these pages is to give these principles more conceptual and practical vigor.

SOME BEGINNING OBSERVATIONS ABOUT STRENGTHS-BASED PRACTICE

These observations are meant to answer some basic questions that have been asked over the years about generic practice from a strengths perspective. First of all, assume that it will take genuine diligence on your part to begin to appreciate and utilize client strengths in practice. The system is against you, the language and metaphors of the system are against you, consumers are sometimes against you because they have been inscribed with the cursor of disease, and, not insignificantly, the culture is against you. Pursuing the ideas that formulate and celebrate strengths, resilience, rebound, challenge, and transformation is difficult because they are not now natural to much of the social service, health, and mental health systems and their membership. Let us begin by examining some of the factors that are implicated consistently in salutary change and development.

The Core Conditions of Growth and Change

In their review and statistical analyses of studies done over the years on the factors that lead to constructive change in psychotherapy, Assay & Lambert (1999) concluded that there are four enduring components of such change. The four ingredients for change include: factors in the matrix of clients' lives (their strengths and resources, contingent factors, etc.); the qualities of good helping relationships; positive expectations, hope and the placebo effect; and the technical operations and principles of theory. Barry Duncan and Scott Miller (2000) offer a precise and straightforward discussion of these factors in *The Heroic Client* (see pp. 55–62).

What Assay & Lambert call extra-therapeutic factors seem to promote the greatest degree of change. These include the strengths, assets, and resources within the individual, the family, and the ambient environment. Supportive kin, determination, insights gained from intimate sources, a rising sense of hopefulness, a lessening of stresses in the environment, and many other things may be involved here. Clearly important factors are contingent ones—luck, fortune, and the play of chance occurrences in one's life. All of these reflect the substance of an individual's or family's daily life—the web of resources in their surroundings, social support networks, their own wiles and wisdom, personal or collective traits and virtues, and the unforeseen in their lives. According to Assay & Lambert, the psychosocial matrix of a person's life may account for 40 percent of therapeutic change.

For years, social workers have emphasized the importance of the helping relationship and the use of self as the medium of change and growth (Shulman, 1992). Half a century ago, Carl Rogers and his associates assured us that truly healing relationships bloomed from the qualities of caring, empathy, positive regard, genuineness, and respect (1951). Over the last 30 years or so, Hans Strupp (1995) has been investigating psychotherapies of all kinds to mine the ore of real and positive change therein. He continually finds that the quality of the helping relationship is the single most important factor across schools of psychotherapy. Practitioners of the strengths perspective add to these the importance of collaboration—developing a mutually crafted project, meant to lay, brick by brick, a path to a person's or family's hopes and dreams. Charles Rapp, one of the most important figures in the development of the strengths perspective, defines the effective helping relationship as purposeful, reciprocal, friendly, trusting, and empowering (1998). Assay & Lambert reckoned that this factor might account for about 30 percent of the positive change in peoples' lives (1999).

Often forgotten, but truly important in promoting beneficial change are hope, positive expectations, and the placebo effect. My expectation that you can do better and prevail through your tribulations translates into the recrudescence of hope, the revival or birth of a dream—no matter how modest. A focus on possibility, an eye cast to a better future, and the creation of justifiable optimism all promote movement toward one's aspirations. Of all these, however, the most intriguing may be the placebo effect (see discussion in Chapter 1). Long known for its use in medical and pharmaceutical research, it has been virtually ignored as a force in bringing about change.

Michael Fisher (2000) reports that in the 1950s at the University of Kansas Medical Center, in order to test a new medical procedure for the treatment of angina, surgeons performed real operations on one group of patients with angina, and a placebo operation on the other group of men with angina. The placebo group was told that they were going to have heart surgery; they were given a local anesthetic, and incisions were made in their chests. But no operation was done, the surgeons just messed around a little bit, and the patients had the scars and postoperative pain to suggest that they actually had surgery. Seventy percent of the people who had the real surgery reported long-term improvement in their angina; but *all* of the placebo group did. Ethical problems with this study aside, the results are just short of amazing.

It is not at all uncommon, in tests of psychoactive drugs, for the placebo groups to show anywhere from 25 percent to 60 percent improvement (Arpala, 2000). As noted, the extent that the real drug is better than the placebo is thought to be the extent that the drug is effective. But it is unknown, for example, just how much the effect of the real drug is also a placebo phenomenon. In more recent years, people have been getting an active placebo in which they experience side effects—look at the drug ads in your magazines and check out the data. People are more likely to get better on active placebos because the experience of side effects convinces them that they are getting a real and powerful drug. Joseph Arpala (2000) reports that a study by Fisher and Greenberg revealed that in 30 percent to 40 percent of all the studies they reviewed of antidepressant drugs and placebos, the placebo was as powerful or therapeutic as the drug. Refer to Chapter 1 for a discussion of the study of the FDA's data on clinical trials of antidepressants.

So what is happening here? Many things no doubt. It could be—and many have proposed this—that when a person is sick and they have an expectation, thanks to a procedure or pill, that they will get better, they mobilize the healing systems within, whether it is the psychoneuroimmune system, endorphins (endogenous morphine produced by the body), relaxation response (which lowers, among other things, the level of cortisol, the production of which is related to stress), or some unknown process. But maybe even more important here is the expectation of the healer that you will get well, the mobilization of hope and possibility that things will be different in the future. We dissipate an awful lot of our possible good will, hinting or directly saying that things will not be better, that once stuck or hurt or disappointed or abused or ill, you will always suffer scars or the effects of these hurts will reverberate, in one way or another, throughout your life. It is not just the person's expectation that they will recover, rebound, do better, it is the unmistakable expectation of the social worker, physician, healer, minister, teacher, or parent that you will do better—the belief in you. As your social worker, I genuinely believe that you can make it, can leap that hurdle, climb that wall, escape that burden. You may need help, it may take time, but my belief in you is steadfast. As a child heretofore defined as at-risk, I define you, as Beth Blue Swadener (1995) suggests, as a child "at-promise." So the placebo effect harbors within it something of considerable persuasive authority.

Consider, too, that it may well be that even the group receiving a real medication may also experience a placebo effect—in some cases to the tune of 30 percent of its supposed efficacy (Brody, 2000). The emotional, nonverbal, and verbal messages that accompany the giving of a placebo appear to be extraordinarily important. Do they galvanize hope, mobilize positive expectations? Creating the expectancy of a healthy, efficacious response would seem to be a part of the potency of the placebo. But the message for practitioners is that you should never underestimate the sway of hope, the belief that things can improve. Such a prospect is vital to those individuals and groups who struggle against the tide of low expectations, little opportunity, belittled self-esteem, and thwarted justice. According to Assay & Lambert's inquiry, these factors may account for as much as 15 percent of positive, dynamic change.

That percentage is about the same as Assay & Lambert attribute to the effect of the technical operations and methods of a theory. These methods clearly are important. It is well known, for example, that cognitive behavioral techniques, and interpersonal therapy both, often in conjunction with antidepressant drugs, are effective in the treatment of moderate to moderately severe depression (Bentley & Walsh, 2001; Gitlin, 1996).[1] For people returning to the community after hospitalization for an episode of schizophrenia, the combination of a neuroleptic threshold dose[2] of antipsychotic medication and vigorous psychosocial and educational interventions is effective. It must be said, however, that in the absence of the first three factors, the techniques and methods of a theory or perspective hold less sway.

In many ways the strengths perspective builds on the mobilization of these factors, in particular the power of possibility and an unstinting and unqualified belief in the person's or group's capacity for change.

---

[1]More evidence is mounting that the therapies without medication are quite effective.

[2]The smallest amount of medication that produces a beneficial effect.

What Are Strengths?

Almost anything can be considered a strength under certain conditions, so this list is not meant to be exhaustive. Nonetheless, some capacities, resources, and assets do commonly appear in any roster of strengths.

What people have learned about themselves, others, and their world as they have struggled, coped with, and battled abuse, trauma, illness, confusion, oppression, and even their own fallibility. People do learn from their trials, even those that they seem to inflict upon themselves. People do not just learn from successes but from their difficulties and disappointments as well. In their recent book, *The Struggle to Be Strong* (2000), Sybil Wolin and Al Desetta report the narratives of adolescents who have been subjected to enormous challenges in their lives. Consonant with Steven and Sybil Wolins' theory that resilience is forged from seven traits and capacities[3] that one might learn in the struggle against adversity, these stories reproduce evidence of those. Youniqiue Symone, living in foster care, at the age of 16 wrote this about the relationship between her and her biological mother:

> I grew up when I realized this: my mother is not going to change because I want her to. She's only going to change when she wants to. I also know deep down in my heart that we are never going to be a real family. . . . I don't want to have children at a young age to show my mother what a "real mother" is. I want to break the cycle. If I don't, I might end up doing the same thing my mother did. (p. 14)

This is an example of more than ordinary insight in a 16-year-old coming to terms with a mother who, for whatever reasons, neglected her. Out of that realization and her particular understanding about its impact on her young life, Youniqiue has determined to walk a different path.

Personal qualities, traits, and virtues that people possess. These are sometimes forged in the fires of trauma and catastrophe, and they might be anything—a sense of humor, caring, creativity, loyalty, insight, independence, spirituality, moral imagination, and patience to name a few (Wolin & Wolin, 1993). These also are the products of living, the gifts of temperament, and the fruits of experience. Whatever their source, these skills and attributes might well become sources of energy and motivation in working with clients.

What people know about the world around them from those things learned intellectually or educationally to those that people have discerned and distilled through their life experiences. Perhaps a person has developed skill at spotting incipient interpersonal conflict or soothing others who are suffering. Perhaps life

---

[3]The seven possible elements of resilience are humor, insight, independence, relationships, creativity, morality, and initiative. People may develop any one or a number of these as they struggle with the challenges of their lives. They are also developmental, each undergoing maturation and sophistication with the passage of time.

has given an individual the ability to care and tend for young children or elders, or it could be that a person could use an artistic medium to teach others about themselves. Maybe personal experience has motivated an individual and shaped a keen ability to help others through the grieving process. Again, we have no way of knowing what it might be without observing and asking.

The talents that people have can surprise us sometimes (as well as surprising the individual as some talents have lain dormant over the years). Playing a musical instrument, telling stories, cooking, home repair, writing, carpentry (who knows what it might be?) may provide additional tools and resources to assist individuals or groups in reaching their goals. In addition, they may be assets that can be shared and given to others to foster solidarity, to strengthen mentorship, or to cement friendship.

> Writing helped me when I was going through difficult times with my family— when they didn't or couldn't understand me, or when they didn't understand why I would cry for no reason. Writing helped me when I needed someone to talk to. Writing is like both my friend and my family, because it's always there for me whenever I need it.
>
> My mother still doesn't believe I can write on my own. She thinks I copy my poems and stories from someone else. . . .
>
> There's another reason why I would like to be a writer. I know that if someone has a problem and they read my story or poem it might make them feel a little (or even a lot) better about themselves. (Desetta & Wolin, 2000, p. 114)

Terry-Ann Da Costa, who wrote this at age 16, understands both her need to write and the gifts that her writing might bestow on others.

Cultural and personal stories and lore are often profound sources of strength, guidance, stability, comfort, or transformation and are often overlooked, minimized, or distorted. It is now often told how the stories of women have been shrouded through domination but how they are, when recounted and celebrated, sources of profound strength and wisdom (Aptheker, 1989). Cultural approaches to helping, to cite another example—whether the sweat lodge, medicine wheel, drumming, chanting, or curanderismo—may be powerful sources of healing and regeneration. Cultural stories, narratives, and myths, accounts of origins and migrations, or trauma and survival may provide sources of meaning and inspiration in times of difficulty or confusion (see Chapter 3). The exploits of cultural heroes, fictional and real, may provide instruction and guidance.

> The new mestiza [a woman of mixed Indian and Spanish ancestry born in the United States] copes by developing a tolerance for contradictions, a tolerance for ambiguity. She learns to be Indian in a Mexican culture, to be Mexican from an Anglo point of view. She learns to juggle cultures. She has a plural personality, she operates in a pluralistic mode—nothing is thrust out, the good, the bad. And the ugly, nothing rejected, nothing abandoned. Not only does she sustain contradictions, she turns the ambivalence into something else. (Anzaldua, 1987, p. 79, cited in Falicov, 1998, p. 15)

Personal and familial parables of falls from grace and redemption, of failure and resurrection, of struggle and resilience may also provide the diction, the metaphors from which one may construct a more vibrant vision of the self and world.

People have pride as well; people who have leapt over obstacles, who have rebounded from misfortune and hardship often have what the Wolins call "survivor's pride." Often this self-regard is buried under an accumulation of blame, shame, and labeling, but it is often there waiting to be uncovered. "Pride drives the engine of change; shame jams the gears!" (Wolin & Wolin, 1994).

The community is frequently overlooked as a physical, interpersonal, and institutional terrain full of riches to be tapped into (see Chapters 11, 12, and 13). The informal or natural environment is an especially rich landscape, full of people and organizations, who, if asked, would provide their talents and knowledge in the service of helping and supporting others. The work of community development (see Chapter 13) and organizing is, in part, dedicated to germinating the saplings of strength and resourcefulness in the community. The efforts of the Search Institute in Minneapolis in identifying those community strengths and assets that shore up the developmental infrastructure for all youth and help reduce risk behaviors is instructive in this regard. Among their many findings is that availability and vitality of community-wide institutions and neighborhood associations—youth groups, churches, synagogues, temples, ethnic associations, and schools—are critical elements of a responsive and working infrastructure for youth development (Benson, 1997).

The idea of *spirituality* is implicit, I think, in the discussions of and allusions to meaning-making. Ed Canda (see Chapter 4) has written with great wisdom about the nature of spirituality. Summarizing his perspective I would say it has three core assertions. First, spirituality refers to the essential, holistic quality of being that transcends the merely biological, psychological, social, political, or cultural but incorporates them all. This quality obliterates categorizations and dichotomies such as that between mind and body, substance and spirit (Canda, 1997). Second, spirituality reflects our struggle to find meaning, a working moral sensibility, and purposes that extend beyond selfish, egoistic concerns. Finally, spirituality refers to an essence that extends beyond the self, that defies ego boundaries, and allows us to join and revere the mysteries and complexities of life. This might be manifest in visions, peak experiences, cosmic revelations, experiences of the numinous and awe-inspiring.

But it is the hopes and dreams, the promise and possibilities of a better life, a different path, that spur many to action and the mobilizing of their resources and assets—often unused and forgotten. Many dreams and hopes have been disregarded, suppressed, distorted by circumstance or distress. But with help, positive expectations, and work they can be recovered, and made more vital.

For many individuals and groups, then, spirituality is a grand bulwark against the demands and stresses, both ordinary and inordinate, of life. It is also a means of discovering or creating meaning withstanding the vexing and sometimes seemingly incomprehensible events of daily life. Finally, it is a sense of the transcendent that can set the possibilities of the future in more hopeful compass.

How Do You Find Out about Strengths?

Sounds difficult, but the discovery of strengths depends on some simple ideas. Look around you. Do you see evidence of client interests, talents, and competencies?

MICHAEL

A student working with a middle-aged man with moderately severe retardation who lived in a group home was visiting "Michael" one day in his apartment and noticed some fabulous maps of the local area, the state, and the nation on the wall. They were extremely detailed, beautifully balanced, and, the student discovered, hand-drawn from memory by—Michael! He had been drawing these maps for years but no one who had worked with him had bothered to ask or show any curiosity about them. They had not looked around. Through the gradually deepening relationship between Michael and his student social worker, and through hard work and deep belief, Michael's maps eventually were exhibited at a museum, and his story was recounted in several newspapers.

Listen to clients' stories instead of zipping through an assessment protocol. Stories and narratives often contain within their plots and characterizations evidence of strengths, interests, hopes, and visions.

BILL

Bill was in his early forties, in and out of state hospitals since the age of 17 with a variety of diagnoses (chronic undifferentiated schizophrenia seemed to be the favorite). Single, living in a big city with no relatives nearby (or very interested in him), he worked as a dishwasher in a midtown bar and grill. He became hooked up with a community support program at the behest of a hospital social worker who was interested in keeping him out of the hospital. Bill was taking haloperidol. He was assigned a first-year MSW student as a case manager. The student was learning the strengths approach to practice and was anxious to try it. She began by encouraging Bill to "tell his stories"—how he got to be where he was, what interesting things he had done, and how he had survived with a serious illness. She learned many interesting things about Bill, and some of his stories clearly revealed a resourceful, motivated person. He had a serious problem with alcohol but quit drinking on his own. Yet he continued to frequent a local bar "because that's where all my buddies are," and being with his buddies was one outpost of connection and stability for him.

Bill also, on one occasion, saved enough money from his modest salary to take a trip to Oslo, Norway. He had seen some of Norway's marvelous statuary in an old *National Geographic* magazine and wanted to experience it for himself. He arranged and took the trip on his own. On his trek, he discovered a joy in flying. A dream began to form in his mind—he could see himself flying a plane.

He revealed his reverie to the social worker, who, given what she had come to learn about Bill, took it to heart. Together they began taking some modest steps toward his desire. In a few months, Bill got a job as a dishwasher at the airport, a busy international terminal, even though it involved an hour-long bus ride each way. He loved being around pilots and planes. At last account, Bill was working toward getting a job on the tarmac, perhaps as a baggage handler. Besides listening to his stories and searching within them for inklings of strength, character, and knowledge, the social worker did something else extraordinarily important to this kind of work: She let Bill know that she was genuinely interested in the hopes and dreams that he nurtured.

DAVID

In discussing her now 44-year-old son, David, who has struggled with a particularly virulent form schizophrenia since his late childhood, clinical social worker and social work educator Mona Wasow (2001) said that it was only when they (parent, foster parent, doctor, and social worker) began to focus on his strengths and attributes that any significant change in his life took place. The change was not brought about by the new, more powerful medications but by a decision to encourage David to harness his talents (music and pottery making—both of which were immanent, not obviously present). She writes:

> A few years ago, at a regular . . . treatment meeting, one of the social workers was reporting on David's considerable deficits. The psychiatrist said, "I don't want to hear all that again. That's his illness and we have not been able to change that for years. Tell me about his strengths; we would do better to work with those."
>
> I remembered hearing David pick out parts of a Bach fugue on his guitar which is pretty good for a guy who has never had a music lesson. And his thoughtful foster mother had suggested pottery lessons because of an interest he seemed to have in a neighborhood pottery studio. My other children were artistic and musical; maybe David had talents, too?
>
> . . . After the first guitar lesson, the teacher said, "Hey, this man is talented!" Now that was worth taking a shower for [one of his symptoms was that he had no interest in bathing]. Maybe the music teacher would say that again. Either way, these lessons would bring the continuing joy of learning to read music and of being able to produce some of those great tunes on the guitar . . . Learn to ride the bus to get to the pottery studio? You bet. Even make a little eye contact with the friendly pottery teacher, who laughed with pleasure at David's newly created ceramic bear sitting in a canoe. The $215 he made in a pottery sale a year later produced even more eye contact" (p. 1306).

In trying to discover the strengths within and around, what sort of questions might one ask? There are several kinds of questions one might ask including:

Survival questions. How have you managed to survive (or thrive) thus far, given all the challenges you have had to contend with? How have you been able to rise to the challenges put before you? What was your mind-set as you faced these difficulties? What have you learned about yourself and your world during your struggles? Which of these difficulties have given you special strength, insight, or skill? What are the special qualities on which you can rely?

Support questions. What people have given you special understanding, support, and guidance? Who are the special people on whom you can depend? What is it that these people give you that is exceptional? How did you find them or how did they come to you? What did they respond to in you? What associations, organizations, or groups have been especially helpful to you in the past?

Exception questions.[4] When things were going well in life, what was different? In the past, when you felt that your life was better, more interesting, or more stable, what about your world, your relationships, your thinking was special or different? What parts of your world and your being would you like to recapture, reinvent, or relive? What moments or incidents in your life have given you special understanding, resilience, and guidance?

Possibility questions. What now do you want out of life? What are your hopes, visions, and aspirations? How far along are you toward achieving these? What people or personal qualities are helping you move in these directions? What do you like to do? What are your special talents and abilities? What fantasies and dreams have given you special hope and guidance? How can I help you achieve your goals or recover those special abilities and times that you have had in the past?

Esteem questions. When people say good things about you, what are they likely to say? What is it about your life, yourself, and your accomplishments that give you real pride? How will you know when things are going well in your life— what will you be doing, who will you be with, how will you be feeling, thinking, and acting? What gives you genuine pleasure in life? When was it that you began to believe that you might achieve some of the things you wanted in life? What people, events, and ideas were involved?

Perspective questions. What are your ideas or theories about your current situation? How do you understand, what kind of sense do you make of your recent experiences and struggles? How would you explain these to yourself, to me, or anyone else?

Change questions. What are your ideas about how things—thoughts, feelings, behavior, relationships, etc.—might change? What has worked in the past to bring about a better life for yourself? What do you think you should or could do to improve your status, your affairs? How can I help?

These obviously do not exhaust likely questions. These questions are not meant to be a protocol, but rather they reflect the kinds of concerns and interests that might arise and direct your attention during conversations with clients or as you hear their stories.

---

[4]Thanks to the practitioners of solution-focused therapy for this terminology. We did not know what to call these kinds of questions (see De Jong, P. & Miller, S. D. (1995, November). How to interview for client strengths. *Social Work, 40,* 729–736).

What Are Some of the Elements of Strengths-Based Practice?

What follows is a representation of some of the stages and phases of practice. In truth, these steps may occur in a different sequence; they even might occur simultaneously. Practice of all kinds is a discursive kind of experience, not necessarily a well-staged and predictable stroll through a set of certainties toward an inevitable destination. What follows is a way to look at the process, knowing that it will be in some ways different every time you engage in helping an individual, or family, or working in a community.

In the Struggle—the Harbingers and Hints of Strength. Clients (individuals, families, and communities) come to you because they feel, perceive, and/or experience discontent, stress, pain, and/or loss. This is their reality at the moment. They must speak to these. They want you to listen. Your professional creed also asks that you begin where the client is—that you hear and honor their story. So far, so good. But in practicing from the standpoint of strengths you also listen for what is almost surely there—as a leitmotif, or maybe swathed in the language of anguish—evidence of capacity, will, determination, and hope, however muted and hesitant. It is common for clients, even as they report their pains and predicaments, to mention decisions they have made, things that they have done that have been healthy or positive. Marshall, troubled by intermittent heavy drinking, said in passing that he did not drink during the week that his son (in the custody of his wife after a recent divorce and very important to Marshall) visited. Statements like this typically are not told to illustrate a strength but simply appear as a part of the recounting of a person's troubles. It is up to you to, at some point, reflect this exemplar of strength back to the individual or family because it does illustrate that people have some power to, at least momentarily, right themselves. You are always listening for the hints and murmurs of resilience and rebound.

Stimulate the Discourse and Narratives of Resilience and Strength. There is often great resistance to acknowledging one's competence, reserve, and resourcefulness. In addition, many traits and capacities that are signs of strength are hidden under the rubble of years of self-doubt, the blame of others, and, in some cases, the wearing of a diagnostic label. Sometimes the problem of discovering strengths lies with the lack of words, sometimes it is disbelief, and sometimes it is lack of trust. The social worker may have to begin to provide the language, to look for, address, and give name to those resiliencies that people have demonstrated in the past and in the present (the Wolins' [1993] language of the seven resiliencies is helpful here). The daily struggles and triumphs of one's life as revealed in stories and narratives are useful (for example, what they have done, how they survived, what they want, what they want to avoid). At some point in this process, people do have to acknowledge their strengths, play them out, see them in the past and the present, feel them, and have them affirmed by the worker and others. In a sense, what is happening at this point is the writing of a better "text." Reframing is a part of this; not the reframing of so many family therapies, but adding to the picture already painted, brush strokes that depict capacity and ingenuity, and that provide a different coloration to the substance of one's life.

The prompting of a discourse and the development of a personal dictionary of strengths and capacities depends on three factors. First, it is incumbent on the practitioner to provide the words and images of strength, wholeness, and capacity where they may be lacking. Second, it is important for the practitioner to be an affirmative mirror, beaming back to the client a reflection of that person's positive attributes, accomplishments, skills, and talents. Last, it is wise to carefully lay out with an individual what might be possible in her or his life—big or small things, it doesn't matter. And all of this must ring true to the person and be grounded in the dailiness of life.

Acting in Context: The Project.   The education continues about the capacities and resilient aspects of the self. Now these are linked up to the person's hopes, goals, and visions, and relevant external resources. The individual is encouraged to take the risk of acting on one's expectancies using the newly found or articulated competencies as well as already active ones. It is through action with the worker—collaborative and continuous—that individuals really begin to employ their strengths as they move toward well-formed, achievable goals. The collaboration with the social worker or practitioner to achieve desired goals using inner and communal resources is, in effect, a project—in the two senses of the word. On the one hand it is an undertaking, on the other it is a *launching of one's self* in the world of relationships, work, and/or play. This is precarious business for many people who have been through a figurative hell. But as they decide and act, they continue to discover and enrich their repertoire of aptitudes. They also discover the limits of their resilience and the effect of still-active sore spots and scars. But, in the end, it is their decision making and activity that lead to changes in thinking, feeling, and relationship that are more congruent with their goals and their strengths. It is also vital that the individual group, or family begins to use naturally occurring community resources—from extended family to local associations and institutions—to move toward their goals.

For the social worker, this means advocacy in the form of discovering what natural or formal resources are available, accessible, and to what extent they are adequate and acceptable to the client (Kisthardt, 1993). The assumption here is that the environment is rich with resources: people, institutions, associations, families who are willing to and can provide instruction, succor, relief, resources, time, and mirroring. When people begin to plan fully to achieve their goals and to exercise their strengths, the effect is synergistic: They can do more personally, and they find themselves more connected to a community. For example, a receptionist at a physician's office begins to help an elderly woman complete her insurance forms, arrange transportation to and from the doctor's office so that she is more likely to keep appointments, and keep a level of health she believes is highly desirable. The synergistic effect is that the receptionist begins to do this for other elders as well and eventually finds other volunteers to assist them. For many of the older persons involved, this is an important support for the maintenance of relative independence—an important strength to be sure (see Chapter 9).

Move toward Normalizing and Capitalizing on One's Strengths.   Over a period of time, often short, the social worker and client begin to consolidate the strengths that have emerged, reinforce the new vocabulary of strengths and resilience, and bolster the capacity to discover resources within and around. The purpose is to cement the foundation of strengths, to insure the synergy of the continuing development and articulation of strengths, and to secure a place for the person to be. For many who have been helped through a strengths-based approach, one important avenue to normalization is teaching others what one has learned in the process. Finally, this is a process of disengagement for worker and client. Done with the assurance that the personal strengths and the communal resources are in place, disengagement is the ritual transition to normalization.

CONCLUSION

In summary, to assume a strengths perspective requires a degree of consciousness raising on the part of social workers and their clients—a different way of regarding what they do together. One thing is certain, however, from reports of many of those people who apply the strengths perspective in their professional work: Once a client is engaged in building up the strengths within and without, a desire to do more and to become more absorbed in daily life and drawn by future possibilities bursts forth. As a means of visualizing the elements of strengths-based practice, the following schema may be helpful (Figure 5.1).

FIGURE 5.1   The Elements of Strengths-Based Practice

RISK FACTORS		**PROTECTIVE/GENERATIVE FACTORS**	
Challenges		*Resources*	
Damage	Internal	Strengths	Internal
Trauma	and	Capacities	and
Disorder	external	Talents	external
Stress		Gifts	
	+		➡
Expectations/possibilities		*Decisions*	
Hopes		Choices and options about	
Dreams		paths to be taken	
Visions		Defining opportunities and	
Goals	➡	setting directions	➡
Self-righting		Gathering resources and	
		mobilizing strengths	
Project			

Mutual collaboration in work toward ➡ A better future

People are always engaged in their situations and are working on them even if they just decide to resign themselves to their fate. Circumstances can overwhelm and debilitate. We know a lot about that. But dire circumstances can also bring a surge in resolve and the blossoming of capacities and reserves. We must know more about that.

DISCUSSION QUESTIONS

1. With a friend or client, use some of the methods for discovering strengths described in this chapter. What was the outcome? How would you personalize such methods so they would be more useful to you?

2. Do you think that the way one goes about finding out about strengths has a different feel to it than methods for determining symptoms or problems? What, if any, is the difference?

3. What do you think of the role of luck and contingency in people's lives? How can it have an impact on your work with individuals, families, groups, or communities?

4. Do you know practitioners who approach clients from a strengths perspective? If so, what do you notice about their practice that is distinctive? Talk to them about how they came to practice in such a way.

5. How do you understand the placebo effect? Have you seen it at work in your professional or personal life?

6. What do you think of the role of hope in helping people create a more satisfying life for themselves?

REFERENCES

Aptheker, B. (1989). *Tapestries of life*. Amherst, MA: University of Massachusetts Press.

Arpala, J. (2000, July, August). Sweet sabotage. *Psychology Today, 32,* 66–67.

Assay, T. P. & Lambert, M. J. (1999). The empirical case for the common factors in therapy: Qualitative findings. In M. A. Hubble, B. L. Duncan, & S. D. Miller (Eds.), *The Heart and Soul of Change: What works in therapy.* Washington, DC: APA Press: 33–56.

Benson, P. L. (1997). *All kids are our kids: What communities must do to raise caring and responsible children and adolescents.* San Francisco: Jossey-Bass Publishers.

Bentley, K. J., & Walsh, J. (2001). *The social worker and psychotropic medication.* (2nd ed.). Belmont, CA: Brooks/Cole.

Brody, H. (2000, July/August). Mind over medicine. *Psychology Today, 32,* 60–65, 67.

Canda, E. R. (1997). Spirituality. In R. L. Edwards, I. C. Colby, A. Garcia, R. G. McRoy, & L. Videka-Sherman (Eds.). *Encyclopedia of social work.* (19th ed., 1997 supplement). Washington, DC: National Association of Social Workers.

Desetta, A., & Wolin, S. (Eds.). (2000). *The struggle to be strong: True stories about youth overcoming tough times.* Minneapolis: Free Spirit Publishing Company.

Duncan, B. L., & Miller, S. D. (2000). *The Heroic Client: Doing Client-Directed Outcome-Informed Therapy.* San Francisco: Jossey-Bass.

Falicov, C. J. (1998). *Latino families in therapy: A guide to multicultural practice.* New York: The Guilford Press.

Fisher, M. J. (2000, October). Better living through the placebo effect. *The Atlantic Monthly, 286,* 16–18.

Gitlin, M. J. (1996). *The psychotherapist's guide to psychopharmacology.* (2nd ed.). New York: Free Press.

Kisthardt, W. E. (1993). A strengths model of case management: The principles and functions of a helping partnership with persons with persistent mental illness. In M. Harris & H. Bergman (Eds.), *Case management for mentally ill patients: Theory and practice.* Langhorne, PA: Harwood Academic Publishers.

Lambert, M. J. (1992). Implications of outcome research for psychotherapy integration. In J. C. Norcross & M. R. Goldfried (Eds.), *Handbook of psychotherapy integration.* New York: Basic Books.

Miller, S. D., Duncan, B. L., & Hubble, M. A. (1997). *Escape from Babel: Toward a unifying language for psychotherapy.* New York: W. W. Norton & Company.

Moxley, D. P., & Washington, O. G. M. (2001). Strengths-based recovery practice in chemical dependency: A transpersonal perspective. *Families in Society, 82,* 251–262.

Rapp, C. A. (1998). *The strengths model: Case management with people suffering from severe and persistent mental illness.* New York: Oxford University Press.

Rogers, C. (1951). *Client centered therapy: Its current practice, theory, and implications.* Chicago, IL: Houghton Mifflin.

Saleebey, D. (1994). Culture, theory, and narrative: The intersection of meanings in practice. *Social Work, 39,* 351–359.

Sampson, E. E. (1993). *Celebrating the other: A dialogic account of human nature.* Boulder, CO: Westview Press.

Shulman, L. (1992). *The skills of helping: Individuals, families, and groups.* (3rd ed.). Itasca, IL: F. E. Peacock.

Strupp, H. H. (1995). The psychotherapist's skills revisited. *Clinical Psychology, 2,* 70–74.

Swadener, B. B. (1995). Children and families 'at promise': Deconstructing the discourse of risk. In B. B. Swadener & S. Lubeck (Eds.). *Children and families 'at promise': Deconstructing the discourse of risk.* Albany: State University of New York Press.

Wasow, M. (Oct. 2001). Strengths versus deficits, or musician versus schizophrenic. *Psychiatric Services, 54*(10), 1306–1307.

Wolin, S. J., & Wolin, S. (1993). *The resilient self: How survivors of troubled families overcome adversity.* New York: Villard.

Wolin, S. J., & Wolin, S. (1994, October). Resilience in overcoming adversity. Workshop for Employee Assistance Program members, Kansas City, MO.

Mannum — 603 836 0197

McCarron — 836 0189

CHAPTER SIX

ASSESSING STRENGTHS

The Political Context of Individual, Family, and Community Empowerment[1]

CHARLES D. COWGER

KIM M. ANDERSON

CAROL A. SNIVELY

Deficit, disease, and dysfunction metaphors continue to shape contemporary social work practice through an emphasis on diagnosis and treatment of problem conditions within individuals, families, and communities. Yet, the proposition that strengths are central to helping relationships continues to gain popularity (Rapp, 1998) and sophistication, especially in regard to practice with diverse, vulnerable, and oppressed populations. Developments in strengths-based practice have included a repositioning of power and authority within helping relationships to encourage ownership in the expression of personal and shared narratives and in decisions of how to seek and receive help. While earlier descriptions of strengths-based assessments have explored issues of power and authority through a discussion of the political nature of the assessment process (Cowger, 1998; Cowger & Snively, 2002), few guidelines were provided to assist the social worker in sharing this political context with the individual or group seeking assistance. A gap between theory and practice is created by a lack of clear recommendations about how to shift the power and control within the assessment process. This gap can be a challenging one for practitioners to bridge, especially those who work within deficit-based systems of care, encounter high demands for work productivity, and are rewarded for using deficit-based classification systems (e.g., reimbursement

---

[1]This chapter is based on Cowger, C. D. (1994). Assessing client strengths: Clinical assessment for client empowerment. *Social Work, 39*(3), 262–268. Copyright 1994, National Association for Social Workers, Inc.

for services rendered). In this chapter, the authors draw on Kim Anderson's work to expand our previous discussion of strengths-based assessment. This chapter addresses how new findings from Anderson's (2001) resiliency research can inform strengths-based assessment strategies and help social workers resist a common tendency to revert to problem description during the assessment process. Examples of strengths-based assessment questions are provided.

MORE DEFICIT, DISEASE, AND DYSFUNCTION?

Sadly, Rodwell's commentary on assessment in social work practice is still relevant. The focus of assessment has "continued to be, one way or another, diagnosing pathological conditions" (Rodwell, 1987, p. 235). Social work assessment literature continues to be concerned with individual, family, and community inadequacies. These inadequacies are reinforced through the practice tools used by social workers. For example, the American Psychiatric Association's *Diagnostic and Statistical Manual*, from volumes I to IV have emphasized pathology. While recent volumes have increasingly considered environmental and cultural influences to psychiatric diagnoses, the purpose of this classification system has always been the identification and categorization of pathological behavior by the individual. No companion text exists for social workers that identifies and categorizes healthy behaviors. Descriptions of strengths-based practice strategies tend to be vague, and minimal empirical research has been conducted to examine the effectiveness of strengths-based practice. This deficit-oriented classification system and a lack of resources regarding effective strengths-based practice strategies influence how direct practice skills are taught to social work students.

Why are so few strengths-based resources available? For the most part, social workers have been negligent in documenting the application of strengths-based principles to divergent practice realms. For example, consider research on direct practice with families. Much of the social work literature in this area and others continues to use psychological dysfunction terminology while ignoring interdisciplinary advances on family strengths (Early & GlenMaye, 2000).

We can only guess how this lack of resources affects social work practice because there continues to be very little empirical evidence indicating the extent to which practitioners consciously make use of strengths in their practice. A few studies indicate that the strengths perspective is not well integrated into practice. Twenty five years ago, Maluccio (1979) found that social workers underestimated strengths and had more negative perceptions of clients than clients had of themselves. Hepworth and Larsen (1990, p. 157) later highlighted this incongruity between social work ideology and practice when they stated, "social workers persist in formulating assessments that focus almost exclusively on the pathology and dysfunction of clients—despite the time honored social work platitude that social workers work with strengths, not weaknesses." Popular practice evaluation strategies have also informed this discussion. Taking a behavioral baseline of individual, family, and community deficits and examining the ability of social work interventions to correct those deficits has continued to be the standard for evaluating the effectiveness of social work practice (Kagle & Cowger, 1984). It seems unlikely then that strengths would have an impact on worker activity, considering the preponderance of deficit assessment instruments as opposed to the dearth of assessment tools that consider strengths. However, Hwang and Cowger (1998) found that when a strengths-specified case was presented to practitioners, they were likely to include strengths in their assessments, though that finding was less likely for workers in mental health settings and for practitioners who identified their theoretical orientation as psychodynamic. Perhaps other unknown factors mitigate the worker's ability to purposefully use strengths in practice.

Not surprisingly, contemporary social workers have become more specialized, are more often held accountable for service outcomes and, in regard to individuals and families, are more involved with managed care, which very often requires a DSM diagnosis for reimbursement (Gibelman, 1999). Thus, there is pressure for social workers to be experts about pathology and demonstrate efficiency in securing remediation of problem symptoms. In light of these trends and research findings, frameworks are needed to assist social workers to creatively and effectively utilize a strengths perspective while working within deficit-focused systems of care. In this regard, the assessment process is very important. Assessment provides an early and ongoing opportunity for the helping partnership to name and rename the "problem," shifting perspectives from deficit to strengths and shifting relational power to the person(s) seeking help. The assessment can also shape the helping process, especially in regard to how the person(s) seeking help understands their behaviors and experiences, as either a result of oppressive social relations or as individual circumstances. In addition to clear and well developed assessment procedures, evaluation of strengths-based assessments are needed to help practitioners understand how, when, and where a strengths-based assessment is most effective. Such knowledge would assist practitioners in refining their practice skills and would provide empirical support for policy changes related to service delivery.

ASSESSMENT AS POLITICAL ACTIVITY

The primary purpose of social work is to assist people in their relationships with one another and with social institutions in order to promote social and economic justice (Council on Social Work Education, 1994). Practice, thus, focuses on developing more positive and promising transactions between people and their environments and ending oppressive social transactions. However, taking seriously the element of promoting social and economic justice in those transactions may not result in conventional models of practice. Indeed, practice that is guided by social and economic justice requires methods that explicitly deal with power and power relationships (see Chapter 10).

The personal empowerment dynamic has been characterized as similar to a traditional clinical notion of self-determination whereby the person(s) seeking help gives direction to the helping process, assumes control in personal decision making, learns new ways to think about their situations, and adopts or adapts behaviors to achieve more satisfying and rewarding outcomes. However, there is an additional political context to personal empowerment. When the helping process focuses on teaching new ways to accommodate to experiences of oppression, personal empowerment will not be achieved. When personal empowerment is an objective, the uniqueness of each situation is acknowledged *and* the political context is illuminated so that the person(s) seeking help can recognize the ways s/he has already fought against oppressive experiences and will begin thinking about how to achieve a socially just result for her/himself and others.

Social empowerment acknowledges that individual behavior and identity is "bound up with that of others through social involvement" (Falck, 1988, p. 30). Empowerment is experienced through interaction with others, a process of gaining power within and through social relationships. Persons, groups, or communities who are socially empowered have the resources and opportunity to play an important role in shaping their environment, and therefore, they positively influence many lives including their own.

Personal and social empowerments are synergistic. Each situation or problem is formed and resolved within a greater, societal context. By fortifying opportunities to achieve success for self and others, those who are gaining personal and social power help to create a more socially just environment in which to live.

This perspective assumes that personal and social power is augmented when any decision making process is shared, that social justice can be achieved, and that empowerment is dependent not only on people making choices but also on people having available choices to make. The distribution of available choices in a society is political. Societies organize systems of production and the distribution of resources, and that differentially affects the choices of individuals, families, groups, and communities. Across societies, production and distribution are based on the degree of commitment to equity and justice: "Some people get more of everything than others" (Goroff, 1983, p.133). Attention to the dynamics of personal power, the social power endemic to the environment, and the relationship between the two is required to realize true empowerment.

One of the important obstacles to empowerment is the traditional roles developed within helping relationships. With the increasing professionalization of services, the power distance between the helper and the person(s) seeking help becomes greater as the social worker assumes the position of expert. The process of developing a professional relationship with a person is a process whereby a role is learned. McKnight refers to this as a process whereby the person or community achieves "client hood" (McKnight, 1995, p. 51). This process has also been referred to as "clientilism" (Habermas, 1981), and "clientification" (Cowger, 1998). Strengths-based assessment has the potential to mitigate the imbalanced power relationship through shared decision making.

Assessment that focuses on deficits presents obstacles to the exercise of personal and social power and reinforces those social structures that generate and regulate the unequal power relationships victimizing vulnerable individuals, families, groups and communities. Goroff (1983) persuasively argues that social work practice is a political activity and that the attribution of individual deficiencies as the cause of human problems is a politically conservative process that "supports the status quo" (p. 134).

Deficit-based assessments target the help seeker as "the problem" because the context of oppression is stripped. Much of professional practice as it is currently conducted shifts the focus of attention from oppressive social systems to individual deficits (Dietz, 2000). The helper addresses the behaviors and feelings presented. Often the person(s) seeking help is not able to see how behaviors, feelings, and circumstances were generated as reactions to oppression. Because of this block, the helper only hears the part of the story where the individual, family, or community is in crisis and does not hear how the circumstances were created for the crisis to occur. For example, from a deficit perspective the person who is unemployed, the family who is homeless or the residents who live in a declining community are "the problem." Social work interventions that focus on what is wrong with the help seeker, for example, why he or she is not working, reinforce the powerlessness the help seeker is already experiencing because he or she does not have a job, a home, or a safe community in which to live. At the same time such an intervention lets economic and social structures that do not provide employment or housing opportunities "off the hook" and reinforces social structures that generate unequal power. To assume that the cause of personal pain and social problems is individual deficiency "has the political consequences of not focusing on the social structure (the body politic) but on the individual. Most, if not all, of the pain we experience is the result of the way we have organized ourselves and how we create and allocate life-surviving resources" (Goroff, 1983, p. 134). Here Goroff is referring to our social not our personal organization as the root of individual problems.

Personal pain is political. Social work practice is political. Diagnostic and assessment metaphors and taxonomies that stress individual deficiencies and sickness reinforce the political status quo in a manner that is incongruent with the promotion of social and economic justice. Practice centered on pathology is reminiscent of "blaming the victim" (Ryan, 1976). Practice based on metaphors of client strengths and empowerment is also political in that its thrust is the development of client power and the more equitable distribution of societal resources—those resources that underlie the development of personal resources.

STRENGTHS AND EMPOWERMENT

Promoting empowerment means believing that people are capable of making their own choices and decisions. It means not only that human beings possess the strengths and potential to resolve their own difficult life situations, but also that they increase their strength and contribute to the well-being of society by doing so. The role of the social worker is to nourish, encourage, assist, enable, support, stimulate, and unleash the strengths within people; to illuminate the strengths available to people in their own environments; and to promote equity and justice at all levels of society. To do that, the social worker helps help-seekers articulate the nature of their situations, identify what they want, explore alternatives for achieving those desires, and then achieve them.

The role of the social worker is not to change people, treat people, help people cope, or counsel people. The role is not to empower people. As Simon (1990) argued, social workers cannot empower others: "More than a simple linguistic nuance, the notion that social workers do not empower others, but instead, help people empower themselves is an ontological distinction that frames the reality experienced by both workers and clients" (p. 32). To assume a social worker can empower someone else is naive and condescending and has little basis in reality. Power is not something that social workers possess for distribution at will. Help seekers, not social workers, own the power that brings significant change in social work practice. A social worker is a resource person, with professional training on the development, accumulation, and use of resources, who is committed to the empowerment of people and willing to share his or her knowledge. The central component to the social work process becomes the practitioner's ability to uncover strengths and to make them accessible in a useful way. The facilitation of strengths emanates from the social worker's practice orientation rather than the application of a specific intervention.

STRENGTHS? OR JUST A NEW SPIN ON OLD PROBLEMS?

Strengths-based practice and resiliency literature are interconnected and similar in many ways. Both emphasize assets and resources of the person(s) seeking help rather than symptomatology and problems (Saleebey, 1997; Wolin & Wolin, 1993). Both recognize that people's ability to live well in the present depends on their ability to recognize and uncover their strengths (Barnard, 1994; Saleebey, 1997). In addition, both understand that people are doing the best that they can with the resources available to them (Saleebey, 1997; Wolin & Wolin, 1993). Finally, both recognize that people may lose sight of their strengths and abilities because their trauma and pain are too great, and the practitioner's role is to assist in uncovering their submerged areas of resilience (Barnard, 1994; Saleebey, 1997). Despite these similarities, strengths and traditional notions of resilience differ regarding environmental context. In this regard, resiliency literature has been criticized for simply "re-packaging" a deficit-based perspective to appear as if it is strengths oriented.

Resiliency literature has emerged over the years from studies in developmental psychopathology that focused on the "adverse" conditions placing children at risk for developing adult pathologies (Byrd, 1994) and the ways in which youth avoid problems despite exposure to adverse conditions. To this end, risk and protective factors have been identified within individual, family, and community domains (Safyer, Griffin, Colan, Alexander-Brydie, & Rome, 1998). Experiences and conditions are categorized as risk factors because their presence deprives youth of important developmental experiences, relationships, and opportunities, making them vulnerable to participation in antisocial activities or ill health (Bowen & Chapman, 1996; Safyer et al., 1998). Some of these adverse conditions studied included poverty (Werner & Smith, 1992), parental mental illness (Beardslee & Podorefsky, 1988), inner-city living (Luthar, 1993), and child abuse and neglect (Farber & Egeland, 1987).

Other experiences and conditions are considered protective in that they encourage healthy development and/or mediate the direct effects of the declined community or dysfunctional family system on adolescent health and well-being (Safyer et al., 1998). For example, the presence of supportive adults can decrease the likelihood of adolescents participating in antisocial behavior by increasing adolescents' exposure to protective factors (Stiffman et al., 1999) and minimizing exposure to risk factors. Both risk and protective factors are thought to have a cumulative effect, or "pile-up . . . as the number of developmental assets increase, risk behavior patterns decrease and thriving behaviors (e.g., school success, affirmation of diversity, prosocial behavior) increase." (Public/Private Venture, 2000, p. 133). Uncovering the attributes that help youth to thrive and resist the negative effects of stress induced by violence, community disorder, and other negative social conditions is often the focus of resiliency research (Anderson, 2001).

While it is helpful to isolate and name which aspects of the environment have a positive or negative influence on youth outcomes, there is disagreement regarding how to think about and name these environmental factors. Some scholars argue that the terms "risk" and "protective factors" imply that the youth is completely malleable by her/his environment and minimizes the youth's capacity to effect change (Medoff & Skylar, 1994). Categorizing experiences and conditions as either inducing problems or saving the youth from problems perpetuates the idea of youth as victims, not competent individuals who can make good choices for themselves, their families, and their communities (Finn & Checkoway, 1998). In contrast, a strengths perspective focuses on competencies, assets of the individual and the environment, as well as the individual's prosocial behavior, e.g., the ways in which the youth has sought to better his/her environment (Snively, 2002).

Despite these differences, Larry Davis (2001, p.6) has also warned us that both resiliency research and a strengths perspective can have negative political implications. The focus on resiliency and strengths, he argues, is "a focus on individual explanations for problems primarily caused by societal shortcomings" and may be used "against the very populations we are attempting to assist." This emphasis in turn has inadvertently served to direct attention away from issues of social injustice and inequality.

In addition, associating the term "at risk" with persons who are of minority status and disenfranchised creates a new label for old stigmas. "In many ways, the wholesale labeling of children of single mothers and inner city children generally, as 'at risk' has become a stigmatizing code word for 'illegitimate'—which also means contrary to law, rules and logic" (Medoff & Skylar, 1994, p. 206). A true strength-based framework avoids this re-packaging of old deficit-based concepts. Terminology that emphasizes assets, such as healthy or positive youth development, competency, capacity, etc., is preferred over older victim terminology. New understandings of resilience as "the individual's active resistance to oppressive circumstances" also emphasizes strengths (Anderson, 2001).

Morris (1997) argues that professional clinical literature has been far too silent on clients' power of resistance, resilience, and their capacity to change and heal themselves after oppressive experiences. The manner in which individuals resist oppression has significant implications for achieving progressive social change. Individually and collectively, vulnerable individuals and groups have responded to oppressive conditions through acts of constructive resistance, including mobilizing effective social change movements to overcome social problems such as poverty, family violence, racism, and homophobia (Wineman, 2003). Exploring perceptions of oppressive experiences assists the helper in understanding how empowerment can emerge from chaos and pain for the individual(s) seeking assistance.

Specifically in regard to assessment, there is a growing body of social work practice literature that reflects a strengths perspective in regard to individual, family and community assessment and helps to re-politicize social work practice with an emphasis on oppressive social relations (Cohen, 1999; DeJong & Miller, 1995; Delgado & Barton, 1998; Early & GlenMaye, 2000; McQuaide & Ehrenreich, 1997; Poole, 1997; Russo, 1999; Solomon, 1976). Notable examples of the application of strengths-based theory to practice and research provides a framework for understanding the experiences of minority families (Billingsley, 1968, 1992; Boyd-Franklin & Bry, 2000; McAdoo & McAdoo, 1985) and research that focuses on adolescents as competent citizens (Finn & Checkoway, 1998).

Findings from resiliency research can help social work bridge the gap between strengths-based theory and practice and further politicize and develop the assessment process. While early conceptualizations of resiliency played an important role in shifting perspectives about problem definition, the language of "risk" and "protective" factors has inadvertently reproduced the deficit helping model. Emerging concepts from resiliency research, such as Anderson's (2001) "resistance to oppression," have greater potential for assisting social workers in exploring the context in which individuals, families, groups, and communities develop the need to seek professional help.

THE RESISTANCE TO OPPRESSION FACTOR

While the resiliency literature has much in common with the strengths perspective and is informative for the social work practitioner, it is particularly limited with its narrow focus on individual circumstances and its exclusion of oppressive social circumstances (Anderson, 2001). The recognition and understanding of oppression and abuse and their relationship to resilience are crucial factors to address while making a holistic assessment. Social ills such as patriarchy, racism, economic brutality, and homophobia all routinely violate individual, group, and community integrity, and in the face of overwhelming personal and institutional forces, people are repeatedly rendered powerless (Wineman, 2003). Yet, "research has confirmed that many social workers understand institutional and social problems at a perceived, discrete micro level, focusing their interventions on individuals while failing to confront institutionalized oppression" (Dietz, 2000, p. 371).

For instance, consider the social problem of incest where the child is dominated by her/his perpetrator and learns that her/his emotional and physical survival depends on her/his acquiescence (Blume, 1990). In the professional literature, incest is often presented as devoid of a context that adequately addresses power relations. Consequently, the effects of oppression, particularly subordination, are often not taken into account in clinical work with incest survivors (Anderson, 2001). Instead, the helper focuses on the pathological symptoms presented by the survivor in response to the oppressive experience of incest. For example, if a child who is being sexually victimized stops eating it is viewed as an eating disorder stemming from depression rather than oppression (Dietz, 2000; Herman, 1992). This perspective is in sharp contrast to how the same behaviors are interpreted for a different group such as prisoners of war whose hunger strikes are viewed as acts of defiance and signs of resistance to their captors' subjugation. Both the children and prisoners are refusing to eat in response to violence, however, societal response to the refusal to eat could not be more different. A prisoner of war who engages in a hunger strike would be regarded as a hero, but the child would be regarded as ill. In response, the helper would typically focus the assessment on the child's eating behavior instead of acknowledging the child's power in drawing attention to her/himself through a creative manner, discovering the reasoning for the hunger strike and educating the child about her/his rights. This focus on sexual victimization as an "individual problem" obscures the societal context of sexual violence toward children and limits how the helper would proceed in the assessment process.

Behaviors are often forged in resistance to subjugation that consequently promotes their survival and perseverance (Anderson, 2001). Individuals typically are resistant to their oppression and use a variety of mental and behavioral strategies to prevent, withstand, stop, or oppose their subjugation and its consequences. Sometimes these behaviors promote health and well-being beyond the initial survival from the oppression. Other times, the behaviors become maladaptive. Social work practitioners can be supportive by encouraging an open expression of the details and implications of their resistance to oppression. Helping people to see how they have actively resisted their oppression is important because they often view their response as passive and blame themselves for the social problems they have experienced. The helper can acknowledge and affirm strategies of resistance as they are illuminated throughout the assessment process. These resilient capacities are often submerged beneath pain and discomfort and are difficult to access if those engaged in the helping relationship are not equipped to view these protective strategies as strengths (Anderson, 2001).

After assessment, the helper can focus on extending these strategies of resistance. Breaking cycles of violence and domination will require help seekers to reflect on the consequences of their oppression, particularly powerlessness, on personal and institutional levels. Consequently, they may come to understand the devastating effects of injurious actions and may resolve to be different from their oppressors. Identifying and building on the positive aspects of the self that had its origins in the resistance of their oppressive experiences then becomes the central focus in treatment. From the beginning of treatment, the social work practitioner and the help seeker consider all the dimensions of one's life story: oppression and resistance.

Understanding resistance as opposition to oppression is useful in developing an intervention plan that builds on these strategies and assists help seekers in management of the difficulties in their current lives. Unfortunately, in social work practice resistance is often defined as a refusal to comply with the advice of professionals or the prescribed process of treatment (Anderson, 2001). Or, the term "resistance" is viewed negatively as used in psychoanalysis as a psychological defense against threatening material in the unconscious mind. In other words, historically, "resistance" has pathology-oriented meanings rather than self-preserving ones. Instead, resistance may be looked as an indicator of health and is "health inducing" (Wade, 1997).

An individual's method to resist oppression may serve not only as a vehicle in individual recovery but in societal transformation as well. Wineman (2003) powerfully addresses the connection between personal healing and the political process:

> Individual recoveries are not enough by themselves to change the structures of oppression, but they are indispensable to social change when they are linked to political consciousness and activism. We need to make as many of these kinds of links as we can, which means finding as many ways as we can to tap our unbearable pain and use it to expand the boundaries of what we had imagined to be possible, personally and politically. (p. 274)

Each time oppressed individuals resolve never to harm anyone the way they have been mistreated, they are using constructive resistance in the service of genuine social change. Consequently, it is important to cultivate ways to assist with the expression of suffering, and to connect such expressions to an analysis of structural oppression (Wineman, 2003). The effects of oppression may never disappear completely; however, focusing on strategies of resistance can promote individual and collective resilience and recovery.

Guidelines for Strengths Assessment

These guidelines for strengths assessment are presented with the understanding that assessment is a process as well as a product. Assessment as process is helping people define their situations (that is, clarify the reasons they have sought assistance) and assisting them in evaluating and giving meaning to those factors that affect their situations. The assessment as a product is an agreement, in many cases a written agreement, between the worker and the person seeking help as to the nature of the problem situation (descriptive) and the meaning ascribed to those factors influencing the problem situation (analytic and interpretative).

A deep source of meaning can be acquired from the stories of individuals that may be used to guide the assessment process, particularly from those who have endured oppression. "The self-narrative is an individual's account of the relationships among self-relevant events across time" (Laird, 1989, p. 430). Composing a narrative reflects efforts to cope with adversity through developing a sense of coherence, continuity, and meaning (Laird, 1989). Individuals' identities are shaped by the sense they make of their own life stories. Providing an opportunity to share their life stories validates help seekers' wisdom and experiences and, at the same time, assists them in developing a deeper understanding of the many dimensions to their life circumstances.

The following guidelines are based on the notion that the knowledge guiding the assessment process is based on a socially constructed reality (Berger and Luckmann, 1966). Also, the assessment should recognize that there are multiple constructions of reality for each person's situation (Rodwell, 1987) and that problem situations are interactive, multicausal, and ever-changing. In addition, they address important aspects in creating a safe environment for people to tell their stories of violation and oppression.

1. **Document the story.** The assessment process allows help seekers ideas, thoughts, and memories to be expressed in their own words, reflects personal and social values, repositions help seekers as experts of their own situations, and places the burden on the helper to gain an understanding regarding the meaning of the situation of those who seek help. Professional and social sciences nomenclature is incongruent with an assessment approach based on mutual participation of the social worker and the person seeking help. Goldstein (1990) convincingly stated, "We are the inheritors of a professional language composed of value-laden metaphors and idioms. The language has far more to do with philosophic assumptions about the human state, ideologies of professionalism, and, not least, the politics of practice than they do with objective rationality" (p. 268). Assessment as a product should be written in simple English and in such a way as to be self-explanatory to all involved. Whenever possible use direct quotes to name and describe the problem and solutions.

2. **Support and validate the story.** Individuals know the depth and reality of what they have experienced in their life journeys. If the social worker demonstrates respect for that ownership, the story will be more fully shared. Individuals/families/groups and communities seeking help need to have their expertise regarding their situations validated. They need to ascribe meaning to their experiences as a way of regaining control and feeling competent. Central to a strengths perspective is a deeply held belief that people ultimately are trustworthy. To prejudge an individual as being untrustworthy is contrary to the social work-mandated values of respecting and recognizing one's dignity, and pre-judgment may lead to a self-fulfilling prophecy. When social workers are involved in cases where the physical welfare of the individual is at risk, such as child protection or domestic violence, the protection of victims of abuse may supersede this guideline.

3. **Honor self-determination.** Professional judgments or assumptions may well be the most detrimental exercises perpetrated on people seeking help. Instead, think of persons seeking help as experts of their own situations or stories. They should not feel "forced" into having to perform for professionals who may have preconceived ideas of what and how healing should take place. Assist in the discovery of their own points of view, choices, and vision. This "letting go" by the social work practitioner may be difficult if they feel people seeking help are incompetent because their victimization has left them too "damaged." If they are perceived as pathological then the strength and courage in one's process of surviving and healing is obscured. Help seekers need to have control over what information they contribute as well as control of the direction of the treatment process. Their control is essential because they are being asked to give something so personal of themselves—their life stories.

4. **Give preeminence to the story.** The help seeking person's knowledge and lived experiences need to be of central importance in guiding the assessment process. Their view of the situation, the meaning they ascribe to the situation, and their feelings or emotions related to that situation are the central focus for assessment. Assessment content on the intrapersonal, developmental, cognitive, mental, and biophysical dynamics of the person are important only as it enlightens the situation presented by the individual. It should be used only as a way to identify strengths that can be brought to bear on the presenting situation or to recognize obstacles to achieving individual and group objectives. The use of social sciences behavior taxonomies representing the realities of the social scientists should not be used as something to apply to, thrust on, or label a person.

5. **Discover what is needed.** There are two aspects of the helping contract. These include: "what is wanted and expected from service?"; and, "what does the person want to change?" This latter want involves the person's goals and is concerned with what one perceives to be a successful resolution to the problem situation.

6. **Move the assessment toward strengths.** The stories of persons seeking help provide numerous examples of strengths as they use their struggles with overcoming their adversity as a catalyst for growth and change. Practicing from a strengths perspective means believing that the strengths and resources to resolve a difficult situation lie within the individual's interpersonal skills, motivation, emotional strengths, and ability to think clearly. A person's external strengths come from family networks, significant others, voluntary organizations, community groups, and public institutions that support and provide opportunities for help seekers to act on their own behalf and institutional services that have the potential to provide resources. Discovering these strengths is central to assessment. A multidimensional assessment also includes an examination of power and power relationships in transactions between the help seeker and the environment. Practitioners need to merge an understanding of individual issues with an awareness of power relations that are embedded in the larger social context. Naming and challenging oppression when it emerges from the narrative in social work practice would involve helping individuals come to terms with oppressive experiences, to examine the effects of oppression, and to uncover ways that oppression was resisted. Explicit, critical examination of such relationships provides a context for evaluating alternative solutions. Obviously there are personal and environmental obstacles to the resolution of difficult situations. However, if one believes that solutions to difficult situations lie in strengths, dwelling on obstacles ultimately has little payoff. People's strengths are the vehicle to creatively negotiate these obstacles.

7. **Discover uniqueness.** The importance of uniqueness and individualization is well articulated by Meyer (1976): "When a family, group or a community is individualized, it is known through its uniqueness, despite all that it holds in common with other like groups" (p. 176). Although every person is in certain respects "like all other men [sic], like some other men, and like no other

men" (Kluckholm, Murray, & Schneider, 1953, p. 53), foundation content in human behavior and social environment taught in schools of social work focuses on the first two of these, which are based on normative behavior assumptions. Assessment that focuses on one's strengths must be individualized to understand the unique situation each person is experiencing. Normative perspectives of behavior are only useful insofar as they can enrich the understanding of this uniqueness. Pray's (1991) writings on assessment emphasize individual uniqueness as an important element of Schön's (1983) reflective model of practice and are particularly insightful in establishing the importance of individual and group uniqueness in assessment.

8. **Reach a mutual agreement on the assessment.** Social workers can minimize the power imbalance inherent in the helping relationship by stressing the importance of the individual's understandings and wants. The worker's role is to inquire, listen, and assist the person in discovering, clarifying, and articulating. The help seeker gives direction to the content of the assessment. The person must feel ownership of the process and the product and can do so only if assessment is open and shared. Rodwell (1987) articulated this well when she stated that the "major stakeholders must agree with the content" (p. 241). All assessment in written form should be written with the person(s) seeking help.

9. **Avoid blame and blaming.** Assessment and blame often get confused and convoluted. Blame is the first cousin of deficit models of practice. Causal thinking represents only one of many possible perspectives of the problem situation and can easily lead to blaming. Concentrating on blame or allowing it to get a firm foothold in the process is done at the expense of moving toward a resolution to the problem. Generally, blaming leads nowhere, and, if relegated to the person seeking help, it may encourage low self-esteem. If assigned to others, it may encourage learned helplessness or deter motivation to address the problem situation and perpetuate oppressive dynamics.

10. **Assess; but do not get caught up in labels.** Diagnosis is incongruent with a strengths perspective as it is understood in the context of pathology, deviance, and deficits and is based on social constructions of reality that define human problem situations in a like manner. While diagnosis is associated with a medical model of labeling that assumes unpopular and unacceptable behavior as a symptom of an underlying pathological condition, it is often required to access services. It has been argued that labeling "accompanied by reinforcement of identified behavior is a sufficient condition for chronic mental illness" (Taber, Herbert, Mark, & Nealey, 1969, p. 354). A diagnosis should not be viewed as the central feature of help seekers' identities or life experiences or the only outcome of an assessment.

ASSESSMENT PROCESS

Our assessment process reflects the two stage process first suggested by Mary Richmond (1917). She proposed that the social worker first study the facts of the situation and then diagnose the nature of the problem. Correspondingly, the first component is a process of clarifying why the person(s) has sought assistance and how the situation would look if satisfactorily changed. The second component involves evaluating and giving meaning to those factors, which impinge on the presenting situation.

Component 1: Defining the "Problem" Situation

Individuals, families, groups, and communities who seek assistance often do so in response to a "problem" situation or experience. The word *situation* or *experience* has a particularly important meaning because it affirms that problems always exist in an environmental context and are often related to oppressive circumstances. To focus on the problem situation is to avoid a perception and subsequent definition of the person as pathological that may lead, for the help seeker, to a self-fulfilling prophecy and, for the worker, to ascribing blame. However, using the word *problem* does not suggest that one therefore assumes environmental or situational pathology and continues with a pathological model by simply redirecting pathological assessment to the relevant environment. *Problem* here refers to mismatch or disequilibrium between the help seeker's needs and environmental demands and resources that is causing difficulty, puzzlement, and often pain. Solely focusing on the person who seeks help is inappropriate and may hinder problem solution. Problem situations have a life of their own and are generated by combinations of unpredicted contingencies, incongruities, and systems disequilibrium. Understanding problem situations in this way allows the worker and help seeker the freedom to capitalize on personal and environmental strengths to resolve the problem.

Unfortunately in practice, the problem situation or experience is often identified as the behavior of the person(s) seeking assistance. Among helpers and seekers of assistance, there is a general lack of understanding for how problematic behavior (e.g., isolation, repetitive behaviors, emotional distancing, substance use) is originally produced within an oppressive context (e.g., violence, abuse, community disorder) as a coping strategy or method of survival (e.g., to escape, to create a sense of control, safety, or belonging). Such a normal and healthy response to an unhealthy situation may become problematic when the behavior is transferred to new situations where the behavior is no longer required for survival.

Consider again the child who stops eating to draw attention to her/his abusive home environment. She or he may continue to starve herself/himself as a means of drawing attention to the self even after being removed from the abusive home life. The tendency in this situation is for the social worker to focus on eating patterns instead of illuminating how her/his control over eating was a form of resistance to her/his abuse. In this manner the helping relationship is organized around changing individual eating behaviors rather than changing the unhealthy living situations that created the need for such coping strategies, encouraging the help seeker to further resist abuse in her/his life, and/or helping others to do the same.

Defining the problem situation or experience is an important first step in the helping process because it guides how the helping process will proceed. To anchor the problem definition within a strengths perspective, it is particularly important at the beginning of the assessment to acknowledge that the person seeking help is in charge of telling his/her/their story. The social worker can help facilitate this process in so far as the person's understanding of the problem situation/presenting issue is honored and not displaced by the social worker's perspective. The following list outlines some ways that the helper can assist the person seeking help to share his/her story or narrative related to the problem situation. Items 4 and 5 are based in part on guidelines developed by Brown and Levitt (1979), and later revised by Hepworth and Larsen (1990), p. 14).[2]

Steps in Defining the Problem Situation or Discovering Why the Client Seeks Assistance

1. Elicit a story about the problem situation.
2. Seek to understand what is wanted and expected from the helper.
3. Seek to understand the meaning that the person(s) ascribes to the problem situation.
4. Seek to understand what life would be like if the problem situation were resolved.
5. Discover who (persons, groups, or organizations) is involved with the problem situation and how they are involved. What happens between the participants before, during, and immediately following activity related to the problem situation?

This outline assumes help seekers know why they seek help. The role of the social worker is to draw out the story from the person seeking assistance. In situations where the person seeking help consists of more than one person (e.g., a family, group, or community), multiple definitions of the problem will exist based on the various members' understanding of the situation. In these cases, it is the role of the social worker to find the common ground in their narratives.

Questions for the Assessment Process: Beyond "What Are Your Strengths?"

In every situation, power relations exist. Domination and brutality inundate our society, at both the personal and institutional levels (Wineman, 2003). Individuals' responses to oppression may serve as a catalyst in the mobilization of individual recovery and societal transformation. The following questions may be used to assist the help seeker to share his/her story and uncover experiences of and responses to oppression:

1. Depending upon what you are comfortable in sharing with me, tell me your story of what happened to you?
2. Has how you think about your life changed over time?

[2]Hepworth and Larsen use items 4 and 5 as ways to identify other people and larger systems that are involved in the problem situation and/or interacting with the problem.

In reflecting upon your life, I would like you to think about how the following areas may have helped you.

3. Is there anything about you that you feel you were born with that has helped you in your life?
4. Is there anything about the way(s) you have coped that has helped you in your life?
5. Are there any relationships that have helped you in your life? How were they helpful?
6. Are there any critical moments or turning points in your life that helped you?
7. Are there any religious or spiritual activities that helped you in your life?
8. Are you involved in any activities that "give back" or help others?
9. Are there any agency services that you have received which have been helpful to you?
10. What advice do you have for other individuals who have experienced similar life circumstances?
11. What could professionals learn from your experience that would help others?

Component 2: Framework for Assessment

The second assessment component involves giving meaning to those factors that influence the problem situation and linking the problem. The model proposed here revolves around two axes. The first axis is an environmental factors versus client factors continuum, and the second is a strengths versus deficits continuum (see Figure 6.1).

When the axes in Figure 6.1 are enclosed, each of the four quadrants that result represents important content for assessment (see Figure 6.2).

Because assessment instruments themselves have tended to focus on the elements of quadrant 4, most practice today emphasizes client deficits. A comprehensive assessment would have data recorded in each quadrant. The version of the assessment axes in Figure 6.2 has been used as a recording tool in teaching, workshops, and agency consultation and has demonstrated that workers and clients can readily identify content for each quadrant. However, quadrants 1 and 2 are *emphasized* when practicing from a strengths perspective.

Exemplars of Client Strengths (Quadrant 2)

Quadrant 2, personal strengths, includes both psychological and physical/physiological strengths. For illustrative purposes, psychological factors are further devel-

Strengths

Environmental factors ———————— Client factors

Deficits (obstacles)

FIGURE 6.1   Assessment Axes

Strengths

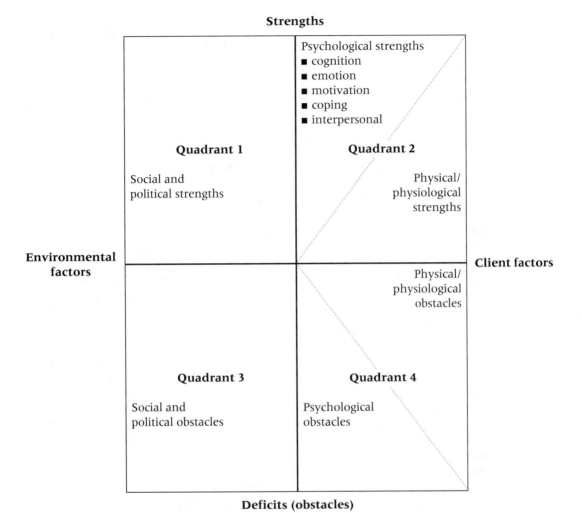

Quadrant 1

Social and
political strengths

Psychological strengths
■ cognition
■ emotion
■ motivation
■ coping
■ interpersonal

Quadrant 2

Physical/
physiological
strengths

**Environmental
factors**

Client factors

Physical/
physiological
obstacles

Quadrant 3

Social and
political obstacles

Quadrant 4

Psychological
obstacles

Deficits (obstacles)

FIGURE 6.2   **Framework for Assessment**

oped here by listing a set of client strength exemplars (see the following section). The taxonomy of strengths—cognition, emotion, motivation, coping, and inter-personal relationships—is used to organize and structure these exemplars. The categories are quite traditional and are not free of conceptual problems. For example, it is important to note that although these items are designated as personal factors, they do not represent intrapersonal attributes devoid of environmental and or physiological interaction (e.g., motivation is dependent on a unique set of environmental and personal dynamics). Physiological factors, which are not included in this list, are particularly important for some clients, such as aging individuals or the disabled. Additions to this quadrant could include aspirations, competencies, and confidence as conceptualized by Rapp (1998).

The previous list suggests exemplars of client strengths workers and clients might consider during the assessment process with individuals and families. These items were arrived at through literature review (for example, Brown & Levitt, 1979; Hepworth and Larsen, 1990) and workshops with agency practitioners.

The framework and outline are proposed as a resource to assist workers and help seekers in considering those strengths and resilient capacities to be exploited in coping with the problem situation presented by individuals and families. In the initial contact, the worker should be able to begin identifying strengths. Workers may wish to have a copy of the exemplars list readily available during an interview. Other workers may find a review of the list helpful during case reflection, recording, and planning. One worker reported to the author that he has used the list by going through it item by item with the person seeking help. Workers may use the list to 1.) stimulate thinking about strengths and their importance in the practice process, 2.) assist in identifying strengths that otherwise would not be thought of, 3.) assist in identifying and selecting positive and supportive content to be shared with help seekers, 4.) provide a foundation for a case plan that is based on help seeker competency and capability rather than inadequacy, and 5.) bolster worker confidence and belief in the person(s) seeking help. The list is intended to be suggestive and heuristic in nature by illustrating the wide range of strengths that any given help seeker might have. Early & GlenMaye (2000) provide a valuable case example of the process by which family strengths are explored and named. The language in the list is somewhat contaminated with professional and middle class notions of reality and the desirable, and therefore will require either interpretation or revision when the assessment process is shared with help seekers, especially those from different cultures.

These exemplars of help seeker strengths are not intended to include all the assessment content and knowledge that a social worker must use in practice. Indeed, important topics such as assessing specific obstacles to empowerment, assessing power relationships, and assessing the relationship between personal empowerment and social empowerment are not considered. Also, community strengths, such as social cohesiveness, social networks, economic investment by community institutions, and community improvement initiatives are not included. In regard to communities, Kretzmann and McKnight (1997, 1993) provide a useful framework for identifying and mapping community assets. The use of these exemplars depends on given practice situations, and professional judgment determines their specific applicability. They are proposed to provide an alternative approach to existing normative and deficit models of intrapersonal diagnosis and treatment. The exemplars may also be of interest to practitioners who wish to use them to supplement existing assessment paradigms they do not wish to give up. A comprehensive assessment would include content from all four quadrants. However, a strengths perspective would emphasize Quadrants 1 and 2, elements often missing from assessment. Items bolded below are additions to previous quadrant two lists (Cowger, 1994; Cowger & Snively, 2000) and reflect Anderson's (2001) resiliency constructs as discussed previously in this chapter.

Assessment of Help Seeker Strengths (Quadrant 2 of Assessment Axes)

A. **Cognition**
   1. Understands that one's problems are related and interactive with other people and other institutions.
   2. Understands that some behaviors and feelings are related to previous life experiences.
   3. Understands that one can take charge of one's life and bring about changes.
   4. Sees the world as most other people see it in own culture.
   5. Has an understanding of right and wrong, from own cultural, ethical perspective.
   6. Is insightful as to how one's own behavior affects others and how others affect him/herself.
   7. Is open to different ways of thinking about things.
   8. Reasoning is easy to follow.
   9. Considers and weighs alternatives in problem solving.
   10. Has the ability to identify/understand injustices and oppression.
B. **Emotion**
   1. Is in touch with feelings and is able to express them if encouraged.
   2. Expresses love and concern for intimate others.
   3. Demonstrates a degree of self-control.
   4. Can handle stressful situations reasonably well.
   5. Is positive about life. Has hope.
   6. Has a range of emotions.
   7. Emotions are congruent with situations.
   8. Has capacity to channel anger into advocacy.
   9. Resists feeling powerless, helpless, isolated.
   10. Resists injustice, maltreatment, and oppression.
C. **Motivation**
   1. When having problematic situations, doesn't hide from, avoid, or deny them.
   2. Willing to seek help and share problem situation with others he/she can trust.
   3. Willing to accept responsibility for his/her part or role in problem situations.
   4. Wants to improve current and future situations.
   5. Committed to overcoming feelings of helplessness, powerlessness, and lack of control.
   6. Ready to identify and fight injustices within the family, community, and broader society.
   7. Committed to opposing maltreatment in whatever form.
   8. Wants to move beyond coping/surviving to empowerment.
D. **Coping**
   1. Is persistent in handling family crises.

  2. Is well organized.

  3. Follows through on decisions.

  4. Is resourceful and creative with limited resources.

  5. Stands up for self rather than submitting to injustice.

  6. Attempts to pay debts despite financial difficulty.

  7. Prepares for and handles new situations well.

  8. Has dealt successfully with related problems in the past.

  9. Confronts injustice and oppression

  10. Holds self and others accountable.

E. Interpersonal

  1. Has friends.

  2. Seeks to understand friends, family members, and others.

  3. Makes sacrifices for friends, family members, and others.

  4. Performs social roles appropriately (e.g., parents, spouse, son or daughter, community).

  5. Is outgoing and friendly.

  6. Is truthful.

  7. Is cooperative and flexible in relating to family and friends.

  8. Is self-confident in relationships with others.

  9. Shows warm acceptance of others.

  10. Can accept loving and caring feelings from others.

  11. Has sense of propriety, good manners.

  12. Is a good listener.

  13. Expresses self spontaneously.

  14. Is patient.

  15. Has realistic expectations in relationships with others.

  16. Has a sense of humor.

  17. Has sense of satisfaction in role performance with others.

  18. Has ability to maintain own personal boundaries in relationships with others.

  19. Demonstrates comfort in sexual role/identity.

  20. Demonstrates ability to forgive.

  21. Is generous with time and money.

  22. Is verbally fluent.

  23. Is ambitious and industrious.

  24. Is resourceful.

  25. Seeks out role models who reflect self-confidence and control over their own lives while being loving and caring toward others.

CONCLUSION

Inherent in these assessment guidelines is the recognition that to focus on help seeker strengths and to practice with the intent of help seeker empowerment is to practice with an explicit power consciousness. Whatever else social work practice is, it is always political, because it always encompasses power and power relationships.

In summary, social work literature has emphasized philosophy and theory that presents a strengths perspective, but continues to lack well-developed practice directives, guidelines, and know-how for incorporating this perspective into practice. Assessment based on a strengths perspective places environmental and personal strengths in a prominent position. Problem situations are understood as coping responses to oppressive experiences. Thus the context of oppression needs to be understood before the helping relationship can focus on strengths. Guidelines for soliciting help seekers' narratives and assessing their strengths have been presented in an attempt to bridge the gap between theory and practice.

DISCUSSION QUESTIONS

1. Choose a client (individual, family, or community) that you have worked with and, using the model in Figure 6.2, fill in the quadrants as best you can. Does this arrangement give you a different picture of your client?

2. What is meant by the politics of assessment? Have you seen it in operation in your practice, agency, or community?

3. How can you use assessment to empower clients? Can you recall a time when you empowered a client? What was it that you did that leads you to think so?

4. Why is it important to give preeminence to the client's perspective and to believe the client? Does this level of belief in clients exist in your agency? How do you know? If the client is the expert on her or his own life, what happens to your role as a professional helper?

5. What are the advantages of focusing on client strengths? Do you see drawbacks?

REFERENCES

Anderson, K. M. (2001). Recovery: Resistance and resilience in female incest survivors. Doctoral dissertation. University of Kansas, *Dissertation Abstracts, 62* (09), 3185A.

Barnard, C. (1994). Resiliency: a shift in our perception? *The American Journal of Family Therapy, 22*(2), 135–144.

Beardslee, W. R., & Podorefsky, D. (1988). Resilient adolescents whose parents have serious affective and other psychiatric disorders: Importance of self-understanding and relationships. *American Journal of Psychiatry, 145*(1), 63–69.

Berger, P. L., & Luckmann, T. A. (1966). *The social construction of reality.* Garden City, NY: Doubleday.

Billingsley, A. (1968). *Black families in White America.* Englewood Cliffs, NJ: Prentice-Hall.

Billingsley, A. (1992). *Climbing Jacob's ladder: The enduring legacy of African American families.* New York: Simon & Schuster.

Blume, S. E. (1990). *Secret survivors: Uncovering incest and its aftereffects in women.* New York: Ballantine Books.

Bowen, G. L., & Chapman, M. V. (1996). Poverty, neighborhood danger, social support, and the individual adaptation among at-risk youth in urban areas. *Journal of Family Issues, 17*(5), 641–665.

Boyd-Franklin, N., & Bry, B. H. (2000). *Reaching out in family therapy.* New York: Guilford Press.

Brown, L., and Levitt, J. (1979). A methodology for problem-system identification. *Social Casework, 60,* 408–415.

Byrd, R. (1994). Assessing resilience in victims of childhood maltreatment. Doctoral dissertation. Pepperdine University, *Dissertation Abstracts International, 55*(03), 1177B. (UMI No. 9417679).

Cohen, B. Z. (1999). Intervention and supervision in strengths-based social work practice. *Families in Society, 80*(5), 460–466.

Council on Social Work Education. (1994). Curriculum policy statement for master's degree program. In *Handbook of accreditation standards and procedures.* Washington, DC: Author.

Cowger, C. D. (1998). Clientilism and clientification: Impediments to strengths based social work practice. *Journal of Sociology and Social Welfare, 25*(1), 24–36.

Cowger, C. D., & Snively, C. A. (2002). Accessing client strengths: Individual, Family & Community Empowerment. In D. Saleebey (Ed.), *The Strengths Perspective in Social Work Practice.* 3rd ed. Boston: Allyn & Bacon, pp. 106–123.

Davis, L. E. (2001). The problem of race: A renewed focus. The Carl A. Scott Memorial Lecture conducted at the annual program meeting of the Council on Social Work Education, Dallas, TX.

De Jong, P., & Miller, S. D. (1995). How to interview for client strengths. *Social Work, 40*(6), 729–736.

Delgado, M., & Barton, K. (1998). Murals in Latino communities: Social indicators of community strengths. *Social Work, 43*(4), 346–356.

Dietz, C. (2000). Responding to oppression and abuse: A feminist challenge to clinical social work. *Affilia, 15*(3), 369–389.

Early, T. J., & GlenMaye, L. F. (2000). Valuing families: Social work practice with families from a strengths perspective. *Social Work, 45*(2), 118–130.

Falck, H. S. (1988). *Social work: The membership perspective.* New York: Springer.

Farber, E., & Egeland, B. (1987). Invulnerability among abused and neglected children. In E. J. Anthony & B. J. Cohler (Eds.), *The invulnerable child* (pp. 253–288). New York: Guilford Press.

Finn, J. L., & Checkoway, B. (1998). Young people as competent community builders: A challenge to social work. *Social Work, 43*(4), 335–344.

Gibelman, M. (1999). The search for identity: Defining social work–past, present, future. *Social Work, 44*(4), 298–310.

Goldstein, H. (1990). Strength or pathology: Ethical and rhetorical contrasts in approaches to practice. *Families in Society, 71*(5), 267–275.

Goroff, N. N. (1983). Social work within a political and social context: The triumph of the therapeutic. In S. Ables & P. Ables (Eds.), *Social work with groups: Proceedings of 1978 symposium* (pp. 133–145). Louisville, KY: Committee for the Advancement of Social Work with Groups.

Habermas, J. (1981). *Theorie de kommunikativen handelns.* Band 2. Suhrkanp. Ausgurg.

Hepworth, D. H., & Larsen, J. A. (1990). *Direct social work practice.* Belmont, CA: Wadsworth.

Herman, J. (1992). *Trauma and recovery.* New York: Basic Books.

Hwang, S. C., & Cowger, C. D. (1998). Utilizing strengths in assessment. *Families in Society, 79*(1), 25–31.

Kagle, J. D., & Cowger, C. D. (1984). Blaming the client: Implicit agenda in practice research? *Social Work, 29,* 347–351.

Kluckholm, C., Murray, H. A., & Schneider, D. M. (Eds.). (1953). *Personality in nature, society, and culture.* New York: Alfred A. Knopf.

Kretzmann, J. P., & McKnight, J. L. (1993). *Building communities from the inside out: A path toward finding and mobilizing a community's assets.* Chicago: ACTA Publications.

Kretzmann, J. P., & McKnight, J. L. (1997). *A guide to capacity inventories: Mobilizing the community skills of local residents.* Chicago: ACTA Publications.

Laird, J. (1989). Women and stories: Restorying women's self-constructions. In M. Goldrick, C. M. Anderson, & F. Walsh (Eds.), *Women in Families* (pp. 427–450). New York: W. W. Norton & Company, Inc.

Luthar, S. (1993). Annotation: Methodological and conceptual issues in research on childhood resilience. *Journal of Child Psychiatry, 34*(4), 441–443.

Maluccio, A. (1979). The influence of the agency environment on clinical practice. *Journal of Sociology and Social Welfare, 6,* 734–755.

McAdoo, H. P., & McAdoo, J. L. (Eds.). (1985). *Black children: Social, educational and parental environments.* Beverly Hills, CA: Sage.

McKnight, J. (1995). *The careless society: Community and its counterfeits.* New York: HarperCollins.

McQuaide, S., & Ehrenreich, J. H. (1997). Assessing client's strengths. *Families in Society, 78*(2), 201–212.

Medoff, P., & Sklar, H. (1994). *Streets of hope: The fall and rise of an urban neighborhood.* Boston: South End Press.

Meyer, C. H. (1976). *Social work practice* (2nd ed.). New York: Free Press.

Morris, C. (1997). Mental health matter: Toward a non-medicalized approach to psychotherapy with women. *Women & Therapy, 29*(3), 63–77.

Palmer, N. (1991). Feminist practice with survivors of sexual trauma and incest. In B. Bricker-Jenkins, N. R. Hooyman, & N. Gottlieb (Eds.), *Feminist social work practice in clinical settings* (pp. 63–89). Newbury Park, CA: Sage publications.

Poole, D. (1997). Building community capacity to promote social and public health: Challenges for universities. *Health and Social Work, 22*(3), 163–170.

Pray, J. E. (1991). Respecting the uniqueness of the individual: Social work practice within a reflective model. *Social Work, 36,* 80–85.

Public/Private Venture. (2000, fall). The science foundations of youth development. In N. Jaffe (Ed.), *Youth development: Issues, challenges, and directions* (pp. 18–64). Philadelphia: K. Pittman, M. Irby, & T. Ferber.

Rapp, C. A. (1998). *The strengths model: Case management with people suffering from severe and persistent mental illness.* New York: Oxford University Press.

Richmond, M. (1917). *Social diagnosis.* New York: Russell Sage Foundation.

Ripple, L. (1964). *Motivation, capacity and opportunity.* Chicago: University of Chicago Press.

Rodwell, M. K. (1987). Naturalistic inquiry: An alternative model for social work assessment. *Social Service Review, 61*(2), 231–246.

Russo, R. J. (1999). Applying a strengths-based practice approach in working with people with developmental disabilities and their families. *Families in Society, 80* (January-February), 25–33.

Ryan, W. (1976). *Blaming the victim.* New York: Vintage Books.

Safyer, A. W., Griffin, M. L., Colan, N. B., Alexander-Brydie, E., & Rome, J. Z. (1998). Methodological issues when developing prevention programs for low-income, urban adolescents. *Journal of Social Service Research, 23*(3/4), 23–46.

Saleebey, D. (1997). The strengths approach to practice. In D. Saleebey (Ed.), *The strengths perspective in social work practice* (pp. 49–57). New York: Longman.

Schön, D. A. (1983). *The reflective practitioner: How professionals think in action.* New York: Basic Books.

Simon, B. L. (1990). Rethinking empowerment. *Journal of Progressive Human Services, 1*(1), 27–40.

Solomon, B. (1976). *Black empowerment: Social work in oppressed communities.* New York: Columbia University Press.

Stiffman, A. R., Hadley-Ives, E., Elze, D., Johnson, S., & Dore, P. (1999). Impact of environment on adolescent mental health and behavior: Structural equation modeling. *American Journal of Orthopsychiatry, 69*(1), 73–86.

Taber, M., Herbert, C. Q., Mark, M., & Nealey, V. (1969). Disease ideology and mental health research. *Social Problems, 16,* 349–357.

Wade, A. (1997). Small acts of living: Everyday resistance to violence and other forms of oppression. *Contemporary Family Therapy: An International Journal, 19*(1), 23–39.

Werner, E., & Smith, R. (1992). *Overcoming the odds: High risk children from birth to adulthood.* Ithaca, NY: Cornell University Press.

Wineman, S. (2003). *Power-under: Trauma and nonviolent social change.* Self-published: Cambridge, MA.

Wolin, S. J., & Wolin, S. (1993). *The resilient self.* New York: Villard Books.

CHAPTER SEVEN

SOLVING PROBLEMS FROM A STRENGTHS PERSPECTIVE

ANN WEICK

JAMES KREIDER

RONNA CHAMBERLAIN

Throughout its history, social work has taken pride in being a seen as a problem-solving profession. At the beginning of the 20th century, social work took root in the concerns of people who were made most vulnerable by the problems of daily living. During this early work of problem-solving, social work learned a hard lesson: that the pressures of poverty, ill health, and unemployment could not be waved away by changing people's personal behavior. Instead, the profession developed a recognition of the factors both within and outside people's lives that had to be taken into account to fully appreciate the nature of human problems. This "dual focus," which incorporates an understanding of both individuals and their environments, has rightly become a hallmark of professional social work practice. While their shapes and definitions have changed, human problems still rivet our professional attention and invite our collective response. However, the activity of "problem solving" has too frequently paid attention to the problem, at the expense of the solution.

The development of the Strengths Perspective (Rapp, 1998; Saleebey, 1992, 1997, 2002; Weick et al., 1989) represents a significant paradigm shift for the social work profession, as well as other professions. Like any paradigm shift, however, it is difficult to leave the old assumptions behind in order to integrate new ways of practicing. For example, it is common to view strengths-based practice as something *added on* to the traditional pathology-based, problem-solving paradigm, whereby an assessment of strengths is used in overcoming barriers and obstacles to achieving goals. Attending to problems and problem-solving at the expense of solutions takes the heart out of the strengths perspective. No matter how competent and dedicated the social worker, a focus on the problem anchors the work firmly in the pathology paradigm. The core assumption of the pathology paradigm is that it is essential to understand the problem before one can know how to proceed toward an intervention. The weight of the DSM IV-TR (APA, 2000), both in authority and in sheer volume, is testament to the power of this assumption. As long as we include "problem" in our assessment, we run the risk of being distracted from client strengths, allowing the power of the problem to stay in the center of the work (Weick and Chamberlain, 2002).

There are costs to focusing on the problem. It costs the people we serve a sense of hopefulness about what they would like to have happen in their lives. It also costs them the sense of competence that comes from being able to discover how to achieve some version of their aspirations and dreams. In addition, it costs workers the sense that they have genuinely contributed to their clients' learning, growth, and development, an experience that is a powerful antidote to worker burn-out.

Attention on human problems has distracted us from considering the other part of the "problem-solving" equation. That other part is the solution and the processes involved in finding them. The Strengths Perspective offers a way to move our focus from the problem to constructive work toward goals (See Weick & Chamberlain, 2002 for more details). When this perspective is enhanced by principles from solution-focused clinical work, the process of finding solutions takes its rightful place as the center of the work.

STRENGTHS AND SOLUTIONS

The development of the Strengths Perspective for social work practice and the development of Solution-Focused Brief Therapy in psychotherapy both grew from a deep discontent with the problem-solving and pathology based models that had long influenced social work and other helping professions. Through much of the 20th century, aided by an evolving array of theories of human behavior, the intent of therapeutic or other professional intervention was to find and accurately identify client or patient problems as the starting point of the work. No matter how sophisticated the approach, the problem was believed to be located within the individual or, at best, within the family group. Social work's historic commitment to a larger environmental perspective was there as a counterpoint but the weight of psychologically-based therapies often focused attention on individual behavior, even in situations where social factors such as poverty, physical abuse, and discrimination clearly limited people's life chances.

The emergence of the Strengths Perspective in social work grew out of the recognition that focusing on the problem does not solve the problem. What a client is left with is a more sophisticated definition of their problem, based on the professional helper's knowledge, biases and favorite theories. When people have problems that affect and seem to fill their entire lives, the challenge of getting beyond the problems seems insurmountable. But that is exactly where the Strengths Perspective had its origins. It grew out of an attempt to work in a more constructive way with people who had severe and persistent mental illness. These were individuals whose problem of mental illness had become all-encompassing through years of hospitalization, crises, and treatment by mental health professionals. Individuals so afflicted knew from the inside-out what their diagnosis was, what their symptoms were, how medications affected them, and how dismal their chances were for a "normal" life. They had, in fact, become their problem.

Early work with the Strengths Perspective came from a kernel of a new idea: that work with people suffering from long-term mental illness should focus on what people wanted in their lives. It was based on the assumption that, despite their mental illness, they could build a life beyond the problem. The bridge to this new life was a shift from the problem to a focus on people's talents, assets, resources, and capacities. The development of a strengths-assessment (Chamberlain and Rapp, 1983; Modrcin, Rapp and Chamberlain, 1985) was the means to document these assets in six life domains so that the person could envision goals that would lead them to a more satisfying life. Through the further development of strengths-based case management (Modrcin, Rapp and Poertner, 1988; Rapp, 1998), mental health workers were trained to focus on people's goals and aspirations, and help build a plan that would lead to success. The companion goal was to make it possible for people to live in their home communities instead of in institutions as way of reducing the stigma and social isolation that had long been associated with mental illness. It was recognized that the existence of a medical condition required some medical management. The ongoing challenges of medication side-effects, of occasional crises requiring hospitalization, and of a lifetime of being stigmatized all required appropriate attention. But the problem of mental illness was seen as contained and manageable. The person's own goals were the focus of the work.

The powerful switch from pathology to strengths brought remarkable results, as initially demonstrated through four non-experimental studies (Rapp and Chamberlain, 1985; Rapp & Wintersteen, 1989; Kisthardt, 1993). Many people who had been categorized as "hopeless cases" began to make improvements in their lives, based on goals that they set. Whether it was finding a job, making new friends, or going by themselves to the grocery store, the focus on what they wanted, as identified by them, began to give a new shape to their lives. The "fuel" for making this change came from the power of their hopes and aspirations, aided by the support and assistance of workers trained in strengths-based management. The role of the case manager was and is to help the person identify goals and the accompanying talents, assets and capacities, as well as the family, neighborhood, and community resources that can help them achieve their goals. Training in strengths-based case management has now occurred in over 45 states, as well as internationally.

Since its beginnings in social work in the early 1980s at the University of Kansas School of Social Welfare, the strengths approach has been extended to many groups of people, particularly those whose life chances have been severely limited by such hope-smothering circumstances as poverty (Jones & Bricker-Jenkins, 2002) physical and sexual abuse (Anderson, 2001; Walsh, 1998), and substance abuse (Rapp, 2002). While the case management approach, with its active connection between personal and community resources, has been particularly helpful for those suffering from serious mental illness, the philosophy of the strengths perspective has permeated many areas of social work practice, including clinical work and family practice (Early and GlenMaye, 2000).

The development of Solution-Focused Behavioral Therapy grew out of the frustration perhaps best described by James Hillman's book title: *We've Had 100*

Years of Psychotherapy and the World is Getting Worse (Hillman and Ventura, 1992). Although the development of psychological theory continued apace through the 20th century, the prevailing focus was on explanations of human problems: their causes, their characteristics, and their complexities, leading to an ever more detailed presentation of the symptoms. While there was great pride in developing a catalog for psychological problems and assigning diagnoses, there was very little demonstrated connection between the diagnosis and treatment. In many cases, the symptoms were seen to be so severe and so protracted that years of psychotherapy were required, and some populations, such as those with persistent mental illness, were consigned to symptom-management, with no hope for a productive life. The advent of powerful psychoactive drugs, while useful in managing symptoms, has done little to erase the sense of hopelessness and denied chances that bedevil people whose lives are still focused on their symptoms. Those who developed Solution-Focused Brief Therapy (SFBT) were influenced by Milton Erickson, the first practitioner to use the term "brief' in talking about therapy. In spite of the prevailing belief that people in need of therapy required extensive time to "work through" their problems, by the 1970's Steve deShazer and Insoo Kim Berg began to realize that most people only stayed in therapy for a brief time. Moving more quickly to solutions became the hallmark of their subsequent development of the Brief Family Therapy Center in Milwaukee.

Commonalities and Differences

The motivation to find a path beyond the problem spurred the development of both the Strengths Perspective and Solution-Focused Behavioral work. In many ways, these approaches share similar radical underpinnings. In the traditional phrasing of social work, both establish the same strong foundation of "starting where the client is." Goals and solutions are the main focus of the work. This conscious attention to what people want is an essential corrective to more traditional approaches that place the professional helper in the driver's seat. In the conventional approach, the practitioner evaluates what people need, not what people want.

Attending to what people want begins an important process of bringing into consciousness the knowledge people have about their own circumstances. In psychologically-based approaches to helping, people's own knowledge is typically viewed as flawed, irrational, or distorted. The solicitation of people's own knowledge is sought primarily in order to identify problematic behaviors and re-package them into an explanation that suits the professional person's own theoretical biases. To trust what clients are saying about their current life but, more importantly, their hopes for a different life, establishes a radically different starting point. Both strengths and solution-focused work intentionally create a partnership designed to explore in detail the shape of a person's life beyond the problem.

In coming to this generative beginning, both approaches share the assumption that knowing about the problem is not related to finding a solution. This idea flies in the face of virtually all psychologically-based theories of human change, which assert that the problem must be clearly and exhaustively identified before moving to a solution. In that respect, both approaches have taken a radical detour away from a century of professional helping. However, Strengths and Solution-focused work have taken different paths. The differences lie in the degree to which problems are acknowledged and in the scope of the resources that can be brought to bear in shaping a different life.

What about Problems?

Social work has been influenced by a problem-solving model, in which the problem is recognized as the initial phase of relationship-building. Because so many human troubles have painful psychological, social and/or physical components, the adage of "starting where the client is" has dictated an initial acknowledgment of the nature of the problem as seen by the person, family, or group affected. Ignoring it entirely has been viewed as disrespectful and even a reflection of worker incompetence. However, strengths-focused practitioners know that the retelling of a problem-based narrative can serve to reinforce a "stuck story," where the person hits the same wall each time. The "unsticking" of the story comes through careful and attentive listening to clues provided by the narrators about their personal resources—their talents and capacities; their social connections: families, friends, neighbors, co-workers and fellow church members; and most importantly, their dreams for a better life. The eventual linking of their aspirations with existing and new resources provides the energy to build a life beyond the problem. Creating the imaginative world where aspirations can be converted to practical goals is a powerful strategy for establishing plans to reach those dreams.

In the Strengths Perspective's early days of working with people affected by persistent mental illness, the development of goal-setting was and continues to be an important strategy in helping clients move away from their understandable preoccupation with what is seen as a chronic, life-burdening problem. In order to begin building a life beyond the problem, life domains form the conceptual structure for the initial assessment. Exploring goals in relation to housing, workplace, income, social relations, leisure time, and health provide a way to future-oriented paths toward a better life.

The solution-focused model of clinical practice offers a helpful corrective to the typical problem-solving approach that characterizes the practice of most of social work and other professional helping professions. It also adds useful extensions to the goal-oriented strategies of practice from the Strengths Perspective. Rather than plan and execute "interventions," the solution-focused model uses questions to guide conversations in a collaborative effort to explore and develop solutions. The model offers several types of questions that can help strength-based workers assist their clients in this solution building, as opposed to traditional problem-solving. By doing so, problems are, in effect, left behind. But doing so requires focusing and refocusing all eyes on solutions, rather than problems.

Solution-Focused Therapy has moved beyond the strictures of the problem-solving approach by skipping the problem definition in order to focus on information about what the person wants *instead of* the problem. In this regard, the approach is fundamentally different than problem-solving models. The practice of focusing on solutions rather than problems as early in the process as possible is based on the assumption that in order to solve any problem, one needs to know more about possible solutions than about problems (deShazer, 1988). This assumption is supported by research from Milwaukee's Brief Family Therapy Center, where the solution-focused model was developed, finding less than a 5 percent correlation between client's problem descriptions and how they described their solutions to their problems (personal communication with deShazer, June 2004). Goals related to problems are different than goals related to solutions.

Solution-focused goals can make a dramatic difference for our clients, helping them identify and reach for their hopes, dreams, and aspirations. Doing so has far broader implications for quality of life than simply solving problems. Consequently, the first step in leaving problems behind in solution-building is simply not to focus on problems, but rather to focus on what people want and what they see as their possibilities.

This idea raises concern about Solution-Focused practice for those who assume that workers must begin building a professional relationship by completely hearing the client's story about their problems (Early & GlenMaye, 2000). Solution-focused work does not ignore relationship-building (De Jong & Miller, 1995). Instead, it begins with a collaborative partnership with clients around what they *want* instead of around their problems, in many cases without ever talking about problems. While it is obvious that it would be neither helpful nor respectful to force clients to stop talking about their problems and instead talk about solutions, many people are so distracted by their problems that they do not realize that it is possible to move toward solutions without a thorough exploration of the problem. The solution-focused model does not assume that all clients must first tell about their problems before they can engage around solution-building. Many clients do initially focus on their problems, but many are also relieved to be assisted in shifting to solutions early on, if not immediately, in the helping conversation. If we assume clients must first talk about their problems, we are likely to ask questions that suggest that they should, and they are in turn likely to respond by assuming that sharing about their problems provides necessary information (Miller and Duncan, 1995). By joining clients in "problem-talk," we run the risk of unwittingly reinforcing the notion that doing so is an important first step in getting to solutions.

On the other hand, in asking questions that probe for information relevant to solution-building as early as possible, clients are likely to share what they want to have happen in their lives (solutions) *instead of* what they don't want to have happen (problems). This is the practical first step in solution-building, as well as a means to developing a relationship that organizes around and affirms people's hopes and desires. Asking about what they want to have happen also makes overt the practitioner's belief they are capable and have the strengths, resources, and abilities that can be marshaled to improve the quality of their lives. This is a central assumption of strength-perspective practice (Saleebey, 1992). However, if workers do not convey this belief through their actions, clients may well doubt their own capabilities. In doubting their capacities, it is less likely that people will try to reach for their hopes and dreams.

"What the client wants from treatment may be the single most important piece of information that can be obtained" (Duncan, Hubble, Miller, & Coleman,

1998). Research is demonstrating the validity of this statement in terms of avoiding "client resistance," capitalizing on motivation, and encouraging client-worker collaboration around presenting problems, ranging from severe substance abuse to dealing with HIV positive status (Gold, 1990; Miller and Rollnick, 2002). In addition, this is relevant for social workers who aspire to have their practice be congruent with professional values regarding the inherent dignity and worth of all people—demonstrated through our commitment to client self-determination.

Solution-focused work skips the broader "assessment" that invariably includes details about and history of problems. Following are some examples of ways to invite conversations that help clients move toward a discussion of solutions:

> "How will you know when your problems are behind you?"
>
> "What will need to happen for you to be convinced that the problems that brought you in here are loosening their grip on your life?"
>
> "How will you know when services are no longer necessary?"
>
> "What will need to be different in your life in order for you to say our work together was successful?"

Gathering information about what "solutions" will look like early in the helping interaction quickly leaves problems behind, as both client and worker become excited about constructing a better future, rather than reviewing a painful past.

While this chapter cannot cover the techniques of Solution-Focused Therapy in detail, (see DeJong and Miller, 1995 for a complete presentation), the key questions used in this approach show how questions are essential to the process of moving beyond problems. Perhaps the most well-known question that connects clients with solutions is the Miracle Question, a very effective way to invite conversations about client's goals. The form asks a person to imagine that their problem has been miraculously solved while they were sleeping and then to detail signs during the next day that the miracle has occurred. Follow-up questions are designed to make this miracle as specific as possible. Even though some workers are initially uncomfortable, feeling silly asking clients to pretend their problems have miraculously disappeared instead of "facing reality," they soon find it an engaging and effective way to help their clients create a "reality" that they are capable of achieving and motivated to take action to create. With a detailed picture of what will need to be different for a more satisfying life, many people quickly fill in how they will need to proceed in order to achieve that future. Since it is their plan, they are more likely to view the plan as viable, to take action on the plan, and to gain a sense of competence, dignity, and worth through experiencing their own success.

A second type of question used by the solution-focused model is the exception question. This question flows out of the assumption that all problems in social systems have exceptions, and those exceptions involve strengths, resources, and abilities (Berg and Miller, 1992). Rather than doing a generic strength assessment in domains that are relevant to the professional but not necessarily to the client, asking about when the problem is less or absent often highlights strengths, abilities, and resources specifically relevant to the client's goals.

Differing Questions

Since solution-building is always searching for a useful difference—a difference that makes a difference—the strengths-based worker will also ask "difference" questions. The purpose of asking the following questions is to help the person assess the usefulness of what they are doing, from their own perspective:

"What difference did doing that make for you?"

"What difference would your spouse (best friend, family, boss) say that made?"

"What difference do you think doing more of that would make?"

For example, when Ms. Greene was mandated into service for hitting her children, she was asked, "When have you been tempted to hit your child and didn't do so?" Realizing that she had the ability to do something different than hit her children when frustrated and overwhelmed helped her feel capable to do something different. Perhaps equally important, this realization helped her reconnect with her intention to be a good parent and to see the hitting as being only an ineffective strategy to do so rather than confirmation that she was a "child abuser." Asking questions that assume that people have resources that can help them achieve their goals not only highlights strengths and abilities, but also directly links together their intentions, goals, and abilities for purposeful action.

Practice in both strengths-based and solution-focused approaches have intentionally broken ties with a preoccupation with the past, in favor of a turn toward the future. The Strengths Perspective tends to emphasize goal-setting as the strategy for moving toward a new future and identifying the strengths that will help lead there. Solution-Focused Therapy emphasizes solution-finding through a strategy of purposeful questions that are intended to develop a detailed picture of a future beyond the problem. While there may be some differences between goals and solutions, the value of solution-focused work is its development of questions that help both the worker and client move quickly beyond the problem to solutions. As mentioned earlier, clinical experience in solution-focused work has provided strong evidence that it is not necessary to know about the problem before moving to solutions. The experience of strengths-based work carries a similar, though perhaps not as strongly stated, assumption. Solution-focused practice shows that the work of letting go of the problem is as much of a challenge to the worker as it is to the client. In order to help the client move beyond the problem, the worker must also let go of the need to analyze the problem.

The art of solution-focused questioning, a unique strength of solution-focused work, is matched in the Strengths Perspective by its full incorporation of the world beyond the client. Because of its roots in social work, the Strengths Perspective has brought to its development the profession's long-standing appreciation of the larger environment within which people live their lives. Thus, the development of goals and the finding of solutions both require a larger network of supportive resources that extend beyond the individual or family. The origins of the Strengths Perspective in the field of mental health, particularly with those who have serious and persistent mental illness, necessitated a community-based perspective. For lives in which medical intervention was a constant factor, strengths-based work required a thoughtful orchestration of supportive networks. As the Strengths Perspective has been extended to many other groups, as well as adapted for clinical practice, the presence of a sustaining environment continues to be an important feature of the approach, matching individual assets and collective resources.

The active inclusion of the resources and possibilities to be found in all domains of life has helped create a large frame for strengths-focused practice and has added to the understanding of the crucial interplay between people's own personal resources and those to be found in the larger social and physical environments within which people live their lives. This larger focus has reinforced social work's skillful command of resource discovery, resource acquisition, and resource development. Strengths-focused practitioners become astute detectives in helping people uncover and celebrate their own myriad resources but also create bridges of connections among individuals, families, neighborhoods, and communities, whether based on geography or common ties. By drawing this larger circle around people whose problems have overwhelmed them, there is increased opportunity for sustaining newly won successes in finding solutions and attaining goals.

EXTENSIONS OF STRENGTHS- AND SOLUTION-FOCUSED PRACTICE

The Strengths Perspective has brought into the vision and the vocabulary of social work a compendium of human qualities that are the building blocks of human change. Its clear focus on human capacity, assets, and aspirations, rather than on deficits and failure, has fundamentally challenged and changed the long-standing dominance of pathology. In a parallel way, solutions-focused work has created valuable tools through the development of questions that help to direct the work and shift attention to what is possible, rather than to what has failed. In this way, the Strengths Perspective and solution-focused practice share important assumptions. Both honor people's capacity to grow more fully into the individuals they were meant to be. Both celebrate the rich personal resources people have developed in their lives, often through great hardship. And both recognize the essential role of hope in imagining a life beyond the problem.

The development of the Strengths Perspective has been notable in its broad conception of human capacity, which places social work practice closer to the profession's long-held values about human potential and the power of personal and communal change. It has laid a generous groundwork for a reconsideration of the strengths of individuals and families. But it has also brought into sharper focus the resources and aspirations of neighborhoods, communities, and organizations. Once one begins to unearth the hidden assets in one domain, others naturally follow. The power of the collective to dream dreams is as palpable as the longing of a family to move beyond the limits of their problems.

The Strengths Perspective offers a way for social workers to move beyond the role of therapy to connect more deeply with the broad roles and goals of the social work profession. The work of reaching out to help people receive sustenance and support from their families, neighbors and community, and to advocate for groups who are diminished by oppressive policies flows from long-held social work value commitments. When one considers the generative resources that exist both within and around people, the focus on strengths becomes a strategic way to keep visible the profession's mission and practice wisdom. When this large view is supported by the practicality of solution-focused questions, it becomes possible to imagine new implications for the merger of strengths and solutions.

Throughout the development of both strengths-based and solution-focused work, the importance of the relationship in the helping effort has been a constant theme. No matter what strategies may undergird the helping process, the nature of the relationship has long been recognized as the medium through which change occurs. This awareness has been bolstered by an extensive literature and framed as a core social work value in the profession's Code of Ethics. But different types of relationships are developed based solely on what is focused upon in the relationship. If a person's dysfunction is the center of attention, following the dominant view of most of the 20th century, the worker inevitably is placed in a position of authority. The person's own knowledge, experiences, and past successes are seen as irrelevant, except to describe the problem. However, by shifting the focus to what clients want to have happen (e.g. goals, solutions) and helping them discover what already works in their lives (exceptions) without ever talking about problems, strength-based practitioners have a very practical way to build on client strengths. Doing so tends to foster the rapid development of a trusting, collaborative relationship where workers consistently demonstrate their commitment to cooperating with clients on what the clients consider important in their lives. When the relationship consistently draws attention to people's strengths and abilities, it holds up a mirror for people to see their own capacities, validating their competence at being able to influence their lives in the directions they want them to go. Rather than using strengths as a way to overcome problems, barriers, and obstacles, and inadvertently drawing attention to them, these "impediments" to having a rewarding life become the opportunities to learn, grow, and develop as clients become the creators of their more rewarding lives.

To collaborate in this process, the practitioner must make a revolutionary shift. Rather than seeing oneself as having expert knowledge about the nature of someone's problem, and therefore able to diagnose it and/or solve it, the practitioner must relinquish this role and, instead, start from a very different place—the place of skilled unknowing. What one learns is that claiming knowledge about people's problems and how to solve them is a false and inevitably frustrating role. In this sense, accepting the role of "not knowing" is an honest and useful one. However, what a strengths-based, solution-oriented practitioner does know is how to help people focus on what they want in their lives and how to uncover and use the resources within and around them to accomplish their goals. The wellspring for this knowledge of process is the practitioner's deep conviction that people do possess much of what they need to construct a more satisfying life. It is this belief in the possible that is the practitioner's most powerful tool in helping others' fashion the life they long to live.

The beauty of this shift toward promise (Saleebey, 2000) is that it not only energizes the person enmeshed in a seemingly intractable problem but it also energizes the practitioner. Rather than being weighed down with cynicism or skepticism in the problem-cycle, the injection of hope provides a powerful antidote to frustration and despair. The act of engaging people in their own solutions, not solutions imposed by the practitioner or outsiders, places them squarely in command of their own lives. For some who have been heavily burdened by a serious, chronic problem, it may be necessary to provide CPR until the spark of hope is ignited. (See Saleebey, Chapter I for more discussion). But for many, the thought that there is a life for them beyond the problem and that the practitioner believes in them and in their capacity to create this is enough to close the door on problems.

Fully embracing this radical stance takes courage. In important ways, the helping professions have been caught in their own problem cycle. Practitioners know that focusing on problems does little to relieve problems and often makes them worse. And yet they continue to pursue, and be required by the mental health establishment to pursue, diagnosis or other problem assessments as the first step in the helping process. Intentionally departing from that expectation can only occur when the practitioner is convinced that finding solutions in the context of people's strengths is the starting point for truly helping people craft a different life. The challenge is to help people find solutions that were there for the finding. By being a collaborator in this process, strength-focused social workers demonstrate a profound recognition of the human capacities for creativity, self-righting, and wisdom that form the deep, sweet core of good social work practice.

DISCUSSION QUESTIONS

1. How do you account for the growing popularity of solution-focused and strengths approaches to practice?

2. What are the key differences between solution-focused and strengths-based practices?

3. How do you get away from clients getting stuck on talking about their problems exclusively?

4. What the client wants is the most important piece of information to be gained from clients. Why is that? What does that mean?

5. Can you see yourself practicing from these perspectives? If so, how? If not, why not?

REFERENCES

American Psychiatric Association (2000). *Diagnostic and Statistical Manual of Mental Disorders IV TR*. Washington, DC: American Psychiatric Association.

Anderson, K. M. (2001). Recovery: Resistance and resilience in female incest survivors. *Doctoral dissertation*. Lawrence, KS: University of Kansas.

Berg, I. K. (1994). *Family based services: A solution focused approach*. New York: Norton.

Berg, I. K., & Miller, S. (1992). *Working with the problem drinker: A solution focused approach*. New York: Norton.

Chamberlain, R. & Rapp, C. A. (1983). *Training Manual for Case Managers in Community Mental Health,* Lawrence, KS: University of Kansas School of Social Welfare.

Cowger, G. (May 1994). Assessing client strengths: Clinical assessment for client empowerment. *Social Work, 39*(4), 262–266.

De Jong, P. and Miller, S. (1995). How to Interview for Client Strengths. *Social Work, 40*(6), 729–736.

de Shazer, S. (1988). *Clues: Investigating solutions in brief therapy.* New York: Norton.

de Shazer, S. (2004). Personal communication.

Duncan, B., Hubble, M., Miller, S., & Coleman, S. (1998). Escaping the lost world of impossibility: Honoring clients' language, motivation, and theories of change. In M. Hoyt (Ed.), *The handbook of constructive therapies,* pp. 293–310.

Early, T. J., and GlenMaye, L. F. (2000). Valuing families: Social work practice with families from a strengths perspective. *Social Work, 45*(2), 118–130.

Gold, N. (1990). Motivation: The crucial but unexplored component of social work practice. *Social Work, 35*(1), 49–55.

Hepworth, D. H., Rooney, R H., and Larson, J. (2002). *Direct Social Work Practice,* 6th Ed. Pacific Grove, CA: Brooks/Cole.

Hillman, J. and Ventura, M. (1992). *We've Had a Hundred Years of Psychotherapy And the World's Getting Worse.* New York: HarperCollins.

Jones, J. & Bricker-Jenkins, M. (2002). Creating strengths-based alliances to end poverty. In D. Saleebey (Ed.). *The strengths perspective in social work practice.* 3rd ed., pp. 186–212. New York: Allyn & Bacon/Longman.

Kisthardt, W. (1993). The impact of the strengths model of case management from the consumer perspective. In M. Harris & H. C. Bergman (Eds.), *Case Management. Theory and Practice.* (pp. 112–125). New York, Longman.

Miller, S., Hubble, M., & Duncan, B. (March/April 1995). No more bells and whistles. *Family Therapy Networker,* 53–63.

Miller, W. R., & Rollnick, S. (2002). *Motivational interviewing: Preparing people for change* (2nd ed.) New York: Guilford Press.

Modrcin, M., Rapp, C. A. & Chamberlain, R. (1985). *Case Management With Psychiatrically Disabled Individuals: Curriculum and Training Program.* Lawrence, KS: University of Kansas School of Social Welfare.

Modrcin, M., Rapp, C. A. and Poertner, John, (1988). "The Evaluation of Case Management Services with the Chronically Mentally Ill, *Evaluation and Program Planning, 11*(4).

National Association of Social workers. (1999). *Code of Ethics of the National Association of Social Workers.* Washington, DC: NASW Press.

Rapp, C. A. (1998). *The strengths model: Case management with people suffering from severe and persistent mental illness.* New York: Oxford University Press.

Rapp, C. A and Chamberlain, R. (September 1985) "Case Management Services to the Chronically Mentally Ill," *Social Work, 30*(5), September 1985, pp. 417–422.

Rapp, C. A. & Wintersteen, R. (1989). The Strengths model of case management: Results from twelve demonstrations. *Psychosocial Rehabilitation Journal, 13,* 23–32.

Rapp, R. C. (2002). Strengths-based case management: Enhancing treatment for persons with substance abuse problems. In D. Saleebey (Ed.), *The strengths perspective in social work practice,* pp. 124–142. New York: Allyn & Bacon/Longman.

Saleebey, D. (Ed.). (2002; 1997; 1992). *The strengths perspective in social work practice.* New York: Allyn & Bacon/Longman.

Saleebey, D. (2000). Power in the people: Strengths and hope. *Advances in Social Work, 1*(2), 127–136.

Walsh, F. (1998). *Strengthening family resilience.* New York: Guilford Press.

Weick, A., & Chamberlain, R. (2002). Putting problems in their place: Further explorations in the strengths perspective. In D. Saleebey (Ed.), *The strengths perspective in social work practice,* pp.95–105. New York: Longman.

Weick, A., Rapp, C. A., Sullivan, W. P., & Kisthardt, W. E. (1989). A Strengths perspective for social work practice. *Social Work, 89,* 350–354.

■ ■ ■ ■ ■

CHAPTER EIGHT

STRENGTHS-BASED CASE MANAGEMENT

Enhancing Treatment for Persons with Substance Abuse Problems

RICHARD C. RAPP

INTRODUCTION

An opportunity to examine the impact of strengths-based case management (SBCM) on reducing attrition from treatment, and improving outcomes among persons with substance abuse problems, presented itself in a 1990 National Institute on Drug Abuse initiative. Over eleven years two projects were developed by addictions researchers at the Center for Interventions, Treatment and Addictions Research (C.I.T.A.R.) at Wright State University's School of Medicine. Led by Dr. Harvey A. Siegal, SBCM was designed as a long-term (up to one year) intervention to encourage crack cocaine users to participate in aftercare (post-primary) services by helping them with a wide array of personal and social problems. Details surrounding the development and implementation of these projects have been discussed elsewhere (Rapp, 1997; Rapp et al., 1993; Siegal et al., 1995).

Over the course of eleven years we have become increasingly knowledgeable about the skill set that is compatible with the implementation of a strengths approach. As a result the description of practice activities has been expanded compared to earlier versions of *The Strengths Perspective in Social Work Practice*. Also present from earlier editions is a presentation of key findings from both qualitative and quantitative studies. These findings directly inform practice activities and provide case managers with ideas that will encourage clients to stay involved in treatment and access needed resources.

The final part of this chapter will discuss our adaptation of SBCM from a long-term approach to a brief model oriented toward accomplishing specific,

Acknowledgment: The projects described here were supported by funding from the National Institute on Drug Abuse (Grants No. DA 06944 and DA15690) and the Centers for Disease Control and Prevention.

focused goals. The first opportunity to develop a brief, five session intervention that would encourage persons who had just been diagnosed with AIDS to follow-through with health care. This multi-site trial (Los Angeles, Miami, Baltimore, Atlanta) was supported by the Centers for Disease Control and Prevention. Early data from the trial suggest that individuals receiving the brief SBCM intervention are more likely to follow-through with medical care.

The second instance of using a brief model of SBCM is currently underway. In the Reducing Barriers Project (DA15690), a National Institute on Drug Abuse project, we are testing the effectiveness of a five session model of SBCM in facilitating treatment linkage and engagement among persons with substance abuse problems. This effort stems from findings that fewer than four in ten clients follow through with treatment following their assessment at a county-wide intake facility. The resulting costs to treatment providers, the community, and individuals are significant.

STRENGTHS-BASED CASE MANAGEMENT WITH PERSONS WHO HAVE SUBSTANCE ABUSE PROBLEMS

A long history of both clinical practice and empirical observations have documented a wide range of needs among persons with substance abuse problems (Oppenheimer, Sheehan, & Taylor, 1988; Westermeyer, 1989). The problems experienced by these individuals are frequently present before the onset of substance abuse and many are a direct result of abuse: homelessness, unemployment, unsafe living environments, and poor health. Several models of case management—generalist, assertive community treatment, strengths-based—have been successfully adapted from the mental health field to assist clients to access and successfully use resources aimed at alleviating these problems (Martin & Scarpitti, 1993; Siegal, Rapp, Li, Saha, & Kirk, 1997; Willenbring, Ridgely, Stinchfield, & Rose, 1991). Each of the case management models rely on practice activities that make up the core functions of assessment, planning, coordination, monitoring, and advocacy.

A strengths approach to the basic case management functions provides a "value added" element to the basic case management functions. Strengths-based case management was originally implemented with persons being discharged from long-term hospitalization for mental illness (Modrcin, Rapp, & Chamberlain, 1985). The spirit of the intervention is found in five principles.

1. *Strengths, abilities, and assets should form the basis for the helping relationship.* Central to SBCM is the belief that clients are most successful when they identify and use their strengths, abilities, and assets. The process of enumerating and using personal strengths allows clients to appreciate their own past efficacy, encourages motivation, and sets the stage for identifying and achieving goals.
2. *Control over goal-setting and the search for needed resources will remain with the client.* All goal-setting is guided by the client's perceptions of their own needs. The role of the case manager is to assist the client in making goals specific, to discuss alternatives, and to identify available resources. Underlying this principle is the belief that clients will participate most fully in treatment if

they are in charge of goals which are really theirs, as opposed to goals which are dictated by others.

3. *The client-case manager relationship is promoted as primary.* The case manager serves as the consistent figure in the client's treatment experience and is thereby able to coordinate fragmented and poorly coordinated resources. A strong relationship allows the case manager to advocate for the client as necessary. Far from being an exclusive relationship, the client and case manager will involve many other persons in the search for resources.

4. *The community is viewed as a resource and not a barrier.* SBCM assumes that a creative approach to use of the community will lead to discovery of needed resources. In working with formal resources—housing agencies, job training programs—case managers assist clients by modeling and practicing behaviors which increase the likelihood of a successful contact. Whenever possible case managers encourage clients to explore informal resources—friends, neighbors, other clients—as a source of assistance.

5. *Case management is conducted as an active, community-based activity.* Office-based contacts are minimized; case managers meet with clients in the community—in their home, at their work site, etc. For the case manager, this activity will inevitably lead to an increased appreciation of the challenges clients face in making changes. For the client these meetings provide an opportunity to develop and master skills where they actually live. In turn, this focus helps clients to break an often too prevalent reliance on institutional settings for assistance.

Using this perspective, case managers can assist clients in any or all of nine life domains encompassing: basic life skills, finances, relationships, leisure, health, internal resources, occupation/education, living situation, and recovery.

THE PRACTICE OF STRENGTHS-BASED CASE MANAGEMENT

While it is relatively easy to articulate general principles concerning "strengths-based practice," it is decidedly more difficult to actually implement an intervention that holds to such principles. The following sections provide ideas for activities that operationalize strengths-based case management. These techniques include actions that occur: 1.) before the case manager meets with a client; 2.) while establishing a relationship; 3.) conducting a strengths-based assessment, and; 4.) engaging the client in a meaningful case management planning process. All of these activities must be viewed in the context of the numerous issues that complicate strict adherence to the ideal, including: workers' training in pathology-based models, resistance from co-workers, and a wide range of organizational and system-based factors (Siegal et al., 1995).

Preparation.   It is imperative to the successful practice of SBCM that case managers are equipped with certain knowledge, skills, and beliefs *before* beginning work with clients. Knowledge and skills should include a thorough knowledge of substance abuse issues, basic counseling and case management skills, as well as empathetic and constructive attitudes toward persons who are substance abusers. Proficiency in intervention approaches such as motivational interviewing and problem-solving approaches are extremely useful.

The case manager should also develop an extensive network of referral sources with formal service providers, as well as natural or informal sources of assistance. This information will affect the degree of trust that clients have in case managers' actions, and ultimately, on how effective case managers are in assisting clients. The steps involved in this activity include:

- Obtaining a directory of generally recognized resources in each area where clients will have needs, including: substance abuse treatment, general and specific health care, mental health treatment, housing, etc.
- Providing a directory of less recognized resources from previous experience and from contacts with other case managers who work with substance abuse clients. These resources are frequently small and may be faith-based and/or operated by individuals who are not part of an agency.
- Contacting as many resources as possible and arranging for a meeting with the staff who are responsible for admitting clients to the resource.
- Asking admitting staff to orient you to the usual application and screening process. If applicable ask to "shadow" the treatment staff.
- Noting significant differences between the actual and "official" requirements for the program.
- Compiling a list of program requirements and personal documents that the client will need to have in order to facilitate admission to needed services.
- Creating an easy to use referral directory for clients that incorporate both the official requirements of resources as well as informal, helpful hints that will be advantageous to the client.

It is critical in preparing to engage clients in a strengths-based relationship for the worker to have a "strengths attitude." While somewhat intangible it can best be recognized in case managers who appreciate the five strengths principles, especially those that call for focusing on client strengths and allowing clients to really identify the goals that they want to work on. An example of a strengths attitude is the case manager's willingness to *not* read the client's substance abuse assessment, case history, or medical record prior to their first meeting with the client. In this way, case managers are less likely to predefine the client in terms of their diagnosis and problems. While ignoring the problems and needs of clients would be negligent, it is an assumption of strengths-based practice that the most appropriate place to hear about those needs is directly from the client and not through the filter of records passed down from previous treatment episodes.

Engagement.   It is critical that case managers begin their first meeting with a client listening to a client's view of why they are seeking services. Every effort should be made to ensure that this activity is central to the meeting. The meeting between case manager and client is vital to the development of a positive working relationship and encouraging clients to stay involved in the helping relationship toward the achievement of the client's goals. In order to stimulate the development of the relationship and initiate the strengths approach several cautions are appropriate:

- Don't be overly concerned about the client's stated motivation for having attended the first contact with the case manager.
- Remember that every client has already surmounted some barriers to follow through with the meeting. In addition to practical considerations, e.g., transportation to the appointment, there are likely a wide range of emotions leading up to this contact, including fear, anger, distrust, helplessness, and fatalism.
- Be cautious about self-disclosure at this point. Until the case manager learns more about their client they cannot know how any disclosure such as, "I'm in recovery" will affect a given client.
- Demonstrate attentiveness to what the client is saying. This can only come from a genuine interest in their situation.

At some time during the session case managers should describe their professional experience, specifically as it applies to helping people gain access to services that they need and dealing with barriers that people have in entering those services. This explanation is meant to encourage the client's confidence that the case manager can be of assistance to them. This point must of course consider the overall program constraints under which the case manager (and the client) must operate.

Case managers should explain the nature of strengths-based work and help the client understand the relationship between identifying their strengths, assets, and skills and being able to acquire the resources that they need. The explanation could be as follows:

> "When we can see ways that we've been successful in the past it can help us to figure out how to be successful again. Knowing how you've been successful will help you plan how to deal with any barriers or problems you might experience."

A tangible example of this can occur when the case manager cites examples of strengths, assets, and abilities that they have already noticed in the client. Common examples in this situation might include coming to the case management appointment, being assertive, etc. The case manager should suggest to clients that they do an assessment that will help them identify their strengths. If sufficient time is available the strengths assessment can be started during the first meeting with the client, if not, case managers should let client know that they will do it during their next meeting.

The case manager should attempt to end this first contact by offering to assist the client in some immediate, tangible manner, such as helping the client's family avoid having electric service disconnected or retrieving clothing from a temporary housing situation.

In closing out the first session it is important to remember that in situations where a great deal of emotional content is present and where a lot of new information has been presented it is likely that the client will miss or forget key pieces of information. As a result the case manager should summarize what has taken place during the session. In some cases the client may be asked to summarize the session.

Strengths-Based Assessment

During this contact it is important that the case manager actively set the stage for what is to follow, an emphasis on client's past and present abilities, skills, assets, and strengths to handle difficult situations. If not started earlier a strengths assessment should be initiated during the second meeting. A strengths assessment is the opposite of most assessments, its aim is to reacquaint, or in many cases acquaint clients for the first time, with their strengths and assets. Discussions are focused on clients' ability to accomplish a task, use a skill, and have or fulfill a goal in a significant area of their life. Discussions of topics such as arrest record, drug use, and failures are avoided.

A strengths assessment is intended to accomplish three critical goals. First, and most importantly, it allows clients an opportunity to consciously and precisely identify instances where they have been successful as a result of their own actions and abilities. Identification of these instances will be used by the client and case manager to identify future needs and the steps necessary to acquiring needed resources.

The interaction that is prompted by a discussion of client strengths and abilities will encourage the development of a positive, trusting relationship between client and case manager. This relationship can serve to encourage client follow-through with treatment. Furthermore, the focus on strengths helps case managers avoid being drawn into the skepticism and hopelessness that frequently is experienced by persons confronting numerous life challenges.

Conducting the Strengths Assessment

A clear introduction of the strengths assessment is important. Although the specific introduction will be guided by the client's particular characteristics, e.g., reading level, cognitive ability, an introduction to the strength assessment might proceed as follows:

> "One of the activities that can help guide you in identifying your needs will be a strengths assessment. This assessment is very different than past assessments that you might have participated in with social service workers. It is designed to help you recognize your strengths, skills, abilities, and things that you're good at doing. We have found that when people can recognize what they are good at it helps them accomplish difficult goals. By recognizing areas where you've been successful you will be in a better position to accomplish goals you want to accomplish and to take the steps necessary to follow-through with treatment. You may already be aware of these strengths; they may be something that you haven't thought about for a long time or never have thought about. It may be difficult to keep the focus on strengths because we are usually taught that it is boasting or bragging to talk about what we've done right. I don't think that's the case. I think it reminds us of how we can get what we need."

Two similar approaches can be taken in conducting the strengths assessment; both can accomplish relationship building, information gathering, and encouraging the client. In the first approach the case manager may open up the discussion with very general questions such as:

- "What strengths do you think you have?"
- "What are you abilities?"
- "When have you successfully faced barriers, and what did you do to face them?"
- "What are you good at?"
- "When was a time that you felt like most things were going well and what were you doing to make them go well?"

A general discussion will allow both case manager and client to note a wide range of strengths, many of which will be applicable to the client's goals.

A second approach to conducting the strengths assessment would have the case manager using a list of strengths, organized by life areas, as a prompt. This approach might be introduced by: "I've found that some of the following strengths are valuable to a person who is facing a situation like yours. Let's go through some of the list and see what fits for you." Such a list is intended to stimulate discussion. The discussion should help to establish a positive relationship and help clients to believe that they possess the ability to directly address the issue of being addicted. This list is not exhaustive, covering strengths in all life areas. The case manager and client need not address every item on the list and can certainly add items that are not on the list. Remind the client that there are no correct answers, and that some of the items on the list may not apply to them.

The case manager should remember two points about the strengths assessment, whether it is conducted as an open-ended discussion or a loosely structured interview. First, if possible, it is valuable to write down the strengths, assets, or skills that the client identifies. The format for doing so is not as important as is the opportunity for the client to see, in writing, a list of their own positive attributes. A copy of the list should be offered to the client.

Secondly, the case manager should remember that the strengths assessment is an on-going process rather than a discrete event. Clients will choose to share on their own terms, possibly at times when the case manager least expects it. For that reason the case manager should continue to emphasize the search for assets and abilities in every contact with a client, whether working on a case management plan or while engaging in general conversation. By doing this the case manager provides the client with every opportunity to pick their own time to share and helps the client understand the day-to-day presence and relevance of their strengths.

Several other critical points should be remembered when conducting the strengths assessment. These include:

- The case manager must believe in the search for strengths and abilities. Most clients, by the nature of the lifestyles that they have led, are extremely adept at spotting someone who is being condescending or patronizing.
- Many of the persons who become addicted have been confronted by numerous negative events in their lives. These events may involve substance abuse,

condemnation of their lifestyle, etc. A strengths assessment stands out as a significantly different approach for addressing their needs. It may be necessary to gently refocus clients back to strengths and away from an endless discussion of problems and deficiencies.

- Case managers should remind themselves and their clients that they are not ignoring important problems in doing strengths assessment. The focus on strengths and abilities will prepare them for the next step, identifying goals that are important to them, and that will also help them follow through with assessment and drug treatment.

- Be careful about reaching too far to find strengths, for instance suggesting to a client that, "You've been a 'successful' sex worker (or drug dealer or homeless person), let's talk about your strengths in that area." If a client suggests such a characteristic is a strength make sure to prompt them to identify how those characteristics can be readily adapted to a healthier lifestyle.

- Clients will sometimes attempt to give someone else the credit for their strengths and/or for times in their lives when things are going well. Emphasize the client's role in making things go right; gently insist that they must have had a hand in things going well.

- Periodically summarize strengths that you have heard, even if the client has not explicitly stated these as strengths. At the same time check out with the client whether they perceive those actions, thoughts, or feelings as strengths. Don't merely impose your view of some characteristic as strength, but assist the client in considering that it might be strength. Ultimately it is the client's perception of something as a positive in their life that will enable them to mobilize it to solve current problems.

- Avoid acting as "inquisitor" or "investigator," assume a role as "consultant" and "facilitator" in the search for abilities.

- Keep the goal of the strengths assessment, i.e., to identify goals that will help the client to seek treatment, an honest part of all discussions. Don't make this a hidden agenda that will prompt the case manager to covertly try to "steer" the client.

Collecting Non-Strengths Information.   Although the emphasis of SBCM is on identifying client strengths it is sometimes appropriate and necessary to good clinical practice to collect information that is not "strengths-based." Examples of this type of information include:

- Suicidal ideation or attempts.
- Risk to do harm to others.
- Physical problems associated with substance abuse, including risk of overdose, delirium tremors, or drug withdrawal.
- Inherent limitations such as not being able to read, having learning difficulties, physical impairments, etc.

When collecting this type of information the case manager should remember to treat the client as an individual and not just as a member of a group with problems.

Case Management Planning

Perhaps the most critical aspect of the case manager-client relationship is identifying needed resources and making plans to secure those resources. While this activity could be merely a verbal agreement between worker and client it is valuable to commit the plan to writing. Doing so provides clients with a tangible, visual document that identifies their goals and the steps necessary to accomplish them. It also increases the importance of the plan by virtue of its being committed to writing. Last, it can provide clients with a firm record of their accomplishments. Even if specific activities are not successfully carried out the written plan can guide the client and case manager in determining what the next steps are in starting over on a goal or objective.

There is no strictly prescribed notion of what a case management plan form should look like. It is useful for the plan to have the following elements though, including places to record them: Goals, Objectives, Strategies, Person responsible for, and target dates for each objective and strategy. If feasible a place where the client can record any potential barriers to the objective being completed might be additionally useful.

It is important to introduce the case management planning tool in a way that demonstrates that it can be a very simple tool, one in which the client senses a personal ownership. An example of introducing the plan might be:

> "One of the activities that can help guide you in accomplishing your goals and the program's goal will be for us to write everything down on a Contact Plan. This plan will help us to organize our work together and make sure that we are anticipating everything we need to work on. We have found that when people can recognize what they are good at it helps them accomplish difficult goals. We'll commit them to writing to remind us of what we're doing; you will always have a copy of your most current case management plan."

Identifying Goals.   From an open-ended question, "What do you need/want to accomplish," clients begin to identify goals in various life domains. Goal statements are written as broad statements, always in the exact words of the client. Using a client's own words decreases the distance between the client and responsibility for accomplishing goals. Further, it eliminates the possibility that case mangers might inadvertently alter the goal to something that they (the case manager) believes is more important. In the end clients must embrace their own goal if they are to be successful. An example of a goal statement might be: "I wanna get a job that I like."

Creating Objectives and Strategies.   Objectives and strategies are the specific working steps necessary to accomplish a client's goals. Both are measurable, identifying a concrete action. Two specific objectives for the goal of "I wanna get a job that I like." might include, "Objective 1: Take and pass the Graduation Equivalency Degree (GED) exam" and "Objective 2: Complete a course on identifying job interests at Smith Vocational School." Strategies are specific activities that lead to accomplishment of an objective. Examples of strategies used to accomplish Objective 1 might include obtaining a GED application, studying a GED work guide ten hours each week and scheduling an appointment for taking the GED. The establishment of target and review dates for each objective and strategy prompts periodic review of client progress.

Detailed attention to the creation of objectives and strategies and systematic review of their outcome is powerful at two levels. First, clients learn an approach to solving problems that is transferable from the treatment setting to their lives outside the treatment milieu. Second, clients have the opportunity to evaluate their own progress in very personal, specific terms. Even in not completing some of their identified tasks clients have support and feedback to learn from the experience. One former client discussed his work with his case manager: "I had a case manager who had me write every little step down, plan out every day what I was gonna do. I was so used to planning on big things and never seein' 'em get done. It was great to see some progress every day" (Brun & Rapp, 2001). The overall effect of this goal setting process specifically and the strengths-based approach generally is that clients are in the position to take responsibility for their own treatment.

While work on goals, objectives, and strategies is always guided by the client's wishes, the case manager lends support to the process of goal-setting by reminding the client of identified strengths, assisting in making objectives specific, discussing alternatives, contributing a knowledge of existing resources, and by advocating for the client as they attempt to access those resources.

Additional Considerations.   Several other points should be considered when completing a case management plan. The case manager should:

- Be attentive to the client's ability to effectively think through a plan, commit it to writing, and then successfully carry it out. While some clients may indeed be very competent at achieving goals, others will engage in wishful thinking, procrastination, and other thought processes that interfere with movement forward in their lives.
- Be precise in helping a client define measurable objectives and the activities necessary to accomplish those objectives. The more specific you encourage clients to be the more likely they are to think through the alternative solutions that they can use to influence their situation.
- Remember to encourage clients to use the strengths they have discussed as the starting point for planning how to accomplish objectives. Periodically summarize strengths that you have heard. At the same time check out with clients whether they perceive those actions, thoughts, or feelings as strengths. Unless the client seems unable to recognize or acknowledge strength don't merely impose your view of something as a strength, but assist the client in making that decision. Ultimately it is the client's perception of something as a positive in their life that will mobilize them to solve current problems.
- Avoid acting as "savior" or "disinterested party"; assume the role of "traveling companion" in the objectives that the client has identified.
- Be creative with clients and when possible come up with a solution that gets at several barriers at once. The fact that they frequently have so many barriers is overwhelming and your ability to help them to deal with several issues at once will be greatly appreciated.

STRENGTHS-BASED CASE MANAGEMENT: MEASURING ITS IMPACT

The goal of two NIDA-funded companion projects, the Enhanced Treatment Project (ETP) and Case Management Enhancements Project (CME), was to assess the impact that a strengths-based model of case management had on: 1.) improving treatment retention among persons with substance abuse problems and 2.) improving treatment outcomes. Besides substance abuse problems, these primarily crack cocaine-involved Vietnam era males suffered from many of the problems which case management has traditionally been expected to address. These problems include homelessness, lack of adequate employment, and uncoordinated involvement with numerous social service agencies.

The initial project (ETP) was designed to have case managers meet with veterans immediately following their entry into primary substance abuse treatment. These contacts with 632 veterans, enrolled between September 1991 and December 1994, were intended to promote clients' continued involvement in the early stages of treatment and establish a relationship between client and case manager that could then serve as the basis for work during the aftercare (post-primary) treatment period. Case managers in the second project, CME, met with more than 400 clients in the latter stages of primary treatment and conducted their work with them from a community-based site rather than medical center grounds. Case management and post-primary services were highly integrated.

Eligibility for both projects was based on the veteran's use of any cocaine or heroin in the preceding six months or being a regular user of other drugs during that time and not being in treatment in the preceding three months. Veterans experiencing substance abuse problems were assigned randomly at entry to treatment to receive one of two treatment conditions, traditional twelve steps, medical model-oriented treatment *or* traditional treatment and a case manager using a strengths-based approach. Follow-up interviews, generally conducted in six month waves, took place with both samples, for five and two years with ETP and CME subjects, respectively.

The following findings primarily provide results from the ETP and some tentative results from the CME. Three areas are covered: case management mediated retention in treatment, outcomes associated with case management, and the characteristics of strengths-based case management that appear to influence retention and outcomes.

SBCM and Retention in Treatment

One of the reasons for implementing strengths-based case management was the belief that the approach would encourage clients to continue their participation in treatment activities, activities related both to primary treatment and aftercare. While a complete discussion of case management's role in retaining clients in treatment is beyond the scope of this chapter, several points warrant mention.

Retention in the Enhanced Treatment Project.   Most ETP clients completed a four-week course of *primary inpatient* treatment (N=349/394; 89%) with little difference between clients receiving strengths case management (N=180/201; 90%) and non case managed clients (N=169/193; 88%). In contrast, attrition was quite high from *primary outpatient* treatment with only 50% of case managed clients completing a six-week course of treatment as compared to 36% of non case managed clients (31/62 vs. 21/58).

Similarities persisted between the two groups when examining participation in *post-primary* treatment. Case managed clients were only somewhat more likely to start relapse prevention treatment than non case managed clients (52% vs. 49%) and on average stayed slightly longer (5.45 weeks vs. 4.54 weeks). In summary, case management did not seem to significantly enhance treatment retention, at least when retention was viewed in the context of participation in relapse prevention.

A closer examination of the case management group during the aftercare period revealed an interesting phenomenon. Case managed clients demonstrated a strong tendency to select participation in case management services during the post-primary period over participation in relapse prevention services. While only 52% of clients in this group attended at least one session of relapse prevention following their discharge from primary treatment, 66% of the case managed clients attended at least one session with their case manager after completion of primary treatment. Thirty-five percent of clients reported up to 20 weeks of contact with their case managers while only 11% of clients attended the same amount of relapse prevention activities. A similar gap, up to 21%, between case management and relapse prevention attendance persisted until the end of the six-month follow-up period.

Explaining Retention among Case-Managed Clients.   A subsequent analysis attempted to determine what characteristics of the case management group (N=313) were related to the selection of case management during the post-primary treatment period. In order to do this, a cluster analytic technique was used to describe the clients in the case-managed group and their use of services following primary treatment (Siegal et al., 1997).

Two variables, weeks in case management and weeks in aftercare treatment, were used to cluster the subjects. Descriptive comparisons among the clusters were conducted using such baseline measures as: 1.) demographic characteristics including age, marital status, ethnicity, gender, and educational level; 2.) measures of psychosocial functioning, including drug use, employment status, criminal justice involvement and; 3.) scales measuring motivation for treatment and psychiatric status.

Clusters were also compared on nine specific indicators representing three dimensions of treatment outcomes: drug use (cocaine, marijuana), participation in self-help groups, and improved social functioning (employment, staying out of the criminal justice system).

Analyses revealed the presence of three distinct groups of clients: 1.) those who quickly dropped out of post-primary treatment services, i.e., both aftercare and case management (N=133); 2.) those who stayed in both aftercare and case management for most of the follow-up period (N=44) and; 3.) those who retained significantly longer contact with their case managers during the post-primary treatment period (N=81).

Three findings were of particular significance. First, all three groups were remarkably similar at the time of admission to treatment on demographic characteristics, level of motivation and the severity of substance abuse, psychiatric, and other problems. This suggests that the search for reasons for treatment retention differences were likely related to what happened *during* treatment and not on *a priori* differences in clients. Practically, this also suggests that there are no obvious pre-existing characteristics that would lead treatment programs to pre-select clients as more or less appropriate candidates for successful treatment.

Second, our data suggest that had it not been for the case management enhancement an additional one-third of the overall sample—those who retained significantly longer contact with their case managers—would have dropped out after primary treatment. Last, at six months following entry into treatment clients who retained contact with only case management services demonstrated outcomes as favorably as clients who remained with *both* case management and aftercare regimens. While case management was implemented as an enhancement, or adjunct to traditional aftercare services, this finding suggests that case management services may also be useful *alternatives* to traditional aftercare.

Together these findings suggested that case manager's time would be spent more productively in improving participation during the post-primary treatment period and assisting veterans in reintegrating into the community. As a result, case management in the successor CME project was attached directly to the aftercare component in a community-based, as opposed to medical center-based, location.

SBCM AND CRITICAL OUTCOMES

Three areas—drug use, employment functioning, criminal justice involvement—are consistently considered measures of the success of clients' recovery from substance abuse problems and thereby important areas which treatment should address. Consequently we examined the impact that SBCM had on these three areas of client functioning.

Multivariate analyses were conducted to explore the relationship between strengths-based case management and drug use (Rapp, Siegal, Li, & Saha, 1998). A second study explored SBCM's relationship with criminal justice involvement (Siegal, Li, & Rapp, 2002). In both cases subjects who received the case management intervention stayed in treatment for longer periods of time. The longer period of treatment engagement was in turn related to lower levels of drug use and less involvement in illegal activities during the six months following discharge from primary treatment. Unlike previous studies that have attempted to explain case management's role in terms of its direct effects on outcomes, we find that its value may lie in encouraging substance abusers to remain longer in treatment during the critical period after primary treatment is completed.

Beyond assisting individuals to reduce their involvement with harmful substances and illegal activities, a central goal of case management was to help individuals become more productive in their employment functioning (Siegal et al., 1996). Veterans from both case managed and noncase managed groups who indicated they were "extremely interested" in assistance with employment problems were selected for comparison. This grouping was used to eliminate clients who were already successfully employed and those who were not considering employment by virtue of a disability or other reason. Among the 193 subjects expressing great interest in employment issues significant differences were found between non-case managed and case managed clients. Case managed clients were employed for significantly more days, reported fewer days of employment problems, felt "less troubled" about their employment status and saw "less need" for employment counseling.

EXPLAINING THE IMPACT OF SBCM

The previously cited studies encouraged researchers and practitioners alike to identify the mechanism of action by which strengths-based case management exerts an influence. Two areas inherent in the strengths approach merit consideration. The first area is the client-driven nature of goal-setting, facilitated by case managers' assistance in teaching clients *how* to set goals. Direct control over the goals they set and the steps taken to accomplish these goals may provide clients an opportunity to mobilize their heightened awareness of personal strengths. A second factor that may have an impact on encouraging substance abusers to remain in treatment and be successful is the nature of the therapeutic relationship formed between case manager and patient. In addressing strengths, encouraging client control over their own treatment, and teaching a process of goal-setting case managers are likely to develop a particularly strong relationship with clients.

Client Driven/Case Manager Facilitated
Treatment Planning

The SBCM case management plan proved to be an especially powerful tool that provided clients an opportunity to identify those areas they saw as most immediate to their well-being and a structure in which to operationalize their abilities as the vehicles for accomplishing that work.

As discussed earlier, development of the case management plan was guided by clients' perceptions of their own needs. Goals were operationalized through the establishment of specific target dates for the objectives and strategies that comprised each goal. In addition client and case manager affixed an outcome of "completed" or "not completed" to each objective and "used" or "not used" to each strategy. "Revised" was used when either an objective or strategy was altered before its termination date.

Almost two thirds of objectives (64%) and strategies (65%) were accomplished by clients. Ranges for completion rates for both objectives and strategies were quite similar ranging from 58% (leisure) to 77% (living arrangements) and 57% (leisure) to 76% (living arrangements) respectively. On average 2.4 objectives were completed for each goal and 2.7 strategies developed for each objective. No comparable measure of goal attainment was available for the work undertaken by clients with other treatment staff, including their substance abuse counselor. While treatment plans were developed as a part of relapse prevention activities, the goals were not created or reviewed in such a way that allowed for systematic measurement of completion.

Another source of information that spoke to the value of creating case management plans came from clients' view of what was beneficial in their work with case managers and with other treatment staff. As part of a series of questions administered at the six-month follow-up interview clients were asked to respond to the question, "What is the single most helpful topic which you worked on?" The question was asked of all clients about their work with their substance abuse counselor and, for those clients who were assigned a case manager, for work with them as well. Client responses were recorded verbatim by project interviewers and then independently classified by two members of the project's scientific team. The raters then arrived at a consensus classification for each response. Although clients were asked to identify a single topic they sometimes identified more than one, in these cases multiple classifications were assigned.

Originally the responses were to be placed into one of the nine life domains or one of two other categories of interest to the team. These two additional categories focused on 1.) "neutral" presentation of cognitive, emotional, or psychological functioning or 2.) presentation of "negative" or deficit-oriented cognitions, emotions, or psychological functioning. In other words, what terms did clients use in presenting their own perceptions of what was helpful to them. It should be noted that "positive," healthy, or constructive terms were coded under the "internal resources" life domain. In addition three other categories developed from client responses. These three categories included: 1.) relationship with their case manager or substance abuse counselor; 2.) no topic seen as most helpful and; 3.) assistance in learning how to set goals. Of significance to our discussion here is the frequent mention of assistance in developing goals relative to work with case managers. Thirty-six percent of clients identified "working on goals," "setting life goals," etc. as the most helpful topic they worked on with their case managers. In contrast only 1 percent of clients recognized this type of assistance in their work with their substance abuse counselor.

These two findings, rate of objective and strategy completion and client perception of the value of goal-setting, illustrate the practical importance of clients' controlling their own course of treatment. Simply put, clients were likely to complete those plans that they had been instrumental in creating and seemed to value the skills they had learned (goal-setting) as well as other forms of assistance, i.e., accessing resources. Obviously, the ability to systematically set goals, and successfully accomplish them, are skills that can be used independently by the client. Of course, some limitations in these findings exist given the inability to compare the outcomes between plans created under SBCM and under the disease concept.

NATURE OF THE CASE MANAGER-CLIENT RELATIONSHIP

A series of ethnographic interviews provided additional information about clients' perceptions of the important elements of strengths-based case management (Brun & Rapp, 2001). The emphasis on individuals' strengths and abilities is the most important principle of strengths-based work and emerged frequently in individuals' stories although "strengths" became "positives" in the lexicon of these individuals. At the same time positives were not always readily accepted by these individuals, although for a different reason than previously anticipated. A practice implication is that strengths-based practitioners have generally assumed that individuals would be uncomfortable with looking at evidence of their own abilities because of guilt and a lack of familiarity with considering their strengths. At least one individual suggested that trusting the positive things that someone says may leave one vulnerable to being taken advantage of by persons in a drug-using culture.

In describing their treatment experience individuals found room for both a discussion of negatives and positives, of pathology and assets. While the remaining presence of pathology in individuals' perceptions about themselves may be disconcerting to strengths-based practitioners, individuals suggest otherwise. The balance that comes from the presence of both approaches—strengths and disease—results from what one client related was the ability to heal after "put[ting] it [negatives about one's use] out on the table." A practice implication is that it is possible that strengths-based staff underestimated the useful role that reflecting on problems, at least problems related to the use of substance abuse, may play in the treatment process.

Individuals described reactions to being asked to remember a time in their life when they were doing well and acting on their strengths. Individual comments included: "I can be creative," "I'm more confident," "I can weigh the positives and negatives," "It gives me my choices back," "I can be a winner," "An addict needs to hear he's doing good," "I haven't been asked about strengths in a long time," and "It [the strengths assessment] showed what I accomplished." One client in particular summed this up best with:

> "You have to bring out the negatives in order to start healing. But there's a time to stop all that negative stuff, too. You know treatment is to get you to put it on the table . . . After it's brought out, you've talked about it, it's kicked around, and it's out in the open, it gets better. You have to get that stuff out before you heal."

The second important principle of the strength-based intervention discerned in this study was the importance of the professional relationship between individuals and the case managers. References to the case manager as a "big sister" who will "check on me" cast the relationship in friendly, intimate terms. Individuals in this study, like the consumers of mental health services noted by Kisthardt (Rapp et al., 1993), indicated that the relational aspects of case management were important in helping them make changes in their lives. Even individuals who were not successful had positive feelings about the assistance they had received from their case manager.

Similarly, clients described the case manager relationship in ways that seem to indicate an intense joining together to accomplish specific tasks: "Someone else is seeing what I need to do," "I don't have to keep it (goals) all in my head," "She becomes a piece of my conscience," "She helps me keep my train of thought," "Hearing her voice motivates me," and "I didn't know nobody would care that much." One client shared the impact that the case manager's commitment had on him:

> "She is like a big sister. She is there checking on me. She says, 'So, you behavin' yourself?' I say, 'Yeah'. She says, 'I haven't heard from you. Are you okay?' That helps that she calls and checks on me like that. I got to keep my nose clean."

An appreciation of the strengths process and sense of a strong positive relationship with their case managers combined at times to create a personal dissonance for individuals. On the one hand they wanted to embrace their own strengths and the relationship with their case manager while at the same time they were being pulled away from both by internal and external pressures. Internal events such as depression and substance abuse, combined with external forces, such as friends and family, can wear away the gains made early in the process.

STRENGTHS-BASED CASE MANAGEMENT AS A BRIEF INTERVENTION

Strengths-based case management was originally conceived as a long-term intervention for clients with significant life challenges. Originally SBCM was used to support clients leaving long-term hospitalization in psychiatric hospitals (Rapp & Chamberlain, 1985). In this instance case management support could continue for years. When SBCM was adapted to encourage retention in treatment among crack cocaine users it was also conceived of as a longer term intervention, lasting up to one year.

During the last two years, researchers at Wright State University's Center for Intervention, Treatment and Addictions Research have been involved in two studies to test the effectiveness of SBCM as a brief intervention. In both studies SBCM was designed to improve the linkage of clients with specific treatment services, in one instance medical care for AIDS and in the second, substance abuse treatment. The time-limited nature of the intervention was driven by the structure of available services and by individual client needs. While the outcomes of these studies are not yet available both have raised specific challenges in adapting a long-term, strengths-based model of case management to a brief format, usually five sessions.

Anti-Retroviral Treatment Access Study (ARTAS). Based on findings that SBCM encouraged substance abusing clients to stay in treatment and achieve improved outcomes, researchers at CITAR developed a brief model of strengths-based case management designed to improve the linkage of newly diagnosed HIV positive persons with medical care. The Anti-Retroviral Treatment Access Study (ARTAS) is a multi-site clinical trial (Los Angeles, Atlanta, Baltimore, Miami) supported by the Centers for Disease Control and Prevention. Early data from the trial suggest that individuals receiving the brief SBCM intervention are more likely to follow-through with medical care.

Reducing Barriers Project.   The second instance of using a brief model of SBCM is currently underway. In the Reducing Barriers Project, a National Institute on Drug Abuse project, CITAR researchers are testing the effectiveness of a five session model of SBCM in facilitating linkage with substance abuse treatment and on-going engagement with treatment. The effort stems from findings that fewer than four in ten clients with substance abuse problem follow-through with treatment following their assessment at a county-wide intake facility.

SBCM—Challenges as a Brief Intervention

Perhaps the most significant challenge in implementing the two brief models of SBCM is the pre-defined nature of the case management goals. In ARTAS case management is expected to encourage clients to follow-through with medical care following their diagnosis of being HIV positive; in the Reducing Barriers Project case managers are to help clients identify barriers to following-through with treatment recommendations. While both goals might seem unconditionally positive not all potential clients will have that perspective on receiving case management services. Any number of barriers, both internal and external, client and system based may lead clients to resist recommendations to seek services.

Following the principles of SBCM the idea of a pre-defined goal, created by program developers and carried out by case managers, is potentially troubling. It is an understood premise of SBCM that clients identify their own goals, objectives, and strategies without interference. Case managers are there to support, offer suggestions, and provide information to clients seeking out their own goals. With a programmatically established goal in place it is difficult for case managers to engage clients based on the offer to "start where the client is at" as opposed to "starting where the program requirements are at."

The dilemma posed by the established program goal is dealt with directly. First, the overall goal of linkage with services is made clear to clients. Case managers provide reasons why following-through might be beneficial to the client. In ARTAS reasons include receiving early medical interventions that could slow the progression of the disease and improve quality of life and qualifying for social services. In the Reducing Barriers Project treatment follow-through could mean alleviation of problems associated with substance abuse. Case managers acknowledge that it is the client's choice to accept the goal or not. Either way case managers will continue to work with clients on objectives and strategies that the client identifies as being important.

Additional challenges are associated with brief SBCM. They include difficulty in quickly establishing a constructive working relationship, multiple problems that clients frequently have, and the challenges of disengaging with clients while supporting their follow-through with other services. In response to these challenges every activity in the five case management sessions was constructed so as to accomplish one or a combination of client-based aims: 1.) help the client appreciate the possible value of the established goal; 2.) establish a short-term, trusting relationship with the case manager; and 3.) draw on any past successes and sense of self-efficacy in addressing current challenges.

CONCLUSION

Several tentative conclusions can be drawn about strengths-based case management implemented with substance abusers. First, it seems that positive outcomes accrue to those clients who receive strengths-based case management, particularly in the areas of drug use, employment, and criminal justice involvement. More specifically, the relationship between strengths-based case management and at least two of the positive outcomes—drug use and criminal justice involvement—seem to be accounted for by the ability of case managers to keep clients involved in services, specifically case management services, following primary treatment. Interestingly, case managers were not particularly effective in keeping clients involved with traditional relapse prevention activities.

Three findings about SBCM's possible mechanism of action—individuals' recognition of the strengths recognition and appreciation process as valuable, an emphasis on the relational aspects of the intervention, conflict between recognizing these elements and effectively implementing them all have significant implications for social workers. Perhaps most significantly social workers need to re-examine the professional detachment that frequently characterizes the relationship between social worker and client. There is no reason to believe that the warm, genuine and mentoring relationship noted by individuals in this study cannot be maintained within the context of appropriate professional boundaries and the realities imposed on social work practice in contemporary settings.

Social workers implementing strengths-based practice must persist in emphasizing strengths throughout the relationship. It is not enough to conduct a strengths assessment early in the intervention and expect that it will effectively support an individual through challenges to their perceptions of personal competency and effectiveness. Social workers should be prepared to integrate the emphasis on strengths into all interactions with individuals, especially during the course of goal-setting activities. The most effective means of maintaining the focus on strengths lies in the social worker's fundamental examination of personal and professional beliefs about those individuals we typically refer to as difficult and resistant. The two themes that emerged from individuals' stories, the value of the helping relationship and a focus on personal strengths, begin to establish a link between the principles of strengths-based practice and the intervention's implementation.

Address correspondence and reprint requests to:

Richard C. Rapp, M.S.W.
Assistant Professor and Co-Principal Investigator
Reducing Barriers Project
Wright State University School of Medicine
215 Medical Sciences
3640 Colonel Glenn Highway
Dayton, Ohio 45435
richard.rapp@wright.edu

DISCUSSION QUESTIONS

1. What does the preparation to do SBCM require of you?

2. Why is it important to understand that the strengths assessment is an ongoing process?

3. What are three critical points to remember when doing a strengths assessment?

4. Why is it good clinical practice to collect information from a client that is not necessarily strengths-based?

5. What are the elements of SBCM that make it effective with people who have substance abuse problems?

REFERENCES

Brun, C., & Rapp, R. C. (2001). Strengths-based case management: Individuals' perspectives on strengths and the case manager relationship. *Social Work, 46*(3), 278–288.

Martin, S. S., & Scarpitti, F. R. (1993). An intensive case management approach for paroled IV drug users. *Journal of Drug Issues, 23*(1), 43–59.

Modrcin, M., Rapp, C., & Chamberlain, R. (1985). *Case Management With Physically Disabled Individuals: Curriculum and Training Program.* Lawrence, KS: School of Social Welfare, University of Kansas.

Oppenheimer, E., Sheehan, M., & Taylor, C. (1988). Letting the client speak: Drug misusers and the process of help seeking. *British Journal of Addiction, 83*, 635–647.

Rapp, C., & Chamberlain, R. (1985). Case management services for the chronically mentally ill. *Social Work, 26*, 417–422.

Rapp, R. C. (1997). The strengths perspective and persons with substance abuse problems. In D. Saleebey (Ed.), *The Strengths Perspective in Social Work Practice*. New York: Longman.

Rapp, R. C., Siegal, H. A., Fisher, J. H., Wagner, J. H., Kelliher, C. W., & Bechtolt, J. A. (1993). A "strengths-based" approach to enhance treatment compliance. *Addiction and Recovery,* (November/December), 22–25.

Rapp, R. C., Siegal, H. A., Li, L., & Saha, P. (1998). Predicting post-primary treatment services and drug use outcome: A multivariate analysis. *American Journal of Drug and Alcohol Abuse, 24*(4), 603–615.

Siegal, H. A., Fisher, J. A., Rapp, R. C., Kelliher, C. W., Wagner, J. H., O'Brien, W. F., & Cole, P. A. (1996). Enhancing substance abuse treatment with case management: Its impact on employment. *Journal of Substance Abuse Treatment, 13*(2), 93–98.

Siegal, H. A., Li, L., & Rapp, R. C. (2002). Case management as a therapeutic enhancement: Impact on post-treatment criminality. *Journal of Addictive Diseases, 21*(4), 37–46.

Siegal, H. A., Rapp, R. C., Kelliher, C. W., Fisher, J. H., Wagner, J. H., & Cole, P. A. (1995). The strengths perspective of case management: A promising inpatient substance abuse treatment enhancement. *Journal of Psychoactive Drugs, 27*(1), 67–72.

Siegal, H. A., Rapp, R. C., Li, L., Saha, P., & Kirk, K. (1997). The role of case management in retaining clients in substance abuse treatment: An exploratory analysis. *Journal of Drug Issues, 27*(4), 821–831.

Westermeyer, J. (1989). Nontreatment factors affecting treatment outcome in substance abuse. *American Journal of Substance Abuse, 15*(1), 13–29.

Willenbring, M. L., Ridgely, M. S., Stinchfield, R., & Rose, M. (1991). *Application of case management in alcohol and drug dependence: Matching techniques and populations* (ADM-91–1766 ed.). Washington, DC: Department of Health and Human Services.

CHAPTER NINE

THE STRENGTHS MODEL WITH OLDER ADULTS
Critical Practice Components

HOLLY NELSON-BECKER

ROSEMARY CHAPIN

BECKY FAST

MARIA

Maria Esperanza had always been a strong and independent woman. At least, that was how those who had known her for the past 30 years she had lived alone in the small inner city brownstone bungalow on Washington Street perceived her. She and her husband were legendary in the community for having kept vacant buildings from hosting street drug transactions and for taking an interest in activities of the youth who would cycle by on warm summer evenings. Her five children had all gone to college on her income as a maid and the factory wages of her husband Carlos. When they graduated, the children had gradually moved away from home as they become more and more successful in their careers. Only Anna, the youngest child, lived nearby. However, even she had to spend what little free time she had caring for her own small children and her disabled mother-in-law who lived with the family. Maria always told the children when they phoned or arrived on rare visits home that she was doing well. They believed her because they wanted to believe it was true.

Maria was an 80-year-old Mexican American woman whose husband had died two years before. Over the past year, Maria had become increasingly frail. She could no longer carry a sack of groceries the two blocks home from the corner grocery store. As a result her diet was now very poor. Her eyesight was not sharp and yesterday, when she had tripped over a rug in her house, she was not able to get up until a neighbor had stopped by the next day and helped. The neighbor notified Anna who rushed over, ready to help her mother sell the house and move into a nearby nursing home where she would be safe.

On the advice of the neighbor who had found her, Anna contacted a social worker at Casa Central, an Area Agency on Aging (AAA) affiliated agency, who was able to meet her at her mother's house. The social worker was licensed as a geriatric care manager. She talked to Maria and learned that her independence was something Maria valued above all else. With the social worker's help, Maria was able to discuss her concerns with Anna, and the social worker was able to present several options for supports so that Maria could choose what she wanted and continue living in her own home. The social worker agreed to Maria's request to continue checking back with her during the transition to service use. Maria observed that the social worker had listened to her and advocated for her with her daughter. She invited the social worker to continue in a case management role.

Maria has entered into the complex web of long-term care services. Luckily, she has a social worker who uses a strengths-based practice model and is skilled at developing rapport. When such an approach is absent, many older adults like Maria will not even consider looking at service options. The strengths model of case management is designed for people like Maria who will require different types of help and levels of intensity in caring and service provision as their health improves or deteriorates. Respect for the dignity and uniqueness of individuals like Maria is operationalized through the model's practice principles and methods. Furthermore, social workers using the strengths model are alert to the additional barriers to service access that Mexican American women may face. Workers operating from a strengths approach are interested in building on the strengths that have helped older adults overcome previous difficult times in their lives.

This chapter describes how the strengths model of case management is implemented in the long-term care of older adults, specifically in the provision of home and community-based services. The application of the strengths model of case management with seniors living at home in the community is beginning to be a focus of theory and research as social workers and others seek to reformulate constructs about aging (Ronch & Goldfield, 2003).

The first section of this chapter presents the conceptual framework that guides and directs the helping efforts with older adults. The next section delineates the critical practice components of a strengths-based case management approach in long-term care, especially practice methods designed to support older adult autonomy, and meet resource-oriented needs while promoting cost-effectiveness and efficiency. The personal stories of individuals who have received case management are included to illustrate the usefulness of the strengths approach within a system accountable for reducing unnecessary institutional costs. The significance of working from a philosophical standpoint of older adult empowerment is discussed, along with the value of incorporating a spiritual assessment component and the need to integrate policy components in case management practice. Finally, the potential of the strengths model in changing long-term care environments is explored.

CONCEPTUAL FRAMEWORK FOR PRACTICE

For over a decade, the professional literature has considered the effectiveness and plausibility of using a strengths-based approach with older adults, children with severe emotional disturbance, and persons with mental illness and/or substance abuse problems (Perkins & Tice, 1995; Poertner & Ronnau, 1990; Pray, 1992; Rapp, Siegal, Fisher, & Wagner, 1992; Ronch & Goldfield, 2003; Sullivan & Fisher, 1994). Strengths-based case management for older adults is derived from the basic principles and functions of the strengths model developed in the 1980s for persons with severe and persistent mental illness living in the community (Rapp, 1992).

Case management has been a part of social work practice since its inception (Johnson & Rubin, 1983). Like all social work practice, strengths-based case management for older adults rests on a foundation of values, knowledge, and skills. But there are several distinguishing features emanating from the values and philosophy of the model that set it apart from other long-term care case management practice approaches. These distinctive features include a shift from traditional models of helping based on medical necessity to a strengths-based model that addresses the whole person in his or her environment. In the strengths framework, discovering, developing, and building on the person's internal and external resources is a focal point. In contrast to many other long-term care case management models, the strengths-based helping process emphasizes consumer participation and decision making.

Medical and rehabilitation models typically emphasize professional diagnosis and treatment of the symptomatology to eradicate or ameliorate the "problem." Authority for and control over decisions lies in the hands of the professional. The unspoken premise is that persons in need of assistance lack knowledge or insight about the identified physical or mental health problem and certainly about how it might be resolved. Professional expertise is needed to assess and treat the troublesome condition (Freidson, 1988).

In contrast, the primary purpose of strengths case management is to recognize the inherent abilities that a person has developed over a lifetime of active effort. The aim of this approach is to help older persons maintain as much control over their lives as possible: to capitalize on what they can do and to compensate for what they cannot do. The goal of strengths case management is to stabilize the older person's routine within the acceptable bounds determined by the individual, often despite advancing disability. Assessment and planning strategies are woven from the social, spiritual, psychological, and physical needs and strengths of an older person. For example, in a medical model case management system, a patient with a broken hip might be hospitalized, have the hip treated, and then be released. The medical needs may have been well met, but matters such as transportation, housing modifications, financial assistance, social isolation, and some physical limitations might never be considered. For most older adults, well-being is more than a medical matter. What is equally significant is the ability to engage in reciprocal interactions, contribute and feel useful, prevent or cope with social isolation, and develop an acceptable routine of daily life despite the disease or illness (Smith & Eggleston, 1989). Even if an individual suffers from a serious chronic condition, where these other needs are addressed, he/she may experience a sense of heightened well-being.

The assumption underlying the medicalization of aging services is that older people, and especially those with chronic disabilities, require the involvement of medical professionals to protect them from further injury and debilitation. In advanced age, chronic rather than acute illnesses are, for the most part, the major medical problems. The leading chronic conditions among older people include heart disease, cancer, stroke, diabetes, chronic obstructive pulmonary disease (CDC, 2004) as well as asthma and osteoporosis (Mader & Ford, 1997). However, these conditions merely annoy some older people who are able to lead relatively normal lives despite aches, pains, and minor physical limitations. Others are not so fortunate and are significantly limited in their ability to carry out both necessary and preferred daily activities, such as cooking, housework, yard work, and getting out of the house to socialize. Of course, many older people also are periodically afflicted with acute illnesses (that is, conditions lasting less than three months).

Over time, the stress inherent in providing and receiving emotional support and getting help with household tasks and personal care are the most pressing challenges during later life transitions for older adults and their families. Medical problems of older persons may remain stable during long periods. The person may even experience years of relative remission, occasionally interspersed with episodes of crisis and declining mental or physical health. Decreased functional abilities—the degree of independence in functioning a person possesses in the face of illness—may overwhelm an individual's coping response. The performance of activities of daily living (ADLs) such as bathing, dressing, eating, toileting, and transferring must be addressed daily while independent activities of daily living (IADLs) such as shopping, preparing meals, managing money, doing housework, and using a telephone, are needs that must be answered regularly. Despite functional deficits, older people demonstrate remarkable resiliency. They often possess an underutilized or untapped capacity for growth and change even in the context of difficult life challenges. Like younger persons with disabilities, some older adults need only minimal assistance to arrange and manage supports and resources so that they can remain in the community and lead the life they choose.

The conceptual framework for the strengths model of case management with older adults places self-determination as the central value; that value directs the focus to personal goal achievement. Consumer power is the preferred balance in the fulcrum of the case management relationship. The older adult as well as the community must be viewed as possessing valuable inherent resources and strengths. Thus, the case managers' task is to help older adults identify and achieve access to both formal and informal resources in order to reach the outcomes they desire. Table 9.1 presents key elements of the strengths model and delineates differences from traditional medical/rehabilitative models of helping.

TABLE 9.1 The Strengths Conceptual Model Contrasted with Traditional Medical/Rehabilitative Models of Helping

FACTOR	STRENGTHS MODEL	MEDICAL/REHABILITATIVE MODELS
Value Base: General Philosophical	Older adults have ongoing potential to grow, heal, learn; Older adults possess ability to identify needs & wants; Older adults have inherent and unique individual strengths as well as environmental strengths/resources;	Medical community has best standpoint to identify problem; Older adult must comply with prescribed treatments as determined by clinical trials and medical expertise;
Value Base: Cultural	Client is a consumer; Ideographic—older adults have ability and authority to determine their best solutions;	Client is a patient—passive recipient of services; Nomothetic and paternalistic—society must take care of older adults who face decreasing physical ability;
Knowledge Base	Case manager brings knowledge of resources & understanding of human capacity for change to client relationship;	Medical community is the custodian and gatekeeper of biological & health knowledge;
Knowledge Base: Problem Resolution	Consumer has decision making capacity; Client knowledge and natural community resources used first; Other resources sought as needed;	Problem resolution dependent upon professional expertise & ability to synthesize vast quantities of information;
Skill Base: General	Professional develops rapport & trust; Professional collaborates with client; Professional combines own resources & environmental resources to help achieve client-identified goals;	Professional assesses nature of person's problem, provides diagnosis, & treatment;
Skill Base: Case Management	Case manager coaches, supports, & encourages; Case manager replaces self when possible with natural helpers; Case manager rejuvenates and creates natural helping networks; Case manager provides services within daily routines.	Professional contact limited to assessment, planning, evaluating functions; Identified problems are managed medically; Patient is taught skills as needed to overcome deficits.

Operationalizing the Strengths Perspective

Common myths about older adults are that they have only problems, are on a course of rapid debilitation, are unproductive, are demanding and difficult, and require more expenditure from society than the assets they render back. Case managers cannot be effective with older clients unless they understand the worth, dignity, uniqueness, and continuing contribution of older people in a society that too often relegates seniors to an inferior position. A first step for those who work with older clients is to suspend beliefs about older adults' lack of resilience and limited capacity for growth and change. This, in essence, means adopting a new concept of the aging process; acquiring an expanded sense of what it means to age in a new time from those who have faced chronic illness or deep personal loss, and yet managed to engage fully and joyfully in the present moment, with whatever resolution or determination that effort may initially require. This new understanding of aging productively and successfully is only possible when case managers are able to confront their own fears about aging and begin to envision their future selves as competent older adults, capable of finding joy in life despite loss. Imagining such a concept of self then allows case managers to join with the older client rather than make plans for someone fundamentally different from them, the "other." Exercises and training materials designed to develop case managers' capacities to use strengths-based strategies with older adults can help expand this understanding of aging as a welcome stage of life (Fast & Chapin, 2000).

Allowing older persons to determine for themselves where they want to go, and when and how, demands belief in their capacity to choose and to handle the consequences of their choices. Such attitudes affirm the dignity and worth of older adults in spite of prevalent myths and stereotypes that clearly represent bias and prejudice against elders. This is a revisionist view of aging.

Despite the strong preference of older adults to remain in their homes as long as possible, family and professional relationships can strongly affect the older adult's sense of self and the type of long-term care s/he decides on. A significant step in this direction is to establish a foundation of genuine dialogue and collaboration (Kivnick & Murray, 2001; Perkins & Tice, 1995). Assisting older persons with identification of the problems at hand while facilitating their participation in finding solutions helps them stay in community-based housing as long as possible. An overarching goal of strengths-based case management, anchored in the value base of client self-determination, is to facilitate consumer involvement and choice. Providing older people with options and including them in decision making about possible institutional placement increases the likelihood of satisfaction with, and relevance of, the choices made. When the older consumer remains active in making medical and social decisions, both the consumer and the providers achieve greater satisfaction.

Asking for additional help can be extremely difficult for an older person. Motenko and Greenberg assert that "the ability to acknowledge the need for help and ask for help is evidence of mature dependence, a crucial transition in late life" (1995, p. 387). These authors suggest that older persons are better able to accept increased dependence if they are given authority to make decisions about the nature of the help needed and how it should be provided. Simply stated, being in charge is essential to personal pride and life satisfaction, particularly for older adults who have been operating independently throughout their lives (Langer, 1989). The more older persons feel in control of their lives by solving their own problems, the less the likelihood of unnecessary dependency and learned helplessness—two outcomes that are too often the fate of older citizens.

In the strengths model, social workers identify consumer abilities and create or find situations to use those abilities in the achievement of personal goals. Lasting change, we believe, can happen only when you collaborate with an individual's aspirations, perceptions, and strengths. Most consumers are competent and able to participate in the planning and delivery processes. Doing so brings renewed self-confidence and independence precipitated by moving with the elder in the direction he or she chooses and in situations and contexts where the person feels capable and willing. If consumers are acknowledged as experts in defining their needs, the role of the social worker must change to reflect a greater appreciation of that consumer expertise.

Helping individuals like Maria manage their own inevitable aging process and the physical and emotional losses involved assists them in being better equipped to make sound decisions regarding what type of help they want. When considering the needs of older persons and their families, risk and security must be carefully balanced. The conflict between the two becomes even clearer for older adults who are more severely disabled. The following case example, supplied by a strengths-oriented case manager, illustrates this dilemma.

SARAH

Sarah Nelson is 82-years-old and lives alone on the family's farm several miles out of town with her six cats and two dogs. Since her stroke, she has fallen several times. At one point she fractured her hip. Even though Sarah is confined to her lazy boy chair during the day, she continues to create dried flower arrangements. She relies on the home health aide to get her in and out of the bath, into bed, and to help with meal preparation. Sarah calls in her grocery list each week and the grocery store delivers her groceries. Her case manager and daughters assist her with finding transportation, managing her finances, and overseeing the upkeep of her home and farm. Her daughter Karen insists that she should move into the assisted-living unit in town. Sarah replies that she would rather lie helpless on the floor for hours than have to share a room and bathroom with a complete stranger. Sarah's daughters are very concerned about her living all alone on the farm. They fear that she will hurt herself and no one will be available to help her.

Over and over again, older people like Sarah state that they value freedom, privacy, and the independence to make risk-laden decisions about their daily life far more than they value living in a safe and protective environment. Sarah, a strong-willed woman, has adamantly resisted her daughters' and her medical providers' pleas that she move into supervised housing, which would prevent her from hurting herself. In this situation, Sarah's decision to remain living in her own home has continued to be respected. Her case manager has helped make it possible by providing her with meaningful choices about long-term care. Sarah's life-long habits of self-care, preferences about daily tasks, and her considerable strength of character are respected through negotiation about the type and level of service she prefers.

Table 9.2 presents a continuum of possible behaviors available to case managers for facilitating higher or lower levels of participation and involvement by the consumer. This table is intended to provide guidance to social workers attempting to foster the participation of frail or disabled older adults who are competent in decisions about their care needs. The continuum ranges from absolute authority (having the locus of control with the case manager) to a self-directed care approach (shifting the control to an informed consumer). The midpoint indicates shared responsibility by both parties for managing the multiple effects of the consumer's disabilities and illnesses, and for individualizing the consumer's resources.

TABLE 9.2   Continuum of Decision-Making

ABSOLUTE AUTHORITY	IMPOSING	JOINT ACTION	LIMITED CONSTRAINTS	SELF-DIRECTED CARE
The case manager pressures the consumer to accept the problems or solutions without input or participation in the decision. The person's understanding of the issues are solicited but the case manager retains absolute authority over decisions.	The case manager defines the problem and selects the solutions that are the most promising. Consumer preferences are taken into consideration.	Together, both parties brainstorm a possible range of solutions. The case manager and consumer are both responsible for identifying consumer strengths and resources for implementing the plan of care. Decisions are not made unless both individuals agree on them.	The consumer offers preferences about the type, role, and the level of service provision. Information and counseling is given by the case manager to assist the consumer in making informed decisions. The consumer retains the final decision within limits defined by the case manager.	Consumer choices are supported through being allowed to choose the mix, frequency, duration, and timing of formal/informal service provision within organizational boundaries. In this system, the case manager becomes a consultant to and resource for consumers to help make viable arrangements.
CASE MANAGER DIRECTED DECISION MAKING		COLLABORATIVE DECISION MAKING		CONSUMER DIRECTED DECISION MAKING

The goal of strengths-based case management is to encourage more active consumer participation in long-term care decisions. The case manager begins where the consumer is and moves with him or her on the continuum to the highest possible level of participation. Professional-directed decision making is seen as the least desirable state. The aim is to expand consumer confidence in making crucial decisions such as when to seek care and what options to select, and to move toward consumer-directed decision making. Maria had never taken care of the finances, the car, or fixing the house before her husband died. She was at a loss initially about how to handle what she saw as traditionally male duties that her husband always had performed. In those arenas, she first wanted family to make more of the decisions. However, she wanted to retain the responsibilities that she had during her marriage. In time, she felt more confident about managing her late husband's duties and subsequently wanted less direction from her family and case manager.

At the self-directed end of the continuum (see Table 9.2) consumers determine what services they need and at what level they need to support themselves in the community. The example of Sarah illustrates how a consumer participated in and negotiated her care service schedule including what service would be performed. She did not want someone coming into her house to clean on a weekly basis. Sarah thought it was unnecessary for her to have a higher standard of living now than she had known previously in her life.

Self-directed care does not preclude the case manager from developing a supportive structure that enables individuals with disabilities, with the assistance of family, friends, and community members, to take responsibility for planning their own lives. Sarah, with the support of her case manager and several women who owned small businesses, was assisted in finding a market for her dried flower arrangements.

One difficulty lies with the minority of older persons whose judgment is so impaired that increased responsibility for care decisions poses a danger to self and others. Questions inevitably arise about whether the person should participate in decision making and at what level. Frail or disabled older adults have the right to be involved in decisions about their long-term care. Even consumers with cognitive or psychiatric disabilities should be afforded as many choices as possible. The challenge is to be thoroughly aware of their rights and the *real* limitations of their physical and mental conditions. Given patience and time, a relationship can be established even with a very frail older person who fades in and out cognitively. His/her fears can be identified, concerns expressed, trust established, and actions taken in which the older adult is a willing partner to the maximum of his or her potential and capacity. Strengths-based case managers strive to understand how their relationship supports or limits the autonomy of older individuals.

CRITICAL PRACTICE COMPONENTS OF EFFECTIVE CASE MANAGEMENT

The purpose of strengths-based case management is to assist seniors in identifying, securing, and sustaining external and internal resources that are needed for customary interdependent (as opposed to independent or dependent) community living (Kisthardt & Rapp, 1991). The strengths model's potential to increase case management effectiveness with older adults occurs through the following practice methods: 1.) personalized assessment and planning; 2.) assertive outreach to natural community resources and services; 3.) emergency crisis planning; and 4.) ongoing collaboration and caregiving adjustments.

Personalized Assessment and Planning

Assessment from a strengths perspective is holistic rather than narrowly diagnostic. Consumer knowledge and motivation rather than professional expertise is the basis of the assessment and planning process (Pray, 1992). A standard functional assessment does not generate a complete picture of the older person's strengths, coping strategies, motivations, and potential for change (Kivnick, 1993). Eligibility for long-term care services based on functional limitations prompts social workers to view their consumers in terms of activities of daily living (ADLs) and instrumental activities of daily living (IADLs) typologies. In fact, so much emphasis is placed on functional limitations that an older person's quality of life is often reduced to *nothing more* than a list of ADLs and IADLs. Vulnerable older adults soon realize that in order to receive help, they too must describe themselves in those terms. In Maria Esperanza's case, an initial focus on the deficits in her ADLs could have reinforced a suspicion that the social worker intended to find her incapable of remaining at home. Careful attention to her desires during the initial relationship building created an environment where functional limitations as well as capacities could be acknowledged and used in the care planning process.

Strengths-based assessment and planning focuses on the optimization of the older person's strengths and resources. Applied helping strategies are implemented to support the individual's sense of control and capacity to function at home. This is accomplished through identifying supports and resources that take the person's limitations into consideration but also counterbalancing them with discovery of strengths and activities that might fit with the individual's desires and interests (Sullivan & Fisher, 1994). For example, in assessing Sarah's strengths, the case manager learned of her past hobby even though it had been years since Sarah had created flower arrangements. She recultivated Sarah's interest in the hobby and helped her buy the necessary supplies. After several months, Sarah's depression lifted, very probably from pursuing her hobby, and her dried flower arrangements even brought in some additional income to fund her home care. The desired resources needed to optimize the individual's capabilities may or may not be available on the menu of services offered by the social worker's agency. Strengths-based care plan development strives to be unrestricted by payment sources. Care planning driven by consumer interests and assets rather than steered by reimbursement is the desired outcome.

Most social workers are indeed committed to acknowledging the consumers' strengths. However, the majority of assessment and care planning tools provide little space or incentive for recording what the older person wants, is doing, has done, and can do to maintain his or her independence. This omission hinders even the best intentions. Rarely, if ever, are consumer strengths seen as integral to the planning process so that services are provided and activities structured to maximize and promote existing or potential strengths. Subsequently, social workers may fail to get to know the older person in a holistic way, whereas an appreciation of the whole person almost always creates a positive interaction. When this kind of relationship is developed, the case manager is better able to assist the consumer in developing an individualized plan of action.

Given system barriers such as large caseloads and organizational policies, the strengths assessment and planning process with senior adults should, at minimum, cover these items:

1. Exploring commonalties: shared values, experiences, interests;
2. Learning how the person has coped with difficulties in the past;
3. Focusing on the strengths within the person and his or her environment; and
4. Visioning together what kind of life the consumer wants.

Basic questions to ask include:

- Who is important to you in your life? (Social support)
- What do you do during a normal day? (Normal activities)
- What makes life worth living for you? (Life satisfaction)
- What has worked well for you in the past? (Coping skill inventory)
- What is going well for you right now? (Present-oriented strengths)
- If things could be different, what would you wish for? (Visioning)

The strengths assessment process is not meant to replace existing standardized assessments for conferring and allocating benefits. However, it is unjust to suppose that the whole picture of a person is captured in diagnostic, functional, or psychotherapeutic assessments. Only through creating *life* plans rather than care plans will an older person be able to live meaningfully in the community. The above focal points and questions can serve as guides for gathering the information needed to develop such plans. An actual strengths assessment and personal plan can be seen in Kisthardt (1997, pp. 103–108).

Assertive Outreach to Natural Community Resources and Services

The strengths perspective on case management practice offers an alternative conception to resource acquisition. Before using formal paid services, the case manager is expected to determine first that naturally occurring, environmental, and community resources are not available. Natural helpers include a collective of supporters to be developed and sustained such as neighbors, apartment managers, grocery store clerks, church or youth groups, adult children, and others with whom the older client comes into contact on a daily or weekly basis. The presence of naturally occurring resources is a strength of all communities and an available resource in all communities when actively pursued (Sullivan, 1997).

The strengths model advocates employing natural helpers and resources whenever possible. From the perspective of older adults, such help may be more acceptable because it is often based on friendship or a perception of mutual need, is easily accessible, lacks stigma, and is usually much cheaper. However, many seniors would rather not encumber their existing social network. In fact, when older adults are asked to help identify their helping networks, they will often tell you that no one is around who can help them. The avoidance of acknowledging dependency, combined with pride, may prevent older people from recognizing their extensive reliance on others for their daily survival. Therefore, it is imperative for strengths-oriented case managers to identify and support these helpers without undermining the older individual's self-esteem and dignity. Assistance from family, friends, employers, and colleagues often is not recognized by the older adult as help because it is extended in a subtle manner. This help is given by informal social helpers as they interact with the individual during the normal rhythms of the day. These social network members may notice that their older friend is having some difficulty with walking, eating, or shopping and, without being asked, help the person with these tasks.

Social supports take on increased significance as older adults become more frail. One of the losses experienced by this population is the shrinkage of the informal support system. Many consumers no longer have a full social support system that can help them. One of the critical functions of the social worker is to help secure and sustain connections to informal resources. The social worker's goal is to facilitate a more adequate fit between the individual's desires and the resources in his or her environment. This includes the social worker's help to recognize and map out what assets are already being used to some degree and to include other community capacities that have not yet been mobilized.

Acquisition of natural community resources is predicated on the belief that including consumers in the decision about who or what entity provides the service will further promote adherence to the form and direction of the help received. The challenge for most social workers is locating and expanding a natural support system for consumers. In Maria's and Sarah's situations, many of their friends and acquaintances, except for their children, were equally frail. They too, had limited physical capability to conduct heavy cleaning or lift objects, and were not able to come and go as they pleased. The social worker needs to be informed about the naturally occurring resources in the wider community, as well as in the consumer's personal network. It is important to generate as many potential resources as possible with consumers and their primary caregivers. Older persons may withhold existing support network information out of pride and a desire to protect their privacy and maintain the appearance of independence.

A useful strategy for case managers to identify natural helpers is to accompany the older person through a typical day in order to learn what help is given, by whom, and how often (Lustbader & Hooyman, 1994). By accompanying the person to the doctor, hairdresser's, etc., and by listening to the conversations, more often than not, a social worker will discover that the older person has more social contact than the social worker realized. Or, the case manager might discover a different interactive style outside the home than that seen at home in the "client" role.

In developing the service mix, caregiver burden is acknowledged. Support networks of family and friends should not feel overtaxed. Assertively working to relieve primary caregiver burden is basic to developing a workable care plan. Ongoing dialogue, assessment of perceived burden, and role adjustment must occur with informal caregivers when they are providing some of the major components of care. One of the chief problems with natural helpers is finding ways to limit their involvement because they are within easy reach on a potentially unlimited basis. Many who could help would rather not get involved because they fear being overwhelmed by the needs that may eventually occur. Occasionally, some older people alienate those who could help by complaining about the help or by expecting too much help.

Despite the emotional bonds linking older adults with their families, friends, and other established caregivers, these individuals often lack the expertise to provide comprehensive long-term care. Further, a previous history of caregiver abuse or neglect in a given situation could necessitate agency assistance to care for and protect the vulnerable adult from informal assistance. However, formal providers, while often equipped with the necessary technical skills, cannot fully satisfy affective needs or deliver the kind of idiosyncratic care that reflects a lifetime of shared values and experiences.

Balancing expensive formal care with less-expensive informal resources can help control costs while ensuring necessary assistance is provided in ways acceptable to the older adult. In Maria's case, the social worker discovered that a man who rented Maria's garage to store an antique car had a daughter in high school. With Maria's agreement, the social worker hired the girl to shop for groceries. Maria prepared a list that the girl's father picked up when he drove by on his way to work (he also usually dropped in to see how Maria was doing on these occasions). When the social worker explored with Maria what her experiences as a Mexican American woman had been in seeking formal service, Maria indicated that she was hesitant to try to negotiate a formal care system primarily staffed by European Americans. Her preference was to rely on friends or relatives to help her obtain services. The high school girl and her father were recognized both as a source of help and as trusted friends who could aid Maria in her efforts to gain access to other resources.

In addition, Maria's son, a school teacher, came to spend a month with his mother in the summer. His work to keep her home repaired relieved many of his mother's concerns about basic household upkeep. The social worker had a chance to become acquainted with him during these visits. At the social worker's suggestion, he accompanied his mother to the community center each week. She continued to attend the center from time to time even after her son returned home. Maria's son now felt more confident his mother could continue to live in the community with the support of the social worker, the center, and other informal resources. If he became concerned about her well-being, he knew he could call his sister nearby or turn to the social worker for help. Undoubtedly, there will never be enough paid formal services to meet the needs of a growing frail older adult population. However, focusing primarily on the deficits in the social environment only further restricts imagination and the number of helping resources realized.

Emergency Crisis Planning

Most older adults come to the attention of a social worker at a time of crisis. Crisis frequently occurs as the result of an acute care hospitalization. This experience leaves frail older adults in a weakened state suffering from depression, anxiety, or a sense of failure if the admission was caused by a fall, medication mismanagement, or lapses in personal care. During these instances, when the person's resilience is low, they are most ready to yield to professional and caregiver choices and goals. Advocating for the person's wishes and increasing older adult involvement in the decision-making process increases the likelihood that alternatives to institutional care will be chosen if available. High care costs often result because the case manager has not had time to deal with the problem before it becomes a crisis or because services are simply allocated to the consumer without trying to fully assess and resolve the situation. Kulys (1983) found that older adults typically do not plan for a health-related crisis. This potential for unwanted institutionalization precipitated by unexpected crises can be mitigated by planning ahead for crisis services.

In the strengths model, an emergency plan is discussed and negotiated with the consumer and the primary caregivers before a health crisis develops. This plan is rehearsed and reviewed. Specific behaviors may be performed to ensure that they can be followed in an emergency. However, as the following examples illustrate, developing an emergency plan involves careful relationship-building. Emergency planning was initiated with a man who had fallen repeatedly. He was not interested in installing a medical alert system that could potentially cause a big scene in his neighborhood. Even though his pride prevented him from using a medical alert system, he did agree to have his mail carrier alert his son if his mail did not get picked up. In Sarah's case, she was willing to wear a medical alert pin that linked her to the small local rural hospital. She and Francis, her neighbor, discussed alternative emergency plans for nonmedical crises. In the event of such a crisis, one of them would alert the on-call worker at the aging social service agency who would then alert the staff nurse or social worker depending on the presenting need.

An established emergency plan takes into consideration that most frail older adults will probably need time-limited, acute-care crisis services at some point. However, at a large number of crisis junctures, either low- or high-cost rapid response mechanisms can be selected, depending on how knowledgeable the consumer and caregivers are about the existing resources and their accessibility. When a structured plan for dealing with crises involving natural and formal resources is not in place, then high-cost services become the simplest and most readily available option. The strengths approach focuses on anticipating key crisis points as a strategy for providing effective case management and helping to contain unnecessary costs.

Ongoing Collaboration and Caregiving Adjustments

In the strengths perspective, monitoring is a continuous process that begins when care goals are established. The social worker frequently contacts and collaborates not only with the older person, but also with her/his family members, friendly visitors, senior citizen groups, nurses, and other support networks. The social worker's role goes far beyond that of "appointments secretary" to that of leader, trainer, and supervisor of a cadre of paid and unpaid helpers.

Skilled and effective case management presupposes that securing resources provides minimal benefits unless they are sustained and individualized to meet consumer preferences. Even after the older adult has gained access to desired services and resources, a lot of effort may need to be expended to sustain that person. The challenge of strengths-based case management is to resolve or at least reduce the interpersonal conflicts within the personal support networks that inevitably arise. Relationship-driven collaboration recognizes the value of each person's input and the benefits of making the helping experience mutually advantageous for everyone. The goal of continuous contact is to strengthen the consumer's self-care capacities and the caregivers' ability to help through the transfer of knowledge and skills by social and medical service providers, all coordinated by the case manager.

For example, an older consumer with hearing difficulty may become extremely frustrated when the taxi driver, whom he calls for rides to the grocery store, leaves after momentarily honking the horn. Facilitation of the resource use frequently involves educating the helper. Attention to building partnerships with resource providers, whether volunteer or paid, is very important. Tailoring the help to meet the needs of the consumer should be done in a nonthreatening way, not only for the sake of the present consumer but for all future consumers who may use that resource.

Ongoing contacts with the consumer and their helpers enable the case manager to influence cost-effectiveness through increasing, decreasing, or terminating any or all services expeditiously. Applebaum and Austin (1990) assert that rapid response to consumer changes can have a dramatic impact on service costs. The overutilization of services typically results from not adjusting prescribed amounts of delivered services to the current situation as it unfolds. Reduction in case management costs as well as paid services can be expected in the strengths model because efforts are reduced and shifted to more frail and needy individuals as other consumers regain increased levels of self-sufficiency.

The Empowerment of Older Adults

The strengths perspective can be used as a philosophical base in guiding case managers to focus on empowerment of older adults. This focus on empowerment is critical for both older men and women who are our clients. However, because demographically the majority of the clients and caretakers whom case managers serve are women, empowerment of older women will be the center of this discussion.

There are many emergent components to the idea of empowerment for older women. Much of feminist literature proclaims the importance of connection and relatedness in the lives of women. Whether biological or a response to oppression in patriarchal social arrangements, friendships, connections, mutual caring, and support networks are sources of power and strength for older women. This is not to say that the idea that women are natural caregivers has not led to exploitation of women's interest in adopting nurturing roles. But "[a] belief in the value of connection and relationships can result in the development of interventions that support the empowerment of the individual and can contribute to group empowerment and societal change through individual empowerment" (Browne, 1995, p. 362).

Another avenue to empowerment is to re-establish bonds with and ties to the community and neighborhood. As we have seen, far too many older women and men are isolated and sequestered away from the communities that they live in. Older adults have much to offer communities: skills built in a lifetime of work, raising families, meeting economic, social, and interpersonal challenges. Their knowledge and experience can lend perspective and wise counsel to members of a community—individuals, families, groups, and associations. They also may have time to donate. Kretzmann & McKnight (1993) give many examples of seniors making contributions to the community. In Chicago, older citizens are involved in the Visiting Important Person program in which they assist less mobile elderly neighbors and by helping them with a variety of problems and needs. They are trained to provide CPR, to recognize drug abuse, to give bed baths, and to help with daily matters like budgeting, menu preparation, and cooking. The oldest participant is an 82-year-old woman. One of the most important signs of neighborhood and community is the evidence of intergenerational relationships—projects, celebration, mentoring, and child care. In *Ordinary Resurrections* (2000), Jonathan Kozol recounts the role of the older women volunteers at St. Anne's church, in making a safe and nurturing after-school environment for the young children in an economically distressed, segregated neighborhood.

> The small dimensions of the church have much to do with the unusual experience of physical and moral safety that attracts children here, and also the feeling of protectedness and intimate religion that is so important to the older women who come here to take care of the children. Several women from the congregation, one of them a great-grandmother, Mrs. Winkle, who is nearly 83 years old, come in the afternoon to congregate around a table at the far end of the afterschool, where they can keep a close eye on the kids and be available to them in times of need. (p.20)

Here these women provide respite for 80 young children who, for the most part, live in siege conditions. Yet none of them think what they do is out of the ordinary, but it is a little something to keep the community's obligation to its children and most vulnerable members alive.

Finally, it is often the older adults who preserve the distinctiveness of the culture—its meanings, tools, rituals, and practices. While youth may be driven away from their culture of origin to adopt the ways of the dominant culture, adult children often find the bridge between the old ways and the new to be built of their elders' wisdom. Celia Jaes Falicov (1998) says this about Mexican American older adults:

The ability to become a 'tough old bird'—energetic, involved, and self-confident—and perceive old age as arriving later than for Anglo-Americans, seems to be preserved among the Mexican American elderly. This finding may stem from the Latino values on collectivism, conservation, cooperation, and continuity. (p. 254)

But older persons are mightily responsible for preserving these important values, values that remain a symbolic and vibrant cornerstone in many communities. Recognition, celebration, and solicitation of this knowledge is a part of the empowerment of older citizens.

None of the above should be interpreted to mean that many older people do not suffer the pains and anxieties, the exclusions and snubs, the marginalization of old age. It does mean that although we have a long way to go to empower the elders in our society and its cultures, we now know more about how to do that than we once did.

It should be noted here that successful aging is always a dialectical process. It is a matter of the adaptive competence and resources of a person and her or his family and the developmental supports and resources of a society, from neighborhood to federal government. In this sense, no one ages alone. "*Successful aging of individuals is related to the functioning and maintenance of communal life as the human ecology changes over time, that is to the successful aging of society through its adaptive competence*" *[authors' emphasis]* (Featherman, Smith, and Peterson, 1990, p. 82).

INTEGRATION OF SPIRITUAL ASSESSMENT AND INTERVENTION IN SOCIAL WORK PRACTICE WITH OLDER ADULTS

Social workers have begun to recapture one of the unique contributions the profession can make through its historical origins in the religious and spiritual movements of the 19th century (Marty, 1980). Incorporation of religious and spiritual assessment routinely and spiritual intervention where requested by older adult clients (Hodge, 2001; Nelson-Becker, Nakashima & Canda, in press), have the ability to support and enrich older adult coping capacity and empowerment, particularly in the current cohorts which generally came of age in a generation of strong religious connections (Koenig, 1994; Pargament, 1997).

Spiritually sensitive practice as detailed in Canda and Furman (1999), promotes attention to those aspects of life that provide meaning and value. While spiritual dimensions may be interwoven in problem-focused narratives that bring older adult clients to seek case management and other kinds of social work help, these dimensions also may form a context that lies beyond satisfaction of immediate concrete needs or development of long-term goals. Older adults typically value the importance of religion and spirituality in their lives, with 58% reporting that religion is very important, the highest rating on a four-point scale in a recent Gallup poll (PRCC, 2001).

Although value is often appraised positively, religion too may hold the bit-terness of social disapprobation (Spilka, 1986) where an older adult may have experienced lack of acceptance or where rigid interpretations of sacred texts may have been the source of personal guilt or shame. Beliefs about religion and spiri-tuality are shaped by individual attributes, by life experience and personal prob-lem solving history, and by the larger societal context in which one matures. To ignore this dimension that has critical importance to many older adults, especially to members of marginalized cultural groups for whom religious centers became a source of social and historical connection as well as a spiritual resource, is to dis-regard a potential resource for healing and managing ongoing challenges in the aging experience.

Many older adults rely on their faith to sustain them as they seek to build competence in new areas. "If you don't want to take [the lesson] over, do all you can not to fail the lesson of the day. I believe in this. God didn't send me here unequipped. I came fully equipped for whatever demand the world makes of me," reported one older African American woman (Nelson-Becker, in press). Others rely on nature-based spirituality to find a larger context to understand and work through immediate problems. "What I see out my window [Lake Michigan] gives me a sense of eternity and my place in it," commented one older Holocaust sur-vivor (Nelson-Becker, 2003, p.94).

Personal religious traditions and rituals should be explored as part of a strength-based assessment focusing on whether religion or spirituality should be engaged to build on personal strengths. Practical philosophies emerge out of a long trajectory of life experience and often contain religious and spiritual aspects. They develop largely because they work; they are effective in meeting a need or pur-pose. Openness to listening to spiritual and religious narratives both in assessment and as one form of intervention offer a resource that until recently, many social workers (who tend as a group to be less religious than their older clients) were hesitant to address. Often, merely creating the space for religious and spiritual conversations can offer great benefit for older adults struggling with spiritual ques-tions and seeking validation and meaning during times of new challenge.

INTEGRATION OF POLICY APPLICATIONS IN SOCIAL WORK PRACTICE WITH OLDER ADULTS

Social workers are expected to engage in policy practice on behalf of clients. Pol-icy practice focuses on trying to change policies that disadvantage our clients in legislative, agency, or community settings. Policy practice approaches infused with the strengths perspective guide us to make sure the voices of our clients are heeded by policy makers at all levels (Chapin, in press). As social workers, we are listening posts—transmitters and interpreters of information—and can help make the challenges, strengths, and goals of our clients known to policy makers who may have little direct contact with the people we—and they—serve.

Policy makers also need to understand the structural barriers that our clients, particularly people of color, face in achieving their goal of remaining in the community. One powerful barrier is the continuing lack of culturally competent health care providers. Another is the personal history of racial discrimination that older clients have experienced with many societal institutions. Claims for benefits and services to overcome these metalevel barriers are formulated based on the right to equal access to resources for citizens regardless of gender, race/ethnicity, age, or disability. One valuable role of the social worker is to win attention for older client perspectives. Another important role is that of helping to produce more equitable policies as a collaborator with older adult activists.

The strengths perspective is premised on social work values of self-determination and social justice. Social policies and programs should build on individual and community strengths and resources and remove structural barriers that disadvantage our clients. Effective policies can lead to empowerment, choice, and opportunity for our clients in keeping with the strength perspective. Older adults can and should be involved throughout the policy development process, including evaluation of a policy's efficacy. For example, it is crucial that social workers make sure elected representatives hear from elders of all backgrounds about their experiences with the Medicare Prescription Drug Cards that were new in 2004. Community ties, detailed in the example of the older Mexican American woman at the beginning of this chapter, may also be a foundation to encourage younger members of the community to talk to policy makers about the efficacy of policies and programs for the elders in their community. Young adults can be encouraged to see the effects on themselves and the entire community when older adults are without needed resources, and then to join with older adults to try to do something about ineffective policies. Ideas for becoming more proficient in policy practice are available from a variety of sources (Jansson, 2003; Schneider, R., & Lester, L. 2001; Chapin, in press). Development of policy practice skills is critical to full incorporation of the strengths perspective into case management with older adults.

UTILITY OF THE STRENGTHS MODEL IN THE CHANGING LONG-TERM CARE ENVIRONMENT

Traditionally, aging has been viewed as synonymous with disease, and a medical framework of care has been implemented to try to cure the problems associated with growing older. Traditional medical/rehabilitative models of helping remain prominent in most community-based, long-term care case management systems. Financial incentives for providers to reduce overutilization of services increases the need for older adults to take responsibility for ensuring that their health care needs are met. As Medicaid and Medicare managed care play a larger role in the aging system, treatment decisions will be closely monitored to conserve clinical and fiscal resources. Many of these plans have been attacked for reducing consumer involvement and authority to direct the course of their help. Older adults have been expected to be passive recipients of care. However, in the changing medical marketplace, the traditional roles of a passive patient and doctor-as-sole-decision-maker are being revised. Case management that focuses on both consumer empowerment and cost consciousness is clearly needed.

Since its inception, case management has been viewed as a potentially significant mechanism for coordinating services and controlling costs to prevent premature institutionalization. In an era of limited resources, private and public payers are demanding accountability for client outcomes and cost (Quinn, 1992). Effectiveness of a case management approach has been frequently evaluated according to its ability to reduce unnecessary institutionalization. However, much less effort has been made to define and measure effectiveness of case management from a standpoint of facilitating consumer involvement and empowerment and its subsequent impact on client outcomes and cost.

The need to first articulate and then to evaluate the effectiveness of strengths-based goals, planning processes, and tasks is imperative if fiscal control becomes the driving force behind case management. Home and community-based care have historically been embedded in the medical model delivery system where critical social, emotional, spiritual, and supportive service needs are often overlooked. The challenge for case management and home-based care becomes one of providing quality services that are acceptable to clients and effective in maintaining functioning while keeping a cost-conscious stance (Kane & Kane, 1987).

More needs to be learned about the effectiveness of case management models. Particular attention needs to be focused on the varying goals, tasks, processes, case management roles, and impact upon the lives of older persons. Long-term care case managers operating strictly from a functional or broker perspective of service provision, as was the case in the Channeling Demonstration Projects, did not employ the strengths model's emphasis on mutual decision making and reciprocity, and they minimized the active pursuit and empowerment of natural helpers (Rose, 1992). Equally, the Channeling Projects failed to carry out a case management process that established a trusting relationship and a purposeful counseling approach for dealing with the emotional stresses accompanying illness and loss of functions (Amerman, Eiserberg, & Weisman, 1985). The model of case management employed influences cost effectiveness.

Although research on the effects of strengths case management with older persons in the long-term care delivery system is still limited, evidence from Medicaid long-term care case managers trained in the use of the strengths model indicates that older adults who participate in strengths-based case management have increased levels of informal support, a more sustainable balance of formal and informal services, and fewer transitions between home and health care facilities (Fast, Chapin, & Rapp, 1994). In other areas research is also beginning to find evidence for the value of reinforcing strengths-based approaches for older adults in the community (Isaacowitz, Vaillant, & Seligman, 2003), in the field of care management (Bartelstone, 2003), in clinical work with older adults who are survivors of trauma (Cook, 2002), and in work with older adults who misuse alcohol (Perkins & Tice, 1999). Case management effectiveness from a strengths approach is embedded in its ability to meet case management's dual mission in long-term care—maximizing client control, dignity, and choice while containing cost.

CONCLUSION

This chapter has explored the essential practice components of the strengths model of case management with older adults in need of long-term care. This model of case management supports self-determination, maximizes consumer choice and interdependence, and can potentially help contain long-term care costs. With the growing number of older individuals in our society and the accompanying concern about health care costs, the importance of self-determination and consumer choice in creating an affordable home and community-based long-term care system should not be overlooked.

Spiritual assessment and possible inclusion of spiritual and/or religious resources constitute an important element of practice, especially with its implications for positive health outcomes. Articulation, implementation, and evaluation of the strengths model of long-term care case management with older adults can help professionals focus on the capacities rather than on the frailty of older adults. Spirituality, in its call to find avenues of meaning and purpose in the aging journey, is one such capacity.

Furthermore, awareness of the value inherent in empowerment of all individuals and the social work imperative to empower older adults through engagement in policy formulation and change, can immeasurably enrich ongoing societal transformation as we become a society that engages the resources of older adults themselves to meet future challenges. May we be successful in that task.

DISCUSSION QUESTIONS

1. How is a vision of aging successfully and productively supported by the strengths model?

2. What are some effective strategies for helping older consumers believe in their own abilities, try out new behaviors, and set and accomplish personal goals?

3. In what ways can case managers involve frail, older consumers in the assessment and planning process?

4. How can case managers help enhance the empowerment of older citizens? What kind of practical steps could they take?

5. In what ways can religion and spirituality serve as both resources and/or barriers for older adults?

6. What kinds of contributions can older adults make to their communities?

7. How can social workers encourage older adults to become involved in influencing policy at the community, agency, and policy levels?

8. Which of your older relatives have aged successfully? Why do you think so? What relatives have not done so well? How are they different?

REFERENCES

Amerman, E., Eiserberg, D., & Weisman, R. (1985). Case management and counseling: A service dilemma. In C. Austin et al. (Eds.), *Experience from the natural long-term care channeling demonstration.* Seattle, WA: Institute on Aging, University of Washington.

Applebaum, R., & Austin, C. (1990). *Long-term care case management: Design and evaluation.* New York: Springer.

Bartelstone, R. S. (2003). Care management: A strengths-based approach to mental wellness with older adults. In J. L. Ronch and J. A. Goldfield (Eds.), *Mental wellness in aging: Strengths-based approaches* (pp. 85–111). Baltimore, MD: Health Professions Press.

Browne, C. V. (1995). Empowerment in social work practice with older women. *Social Work, 40,* 358–364.

Canda, E. R. & Furman, L. D. (1999). *Spiritual diversity in social work practice.* New York: Free Press.

Centers for Disease Control, (CDC). (2004). Chronic Disease Overview. Retrieved June 16, 2004 from http://www.cdc.gov/nccdphp/overview.htm.

Cook, J. M. (2002). Traumatic exposure and PTSD in older adults: Introduction to the special issue. *Journal of Clinical Geropsychology, 8*(3), 149–152.

Chapin, R. (In press). *Social policy.* Boston: McGraw Hill.

Falicov, C. J. (1998). *Latino families in therapy: A guide to multicultural practice.* New York: The Guilford Press.

Fast, B., & Chapin, R. (2000). *Strengths case management in long term care.* Baltimore: Health Professions Press.

Fast, B., Chapin, R., & Rapp, C. (1994). *A model for strengths-based case management with older adults: Curriculum and training program.* Unpublished manuscript, The University of Kansas at Lawrence.

Featherman, D. L., Smith, J., & Peterson, J. G. (1990). Successful aging in a post-retired society. In P. B. Baltes & M. M. Baltes (Eds.), *Successful aging: Perspectives from the behavioral sciences.* Cambridge, UK: Cambridge University Press.

Freidson, E. (1988). *Profession of medicine.* Chicago: University of Chicago Press.

Hodge, D. R. (2001). Spiritual assessment: A review of major qualitative methods and a new framework for assessing spirituality. *Social Work, 46*(3), 203–214.

Isaacowitz, D. M., Vaillant, G. E., & Seligman, M. E. (2003). Strengths and satisfaction across the adult lifespan. *International Journal of Aging and Human Development, 47*(2), 181–201.

Jansson, B. (2003) *Becoming an effective policy advocate,* 4th ed. Pacific Grove, CA: Thomson/Brooks Cole.

Johnson, P. J., & Rubin, A. (1983). Case management in mental health: A social work domain? *Social Work, 28,* 49–55.

Kane, R. A., & Kane, R. L. (1987). *Long-term care: Principles, programs, and policies.* New York: Springer.

Kisthardt, W. E. (1997). A strengths model of case management: Principles and helping functions. In D. Saleebey (Ed.), *The strengths perspective in social work practice.* (2nd. ed.) New York: Longman.

Kisthardt, W., & Rapp, C. A. (1991). Bridging the gap between principles and practice: Implementing a strengths perspective in case management. In S. M. Rose (Ed.), *Social work practice and case management.* White Plains, NY: Longman.

Kivnick, H. Q. (1993, Winter/Spring). Everyday mental health: A guide to assessing life strengths. *Generations,* 13–20.

Kivnick, H. Q., & Murray, S. V. (2001). Life strengths interview guide: Assessing elder clients' strengths. *Journal of Gerontological Social Work, 34*(4), 7–32.

Koenig, H. G. (1994). *Aging and God: Spiritual pathways to mental health in midlife and later years.* New York: Haworth Press.

Kozol, J. (2000). *Ordinary resurrections: Children in the years of hope.* New York: Crowne Publishers.

Kretzmann, J. P. & McKnight, J. L. (1993). *Building communities from the inside out: A path toward finding and mobilizing a community's assets.* Chicago: ACTA Publications.

Kulys, R. (1983). Future crisis and the very old: Implications for discharge planning. *Health & Social Work, 8,* 182–195.

Langer, E. J. (1989). *Mindfulness.* Cambridge, MA: Perseus Books.

Lustbader, W., & Hooyman, N. (1994). *Taking care of aging family members.* New York: Free Press.

Marty, M. E. (1980). Social service: Godly and Godless. *Social Service Review, 54(4),* 463–481.

Motenko, A. K., & Greenberg, S. (1995). Reframing dependence in old age: A positive transition for families. *Social Work, 40(3),* 382–389.

Nelson-Becker, H. (2003). Practical Philosophies: Interpretations of Religion and Spirituality by African-American and Jewish Elders. *Journal of Religious Gerontology, 14(2/3),* 85–99.

Nelson-Becker, H. (In press). Meeting life challenges: A hierarchy of coping styles in African-American and Jewish-American older adults. *Journal of Human Behavior in the Social Environment.*

Nelson-Becker, H., Nakashima, M., & Canda, E. R. (In press). Spiritual assessment in aging: A framework for clinicians. *Journal of Gerontological Social Work.*

Pargament, K. I. (1997). *The psychology of religion and coping.* New York: Guilford Press.

Perkins, K., & Tice, C. (1995). A strengths perspective in practice: Older people and mental health challenges. *Journal of Gerontological Social Work, 23(3/4),* 83–97.

Perkins, K., & Tice, C. (1999). Family treatment of older adults who misuse alcohol: A strengths perspective. *Journal of Gerontological Social Work, 31(3–4),* 169–185.

Poertner, J., & Ronnau, J. (1990). A strengths approach to children with emotional disabilities. In D. Saleebey (Ed.), *The strengths perspective in social work practice.* White Plains, NY: Longman.

Pray, J. E. (1992). Maximizing the patient's uniqueness and strengths: A challenge for home health care. *Social Work in Health Care, 17(3),* 71–79.

Princeton Religious Research Center (PRCC). (2001, March). Index of Leading Religious Indicators Remains at High Level. *Emerging Trends, 23(3).*

Quinn, J. (1992). Case management: As diverse as its clients. *Journal of Case Management, 1(2),* 38.

Rapp, C. A. (1992). The strengths perspective of case management with persons suffering from severe mental illness. In D. Saleebey (Ed.), *The strengths perspective in social work practice.* White Plains, NY: Longman.

Rapp, R. C., Siegal, H. A., Fisher, J. H., & Wagner, J. H. (1992). A strengths-based model of case management/advocacy: Adapting a mental health model to practice work with persons who have substance abuse problems. In R. Ashery (Ed.), *Progress and issues in case management* (Research Monograph no. 127, pp. 79–91). Rockville, MD: National Institute on Drug Abuse.

Ronch, J. L., & Goldfield, J. A. (Eds.). (2003). *Mental wellness in aging: Strengths-based approaches.* Baltimore, MD: Health Professions Press.

Rose, S. M. (1992). *Case management social work practice.* White Plains, NY: Longman.

Schneider, R., & Lester, L. (2001). *Social work advocates.* Belmont, CA.: Brooks/Cole.

Smith, V., & Eggleston, R. (1989). Long-term care: The medical model versus the social model. *Public Welfare, 47,* 27–29.

Spilka, B. (1986). Spiritual issues: Do they belong in psychological practice? Yes-but! *Psychotherapy in Private Practice, 4(4),* 93–100.

Sullivan, W. P. (1997). On strengths, niches, and recovery from serious mental illness. In D. Saleebey (Ed.), *The strengths perspective in social work practice* (2nd ed.). New York: Longman.

Sullivan, W. P., & Fisher, B. J. (1994). Intervening for success: Strengths-based case management and successful aging. *Journal of Gerontological Social Work, 22(1/2),* 61–74.

U.S. Bureau of the Census. (1991). *Statistical abstract of the United States.* Washington, DC: U.S. Government Printing Office.

CHAPTER TEN

THE OPPORTUNITIES AND CHALLENGES OF STRENGTHS-BASED, PERSON-CENTERED PRACTICE

Purpose, Principles, and Applications in a Climate of System's Integration

WALTER E. KISTHARDT

The essential political problem is that of ascertaining the possibility of constituting a new politics of truth . . . not changing peoples' consciousness, or what's in their heads—but the political, economic, institutional regime of the production of truth.
—Michel Foucault

INTRODUCTION

The Strengths Perspective, and concomitant "strengths-based" practice, continues to interest, intrigue, and challenge front-line workers, policy-makers, funders, and those who administer a wide range of programs designed to assist people in achieving their goals (Anderson & Carter, 2003; Glicken, 2004; Krogsrud-Miley, O'Melia, & Dubois, 2004; Pulin, 2005). For many, the dilemma has been finding ways to integrate a strengths approach with prevailing medical and problems-based frameworks related to medical necessity and funding. For others, the challenge has been to develop and deliver training curricula that capture the complexity of what initially appears to be a straightforward and simplistic approach to practice. In recent years the Purpose and Principles of Strengths-Based, Person-Centered Practice have been embraced as a potential "truth" that may serve to foster true integration of multiple service systems on behalf of each service participant.

171

In this chapter I identify key concepts regarding the nature of our ultimate purpose in entering the collaborative helping process. What is our political agenda? What do we want to happen? What do our programs want to happen? How do we measure success? By counting units of service or by documenting social outcomes realized by those who are disenfranchised? I shall illustrate diverse practice applications and suggest that six core principles of strengths-based person centered practice may serve to guide and direct the efforts of multiple stakeholders and diverse systems of care. I will draw upon my collaboration with a wide range of programs interested in implementing the strengths approach and achieving systems integration in their work with service participants. These populations include people living with HIV/AIDS, adults with persistent mental illness, adults with developmental disabilities, and persons struggling with substance abuse/addictions or co-occurring disorders. I then examine some practical applications that seem to promote a collaborative power sharing interpersonal helping relationship. I conclude with some reflections regarding the current trend toward service and systems integration and what challenges lie ahead.

THE PURPOSE OF THE STRENGTHS APPROACH

In order to be effective and efficient practitioners, a clear understanding of the purpose of our helping efforts is essential. I have used the following statement of purpose with my social work graduate students and providers across the country in training seminars (Kisthardt, 2002, p. 164).

> To assist individuals, families, and communities within the context of a mutually enriching, collaborative partnership, to identify, secure, and sustain, the range of resources, both external and internal, needed to live in a normally interdependent manner in the community.

There are several key contrasts that this statement of purpose suggests to providers. First, we strive in a strengths approach to "help" people achieve the goals that they *want* to achieve, not the goals that someone else believes they *need* to achieve. Second, the strengths approach does not suggest that "anything goes." That whatever the service participant "wants" is agreed with and used to fuel the helping plan. This is where the notion of "normal interdependence" becomes crucial.

The strengths-based practitioner is keenly aware of the social/cultural/legal constraints on individual behavior within a given community. Behavior that is normally interdependent (and I use the term "normally" sociologically) is tolerable, acceptable, and ultimately, legal. The provider who embraces the concept of normal interdependence seeks to influence others, within the context of the professional helping relationship, to make choices that are likely to be healthier for them, and that are respectful of other citizens. If our focus is upon the "problem" this begs a very important question: What problem do we focus on first? Medical management and adherence to the medical regimen for symptom management? Mental health diagnosis and compliance with psychoactive neuroleptics? The problematic use of alcohol as indicated by the person's score on the addictions severity index? Consider the following situation:

> Let's say that you have asked a service participant, who happens to have co-occurring diagnoses of mental illness and substance abuse, and who also is living with AIDS, "what do you want in your life?" The person states that he wants to work, but that his anti-retroviral medication is causing nausea. He notes that one of the ways he copes with his illness is by using alcohol. He has been arrested once for driving under the influence. His probation plan requires that he completes a residential substance abuse treatment program. He tells you that he has "been down these roads before" and that what he really wants is to get a job so that he can get his own place and get on with his life. How do you respond?

This example typically engenders much discussion and even heated debate. Treatment providers will tend to have different viewpoints which appear to be related to their training and experience. Some may say that the initial focus should be upon the substance abuse, as this is the core problem that will continue to negatively affect all other aspects of one's life unless it is directly confronted and addressed through planned intervention. Others will suggest that the substance abuse is related to clinical depression and that once the depression is understood and treated the use of substances as a self-medicating mechanism will no longer be needed. Others will argue that we must develop programs to treat both of these disorders simultaneously in order to be effective. Still others will suggest that due to the diagnosis of HIV/AIDS that the person should be referred to the Ryan White case management program for initial evaluation and brokerage case management services.

This example illustrates the systemic fragmentation and multivariate and complex nature of peoples' lives demanding the attention of advanced generalist social work practice (Derezotes, 2000). By developing approaches that place the "person" not the "problem" at the center of our deliberations, we are more likely to meet the person in the middle and to discuss and develop a plan that both provider and service participant can live with. This requires that strengths-based practitioners, regardless of their theoretical and methodological stance ask the following question . . . how am I contributing to the *social* outcome that has been articulated by the person? I submit that medical, behavioral, and psychological outcomes (medication adherence, sobriety, insight and cognitive restructuring) are incomplete without concomitant changes and gains in one's social world. Examples of these outcomes might include meaningful employment, increased social support network, achieving a permanent home of one's choosing, gaining opportunities for leisure, and having opportunities for spiritual growth and connectedness.

The concept of normal interdependence should ultimately determine whether or not we affirm and support each person's own aspirations. I submit that if we choose not to help someone with a goal that is normally interdependent, then this reflects a stance of oppression and a fundamental difference of opinion regarding values (Foucault, 1980). In a strengths-based approach, our task becomes helping others engage in behaviors that respect the wants and needs of

other citizens in the community, while at the same time promoting personal gratification, satisfaction, and sense of accomplishment. As a supreme court judge
once ruled "individual liberty ceases, where public peril begins." In the spirit of
eco-systemic theory this perspective involves "the creation of structural conditions
under which people can choose to give to their community as well as to take from
their community" (Breton, 1994, p. 29). The treatment or helping process should
enrich a sense of citizenship, inclusion, and meaning; a sense of autonomy and
social responsibility, a shift from valuing independence to affirming and valuing
interdependence (Capra, 1996).

The six principles of strengths-based practice serve to guide and direct the
range of helping efforts related to this purpose. I have found that there is often disagreement on one or more of these principles not only between different systems,
but within different components of the same agency. If providers are not able to
agree on these principles, integration, consistency and continuity of care becomes
far more difficult, if not impossible to achieve. We now examine these principles,
incorporating examples from programs where I have provided training and/or
technical assistance.

THE SIX PRINCIPLES OF STRENGTHS-BASED HELPING

1. The initial focus of the helping process is on the strengths, interests, abilities, knowledge, and capabilities of each person; not on their diagnoses, deficits, symptoms, and weaknesses as *defined by another.*

The human beings who enter your life as a service provider are so much more
than a collection of symptoms and an amalgam of problems. They are survivors.
They are exceptionally adaptive. Despite the effects of poverty, oppression, discrimination, illness, disappointments, public apathy and even at time hostility,
people who are described as being at-risk and/or vulnerable still resolve to live
each day as best they can. They are creative, resilient, persistent, and courageous.
They have not given up, but have decided to press on despite external challenges
and internal conflict and pain.

This principle suggests that people decide for themselves what they want in
life. Even if this statement is something as basic as "I want to live," to be able to
express one's personal aspirations and desires is an important strength. Once this
statement is made, then attention to deficits and various other "needs" assumes
meaning for them. For example, I have reviewed many treatment plans that list
the goal as "medication compliance." Whose goal is this? In many instances, it is
the providers' goal. They are focusing on what they believe the person "needs."
Most service participants I speak to would rather not take their medications. A
person may ultimately decide to take their medication because it helps them to
achieve something that they want. Medication, therefore, is viewed as a means

toward some other socially-oriented end. One person once shared, "I want to keep my job. I really love it, and I know I need to take my medications to help me stay healthy." Still another person told me "I didn't want to work anymore, so I went off my medication and I lost the job." If the fact that this person no longer wanted to work had been identified, he could have been counseled to leave the job in a normally interdependent manner, giving notice and getting a letter of reference. What happened, however, was that his "illness" and "medication non-compliance" were cited as the reasons why he "lost" his job.

This principle challenges us to assume a stance of respect and admiration for people. We are challenged to assume the role of "student" interested in learning about this person's hopes and dreams, rather than as the "expert" who purports to know more about what motivates a person than the person does (Miller & Rollnick, 2002). We are committed to get to know all persons as unique and valuable beings, to learn what things they want in their lives, what holds meaning for them, and to then collaborate on what needs to happen in order for them to be successful. One service participant remarked:

> Mary (social worker) was the first person I ever worked with who asked me what I wanted to do. She told me that she admired me because of how I have been able to cope with my mental illness and still get what I need each day. She told me she had a lot to learn from me. She said I have a lot of strengths, and I guess she's right . . . but I didn't see them as strengths . . . but I do now.

A "focus" on strengths does not mean one ignores or deliberately turns a blind eye to the realities of decisions people make regarding behaviors that may indeed not be conducive to their wellness and/or the wellness and safety of others. In the era of managed care the challenge is to balance attention to symptoms, problems, deficits, and medical necessity with attention to the development of individualized plans of care which demonstrate evidence that the intervention is making a difference. This principle reminds providers that every helping intervention is grounded in the meaning ascribed to the process by each individual (Finn & Jacobson, 2003). As these authors suggest, practice rooted in a social justice framework must integrate meaning, context, history, possibility, and power. This principle is summed up nicely by a young woman who shared "the first thing is to get to know me . . . I am not a collection of problems, pathology, and failures . . . I have hopes and dreams and visions for what I want in my life . . . you are not living my life . . . I am different from everyone else you will encounter . . . show respect for that difference, honor it . . . and I'll let you in . . . ignore it, or come off like you know more about me than I do, and it will do no more than to frustrate us both."

2. The helping relationship becomes one of collaboration, mutuality, and partnership. Power with another, not power over another.

Power is a socio-political construct (Anderson & Carter, 2003). Foucault (1980) has suggested that power is "co-extensive with the social body . . . that power is relational, and that relations of power are interwoven with other kinds of relations for which they play at once a conditioning and conditioned role" (p. 142). Power is expressed through influence. It is "the ability to get things done the way one wants them done . . . the ability to influence people" (Shafritz & Ott, 1996, p. 354). For example, professors may feel powerful when a student shares that their comments have influenced them to reconsider some notions they have held regarding a certain group of people. In a like manner, students may feel powerful when they suggest an alternative assignment that will help them to more fully experience and learn about a given concept and the proposal is accepted by the professor. How do we respond when a "client," "patient," or "consumer" suggests that what we have recommended is not what they want or believe that they need at this time in their lives? I have frequently used the example that if professionals recommend a certain set of protocols in an attempt to influence a service participant it will likely be thought of as "assessment and treatment." Whereas, if the person disagrees, and shifts the attention to some other set of protocols which they believe will be helpful, this may be interpreted as "manipulation." This double standard runs antithetical to a true notion of mutual influence, true collaboration, and power sharing (Mattaini, 2001). Relationships where power, as reflected in influence and decision making, is skewed in one direction disproportionately, may eventually lead to oppression. As Friere suggests, human beings are not liberated through revolution, but through "communion" with each other (1994, p. 114).

This principle challenges us to develop helping plans with people not for them. It challenges us to share power and decision making as we journey with another human being. The challenge of implementing this principle in practice demands that we expand the boundaries of the helping enterprise. Who decides where meetings take place? Who decides what the treatment goal is to be? Who decides how long the meetings take place? Who decides if there can be communication between regularly scheduled meetings? Who decides which questions are "appropriate" and which are not? Who decides whether there will be "self-disclosure" on the part of the provider? These are but a few of the important questions to ask as we strive to make the helping relationship more collaborative and more strengths-based. A service participant shared these thoughts with me regarding the power of this type of relationship:

> My case manager was more like a friend than other workers in my past. She really seemed to care about me, and she did not force me to do things. We talked about our mothers, we smoked and laughed together. She helped me get my own place and she came to AA meetings with me. Now I go without her. She has been a gift from heaven, a real miracle in my life. When I think about drinking now . . . and I do, pretty much every day . . . I realize I want to keep my apartment more than I want to drink and I get busy with other things that bring me a sense of joy . . . if I was still living with my mother I'd probably resort to drinking again. She helped me to get something in my life I didn't want to lose."

Strengths-based practitioners have realized the importance of expanding traditional "boundaries" of the helping relationship. As Derezotes (2000) notes, "in a reciprocal relationship the client and worker share co-responsibility for the work process . . . the worker and client view themselves as equals . . . (they) co-create the practice goals, objectives, and tasks (p. 79). The ideal situation in any helping encounter is when both workers and service participants, having been guided by the wants and needs of those helped, come away from the process enriched. Strengths-based practitioners do not have more invested in the process and outcomes than do service participants. There is a belief in the resourcefulness, determination, and resiliency of all people, regardless of illness, disability, or personal history.

3. Each person is responsible for their own recovery.
The participant is the director of the helping efforts.
We serve as caring community living consultants.
The healing process takes place on many levels.

People constantly make decisions. Do I take one drink or not? Do I change the baby now or wait until later? Do I take my medications? Do I get out of bed today? A strengths perspective recognizes that decisions are being made. The question here is not whether someone is conscious that they are making a decision. Their behavior becomes a *de facto* indication of the decision that has been made. If we are to influence and promote other decisions that are more normally interdependent, the first step is to help people realize that they are in fact making these decisions. And that if these decisions continue, they may not attain the goal they have articulated. This view certainly recognizes that bio-neurological realities affect human behavior. It suggests, however, that this variable is not exclusively the "cause." Environmental, cultural, spiritual, economic, psychological, and ethno-cultural factors also warrant the strengths-based practitioner's attention and consideration.

The example of the young single parent who refuses to get help for a chemical addiction is a prime example. She has stated that she *wants* to be reunited with her infant who has been placed in foster care. This goal becomes the ultimate focus of the work. She refuses, however, to participate in treatment and the providers, who have a duty to the baby and the larger community, petition to terminate parental rights. The young parent may "blame" social services for "taking" her baby. In point of fact her decisions, as reflected in her behavior, suggest that competing desires are at play. She directed and determined the course of events, the workers responded. I have spoken with many providers who were convinced that what some of these young people may truly have wanted was to not be a parent. By making certain decisions they accomplished that goal in a manner where the responsibility and blame could be shifted to the state department of children and family services.

A recent collaboration with a residential treatment facility for people struggling with chemical addictions provided me with renewed insights regarding the nature of recovery and the compatibility of this concept with strengths-based practice. After providing a two-day training on strengths-based, person-centered care, I spent time at the facility observing intake, and a wide range of psycho-educational treatment groups. It seemed clear from my observations that tasks tended to be "assigned" by counselors, not generated from a discussion of a range of options relating to the social goals that each person held for themselves. As the staff began to implement Person-Centered Strengths Assessments, and Personal Wellness Plans, they reported increased enthusiasm and follow-up on the part of those receiving treatment. They also reported feeling less "pressure" to constantly generate treatment plans and tasks for people. As one counselor stated, "you have really challenged me to get out of my box . . . it's not comfortable . . . I like staying in my box, it's what I know and what I believe . . . but I realize how this approach is actually freeing and healthier for me . . . if they don't own it, it's not going to work."

As a result of this process, service participants began to attend and participate in the staff discussion of their plans where they had not been involved before. The idea was generated that each person who received care should leave the facility with their own "Personal Recovery Plan" that had been developed at the residential facility. The community case manager had also been involved in the training, and was in a much better position to continue the process as each person was discharged from the facility.

4. All human beings have the inherent capacity to learn, grow and change.

The human spirit is incredibly resilient. Despite the hardships, trauma, experience of repeated psychiatric hospitalizations, years of living on the streets, years of experiencing the negative effects of poverty, physical or neurological disability, structural oppression, stigma and discrimination, each person, at the time you begin the collaboration, may be on the verge of making important changes in his/her life (Prochaska, DiClemente, and Norcross, 1992). This principle challenges us to harness the motivating power of positive expectations—the healing power that often is the product when the faith, hope, and love conveyed by one person, ignites the fire of potentials and possibilities for another.

I have encountered service providers in training seminars who suggest that this principle is fine for those who are "higher functioning," but the majority of the people they work with have "severe disabilities" and may not even be able to tell you what they want. In these types of situations it becomes important to shift our focus from asking questions to patiently observing. A strengths perspective suggests that people will indicate their preferences by their behavior. Moreover, we should constantly attempt to try something new and different with people who may seem to have very little potential to accomplish new tasks or to engage in certain behaviors. The following experience illustrated the essence of this principle, and it is an image I will never forget.

> I was providing two days of training for staff at Tachachale, a residential treatment facility in Gainesville, Florida. Prior to the training the staff was taking me on a tour of the cottages. In one cottage was a young man who was lying in a hospital bed face down and reclined at a 45 degree angle, with his head about two feet from the

floor and his feet elevated. He was not able to speak, as he had experienced significant neurological impairment due to traumatic brain injury. This position assisted with postural drainage. As the staff stopped to introduce me he began to make low guttural vocalizations. It seemed clear that he heard the staff member, and was responding as best he could. Acting on an impulse, I laid down on the floor where he could see my face and said, "Hi Jimmy, it's nice to meet you." At which point Jimmy began to make much louder vocalizations which the staff agreed was laughter! They stated that they had never heard him respond in this manner. I asked them if they had ever lain down on the floor to talk to him when he was in this position. They had not. They decided that they would start doing this, especially on those days when it seemed to them that he was having one of his "off" days.

If we believe that all people possess the capacity to learn, grow, and change, then we will constantly be seeking new and different strategies to create opportunities for this growth to occur. At every helping session we should strive to learn something about the service participant(s) that we did not know before. Each new piece of information may serve as a key that unlocks the potential that resides in all people. Sometimes when staff has worked a person for several years they may get to the point where they think they know "everything" about the person. Many times, when I have done an actual demonstration of engagement, strengths assessment, and planning with a current service participant at a particular program, I have learned things about them in 20 minutes that no one at the agency knew. The following example illustrates this point.

> At a recent training in Iowa, I spoke with a man who has a developmental disability at a workshop in Fort Dodge. There were over 100 people at the seminar, and this gentleman agreed to come up front and work with me to demonstrate the engagement and strengths assessment process. During our conversation, I asked him if spirituality was an important part of his life. He hesitated, looked around the room, and then shared that he wanted to get baptized into the Lutheran faith. There was a marked buzzing in the room, and it became clear that this desire had never been shared with anyone at the program. I asked him if his family (especially his father who was his legal guardian) would be supportive of this. He said that he told his grandmother and she thought it was a good idea, but that he was afraid to ask his father as he was not sure how he would react. The staff later said they would work with him on a plan to share this desire with his father at his next circle of support meeting.

As I said, when we work with people day in and day out, for a period of many months or even years, we may come to believe that we know everything about them. Coming to this conclusion serves as a barrier to integrating a strengths perspective in our work. There is always something new to learn. There is always a different question to ask. We must assume the perspective of an explorer, and enter into a voyage of discovery. The more we learn about the uniqueness, talents, skills, accomplishments, desires, and knowledge people possess, the more creative we may be in mutually developing helping plans that are truly individualized and hold particular meaning for them.

5. Helping activities in naturally occurring settings in the community are encouraged in a strengths-based, person-centered approach.

Models of community care with vulnerable and multiply challenged populations suggest that working with people in naturally occurring settings whenever possible is an effective component of effective and efficient practice (Bentley, 2002). A common characteristic of each of these models is the fact that case managers as well as therapists are expected to work with people in various locations in the community as well as in their homes whenever possible unless there are legitimate concerns regarding safety. In this manner, providers may observe skill sets not demonstrated at the program or agency. In addition, the environmental strengths in terms of natural helpers, employment opportunities, and a range of other potential connections may be discovered.

In my conversations with providers several benefits of meeting with people out of the mental health center or program building are frequently noted. First, we are able to observe firsthand some of the realities of the person's day to day living circumstances. Second, people often feel more comfortable and share more detailed personal information in the context of completing tasks together in the community. Third, people with disabilities are more visible in the community, and this serves to break down myths, stereotypes, and the discrimination that is often a result of these biases. In addition, many case managers state that they would much rather be out of the office, so there is a feeling of satisfaction and even joy that accompanies the challenges of holistic, comprehensive helping. Finally, providers often report a marked change in people's behavior when they are in naturally occurring settings in the community. People behave less like "patients" or "clients" (Mead, 1934) and more like collaborators and partners in completing the helping tasks. The goals related to community activities should always be documented on the Person Wellness Plan with the service participant or guardian signing off, thus reflecting informed consent (Hepworth, Rooney, & Larsen, 2002, p. 69).

Strengths-based practice rekindles and invites even further application of eco-systems theory in our work with people. As we discovery the desires, talents, and interests of each person, we discover locations in the environment where the goal is to enhance the "reciprocal interactions" (Krogsrud-Miley, O'Melia, & Dubois, 2004, p. 30). The focus of our efforts shifts from seeking to promote some sort of "change" within the person or within environments. We hone our skills in recognizing, appreciating, valuing, and utilizing that which is already there. In a sense, we co-create with individuals and various social settings a mutually enriching partnership and exchange. Indeed, there may be aspects of the person and aspects of environments which may suggest change and transformation. Greif views this transformation as a "dynamic process between people and their environments as people grow, achieve competence, and make contributions to others" (Krogsrud-Miley, O'Melia & Dubois, 2004, p. 30). Principle number six expands upon these points.

6. The entire community is viewed as an oasis of potential resources to enlist on behalf of service participants. Naturally occurring resources are considered as a possibility first, before segregated or formally constituted "mental health" or "social services".

This principle challenges providers to avoid the "knee jerk" reaction that sometimes accompanies the planning and referral process. For example, the person sets a goal of finishing her/his high school equivalency (GED) and the provider refers the person to a GED study group at the "partial hospital" day program. Before this referral should be made, the provider might encourage enrollment in a review course offered by the local junior college, or see if there is a mentoring program where the participant may study one-on-one with a retired teacher who is willing to volunteer his or her time. This may actually be more comfortable for those who do not do well in formal classroom-like settings. Seeing the entire community and the potentials and possibilities for resource development is an essential perspective of the strengths-based practitioner. The strengths perspective transcends the individual, to neighborhood, organization, and larger community (Sullivan & Rapp, 2002).

One major disincentive to implementing this principle in mental health practice has been the prevailing policy of "fee for service." If the center is billing for "services" provided at their program and they cannot bill for services provided by a natural helper, the choice for administrators is fairly clear cut. If they are to achieve their goal of sustaining the program, revenues are needed. The landscape of funding services for people with persistent mental illness, however, has shifted markedly in recent years.

The onset of managed care, capitated financing schemes, and case management options through Medicaid now provide incentives for providers to expand traditional notions of "therapeutic" and "clinical" care (Maguire, 2002). For example, in a capitated arrangement providers receive a set annual dollar limit for each person who meets the criteria of persistent mental illness. Person-centered outcomes will drive the work. How each individual meets the needs related to these outcomes will vary. The point is—providers will be more likely to use a wider range of natural supports if their funding is not totally dependent on formally constituted clinical services.

The onset of "supportive housing" is another example of this principle (Ridgeway and Zipple, 1990). Often a person desires to secure his/her own apartment and others, family and/or treatment team sees this goal as "unrealistic." A plan is then suggested where the person lives in a group home or other "supervised housing" arrangement as a "transitional" step. For some individuals, this approach works well. For others, however, it is not effective and often leads to "acting out" behaviors. Anyone who has ever lived in the same space with six or more non-relatives for a period of time knows first hand how stressful congregate living may be.

This principle challenges providers to creatively and directly identify and strive to remove barriers so that each person may live where they want to live. As one service participant shared: "I was in a group home and I couldn't take it. I can't be around people. I don't like people. I went back to the hospital (state psychiatric hospital), I had more freedom there. My case manager helped me to get my own place. It's not much, just one room, but it's mine."

Each of these principles serves to guide and direct strengths-based, person-centered helping. By identifying and honoring individual aspirations, skills, resiliency, resourcefulness, and potential for growth, we gain a fuller picture of the person. As Sir William Osler, pioneering physician once said, "it is more important to know what sort of patient has the disease, than it is to know what sort of disease the patient has." By realizing that there is more in our shared experience as human beings that make providers more like participants than different from them, we gain the courage to be warm, caring, empathic, and genuinely affirming of people's own visions (Kisthardt, 1996). In this spirit of connection, we expand the boundaries of "therapy" and strive to assist in ways that are "therapeutic." When this happens, both provider and participant come away from the process enriched, fulfilled, and gratified. One participant became tearful as he shared his experience with his provider:

> He's like a brother to me. I know he care (sic) about me. He checks on me, comes to my place, makes sure I get my medicine . . . he send me a card at Christmas. I never got a card at Christmas . . . it meant so much. . . .I showed it to my mom. I'm gonna keep the card forever . . . Tom's (provider) gone now, but I'll never forget him.

A strengths-based practitioner understands that people we work with make decisions. The essence of helping is to help people bolster their internal and external resources so that more choices may be available to them. We strive, through the collaborative partnership and caring relationship, to influence decision making that may lead to healthier, more satisfying lives. We recognize that the first meetings play an important role in whether or not people choose to work with us. My research on the service participant perspective regarding the factors that promote effective engagement suggests the following strategies.

STRATEGIES THAT PROMOTE EFFECTIVE ENGAGEMENT FROM THE PERSPECTIVE OF THE SERVICE PARTICIPANT

We have entered into the era of "targeted populations." For example, people with the coexisting disorders of mental illness and substance abuse, people who are receiving TANF (Temporary Assistance for Needy Families), people with developmental disabilities, people who are homeless, people who have been diagnosed with HIV/AIDS, or people who are mandated to receive services by order of the correctional system, may become the focus of helping efforts. Engaging these individuals, who are confronted with many challenges, not the least of which are related to poverty and structural discrimination, is not an easy task.

By talking to people who receive services as well as to experienced community care providers across the country, the following strategies appear to contribute to effectively engaging people in the helping process. I will use examples from work with many different populations. These experiences were shared during time I spent at different service agencies providing training and technical assistance in the Strengths Model.

Focus more on conversational skills than interviewing skills.   Service participants seem to respond more fully to providers who come across as "real people." It is not possible to have a conversation with another person if I am not willing to "self-disclose." I have heard from many providers who share that they have been trained not to self-disclose to a "patient, client, etc." and indeed, that many of their programs have policies that prohibit such activity. Despite this reality, many seasoned providers have learned that they will get much more information if they are willing to share personal information is timely, relevant, and designed to foster trust and collaboration. The following example from a training session I conducted for the staff at the Department of Corrections in Kansas illustrates this point:

> After an exercise where the people at the training were asked to spend a few minutes with a colleague identifying as many things as they could that they had in common we reconvened. One of the uniformed corrections officers (complete with standard issue sidearm neatly holstered by his side) stood up and said, "if you are asking us to do this type of thing with prisoners we would be in direct violation of the Department of Corrections Policy and Procedures Manual which clearly states, "at no time disclose personal information to any of the inmates." After I thanked him for sharing this information I said "now, given that reality, may I ask if you have ever shared something about yourself with an inmate?" He hesitated, and then said "yes, I have." I then asked all of the other uniformed officers in the room if they had ever "self-disclosed" in their interactions with inmates. All of their hands went up. Our discussion then centered on how they made decisions regarding what specifically might be shared, under what circumstances, and to whom. One officer summarized our discussion by saying "we're much less likely to have trouble with inmates if we treat them with respect, like human beings, and to affirm that we may have common interests as human beings."

Send a clear message that you are not there to make negative judgements, to try to change them, but rather to affirm their own aspirations and work together toward making those dreams a reality.   This is accomplished by integrating questions from a Person-Centered Strengths Assessment right from the start of the work (see figure 10.1). This process seeks to identify what people "want" in their lives, before identifying what they "need" in their lives from your perspective. The shift from focusing on what someone else thinks the person needs to the person's own motivation (what they really want) seems to be an essential component of effective engagement. The following example from a case manager working with a person with coexisting disorders clearly illustrates this shift. He shared this with me six months after going through the strengths perspective training at his agency.

> I started working with a guy who had a long history of mental illness and substance abuse. At our first meeting I asked him if he was still drinking and he said

"occasionally." I asked him if he would be willing to accept a referral for in-patient detox after which we could start working on some other things in his life. He said, "I can handle it, I don't have a problem with it." My first thought was that he was clearly in denial. I then thought about shifting the focus and I said, "OK, you don't want to work on that and you don't think you need to, what is it that you do want?" He said, "I want my own apartment." I asked him to write that goal on the top of the personal wellness plan. He did. Then we talked more specifically about finances, location, etc. I agreed to meet him the following week to begin to develop the plan to achieve this goal. I then said, "OK, our meeting is at 11 a.m. You need to know that I will be sober when I get there. I also expect you to be sober, because this is your goal, not my goal, and if you really want it you have got to make some important decisions about your drinking. If you have been drinking before I get there, I'm going to leave." He agreed. When I showed up he was ready and indeed had not been drinking. This was the first time in a long time that he had not taken a drink before noon. The weeks went by and he worked hard to complete the short term goals related to getting an apartment. When he moved in he was so proud and said he had never really had his own place. I said, "if you want to keep it, you might think about watching how much you drink. It would have been better, I believe, if he would not be drinking at all, and working on sobriety. This however, was not his goal yet. He has been in the apartment for three months and seems to be doing well. He reports that he is still taking a drink every now and then, but that he has "really cut down, because I don't want to get sick again and lose this great apartment."

Engage in activities you both enjoy.   Providers who work with children have known for years how important it is to get on the floor with kids and engage through games and activities that the children enjoy and that make them comfortable. What happens to that strategy when we are working with adults? Why is it sometimes considered "unprofessional" or even "unethical" to engage in activities with a participant that are enjoyable, while at the same time doing an assessment, getting ideas for possible helping plans, monitoring and evaluating their progress, etc.? When we ask people where they would like to meet, if they would like to walk while we talk, if they would like to throw a ball back and forth while we get to know each other, these are truly examples of starting where the "client" is. The following vignette, shared by an income maintenance case manager/advocate from Kansas City, is still the best example I have heard of creative use of self in an effort to engage an assertively reluctant participant.

A case manager was working with a program to attempt to engage with noncustodial fathers (The Futures Connection) throughout the city. Each time the case manager found this particular gentleman he was not willing to talk at any length and would not remain very long. The case manager sometimes spent hours just trying to find him, and often he did locate him at the neighborhood basketball court, where he was known for his skill. The case manager then got an idea. He told the man that he had a proposition for him. They would play one-on-one to 21 points. If the participant won, the case manager would "not bother him" any more. But, if the case manager won, the participant would become involved in the program. The person agreed. The case manager won the game! The participant, bound now by the agreement made on the basketball court, was true to his word and became involved in skill training, job readiness, and case management. When the participant completed the program, he got a full-time job, with benefits, driving a Pepsi truck and making $14.00 per hour. He had re-established contact with his children, and was regular in his child support payments to their mother.

Be sensitive to cultural factors . . . honor diversity and seek to assist people in involvements that hold meaning for them.   The strengths approach, by its very nature, attempts to be sensitive to the importance of culture in people's lives. A strengths-based practitioner is like an ethnographer. The goal is to learn about one's lived experience, meaning, and future visions that hold meaning and value (Anderson & Carter, 2003). When we gain an appreciation for worldview that is different from ours, we will join people in generating plans that reflect outcomes that resonate on multiple levels. The following example shows the power of culturally sensitive engagement.

> A social worker who was a case manager at a community support program for people with persistent mental illness was attempting to engage with a young man by doing outreach in Lawrence, Kansas. During the first few visits the case manager's agenda was to influence the young man to come in to the mental health center for intake, evaluation, and to become involved for "socialization" at the partial hospital program. The young man was cordial and polite, but refused to go to the center. As the case manager grew to know him better they talked of his Native American roots. They talked of things he had done in the past related to the culture of his people. He shared that he used to get much from attending sweat lodge ceremonies. The case manager then got the idea of connecting him with some people at the Haskell Indian School located in Lawrence. He said he would agree to this plan. They both went to meet some students at the school, and he quickly became involved in a regular sweat ceremony. He also eventually became more involved with the services the mental health center had to offer.

Seek to incorporate humor, joy, and laughter into the helping process.
To be sure, many people we attempt to help are in very serious situations and struggle with the harsh realities of poverty, illness, addiction, sadness, and loss. Our field is becoming increasingly aware of the healing power of humor, joy, and laughter. As Sigmund Freud once said, "Like wit and the comic, humor has a liberating element. It is the triumph of narcissism, the ego's victorious assertion of its own vulnerability. It refuses to suffer the slings and arrows of reality" (1905). It is somewhat unfortunate, that many service providers equate the presence of humor and laughter in the helping process as being callous, uncaring, heartless, and indifferent. I recently spoke to an emergency room nurse who was "written up" because her supervisor heard her laughing, and the ER was "no place for laughter."

It seems clear from feedback I have gathered from people on the receiving end of our ministrations, that a sense of humor, honesty, and joy are perceived as important characteristics of people who would attempt to help them. And, as one participant shared with me "this does not mean they try to do a ten minute monologue to try to make me laugh, and it does not mean that they use humor as a substitute for knowledge, skills, and professionalism."

FIGURE 10.1   Person-Centered Strengths Assessment

Participant _____ Case Manager _____ Date _____

Housing/A Sense of "Home":

Where are you living now?

What do you like about your current living situation?

What things don't you like about where you are living now?

For now, do you want to remain where you are, or would you like to move?

Describe the housing situation you have had in the past that has been the most satisfying for you.

Transportation/Getting Around:

What are all the different ways you get to where you want or need to go?

Would you like to expand your transportation options?

What are some of the ways you have used in the past to get from place to place?

If you could travel anywhere in the world, where would you go? Why?

Financial/Insurance:

What are your current sources of income, and how much money do you have each month to work with?

What are your monthly financial obligations?

Do you have a guardian, conservator, or payee to help you with your finances?

What do you want to happen regarding your financial situation?

What was the most satisfying time in your life regarding your financial circumstances?

FIGURE 10.1   Continued

Vocational/Educational:

Are you employed full or part time currently? If so describe where you work and what you do at your job.

What does your job mean to you? If you do not have a job now, would you like to get one? Describe why you would or would not like to get a job at this time.

What activities are you currently involved in where you use your gifts and talents to help others?

What kinds of things do you do that make you happy and give you a sense of joy and personal satisfaction?

If you could design the perfect job for yourself what would it be? Indoors or outdoors? Night or day? Travel or no travel? Alone or with others? Where there is smoking or no smoking? Where it is quiet or noisy?

What was the most satisfying job you ever had?

Is it harder for you to **get** a job, or harder for you to **keep** a job? Why do you think this is so?

Are you currently taking classes that will lead to a degree or taking classes to expand your knowledge and skills?

What would you like to learn more about?

How far did you go in school? What was your experience with formal education?

What are your thoughts and feelings about returning to school to finish a degree, learn new skills, or take a course for the sheer joy of learning new things?

Do you like to teach others to do things? Would you like to be a coach or mentor for someone who needs some specialized assistance?

(continued)

FIGURE 10.1   Continued

Social Supports, Intimacy, Spirituality:

Describe your family.

What are the ways that members of your family provide social and emotional support for you and help to make you feel happy and good about yourself?

Is there anything about your relationships with family that makes you feel angry or upset?

What would you like to see happen regarding your relationships with family?

Where do you like to hang out and spend time? Why do you like it there?

What do you do when you feel lonely? Do you have a friend that you can call to talk to or do things with? If not, would you like to make such a friend?

Do you have the desire to be close to another in an intimate way? Would you like to have this type of relationship?

What meaning, if any, does spirituality play in your life? If this area is important to you, how do you experience and express your spiritual self?

What are your thoughts and feelings about nature?

Do you like animals?

Do you have a pet?

If not, would you like one? (if so, describe)

Have you ever had a pet? (elaborate)

Health:

How would you describe your health these days?

FIGURE 10.1   Continued

Is being in good health important to you? Why or why not?

What kinds of things do you do to take care of your health?

What are your patterns regarding smoking? Using alcohol? Using caffeine? What effect do these drugs have on your health?

What prescription medications are you currently taking? How do these medications help you?

How do you know when you're not doing too well? What is most calming and helpful for you during these times?

What limitations do you experience as a result of health circumstances?

What do you want and believe that you need in the area of health?

Leisure Time, Talents, Skills:

What are the activities that you enjoy and give you a sense of satisfaction, peace, accomplishment, and personal fulfillment?

Would you like the opportunity to engage more frequently in these activities?

What are the skills, abilities, and talents that you possess? These may be tangible skills such as playing a musical instrument, writing poetry, dancing, singing, painting, etc. or intangible gifts such as sense of humor, compassion for others, kindness, etc.

What are the sources of pride in your life?

Are there things you used to do regularly that gave you a sense of joy that you have not done in recent years?

Which of these activities would you consider rediscovering at this time in your life?

(continued)

FIGURE 10.1   Continued

Prioritizing

After thinking about all of these areas of your life, what are the two personal **DESIRES** that are most meaningful for you at this time?

1999 Wally Kisthardt, Ph.D., UMKC Graduate Social Work Program: 816-235-2203 kisthardtw@umkc.edu

FIGURE 10.2   Personal Wellness Plan

Participant _____   Case Manager/Clinician _____

Participant's Aspiration (motivation—may be concrete or abstract):

Intermediate Concrete Goal Related to Aspiration (3 to 6 months):

Short-Term Goals (What NEEDS to get done to accomplish above?):

Goal/Task/Objective   Target Date /// Date Achieved

_____   _____   _____
      PARTICIPANT   PROVIDER   COLLATERAL

1999 Wally Kisthardt, Ph.D., UMKC Graduate Social Work Program: 816-235-2203 kisthardtw@umkc.edu

During the engagement process providers gather data and seek to begin documenting the helping/service plan. Many providers are now incorporating the Person-Centered Strengths Assessment and the Personal Wellness Plan in their daily work with participants. The last section of this chapter examines these helping tools in greater detail.

THE PERSON-CENTERED STRENGTHS ASSESSMENT AND PERSONAL WELLNESS PLAN

Providers in many different venues and with many different populations have used the Person-Centered Strengths Assessment and Personal Wellness Plan (see Figures 10.1 and 10.2). In consulting with providers who have worked with these tools the following points seem to be related to successful implementation.

   1. *Both documents must reflect the dynamic nature of the helping process.* Many programs have become accustomed to writing a "treatment plan" for a service participant that often is not reviewed until some time in the future. In some programs it is an annual review. Seasoned clinicians know that gathering relevant information (assessment) and working towards goals the service participant has articulated occurs at each and every helping session. Therefore, new information regarding the person's life should be documented as the helping process evolves. Moreover, shifts in the service participant's priorities and incremental gains made toward stated goals should be recorded at each visit. I have suggested that both these tools be used when meeting with the person. Many clinicians do their "paperwork" after the person has left the office. Providers who have begun to use the person-centered strengths assessment and personal wellness plan at each meeting report that this is an effective strategy to "draw the person in" to the collaborative helping partnership. Some providers have shared that they now complete their progress notes in the presence of the service participant. One provider shared "this really helps me to be more descriptive and less jargony . . . I also tend to use more strengths-based language . . . rather than stating the client is resistive, manipulative, non amenable to treatment . . . I will say . . . client continues to have strong feelings about what they want and need and has remained steadfast in his decision not to follow through on my recommendations."

   2. *These documents are designed to be "user friendly." Therefore, service participants should be encouraged to actually write the information and record the plans.* I have suggested that providers give people a copy of the assessment to take home with them to work on at their own pace. Many providers have reported being "amazed" at how much information people write when they have a chance to take the form with them. I recall an experience I had doing training at a state hospital in Kansas. A patient from one of the wards volunteered to join me in a demonstration of how I would conduct the first meeting using a strengths approach. At the conclusion of our conversation, I showed him a copy of the Person-Centered Strengths Assessment. I pointed out that I had asked him many of the questions during our talk just as they appear on the assessment. I invited him to take the form back to the ward, and I encouraged him to work on it if he felt up to it. I then asked him to consider sharing it with his treatment team next time they met. The following day at the training the group had quite a surprise. The young man had finished the entire assessment and had asked one of the nurses if he could come to the training building again to show me how well he had done. As I shared some of what he'd written the treatment team was quite impressed by the fact that he was able to concentrate for this period of time and that he had recorded meaningful information that was not included on their diagnostic, problems-based intake assessment.

3. *These documents honor and document the person's wants, desires, and aspirations first. Once this data has been gathered, the needs are discussed and negotiated in the helping process.* As you can see as you examine the strengths assessment it does not focus on what someone "needs" from another person's perspective. It focuses on what people have going for them now, what they *want* in the future (and for some people they write, "I want to keep things just the way they are"), and what people have accomplished in the past. The areas of people lives, or life domains, provide a holistic, comprehensive picture of person and environment. If the person is not able to write I encourage the provider to record their responses in their presence, using their own words. If the person is not able to talk, I have encouraged providers to record their observations in each of these areas, as people will tend to gravitate to activities that are enjoyable or pleasant for them.

One of the most frequently noted "barriers" to using a strengths approach, especially in work with people who suffer from neurological impairments or other developmental disability, is the question of safety. The following example from a workshop I provided in Indiana illustrates how we can negotiate with people around this concern once we have affirmed their agenda and motivation.

A 27-year-old woman with a developmental disability agreed to work with me to demonstrate the strengths approach in front of over 50 of the staff as well as her mother (her legal guardian) who attended the training. I asked her what she really liked to do during the day. Before she answered, she slowly looked around the room, smiled, and then said with some conviction "I like to go to Scott's grocery store." I heard a bit of rumbling in the room and bits of comments shared between the staff in the room. I then invited her to write that down on the assessment. The rumbling grew a bit louder. She agreed, and I gave her the letters and she wrote them on the assessment. She talked about how she likes the people at Scott's, how they make her laugh, and how she buys Twinkies. She then said, "I take the Twinkies back to my room, and eat them before my program manager gets there!" Now the group was laughing loudly. As I learned in processing this encounter, the staff was actually trying to keep her from going to Scott's through a contingency management plan. They thought it was not safe, and they were concerned that she was overweight and they knew she liked to get Twinkies. What took place was rethinking her plan, and making a deal with her that they would not try to stop her from going to Scott's if she agreed to buy one Twinkie, not three, and to buy one apple. She happily agreed to this plan. I heard from the staff at this program some months later that they were working on helping her to get a part-time job at Scott's as she was unhappy at the sheltered workshop and shared that she wanted a "real job."

CLOSING THOUGHTS

This chapter has briefly examined a statement of purpose, six principles, and practical tools to aid in the integration of a strengths perspective in interpersonal helping. Concepts such as normal interdependence, personal autonomy, personal freedom, citizenship, accountability, reciprocity, community resources, the fundamental difference between what we want in our lives versus what we truly need in our lives, negotiated plans, partnership, collaboration, and mutual enrichment (provider and service participant) become essential to consider as we become more strengths-based and person-centered. For some providers, this process entails some profound shifts in perspective and practice. For others, however, these notions have served as a welcome affirmation of beliefs and helping activities that have long been integral components of their community-based helping efforts.

Policy makers and funders are challenging providers to integrate and coordinate their services on behalf of people who are involved with multiple systems. People are frequently involved with corrections, addictions, mental health, Social Welfare (TANF), etc. The strengths perspective has been suggested as a philosophical and conceptual bridge that may serve to span systems. I was involved with a recent yearlong SAMHSA study in Oklahoma that demonstrated that providers from different and often disparate theoretical perspectives can achieve consensus on a common purpose and set of practice principles. The growing research and anecdotal evidence suggests that further refinement, development, and evaluation of a strengths-based model is indicated. If service participants are welcomed as key informants and legitimate stakeholders in this enterprise, we will generate deeper and more valuable knowledge.

One of the most common concerns I have heard regarding strengths-based, person-centered practice is that of safety and potential liability. Providers and agency administrators often express a fear that affirming a goal that engenders some risk for the participant may leave them open to litigation should some harm or injury take place during the helping process. Concepts such as informed consent, inclusion of guardians, wrap around services, incremental short-term goal attainment, risk assessment and risk management, harm reduction, experiential learning, and individual guarantees and rights under the Constitution all need to be continuously explored and considered as we engage more fully in person-directed, strengths-based helping approaches.

We will be challenged to continue to gather data from multiple sources through research, both qualitative and quantitative methods, that provide evidence regarding the effectiveness of innovative, creative, strengths-based models. As practitioners we must continue to view ourselves as researchers, and every helping situation represents the opportunity to contribute to the knowledge base of the profession. Some may design large experimental studies with random assignment to determine effectiveness. Others may use strengths assessments and personal wellness plans from one helping situation to contribute to our understanding of the helping process. We must also never discount each service participants' own perspective as a contributing expert in striving to more fully understand what works and what does not (Kisthardt, 1993; Brun & Rapp, 2001).

We must continue to work with and educate funders who may tend to operate from a medically oriented treatment paradigm about the nature of strengths-based work and the rationale behind a broader range of creative community based initiatives. Current trends suggest the importance of tying funding to performance and outcomes rather than funding provision of services. If this is to be accomplished all stakeholders must share a common vision regarding the goals and principles which guide and direct our helping efforts. Toward this end more counties are developing cross training, where all levels of the system gather to engage in a conversation regarding their desires for people with disabilities and how best to maximize resources to provide services in a more integrated, efficient, and effective manner. For example, at a recent training on strengths-based, person-centered practice in Indiana in attendance were mental health case managers, vocational rehabilitation counselors, probation officers, the chief of police, substance abuse counselors, family members, service participants, teachers and school principals, therapists, and state planners. I have had similar experiences in Florida, Iowa, North Carolina, and Oklahoma. True integration can only take place when different systems come together and engage in critical dialogue and come to some consensus regarding outcomes and value-based concepts related to services and treatment.

This chapter has attempted to identify and clarify some key concepts related to strengths-based, person-centered practice. This discussion has certainly not been exhaustive. My hope is that your reading has generated thoughts and feelings regarding your work with people and how you respond to each unique person and situation. Consider the following poem from my book "You Validate My Visions: Poetic Reflections of Helping, Healing, Caring and Loving" (1996) and the questions for discussion which follow.

WHAT IS PERSON CENTERED?
What is "person centered?" an important question today.
As we strive to help another, as she travels on her way.
As we try to know the spirit that makes people what they are.
As we encourage one, whose arms are weary, to reach for one more star,
Person-centered is seeing beyond labels which have been worn.
A person is more than symptoms, and the problems he has born.
A person cannot be fully understood, by calling her a name.
Schizophrenic, Borderline, or Bi-Polar . . . people are not the same.
To be person-centered is a challenge; it is not an easy task.
The nature of our sharing, the questions that we ask.
What are your gifts? What are your joys? What holds meaning on your quest?
What are your dreams? What makes life real? What is it you request?
A person is a producer, a person also consumes.
A person may have more potential than prognosis may assume.
A person is entitled to express his own opinion,
Without fear of reprisals, when another holds dominion.
A person has the right to fail, as she risks something new,
Without another telling her "that goal is unrealistic for you."
A person is a fluid being, ever changing, ever free.
A person makes his own decisions, though others may disagree.
A person is a spirit, whose energy is divine.

A person is a work of art, that the brushes of life refine.
More than a "stage," more than a "phase," more than "old" or "young."
More like a song, drifting on the wind, both singer, and that which is sung.
A person may make plans one minute, and then decide to change them.
A person may order things a certain way, then turn, and rearrange them.
A person may not grasp some things, while with others, they are clever.
A person is the moment . . . a person is forever.
Person centered is being grateful, for the gifts that others share.
Person centered is valuing the opportunity to care.
Person centered is cherishing the wonder of each being.
Person centered is joyful, it is enriching, and it is freeing.

DISCUSSION QUESTIONS

1. Consider the assessments used at your agency. To what extent are they oriented toward the interests, desires, talents, skills, and knowledge of each person? If you only had five questions to ask someone as you begin work with them, what would you ask?

2. Examine the policies of your agency. In what ways do you think these policies promote strengths-based, person-centered work? For example, is there a policy that workers cannot accept gifts from "clients." What if a part of that person's culture is to share something with another who helps them and they bake a loaf of bread for you? What if they invite you to their home to share a meal? How do we respond? Why?

3. Identify strategies your agency has in place currently to meet regularly with providers from other systems who are also involved with people your agency is working with. To what extent has service integration occurred?

4. You are sitting in your office and the service participant states that she/he would rather meet outside at a picnic table to talk about their situation as they do not like closed spaces. How do you respond? Why? How is your response "person-centered?"

5. Listen and observe a staff meeting where a person or family's situation is being discussed. To what extent is the conversation balanced between problems, deficits, needs, and person-centered goals, skills, accomplishments, etc.?

6. What does power-sharing mean to you? In a small group share examples of times when you have not been in a power-sharing relationship and times when you have been. Discuss the difference.

REFERENCES

Anderson, J., & Carter, R. W. (2003). *Diversity perspectives in social work practice.* Boston: Allyn & Bacon.

Bentley, K. J. (Ed.). (2002). *Social work practice in mental health care.* Pacific Grove, CA: Brooks/Cole.

Breton, M. (1994). On the meaning of empowerment and empowerment-oriented social work practice. *Social Work with Groups, 17,* 23–37.

Brun, C., & Rapp, R. C. (2001). Strengths-based case management: Individuals' perspectives on strengths and the case manager relationship. *Social Work, vol. 46, No. 3,* July 278–288.

Capra, F. C. (1996). *The web of life.* New York: Doubleday.

Derezotes, D. S. (2000). *Advanced generalist social work practice.* Thousand Oaks, CA: Sage.

Finn, J., & Jacobson, M. (2003). *Just Practice: A social justice approach to social work.* Peosta, IA: Eddie Bowers Publishing.

Foucault, M. (1980). *Power/knowledge: Selected interviews and other writings.* Colin Gordon (Ed.). New York: Pantheon Books.

Freud, S. (1905). *Jokes and their relation to the unconscious.* (J. Strachey, trans.) New York: Norton. (Original Work Published 1960).

Friere, P. (1994). *The pedagogy of the oppressed.* (rev. ed.). New York: Continuum.

Glicken, M. D. (2004). *Using the strengths perspective in social work practice.* Boston: Allyn & Bacon.

Hepworth, D. H., Rooney, R. H., & Larsen, J. A. (2002). (6th ed.). *Direct social work practice: Theory and skills.* Pacific Grove, CA: Brooks/Cole.

Kisthardt, W. E. (1993). An empowerment agenda for case management research: evaluating the strengths model from the consumers' perspective. In M. Harris and H. Bergman (Eds.), *Case Management: Theory and Practice.* Langhorn, PA: Harwood Academic Publishers: 165–182.

Kisthardt, W. E. (1996). *You validate my visions: Poetic Reflections on Helping, Healing, Caring, and Loving.* Author is publisher.

Kisthardt, W. E. (2002). The strengths perspective in interpersonal helping. In D. Saleebey, (Ed.), *The strengths perspective in social work practice* (3rd ed). Boston: Allyn & Bacon. 163–185.

Kisthardt, W. E. (1993). The impact of the strengths model of case management from the consumer's perspective. In M. Harris & H. Bergman (Eds.), *Case Management: Theory and Practice.* Langhorn, PA: Harwood Academic Publishers: 165–182.

Krogsrud-Miley, K., O'Melia, M., & Dubois, B. (2004). *Generalist social work practice: An empowering approach.* (4th ed). Boston: Allyn & Bacon.

Maguire, L. (2002). *Clinical social work: Beyond generalist practice with individuals, families, and groups.* Pacific Grove, CA: Brooks/Cole.

Mattaini, M. A. (2001). The foundation of social work practice. In H. Briggs and K. Corcoran, (Eds.), *Social Work Practice.* Chicago, IL: Lyceum Books. 15–35.

Mead, G. H. (1934). *Mind, self, and society.* Charles W. Morris (Ed.). Chicago, IL: University of Chicago Press.

Miller, W. R., & Rollnick, S. (2002). *Motivational Interviewing: Preparing People to Change Addictive Behavior* (2nd ed). New York: Guilford.

Prochaska, J. O., DiClemente, C. C., & Norcross, J. C. (1992). In search of how people change: Applications to addictive behaviors. *American Psychologist, 47*(9), 1102–1114.

Pulin, J. (2005). *Strengths-based generalist practice.* (2nd ed). Belmont, CA: Brooks/Cole-Thompson Learning.

Ridgeway, P., & Zipple, A. M. (1990). The paradigm shift in residential services: From the linear continuum to supported housing approaches. *Psychosocial Rehabilitation Journal, 13,* 11–31.

Shafritz, J. M., & Ott, J. S. (1996). *Classics of organizational theory.* (5th ed). Fort Worth, TX: Harcourt College Publications.

Sullivan, W. P., & Rapp, C. A. (2002). Social workers as case managers. In Kia Bentley, (Ed), *Social work practice in mental health.* Pacific Grove, CA: Brooks/Cole 180–210.

Walter E. Kisthardt, Ph.D. is currently an Assistant Professor at the School of Social Work at the University of Missouri Kansas City. He teaches Advanced and Foundation Practice, Social Work in Mental Health and Substance Abuse, and the Integrative Seminar. He has provided training and technical assistance with programs in 42 states, England, and New Zealand. His original music and poetry have served to affirm and promote the principles of strengths-based practice.

CHAPTER ELEVEN

USING STRENGTHS-BASED PRACTICE TO TAP THE RESILIENCE OF FAMILIES[1]

BONNIE BENARD

The last 10 years have been pivotal for all strengths-based movements in education, prevention, and other human services. We now have considerable research and practitioner interest in resilience—in how people have overcome adversity to lead healthy and successful lives, as well as in youth development, asset-building, positive psychology, wellness, health promotion, restorative justice, strengths-based social work, health realization, social capital and its sub-categories, multiple intelligences with more recent spin-offs into practical and spiritual intelligence, and, the really big one in the 1990s, EQ or emotional intelligence. Obviously, people in professions, such as social work, known for studying and ameliorating human problems, are increasingly attracted to what has become a new paradigm, a new way of thinking about and working with human beings across the lifespan that focuses on assets instead of deficits and on working in partnership "with" instead of doing "to." Of most recent relevance for social workers is the priority that states across the nation have placed on redesigning their welfare systems to build on family strengths and work in partnership with families and community-based organizations.

This perspective comes none too early in that not much has changed in the last decade in terms of children and families living with multiple risks and stressors in their lives. According to a KidsCount report from the Annie E. Casey Foundation (March 2002) showing how children faired in terms of eight family risk factors for the period 1990–2000, the percent of children living in "high-risk" families improved 1% over this decade, going from 13% to 12% (2002, www.kidscount. org). Similarly, Sam Halperin, whose two documents about *The Forgotten Half* (non-college bound youth and young families in America) stirred the education and youthwork world in 1988, said this last decade has not brought much improvement for older adolescents—whom are often young parents—either (1998). "Overall, the record of advances in the last decade . . . —whether family life, schools, communities, employment, national service, or youth development—provides but a slim reed of hope for a better deal for much of the nation's youth and young families (1998, p. 1).

These fairly grim statistics clarify why resilience matters, why it is imperative that we learn about, adopt, and assess practices and policies in all of human services, especially that of social work, that are focused on "protective" factors, the critical supports and opportunities present in families, schools, and communities, that protect children and families from harm's way and promote their healthy and successful development, even in the face of the multiple risks and stressors our society places on them everyday. As social workers, it is especially critical that we apply a resilience-lens, that is, a strengths-based practice approach, in our work with families, be they biological, adoptive, or foster, for they are truly our children's first teacher. After a brief overview of resilience research and its application to families and those of us working with families, we will examine the critical family protective factors/strengths associated with healthy child outcomes as well as social work practices that tap these family strengths.

RESILIENCE RESEARCH

When followed into adulthood (and even into later adulthood) resilience researchers worldwide have documented the consistent and yet amazing finding that most children and young people, even those from highly stressed families or resource-deprived communities do "somehow" manage to become not only successful by societal indicators but to develop social, emotional, intellectual, moral, and spiritual strengths as well (Werner & Smith, 2001). In fact, for just about any population of children research has found to be at greater risk for later problems— children who experience divorce, step-parents, foster care, loss of a sibling, attention deficit disorder, developmental delays, delinquency, running away, religious cults, and so on—more children make it than don't (Rhodes & Brown, 1991). However, in most studies the figure seems to average 70 to 75 percent for children in foster care (Festinger, 1984), from gangs (Moore, 1991; Vigil, 1990), children from substance-abusing families (Beardslee & Podoresfky, 1988; Chess, 1989; Watt et al., 1984; Werner, 1986; Werner & Smith, 2001); children growing up in poverty (Clausen, 1993; Schweinhart et al., 1993; Vaillant, 2002). children born to teen mothers (Furstenberg et al., 1998), and even children who have been sexually abused (Higgins, 1994; Wilkes, 2002; Zigler & Hall, 1989). Even in the worst case scenarios, when children experience multiple and persistent risks, still half of them overcome adversity and achieve good developmental outcomes (Rutter, 1987, 1989).

Resilience research is indeed a gift to all the human services. First of all, resilience research gives practitioners a scarce commodity these days: hope. By the above percentages alone, these studies provide evidence that protective factors are indeed more powerful than risk factors in the lives of children and families. This is attributed to the discovery in resilience and resilience-related research that resilience is a "self-righting" capacity for healthy growth and development—even in the face of challenges, a capacity hard-wired into our species. All that this natural developmental process requires to produce good developmental outcomes is a protective or nurturing environment in which people—young and old—can meet their inborn developmental needs to be safe, to love and belong, to be respected, to have challenges, to achieve a sense of control, and to have hope (Werner & Smith, 1992, 2001). Adversity and risk are now seen by the leading resilience researchers as coming from threats to satisfying these needs (Masten & Reed, 2002; Sandler, 2001). According to Masten and Reed (2002), "The findings on resilience suggest that the greatest threats to children are those adversities that undermine the basic human protective systems for development" (p. 83).

Another gift from resilience research is that it gives all who work with children and families research-based answers to the questions: How can families prevent negative developmental outcomes in children facing multiple stressors? What do families need to do to nurture these inborn developmental systems? How best can we as social workers intervene to support families in supporting their children? Resilience research provides the answers by identifying the specific protective factors, the developmental supports and opportunities, that have facilitated both children and their families in not only coping with their challenges but using their challenges as opportunities to engage their innate resilience and turn their lives around.

ENVIRONMENTAL PROTECTIVE FACTORS

> The life stories of the resilient youngsters now grown into adulthood teach us that competence, confidence, and caring can flourish, even under adverse circumstances, if children encounter persons who provide them with the secure basis for the development of trust, autonomy, and initiative. From odds successfully overcome springs hope—a gift each of us can share with a child—at home, in the classroom, on the playground, or in the neighborhood. (Werner & Smith, 1992, p. 209)

The above quote provides the very simple, commonsense answer to the question resilience researchers have asked for over two decades: How do people facing so many challenges manage to grow up to "love well, work well, play well, and expect well?" Who or what helps them tap their innate potential for healthy growth and development, for transformation and change?

No matter whose conceptualizations we examine, these protective factors or systems, comprise a very simple recipe—albeit not an easy one!—of *caring relationships, high expectation messages,* and *opportunities for participation and contribution.* These three environmental "protective factors" were first conceptualized in Benard's 1991 paper, *Fostering Resiliency in Kids: Protective Factors in the Family, School, and Community.* Not only have they held up under scrutiny of research, they have formed the guiding principles of many prevention and education efforts over the last 10 years. They basically describe what the youth development field refers to as "supports and opportunities" (Pittman & Zeldin, 1995) and match well to the Search Institute's categories of "external assets" (Benson, 1997) as well as to what family process researchers have identified as "family strengths" associated with children's success and well-being (Baumrind, 1971; Steinberg, 2000). Perhaps most importantly, they match precisely what young people say they want from their parents/caregivers (Resnick et al., 1997) and especially salient to social workers, these protective factors are what youth in the foster care system tell us they want from their foster families as well as their child welfare workers (Bernstein, 2002; Foster Care Work Group, 2004). They are also commonly referred to as "social capital," the interpersonal resources necessary for healthy development and life success. After a brief general (that is, applied across the lifespan and all environmental systems) definition of each of these protective factors, we'll look at research validating them in the family system and then at how we as social workers can apply them in our work with families.

Keep in mind that while we discuss each of these as if it were a separate entity, they each are one aspect or component of a dynamic protective *process* in which they work together. Caring relationships without high expectations or opportunities for meaningful participation foster dependency and co-dependency—not positive human development. High expectations without caring relationships and support to help a person meet them is a cruel "shape-up or ship-out" approach associated with negative outcomes. And one more example: caring relationships with high expectation messages but no opportunities for a person's active participation and contribution creates a frustrating situation that blocks the natural process of human development.

Caring Relationships

Caring relationships convey loving support—the message of being there for a person, of trust, of unconditional love. Resilient survivors talk about relationships characterized by "quiet availability," "fundamental positive regard," and "simple sustained kindness"—a touch on the shoulder, a smile, a greeting (Higgins, 1994, pp. 324–325). Higgins' subjects "strongly recommended that those of you who touch the life of a child [or adult] constructively, even briefly, should *never* underestimate your possible corrective impact on that child [or adult]" (p. 325). Even respect, having a person "acknowledge us, see us for who we are—as their equal in value and importance" figures high in "turnaround" relationships and places (Meier, 1995, p. 120).

These caregivers also convey a sense of compassion—nonjudgmental love that looks beneath a person's negative behavior and sees the pain and suffering. They do not take the person's behavior personally. They understand that no matter how negative a young person's behavior, s/he is doing the best s/he can given how s/he *sees* the world.

Finally, being interested in, actively listening to, and getting to know the gifts of people young and old conveys the message, "You are important in this world; you matter." Alice Miller's account of resilient survivors of childhood sexual abuse and trauma validates the healing power for victims of telling their story to someone who believes them: "It turns out in every case [of successful adaptation] that a sympathetic and helpful witness confirmed the child's perceptions, thus making it possible for him to recognize that he had been wronged" (1990).

According to the Institute of Medicine, "Supportive relationships are critical 'mediums' of development. They provide an environment of reinforcement, good modeling, and constructive feedback for physical, intellectual, psychological, and social growth." Furthermore, "The attentive, caring, and wise voice of a supportive adult gets internalized and becomes part of the youth's own voice" (Eccles & Gootman, 2002, p. 96).

High Expectations

At the core of caring relationships are clear and positive person-centered expectations. Clear expectations refer to the guidance and regulatory function that caregivers must provide developing young people. This means creating a sense of structure and safety through rules and disciplinary approaches that are not only perceived as fair by young people but that include youth in their creation.

Positive person-centered messages are those that communicate the caregiver's deep belief in the person's natural resilience and self-righting capacities and challenge the person to become all she can be. "She believed in me when I didn't believe in myself" is a common refrain echoed by adults reflecting on transformative messages in their lives in the author's workshops. A consistent description of turnaround caregivers is their *seeing the possibility:* "They held visions of us that we could not imagine for ourselves" (Delpit, 1996, p. 199). These family members, teachers, youth workers, counselors, and social workers follow up this belief message with a challenge message: "You can make it; you have everything it takes to achieve your dreams; and I'll be there to support you." This message is consistently documented by young people of color who have survived poverty, poor schools, and discrimination to become highly successful adults (Clark, 1984; Gandara, 1995).

An often-ignored subtlety of this now cliched term is that caregiver's high expectations must be person-/youth-centered. They must be based on the strengths, interests, hopes, and dreams of the person—not what the caregiver wants the person to do or be. These strengths-based, person-centered caregivers not only see the possibility and communicate the challenge message, they *recognize existing strengths, mirror them back,* and help people see where they are strong. They use the person's own strengths, interests, goals, and dreams as the beginning point for learning and helping. Thus, they tap people's intrinsic motivation, their existing, innate drive for learning and personal growth. John Seita, who grew up in multiple foster homes, tells the story of his turnaround social worker: "Mr. Lambert, who was a recent graduate of college when he first met me, had no training in bonding with relationship-resistant youth. Few of us do. But he reached me through the back door. He doggedly attempted to find a *special interest* of mine, namely my dreams of being a sports hero. Although I did not trust other adults, he connected with me through a special interest" (1996, p. 88).

Turnaround caregivers assist their children or those they serve, especially those who have been labeled or oppressed, in understanding their innate resilience, their personal power to reframe their life narratives from damaged victim to resilient survivor (Wolin & Wolin, 1993). Turnaround people help youth see the power they have to think differently about and construct alternative stories of their lives. They help them 1.) to not take *personally* the adversity in their lives ("You aren't the cause, nor can you control, your father's drinking/your friend's racist remarks");

2.) to not see adversity as *permanent* ("This too shall pass"); and 3.) to not see set-backs as *pervasive* ("You can rise above this"; "This is only one part of your life experience") (adapted from Seligman et al., 1995).

Opportunities for Participation and Contribution

Creating the *opportunities for youth or client's participation and contribution* is a natural outgrowth of relationships based on caring and high expectations. This category consists of providing people with the chance to participate in engaging, challenging, and interesting activities or "flow" experiences as well as job opportunities through which they can develop critical life skills and resilience strengths. Werner and Smith found that while their resilient survivors weren't unusually talented, "They took great pleasure in interests and hobbies that brought them solace when things fell apart in their home lives" (1992, p. 205).

This category also refers to providing opportunities to youth and clients to participate in activities that allow them to belong, "to be a part of a cooperative enterprise, such as being a cheerleader for the home team or raising an animal for the 4-H Club [as well as] active involvement in a church or religious community"—activities that fulfilled their need to belong, that connected them to a group that became a surrogate family (Werner & Smith, 1992, p. 205). In working with families this especially means interventions that incorporate family peer support (Layzer et al., 2001).

Another important kind of participation involves having opportunities for reflection and dialog around issues meaningful to youth and clients. Discussing issues around sexuality, drug use, and family communication—is continually identified by adolescents and youth as what they want to do in their families, schools, and communities—especially in a small group context (Brown & D'Emidio-Caston, 1995). For families, the issues often involve ones around parenting as well as around accessing social and economic resources (Benard & Quiett, 2002; Mills, 1995; Walsh, 1998). When youth and families are given the opportunity—especially in a small group context—to give voice to their realities and tell their "stories"—to discuss their experiences, beliefs, attitudes, and feelings—and encouraged to critically question societal messages—those from the media and their own conditioned thinking around these issues—we are empowering them to be critical thinkers and decision-makers around the important concerns in their lives.

Opportunities for creative expression through all forms of the arts—writing, storytelling, and the performing and visual arts—are a vital component in youth and client participation and in the turnaround process. By providing people with ways to use their creativity and imagination—instead of their conditioned thinking—caregivers help them develop transformative resilience and strengths. The power of creative arts programs in prisons have clearly demonstrated their role in moving individuals from risk to resilience (Lamb, 2003).

Opportunities for participation also include having chances to problem-solve and make decisions, to have some freedom and self-determination, i.e., control over the one's self direction. In this way, youth develop autonomy and self-control. Providing authentic decision-making and leadership responsibilities are often the characteristics distinguishing successful from unsuccessful youth programs and settings

(Gambone & Arbreton, 1997; McLaughlin et al., 1994; Tierney et al., 1995; Werner & Smith, 1992) as well as effective programs serving families (Schorr, 1997).

Opportunities for contribution, to do things that matter, that are meaningful to one's self, family, school, and community are also key components of this category of protective factors. When youth and clients have the opportunities to "give back" their gifts to their families, schools, and communities, they see themselves as no longer just recipients of what we adults have to offer—even if it is the good stuff of caring and positive beliefs—but as active contributors to the settings in which they live. Giving back is a powerful "hook" for all individuals, especially for those not used to thinking of themselves as successful. It helps them reframe their self-perceptions from being a problem and *receiver* of services to being a resource and *provider* of services.

In all of these ways—having the opportunities to be heard, to voice one's opinion, to make choices, to have responsibilities, to engage in active problem-solving, to express one's imagination, to work with and help others, and to give one's gift back to the community—people develop the attitudes and competencies characteristic of healthy development and successful learning: social competence, problem-solving, a positive sense of self, and a sense of purpose and future. This is the final component of the protective process that connects people young and old to themselves and to their families, schools, and communities.

Understanding the power of these "protective motivational systems," as Ann Masten (Masten & Reed, 2002) refers to them, is important to social workers on two levels. First, this empowering information needs to be conveyed to the families we serve so they can relax and focus on what really matters in their parenting—and not on their family structure or family socioeconomic status. Second, for social workers to intervene effectively with families and to engage the resilience of family members and the family itself, we need to relate to the family with caring relationships, to communicate high expectation messages, and to provide opportunities for participation and contribution.

WHAT RESEARCH SAYS ABOUT FAMILIES

Do parents matter? This was the critical question addressed by family research in the past decade. Psychologist Judith Harris's controversial book, *The Nurture Assumption: Why Children Turn Out the Way They Do* (1998), made the case that parents, especially as traditionally defined, have a more limited effect on a young person's development than is commonly believed in our culture. Similarly, Stephanie Coontz's earlier historical account of family life, *The Way We Never Were: American Families and the Nostalgia Trap* (1992), challenged the idea that the nuclear family, a very recent organization in terms of human history, is the only and "best" structure for rearing our children.

While armies of researchers and advocates have lined up on both sides of this values-laden controversy, much of the research cited in both books (several hundred studies) supports the findings of resilience research—in other words that, yes, the family and parenting do matter, but, no, they are not the only nor even always the most potent influence (Barber & Olsen, 1997) on young people. A child grows up in many settings beyond the home—preschools, schools, community-based organizations, youth groups, and friendship groups, which can also play a powerful role in their healthy and successful development. If this were *not* the case, we would not see resilient survivors of abusive, drug-using, mentally ill, or absent families nor would we see healthy adults who grew up in nontraditional families—divorced, gay/lesbian, single-parent, or foster families.

Much of this controversy, especially as it has focused on single-parenting, can be resolved by closely examining the numbers and percentages of children who actually experience adverse outcomes (psychological, behavioral, social, and academic) as a result of their living in a single-parent home. For example, a recent rigorous study comparing children in single- and two-parent households in Sweden did indeed find the former at roughly twice the risk for developing a psychiatric illness, killing themselves or attempting suicide, and developing an alcohol-related disorder (Weitoft et al., 2003). This study was highly publicized in newspapers across the country in headlines such as "One Parent, Twice the Trouble (Ross, 2003). However, what was not addressed either by the researchers or the reporters were the actual numbers or percentages of youth with adverse outcomes. Upon examining the tables in the actual study, one finds that only 2% of the girls and 1.5% of the boys from single-parent families developed psychiatric problems as children and adolescents and only .9% and .7% as young adults. This is indeed twice the adversity than that experienced by individuals growing up in a two-parent household. However, the untold story is that 98% of children and adolescents in single-parent families did *not* have psychiatric disorders. Similarly, 98% of the girls and 99% of the boys did *not* commit suicide; 99% of the girls and 98.8% of the boys did *not* commit a violent act; 99% of the girls and 98.8% of the boys did *not* develop an alcohol-related disorder, and so on (Weitoft et al., 2003).

Even while acknowledging that children can succeed regardless of their families, findings from the huge National Longitudinal Study of Adolescent Health (Add Health, 2000) point to the importance of the parent. This study surveyed 90,000 middle and high school students and interviewed a 20,000-student sample plus their parents. Blum and the other Add Health researchers (2000) concluded that commonly regarded "predictors" of adolescent behavior—race/ethnicity, family income, and family structure—turn out to be relatively weak (and "not especially amenable to change"). Instead, in a more fine-grained analysis of the data, Blum et al. report, "The one most consistently protective factor found was the presence of a positive parent-family relationship."

The effect of parents as a protective factor for children is most dramatic in extreme conditions—for children growing up in dangerous or resource-poor communities or in the midst of war—when the family often is a child's only reliable resource (Garbarino et al., 1992; Richters & Martinez, 1993). In their studies of resilience in violent communities, Richters and Martinez found that "The odds of early adaptational failure among children from stable and safe homes were only about 6 percent; these increased by more than 300 percent for children from homes rated as either unstable or unsafe, and by more than 1,500 percent for children from homes rated as both unstable and unsafe" (1993, p. 625).

Because divorce is a factor in so many families, and usually contributes at least initially to family instability, the research represented in E. Mavis Hetherington's three-decade-long study of almost 1,400 families and more than 2,500 children, *For Better or For Worse: Divorce Reconsidered* (2002), is another important lens for viewing the role of parents and families in children's development. Her study, which included a control group of intact families, documented that 75 to 80 percent of children from divorced homes are "coping reasonably well and functioning in the normal range" and "go on to have reasonably happy or sometimes very happy lives." Given that Hetherington's research methods are regarded by her peers as the "gold standard" (K. Peterson, 2002), her study convincingly refutes less rigorous but widely reported research indicating less positive outcomes for children from divorced families (Blakeslee & Wallerstein, 1989; Wallerstein et al., 2000).

Teenage single mothers have also been surprisingly successful, in terms both of their children's well-being and their own. Furstenberg and his colleagues (1998) studied 500 teenage mothers and their children in an urban environment. They found that most of the children were doing well, and so were their mothers. Furthermore, they found that the children's successful adolescent development was directly related to the economic and social support services (not necessarily income) provided to teen mothers. Werner and Smith's (2001) 26-year follow-up analysis of the teen mothers in their cohort found parallel outcomes with 92% of their teen moms staging a "remarkable metamorphosis" by mid-life (p. 93).

The commonsense, good news from all this research for social workers and other caregivers, as well as for policymakers, politicians, and advocates, is that the critical issues in supporting children's healthy development have been identified. If we truly want to improve the lives of children, first, our society must support all family caregivers, regardless of family structure. As Coontz states, "Both contemporary studies and historical experience show that children are resilient enough to adapt to many different innovations in family patterns: When they cannot adapt, this is caused more often by the economic and social context in which those innovations take place than by their parents' 'wrong turns' away from traditional family patterns" (1992, p. 206).

Second, we must support those outside of families who serve as children's caregivers. As documented by Werner and Smith, the most powerful protective factor in the life histories of resilient children was the presence of one caring adult in the child's life, most commonly a parent but more often than one might suspect a mentor or surrogate parent (1992). This is incredibly empowering information for our foster family caregivers as well as teachers, youth workers, mentors, and for us as social workers who support both children and their families.

Third, because families do not and cannot provide all the support that young people need, the other settings in which children grow up—schools and communities—must recognize as their primary role the fostering of the healthy physical, social, emotional, and cognitive development of young people. The fundamental and comprehensive aspects of this role are not always appreciated. Schools and communities are powerful and even transformative developmental influences in the lives of children, especially when they are called on to compensate for deficits in the family setting (Barber & Olsen, 1997; Masten & Coatsworth, 1998; Werner & Smith,

1992). This behooves us as social workers to connect the children we serve to school and community resources such as after-school programs, mentoring and tutoring opportunities, and community-based organizations like Boys and Girls Clubs.

Helping the families we serve understand the help that others provide in their children's development—or the limits of their own influence—can help them to relax and tap into their common sense in parenting. As Harris points out, "The nurture assumption [the idea that parents are totally responsible for how their children turn out] has turned children into objects of anxiety. Parents are nervous about doing the wrong thing, fearful that a stray word or glance might ruin their child's chances forever" (1998, p. 352). In contrast, Furstenberg found that when parents felt a sense of self-efficacy or had "beliefs of mastery as a parent," their adolescents did better in school and were able to avoid social- and health-risk behaviors (1999, p. 121).

The Role of Parenting Style

> We believe that the concept of resilience defines a process of parenting that is essential if we are to prepare our children for success in all areas of their future lives. Given this belief, a guiding principle in all of our interactions with children should be to strengthen their ability to be resilient and to meet life's challenges with thoughtfulness, confidence, purpose, and empathy. (Robert Brooks & Sam Goldstein, *Raising Resilient Children,* 2001)

Research into the qualities that differentiate effective and ineffective parenting has burgeoned along with a general interest beginning in the 1980s into the *qualities* of all the contexts that contribute to healthy adolescent development. In terms of protective factors, "Parenting style rather than family structure has been found to be the main determinant of effective family functioning and adolescent well-being" (McFarlane et al., 1995). In terms of risk factors, parental conflict (parent-to-parent) continued to be identified as the major family risk factor and source of stress for adolescents (Henricson & Roker, 2000).

Most of the research on parenting has continued to validate the three-pronged approach advocated a decade ago in *Fostering Resiliency in Kids* (Benard, 1991) and reiterated in this article: caring relationships, high and *youth-centered* expectations, and opportunities for participation and contribution. According to ChildTrends researchers, these are, in essence, critical family strengths that are "often overlooked, but real. . . .We think of family strengths as the relationships and processes that support and protect families and family members, especially during times of adversity and change" (Moore et al., 2002, p. 1).

An impressive body of research on the role of the family in adolescent development and school success has flowed over the last 10 years from a team of researchers at Stanford University, the University of Wisconsin, and the University of Pennsylvania. They have identified three key qualities of the parent-child relationship—warmth/connection, guidance/regulation, and psychological autonomy-granting (Steinberg, 2000)—that map well to our three protective factors (caring relationships, high expectations, and opportunities for participation and contribution). Similarly, other bodies of research, including the Seattle Social Development Project (Hill et al., 1999), the Rochester Youth Development Study (Thornberry, 1998), and the Pittsburgh Youth Study (Lahey et al., 1999) have all found adverse adolescent outcomes associated with the lack of a caring parent-adolescent relationship and poor parental regulation or family management practices.

"Authoritative" is the term Steinberg and his colleagues use (building on the pioneering research of Diana Baumrind, 1971) to describe a parent who is "warm and involved, but is firm and consistent in establishing and enforcing guidelines, limits, and developmentally appropriate expectations" and "encourages and permits the adolescent to develop his or her own opinions and beliefs" (Steinberg, 2000, p. 173). As Steinberg continues in this important review article, "Each component of authoritativeness—warmth, firmness, and psychological autonomy-granting—makes an independent contribution to healthy adolescent development, in overlapping, although slightly different ways" (2000, p. 173). According to Steinberg, "Perhaps the most important conclusion to emerge from our work is that adolescents raised in authoritative homes continue to show the same sorts of advantages in psychosocial development and mental health over their non-authoritatively raised peers that were apparent in studies of younger children" (2000, p. 173). In another study, Masten and her colleagues followed over 200 children for 10 years and found that parenting quality, measured as a combination of "warmth, expectations, and structure" was a major protective factor sustaining healthy development in the face of adversities such as poverty and personal traumas, from both the parents' and teens' perspectives (1999).

In terms of cultural differences in parenting style, Steinberg's review of the literature holds that "Minority youngsters raised in authoritative homes fare better than their peers from non-authoritative homes with respect to psychosocial development, symptoms of internalized distress, and problem behavior" (2000, p. 175). Several researchers have challenged the efficacy of authoritativeness with African American and Asian American youth, proposing that a more structured, "authoritarian" parenting style, which features higher levels of behavioral and psychological control, is more protective (Baldwin et al., 1993; Chao, 1994, 2001; Walker-Barnes & Mason, 2001). Interestingly, Ruth Chao found positive effects of authoritative parenting for second-generation Chinese Americans but not for first-generation Chinese (2001). Perhaps some of these discrepant findings can be explained as Chao (1999) and others (Walker-Barnes & Mason, 2001) have by the fact that parental emphasis on obedience and respect have different *meanings* in Asian and African American cultures than in American culture generally. In African American and Asian cultures, parents see an emphasis on obedience and respect more often as an attribute of caring and "relationship closeness" than as an attribute of control.

In Steinberg's review, the one area in which authoritative vs. authoritarian parenting style outcomes are ambiguous for African American and Asian American youth is that of school performance. On the other hand, Furstenberg et al.'s longitudinal study of primarily African American Philadelphia neighborhoods associates an authoritative pattern of parenting with better academic outcomes (1998). (The effects of cultural differences are also at issue in our later discussion of autonomy and opportunities to participate and contribute.)

Apparently, so long as adolescents feel "connected" to their families (operationalized as feeling close to parents, feeling satisfied with family relationships, and feeling loved and cared for), the Add Health researchers found this "connected" relationship was protective against every adolescent health-risk behavior from alcohol, tobacco, and other drug use to emotional distress, violence, and risky sexual behavior (Resnick et al., 1997). Likewise, the California Department of Education's Healthy Kids Resilience & Youth Development Module, which is based on the resilience framework developed by Benard (1991) and presented here, has found similar relationships between family protective factors and the risk behaviors so far examined: binge drinking, tobacco smoking, marijuana use at school, and bringing a weapon to school (Benard, 2002). The greater the levels of caring relationships, high expectation beliefs, and meaningful participation in the family, the less young people are involved in these health-risk behaviors.

Caring Relationships in Families

Few would have predicted that 14-year-old Lauren Slater, with bandages on her wrists, alone in a psychiatric hospital bed, would later be a Harvard graduate with awards for her writing and administrative duties as the director of a mental health facility. This young woman was hospitalized repeatedly for suicide attempts as a teenager. At the age of 14 she was given over as a ward of the state by a mother who had abused her and no longer wanted her. However, she credits the four years she spent in foster care with an unfailingly loving foster mother for her eventual decision to giver herself a chance at health and happiness. (Sylvia Rockwell, 1998, p. 16)

What describes a caring parent? Words like emotionally supportive and responsive, nurturing, warm, empathic, accepting, and unconditional are common in the literature. "Unfailingly loving" would apply to Lauren Slater's foster mother. Rak's case studies (2002) of "heroes in the nursery" document the findings of earlier resilience research (Anthony, 1974; Werner & Smith, 1982; Rutter's (1979) in terms of the power of one caregiver early in the child's life who "provided a good-enough nurturing and bonding experience" (Rak, 2002, p. 258). In the Mother-Child Project, a longitudinal study of high-risk children and families, researchers found that the major protective factor for children growing up in poverty and its attendant lack of resources was the "emotionally responsive caregiving" available in the family (Egeland et al., 1993). As Add Health researchers have reported, family "connectedness," consisting of "feelings of warmth, love, and caring from parents" (Resnick et al., 1997, p. 830) was equally protective whether the parent was custodial or noncustodial; the critical issue was that the adolescent felt listened to, paid attention to, and special.

Steinberg and his colleagues found that parental warmth is "a general facilitator of mental health, academic competence, and overall psychological functioning" (2000, p. 173). Barber and Olsen (1997) found a direct association between warmth and care in the family and adolescent social competence (1997). "Consistent, stable, positive, emotional connections with significant others, like parents, appear to equip children with important social skills as well as a sense that the world is safe, secure, and predictable" (Barber, 1997, p. 8). Henry and others found that parental encouragement, warmth, and praise were associated with adolescents' higher levels of empathy and caring for others (1996). Herman and her colleagues found a direct positive relationship between teens who experienced caring relationships in their families and their academic achievement (1997).

Parental empathy is a primary first step in developing a caring relationship, according to Brooks and Goldstein in *Raising Resilient Children* (2001). Empathy, they point out, helps parents accept their children for who they are and provides them with the unconditional acceptance that children need in order to develop a basic sense of trust. Fortunately, according to the theory proposed by Thomas Lewis and his colleagues in *A General Theory of Love* (2000), empathy is a built-in biological capacity of the limbic system—"a sensory system inside the brain designed to [provide] information about the emotional state inside someone else's brain" (Ellis, 2001, p. 50). As identified in research about the Health Realization approach to parenting (Mills, 1995), one of the most effective ways to help parents love and care for their children is to teach them to relax enough to allow this natural empathic process to occur.

High Expectations in Families

> I've always had the sense that by [my grandmother's] allowing me to watch how she did things and treating me as though she thought I could be like her, there was a message: "You can do this. Somewhere in you is all the right stuff. You've just got to find it, and you'll do it, and I'll love you. I'm your grandmother, and so I'll be there; but . . . this is your job, and you can do it and you *will* do it." (Joanna in Gina O'Connell Higgins, *Resilient Adults: Overcoming a Cruel Past,* 1994)

High expectations in families can provide the guidance that contributes to a young person's safety, can communicate an attitude of believing in the child's worth and competence, and can be the catalyst for helping a young person to find her or his strengths.

In our typology, the regulatory function of parenting—providing clear expectations in the form of guidance and structure for behavior—meets children's and adolescents' needs for safety. This function goes by many terms in the literature: parental regulation, parental monitoring, family management, and supervision, to name a few. Steinberg and his colleagues found that a parenting style characterized by "firmness" in setting expectations was protective in promoting positive youth outcomes, especially by preventing antisocial behavior such as drug and alcohol abuse and delinquency, but also in contributing to academic competence (2000, p. 173).

Another component of high expectations is the positive belief on the part of parents that their children will be successful, that they have "what it takes." The above quote provides a powerful example of this simple affirmation. According to Brooks and Goldstein, "When parents convey expectations in an accepting, loving, supportive manner, children are often motivated to exceed those expectations" (2001, p. 134).

High expectations on the part of parents and other family caregivers for their children's school success has remained a consistent predictor of positive health and academic outcomes for youth over the years, and increasingly so for children in minority families (Clark, 1984; Gandara, 1995; Herman et al., 1997; Kim & Chun, 1994). All of these studies identified parents who not only had high educational expectations for their children but also were willing to actively advocate for their children. The Add Health study found that high parental expectations for their child's school achievement were moderately protective against children's emotional distress (Resnick et al., 1997).

Parental high expectation beliefs are not limited to academic success; they include encouraging children to find their strengths, their calling, their special interest and gift. Parents nurture these strengths by connecting children to programs, people, and places that will help them develop their calling. John Seita and his colleagues refers to this as "talent scouting" (1996). Brooks and Goldstein refer to this aspect of raising resilient children as helping children find their "island of competence" (2001). Furstenberg and his colleagues found that the most successful African American parents in their longitudinal study were actively engaged in these "promoting" strategies that connected their children to outside resources and supports to further develop their interests and competencies (1999).

Sometimes talent scouting requires good detective work, for many children's strengths are embedded in what may appear to be a deficit. Continual clowning around, for example, is often punished in families and schools. However, as resilience research has documented (Benard, 2004), humor remains one of the most protective strengths a person can have in terms of physical and mental health. The challenge for parents and other caregivers is to find an appropriate channel for what can be annoying behavior so that this potential asset is not shamed out of existence. Many books over the last decade have focused on how to do this reframing with especially challenging children. *Raising Your Spirited Child* (Kurcinka, 1992) remains one of the best and most popular examples.

Opportunities for Participation and Contribution in Families

> Children's inborn need to help is an obvious fit with reinforcing a sense of responsibility and compassion. Engaging in the task of helping others strengthens children's self-esteem and feeling of ownership and instills the message that what they do contributes to the well-being of other people—all elementary to a resilient mindset. (Robert Brookes & Sam Goldstein, *Raising Resilient Children*, 2001)

In families, the protective factors of participation and contribution depend on parents being able to provide children with both responsibility and autonomy. The degree to which a child experiences either must be developmentally appropriate but also, researchers are finding, sensitive to conditions in the child's particular environment.

While being able to contribute by having valued responsibilities and roles within the family has not been a focus of research attention this last decade, historically it has been associated with positive developmental (including health) outcomes for youth (and adults) and good parenting (see Benard, 1991, for a summary). Janice Cohn's book, *Raising Compassionate, Courageous Children in a Violent World* (1997), cites several studies documenting higher levels of well-being and life satisfaction for individuals who are involved in something beyond themselves. Similarly, Werner and Smith (1992) found that "acts of required helpfulness," such as caring for younger siblings or managing the household when a parent was incapacitated, were positively associated with overcoming a challenging childhood and with life success.

Young people's opportunities to participate in the family are often tied to parenting style, and especially to parents' granting of autonomy. Parents who create opportunities for their children and adolescents to have some decision-making power and to solve problems on their own help meet their children's basic need for psychological autonomy. Likewise parents who listen to their children as people deserving respect and attention grant them psychological autonomy. According to Steinberg, "Psychological autonomy-granting functions much like warmth as a general protective factor, but seems to have special benefits as a protection against anxiety, depression, and other forms of internalized distress" (2000, p. 174). Eccles et al. also found "positive associations between the extent of the adolescents' participation in family decision making and indicators of both intrinsic school motivation and positive self-esteem" (1993, p. 98). This fits nicely with research on self-efficacy (Bandura, 1995; Maddux, 2002) since it is through autonomy experiences that individuals develop a sense of their own power and control, known moderators against anxiety and depression.

The gradual granting of autonomy experiences (or opportunities for participation) and the need to balance autonomy with guidance and control is perhaps the most challenging aspect of parenting, especially during the adolescent years when the biological need for autonomy asserts itself as a primary drive. As prominent adolescent researchers have written, "It is not easy for parents to determine the optimal level of autonomy versus control for their children at all ages. One would predict strained relationships wherever there is a poor fit between the child's desire for increasing autonomy and the opportunities for independence and autonomy provided by the child's parents" (Eccles et al., 1993, p. 97).

Parents whose efforts, however imperfect, are at least on the continuum of granting their children appropriate psychological (and behavioral) autonomy stand in sharp contrast to parents who wield psychological control. Psychological control appears to be a particularly destructive way *not* to grant psychological autonomy. This last decade has witnessed a burgeoning of interest, led by Brian Barber and his colleagues, in the concept of parental psychological control (Barber, 1996; Barber & Olsen, 1997; Barber, 2002). "Psychological control refers to parental behaviors that are intrusive and manipulative of children's thoughts, feelings, and attachments to parents" (2002, p. 15). In characterizing parental psychological control as a violation of the child's psychological self, these researchers point to terms in the literature, including manipulative, constraining, guilt-inducing, love withdrawal, anxiety-instilling, possessive, dominant, and enmeshing, that refer to psychological control.

In the edited volume *Intrusive Parenting: How Psychological Control Affects Children and Adolescents* (2002), Barber and his colleagues marshal convincing evidence that parental psychological control is associated with disturbances in psycho-emotional boundaries between the child and parent and, hence, with the development of an independent sense of self and identity. They report that besides these negative effects on children's self well-being processes (the resilience strengths of autonomy, identity, self-awareness, self-efficacy, etc.), psychological control also increases children's internalized problems, such as depression, suicidal ideation, withdrawn behavior, eating disorders, and passive resistance. Similarly, they found a consistent positive relationship between psychological control and externalized problems (delinquency, substance abuse, aggression, defiance, and deviance) as well as with decreased academic achievement.

The research reported in *Intrusive Parenting* looks at parental control across cultures and, as Barber and Harmon report, "The findings are consistent in showing that perceived psychological control is associated positively and significantly to both forms of problem behavior [internalized and externalized] in all nine cultures [we've examined]. Particularly noteworthy is that these patterns hold in two collectivist cultures—India and Gaza—in which less emphasis is placed on individual autonomy than is in more individualistic cultures" (p. 45).

The thesis advocated here is that while autonomy support may look different in different cultures and may vary in degree, autonomy is a basic human need and, thus, healthy development requires autonomy-supportive environments. The research reported by Barber leads him to make a similar assertion: "The effects of parental psychological control are as ubiquitous as they have recently been shown to be because this behavior intrudes on a basis human drive for some form of psychological and emotional autonomy, and that therefore, these negative effects should be found broadly across cultures" (p. 44).

Referring back to our discussion of authoritarian and authoritative parenting, it should be pointed out that authoritarian parenting, while more controlling than authoritative parenting, is not synonymous with parental psychological control. Autonomy-granting can be problematic for parents living in dangerous and under-resourced communities, but restricting children's autonomy need not be manipulative in the ways associated with parental psychological control. Parents' concern for their children's safety in dangerous neighborhoods often takes precedence over giving their children more freedom. Research on adolescents in dangerous neighborhoods finds a major strategy employed by parents is *not* allowing their children to have so much freedom (Furstenberg, et al., 1999; Sampson et al., 1997). As Furstenberg and his colleagues found, "In general, African-American parents were more engaged in family management strategies that minimize danger and maximize opportunity than white parents, regardless of socioeconomic status. They were more inclined to protect their children from street influences by restricting their freedom, taking measures to confine them to the household after school and on weekends" (1999, p. 142).

In fact, Boykin and Allen's (2001) study of adolescents in both low- and high-risk contexts found *negative* developmental outcomes for teens in high-risk communities who are more autonomous. While they found social competence benefits for low-risk teenagers who exhibited autonomy, teenagers in high-risk environments who exhibited autonomy reported increased levels of delinquent activity. Boykin and Allen hypothesize that this is due to a combination of the many opportunities surrounding teenagers in high-risk contexts to engage in deviant behavior and the absence of other, safe opportunities to gain autonomy. In high-risk contexts, the natural developmental process of adolescent autonomy seeking is often blocked or misdirected. Boykin and Allen report, "High-risk teens may have fewer opportunities to gain autonomy from a part-time job, scholastic success, or extra-curricular activities, and thus for these teens, problematic behavior may be one easily accessible arena through which they can assert themselves and gain independence" (2001, p. 232).

In view of all this sometimes conflicting research, one recommendation seems in order for parents trying to respond to their children's autonomy needs when safety is an issue. Given that more-than-ideal regulation or *behavioral* control measures may be required, parents should try to support their adolescents' *psychological* autonomy as much as possible. This means including them in shared decision-making, talking with them about salient issues of daily life, and supporting their problem-solving and personal planning efforts, and connecting them to community resources where they can do service to others.

While several studies have made a good case for the differing effects of warmth, rules/expectations, and decision-making power in promoting health and academic achievement (Herman et al., 1997), a safe conclusion from the literature is that all three family protective factors are important, albeit, perhaps in different proportions, not only to different cultural groups but based on individual and *contextual* differences as well. It remains for the parent or family caregiver to keep all three protective factors in a dynamic balance depending on the specific child and the specific context. This means loving our kids and using our intuition and common sense to keep regulations and rules from becoming a form of emotional control. Perhaps it is up to each parent or family caregiver to consider the following questions from Brooks and Goldstein: "When you interact with your children, do you ask yourself if they are gathering strength from your words and actions? When you put your children to bed at night, do you think about whether they are stronger people because of the things you have said or done that day? Have they gathered strength from you that will reinforce their sense of self-worth and resilience?" (2001, p. 88).

FAMILY RESILIENCE

A growing movement over the last decade that really sheds light for us as social workers in how best to support the families with whom we work has been that of family support programs, that attempt to redress the limitations of a "narrow focus on individual resilience [that] has led clinicians to attempt to salvage individual 'survivors' without exploring their families' potential, and even to write off many families as hopeless" (Walsh, 1998, p. 23). Family support programs see that the best and most effective ways to foster resilience in youth is to foster it in the family caregivers. This approach acknowledges the family as the child's first and foremost environment and is based on nurturing family resilience as well as the resilience of individual family members. In the vignette reported by Katy Butler (1997) below, it is clear, for example, that Patty Tachera's children also benefit from the personal strengths she has developed with the help of a family support program:

> Late last summer, at a table in the cafeteria of Kauai Community College, Connie Bunlaga, a carefully dressed, white-haired older Filipina woman, was holding Patty Tachera's hand. Connie is Patty's support worker from Healthy Start. Patty, 41, is a single mother now studying to be a teacher. Her only island relatives are the four children she is raising alone. Born in Florida, she was 20 when she followed a surfer friend to Hawaii and stayed on. She married a man who beat her and, later, their son and daughter. After eight years she fled, only to have two sons with another, emotionally abusive man. Her daughter, now in her early teens, has not beaten the odds: she is living in therapeutic foster care because of her uncontrollable violence toward Patty and the other children. Patty signed up for Healthy Start and met Connie two years ago, shortly after giving birth to her youngest son. "I had a one-year-old and a newborn and no support," she says. "I lived through the men in my life. I was overweight. I cried all the time. I couldn't sleep. You get so low you can't pick yourself back up. In a very mellow, calming way, Connie kicked me in the butt."
>
> Over the next year, Patty experienced the sort of upward spiral that characterizes the lives of resilient children who meet good mentors. Connie came to see her every week. Patty lost 30 pounds. . . . Patty decided to become a teacher and went back to school; Connie helped her get aid from a state rental subsidy program. Finally, Patty kicked out her emotionally abusive boyfriend.
>
> "She's like my mother," Patty says. . . . "She has a calming effect on me. . . . I don't think I was ever happy before, but I am now," she continues, "I'm much more patient with the babies. I don't find myself yelling as much. It's so important to have somebody who you know cares about you." (pp. 22–31)

Treating the family as the unit of change, family support programs apply to the family the protective approaches for nurturing individuals— caring, high expectations, and opportunities for participation (Patterson, 2002; Walsh, 1998)— recognizing that many of the resilience strengths found in young people—social competencies like caring, empathy, trust, and connections to others; collaborative problem-solving skills, flexibility, and resourcefulness; sense of self-efficacy, self-awareness, and resistance; and sense of purpose and meaning or faith—can be tapped in practice with families as well (Benard, 1997; Walsh, 1998). Strengths-based social work with families reflects the same practices as those with youth advocated in the 3rd edition of this book (Benard, 2002):

- Listen to their story
- Acknowledge the pain
- Look for strengths
- Ask questions about survival, support, positive times, interests, dreams, goals, and pride
- Point out strengths
- Link strengths to families'/members goals and dreams
- Link family to resources to achieve goals and dreams
- Find opportunities for family/members to be teachers/paraprofessionals (p. 217).

A wonderful aspect of the family support movement is that these hundreds of family support programs are incredibly diverse, arising locally but applying global resilience principles. While family support programs look different structurally—and range from family centers to programs that are part of larger organizations such as Boys and Girls Clubs, to organizations that infuse family support principles into their mission, to community-level systems of care in which family support sites form an integrated network of care, to actual comprehensive community collaborative structures that plan and organize human services at the community level (Diehl, 2002)—they are all based on caring relationships of staff to family, high expectations that the family not only has strengths to nurture but also has innate resilience and the capacity to grow and change, and that the most effective way to work with families is through a strengths-based approach, a partnership with them that welcomes the family's gifts and contributions (Family Support America, 2000; Schorr, 1997). The Family Resource Coalition of America (www.familysupportamerica.org), for example, lists the following principles that guide their Family Support Centers, principles that are at the heart of working from a strengths perspective with families:

- Staff and families work together in relationships based on equality and respect. Participants are a vital resource.
- Staff enhance families' capacity to support the growth and development of all family members: adults, youth, and children.
- Programs affirm and strengthen families' cultural, racial, and linguistic identities and enhance their ability to function in a multicultural society.
- Programs are embedded in their communities and contribute to the community-building process.
- Programs advocate with families for services and systems that are fair, responsive, and accountable to the families served.
- Practitioners work with families to mobilize formal and informal resources to support family development.
- Programs are flexible and continually responsive to emerging family and community issues.
- Principles of family support are modeled in all program activities, including planning, governance, and administration.

Not only are the above principals at the heart of strengths-based work with families, they already are at the heart of good social work practice.

Evaluations of family support programs, such as of California's Healthy Start, consistently document positive adult and child outcomes from these efforts (Wagner & Golan, 1996). A meta-analysis of 665 studies representing 260 programs, the 2001 National Evaluation of Family Support Programs, computed effect sizes for nine possible outcomes, including the major goals of these programs—improved parenting and enhanced child development. The researchers found that effect sizes *doubled* when the programs used family support best practices as outline above (Layzer & Goodson, 2001). It is *how* we do what we do that ultimately makes the difference.

The family support field, like most others in the human services, has faced increasing pressures for accountability over this last decade. According to the Harvard Family Research Project, probably the major source of knowledge for the family support field, two other major assessment projects are underway: the National Family Support Mapping Project and the Promotional Indicators Project. The former is an effort to locate and collect information on every family support program in the country and to create a comprehensive national database that would answer "simple but important questions: How many family support programs are there? What families are they serving? What are the services and programs being offered? What are the funding sources for these programs?" (Diehl, 2002, p. 14). The latter project will develop indicators for measuring family strengths and capacities, instead of using deficit-based indicators that measure the negative aspects of families.

It is to be hoped that with all of this assessment activity, the family support field, perhaps working in collaboration with social work organizations, can form a viable lobby for social and economic policies that support families and children. A recent finding with dire implications for children's well-being is that mothers participating in the welfare-to-work programs of the last several years display twice the rate of clinical depression—two mothers in every five—compared to the general population. According to these researchers, "Maternal depression sharply depresses their young children's development" (Fuller et al., 2002). Given that the 2001 meta-analysis discussed above found a positive long-term effect size of .39 for family economic self-sufficiency, it seems likely that a family support approach would provide a more developmentally supportive, resilience-enhancing, and, in the long run, economically viable approach to helping families in poverty. Moreover, it would offer the strong possibility of creating a healthy next generation, one reflecting the most powerful protective factor in a child's development—having a quality care-giving experience in the family (Werner & Smith, 2002).

DISCUSSION QUESTIONS

1. In your own family can you see evidence of the three resilience factors: caring relationships, high expectations, and opportunities for participation.

2. In the families of clients that you see, which of these three factors seems most durable?

3. In families that seem on the surface to be in trouble (e.g., single-parent families), what are their sources of resilience and rebound?

4. How can you as a worker contribute to the strengthening of these three resilience factors?

REFERENCES

The Annie E. Casey Foundation. (n.d.). *PRB/KIDS COUNT special report: A first look at Census 2000 supplementary survey data* (p. 24). Retrieved from http://www.aecf.org/kidscount/c2ss/pdfs/front/national_profile.pdf

Anthony, E. J. (1974). The syndrome of the psychological invulnerable child. In E. J. Anthony (Ed.), *The Child in His Family, Vol. 3: Children at Psychiatric Risk* (pp. 29–544). New York: John Wiley and Sons.

Baldwin, A., Baldwin, C., Kasser, T., Zax, M., Sameroff, A., & Seifer, R. (1993). Contextual risk and resiliency during late adolescence. *Development and Psychopathology, 5,* 743–761.

Bandura, A. (Ed.) (1995). *Self-Efficacy in Changing Societies.* Cambridge, UK: Cambridge University Press.

Barber, B. (1996). Parental psychological control: Revisiting a neglected construct. *Child Development, 67,* 3296–3319.

Barber, B. (1997). Introduction to special issue: Adolescent socialization in context—The role of connection, regulation, and autonomy in the family. *Journal of Adolescent Research, 12,* 5–11.

Barber, B. (Ed.). (2002). *Intrusive Parenting: How Psychological Control Affects Children and Adolescents.* New York: American Psychological Association.

Barber, B. & Harmon, E. (2002). Violating the self: Parental psychological control of children and adolescents. In B. Barber (Ed.), *Intrusive Parenting: How Psychological Control Affects Children and Adolescents* (pp. 15–22). New York: American Psychological Association.

Barber, B. & Olsen, J. (1997). Socialization in context: Connection, regulation, and autonomy in the family, school, and neighborhood, and with peers. *Journal of Adolescent Research, 12,* 287–315.

Baumrind, D. (1971). Harmonious parents and their preschool children. *Developmental Psychology, 4* (1), 99–102.

Beardslee, W. & Podoresfky, D. (1988). Resilient adolescents whose parents have serious affective and other psychiatric disorders: The importance of self-understanding and relationships. *American Journal of Psychiatry, 145,* 63–69.

Benard, B. (1997). Focusing therapy on what families do right: An interview with Steven Wolin. *Resiliency In Action,* Spring, pp. 17–21.

Benard, B. (1991). *Fostering Resiliency in Kids: Protective Factors in the Family, School, and Community.* Portland, OR: Northwest Regional Educational Laboratory.

Benard, B. (2002). Turnaround people and places: Moving from risk to resilience. In D. Saleebey (Ed.), *The Strengths Perspective in Social Work Practice* (3rd. ed., pp. 213–227). Boston: Allyn & Bacon.

Benard, B. (2004). *Resiliency: What We Have Learned.* San Francisco: WestEd.

Benard, B. & Quiett, D. (2002). *Nurturing the Nurturers: The Importance of Sound Relationships in Early Childhood Intervention.* San Francisco: WestEd.

Benson, P. (1997). *All Kids Are Our Kids: What Communities Must Do To Raise Caring and Responsible Children and Adolescents.* San Francisco: Jossey-Bass.

Bernstein, N. (2000). *A Rage to do Better: Listening to Young People from the Foster Care System.* San Francisco: Pacific News Service.

Blakeslee, S. & Wallerstein, J. (1989). *Second Chances: Men, Women and Children A Decade After Divorce.* Boston: Tichnor and Fields.

Blum, R., Beuhring, T., Shew, M., Bearinger, L., Sieving, R., & Resnick, M. (2000). The effects of race/ethnicity, income, and family structure on adolescent risk behaviors. *American Journal of Public Health, 90,* 1879–1884.

Boykin, K. & Allen, J. (2001). Autonomy and adolescent social functioning: The moderating effect of risk. *Child Development, 72,* 220–235.

Brooks, R. & Goldstein, S. (2001). *Raising Resilient Children: Fostering Strength, Hope, and Optimism in Your Child.* New York: McGraw-Hill/Contemporary Books.

Brown, J. & D'Emidio-Caston, M. (1995). On becoming at-risk through drug education: How symbolic policies and their practices affect students. *Evaluation Review, 19* (4), 451–492.

Butler, K. The anatomy of resilience. *Networker,* pp. 22–31, March/April 1997.

Chao, R. (1994). Beyond parental control and authoritarian parenting style: Understanding Chinese parenting through the cultural notion of training. *Child Development, 65,* 1111–1119.

Chao, R. (2001). Extending research on the consequences of parenting style for Chinese Americans and European Americans. *Child Development, 72,* 1832–1843.

Chess, S. (1989). Defying the voice of doom. In Dugan, T. & Coles, R., (Eds.), *The Child in Our Time: Studies in the Development of Resiliency* (pp. 179–199). New York: Bruner-Mazel.

Clausen, J. (1993). *American Lives: Looking Back at the Children of the Great Depression*. New York: Free Press.

Clark, R. (1984). *Family Life and School Achievement: Why Poor Black Children Succeed or Fail*. Chicago: University of Chicago Press.

Cohn, J. (1997). *Raising Compassionate, Courageous Children in a Violent World*. Atlanta, GA: Longstreet Press.

Coontz, S. (1992). *The Way We Never Were: American Families and the Nostalgia Trap*. New York: Basic Books.

Delpit, L. (1996). The politics of teaching literate discourse. In *City Kids, City Teachers: Reports from the Front Row*, edited by W. Ayers and P. Ford. New York: New Press.

Diehl, D. (2002). Family Support America: Supporting "family supportive" evaluation. *The Evaluation Exchange, 8*(1), 14–15.

Eccles, J. & Gootman, J. (2002). *Community Programs to Promote Youth Development*. Washington, D.C.: National Academy Press, Institute of Medicine.

Eccles, J., Midgley, C., Buchanan, C., Wigfield, A., Reuman, D., and MacIver, D. (1993). Development during adolescence: The impact of stage-environment fit on young adolescents' experiences in schools and in families. *American Psychologist, 48*(2), 90–101.

Egeland, B., Carlson, E., & Sroufe, L. (1993). Resilience as process. *Development and Psychopathology, 5*, 517–528. Cambridge University Press.

Ellis, N. (2001, Summer). Tuning in. *Hope, 6*, 48–50, 61.

Family Support America (2000). *Family Support Centers, Volume I: Program Planning and Evaluation, A Program Manager's Toolkit*. Chicago: Family Support America.

Festinger, T. (1984). *No One Ever Asked Us: A Postscript to the Foster Care System*. New York: Columbia University Press.

Foster Care Work Group (2004). *Connected by 25: A plan for investing in successful futures for foster youth*. Washington, D.C.: Youth Transitions Funders Group.

Fuller, B., Kagan, S., & Loeb, S. (2002). *New Lives for Poor Families? Mothers and Young Children Move through Welfare Reform*. University of California-Berkeley: Graduate School of Education-PACE.

Furstenberg, F., Cook, T., Eccles, J., Elder, G., & Sameroff, A. (1998). *Managing To Make It: Urban Families and Adolescent Success*. Chicago: University of Chicago Press.

Gambone, M. & Arbreton, A. (1997). *Safe Havens: The Contribution of Youth Organizations to Healthy Adolescent Development*. Philadelphia: Public/Private Ventures.

Gandara, P. (1995). *Over the Ivy Walls: The Educational Mobility of Low Income Chicanos*. New York: SUNY Press.

Garbarino, J., Dubrow, N., Kostelny, K. & Pardo, C. (1992). *Children In Danger: Coping With the Consequences of Community Violence*. San Francisco: Jossey-Bass Inc.

Halperin, S. (Ed.). (1998). *The Forgotten Half Revisited: American Youth and Young Families, 1988–2008* (pp. 1–26). Washington, D.C.: American Youth Policy Forum.

Harris, J. (1998). *The Nurture Assumption: Why Children Turn Out the Way They Do*. New York: Touchstone.

Henricson, C. & Roker, D. (2000). Support for the parents of adolescents: A review. *Journal of Adolescence, 23*, 763–783.

Herman, J. (1997). *Trauma and Recovery*. New York: Basic Books.

Herman, M., Dornbusch, S., Herron, M., and Herting, J. (1997). The influence of family regulation, connection, and psychological autonomy on six measures of adolescent functioning. *Journal of Adolescent Research, 12*, 34–67.

Hetherington, M. & Kelly, J. (2002). *For Better or Worse: Divorce Reconsidered*. New York: Norton.

Higgins, G. O. (1994). *Resilient Adults: Overcoming a Cruel Past*. San Francisco: Jossey-Bass.

Hill, K., Howell, J., Hawkins, J., & Battin-Pearson, S. (1999). Childhood risk factors for adolescent gang membership: Results from the Seattle Social Development Project. *Journal of Research in Crime and Delinquency, 36*, 300–322.

Kim, U. & Chun, M. (1994). Educational "success" of Asian Americans: An indigenous perspective. *Applied Behavioral Development, 15*, 328–342.

Kurcinka, M. (1992). *Raising Your Spirited Child: A Guide for Parents Whose Child Is More Intense, Sensitive, Perceptive, Persistent, and Energetic*. New York: Perennial.

Lahey, B., Gordon, R., Loeber, R., Stouthamer-Loeber, M. & Farrington, D. (1999). Boys who join gangs: A prospective study of predictors of first gang entry. *Journal of Abnormal Child Psychology, 27,* 261–276.

Lamb, W. (2003). *Couldn't Keep It To Myself.* New York: HarperCollins.

Layzer, J., Goodson, B., Bernstein, L., & Price, C. (2001). *National Evaluation of Family Support Programs: Final Report.* Prepared for the Federal Administration for Children, Youth, and Families. Cambridge, MA: Abt Associates.

Lewis, T., Amini, F., & Lannon, R. (2000). *A General Theory of Love.* New York: Random House.

Maddux, J. (2002). Self-efficacy: The power of believing you can. In C. Snyder & S. Lopez (Eds.), *Handbook of Positive Psychology* (pp. 277–287). New York: Oxford University Press.

Masten, A. & Coatsworth, D. (1998). The development of competence in favorable and unfavorable environments: Lessons from research on successful children. *American Psychologist, 53,* 205–220.

Masten, A., Hubbard, J., Gest, S., Tellegen, A., Garmezy, N., & Ramirez, M. (1999). Competence in the context of adversity: Pathways to resilience and maladaptation from childhood to late adolescence. *Development and Psychopathology, 11,* 143–169.

Masten, A. & Reed, M. (2002). Resilience in development. In C. Snyder and S. Lopez (Eds.), *Handbook of Positive Psychology* (pp.. 74–88).New York: Oxford University Press.

McFarlane, A., Bellissimo, A., & Norman, G. (1995). Family structure, family functioning and adolescent well-being: The transcendent influence of parental style. *Journal of Child Psychology and Psychiatry, 36,* 847–865.

McLaughlin, M., Irby, M., & Langman, J. (1994). *Urban Sanctuaries: Neighborhood Organizations in the Lives and Futures of Inner-City Youth.* San Francisco: Jossey-Bass.

Meier, D. (1995). *The Power of Their Ideas.* Boston: Beacon Press.

Miller, A. (1990). *The Untouched Key:Tracing Childhood Trauma in Creativity.* New York: Anchor Books.

Mills, R. (1993). *The Health Realization Model: A Community Empowerment Primer.* Alhambra, CA: California School of Professional Psychology.

Mills, R. (1995). *Realizing Mental Health.* New York: Schulzberger and Graham.

Mills, R. & Spittle, E. (2001). *Wisdom Within.* Auburn, WA: Lone Pine Publishing.

Moore, J. (1991). *Going Down to the Barrio: Homeboys and Homegirls in Change.* Philadelphia: Temple University Press.

Moore, K., Chalk, R., Scarpa, J., & Vandivere, S. (2002). Family strengths: Often overlooked, but real. *Child Trends Research Brief,* August.

Patterson, J. (2002). Understanding family resilience. *Journal of Clinical Psychology, 58,* 233–246.

Pittman, K. & Zeldin, S. (1995). *Premises, principles, and practices: Defining the why, what, and how of promoting youth development through organizational practice.* Washington, D.C.: Academy for Educational Development, Center for Youth Development & Policy Research.

Polokow, V. (1993). *Lives On the Edge: Single Mothers and Their Children in the Other America.* Chicago: University of Chicago Press.

Rak, C. (2002). Heroes in the nursery: Three case studies in resilience. *Journal of Clinical Psychology, 58,* 247–260.

Resilience & Youth Development Module Report (2002). California Healthy Kids Survey, San Francisco: WestEd, Health & Human Development Program (www.wested.org/hks).

Resnick, M., Bearman, P., Blum, R., Bauman, K., Harris, K., Jones, J., Tabor, J., Beuring, T., Sieving, R., Shew, M., Ireland, M., Bearinger, L., & Udry, J. (1997). Protecting adolescents from harm: Findings from the National Longitudinal Study on Adolescent Health. *Journal of the American Medical Association, 278,* 823–832.

Rhodes, W. & Brown, W. (Eds.). (1991). *Why some children succeed despite the odds.* New York: Praeger.

Richters, J. & Martinez, P. (1993). Violent communities, family choices, and children's chances: An algorithm for improving the odds. *Development and Psychopathology, 5,* 609–627.

Rockwell, S. (1998). Overcoming four myths that prevent fostering resilience. *Reaching Today's Youth: The Community Circle of Caring Journal, 2*(3), 14–17.

Ross, E. (2003, January 26). One parent, twice the trouble. *Contra Costa Times.*

Rutter, M. (1979). Protective factors in children's responses to stress and disadvantage. In M. Kent & J. Rolf (Eds.), *Primary Prevention of Psychopathology, Vol. 3: Social Competence in Children* (pp. 49–74). Hanover, NH: University Press of New England.

Rutter, M. (1987). Psychosocial resilience and protective mechanisms. *American Journal of Orthopsychiatry, 57,* 316–331.

Rutter, M. (1989). Pathways from childhood to adult life. *Journal of Child Psychology and Psychiatry, 30,* 23–54.

Sampson, R., Raudenbush, S., & Earls, F. (1997). Neighborhoods and violent crime: A multilevel study of collective efficacy. *Science, 277,* 918–924.

Sandler, I. (2001). Quality and ecology of adversity as common mechanisms of risk and resilience. *American Journal of Community Psychology, 29,* 19–61.

Schorr, L. (1997). *Common Purpose: Strengthening Families and Neighborhoods to Rebuild America.* New York: Anchor Books.

Schweinhart, L., Barnes, H., & Wiekart, D. (1993). *Significant Benefits: The High/Scope Perry Preschool Study Through Age 27.* Ypsilanti, MI: High/Scope Press.

Seita, J., Mitchell, M., & Tobin, C. (1996). *In Whose Best Interest? One Child's Odyssey, A Nation's Responsibility.* Elizabethtown, PA: Continental Press.

Seligman, M., Reivich, K., Jaycox, L., & Gillham, J. (1995). *The Optimistic Child: A Revolutionary Program That Safeguards Children Against Depression and Builds Lifelong Resilience.* Boston: Houghton Mifflin.

Steinberg, L. (2000). The family at adolescence: Transition and transformation. *Journal of Adolescent Health, 27,* 170–178.

Thornberry, T. (1998). Membership in youth gangs and involvement in serious and violent offending. In R. Loeber & D. Farrington (Eds.), *Serious and Violent Offenders: Risk Factors and Successful Interventions* (pp. 147–166). Thousand Oaks, CA: Sage.

Tierney, J., Grossman, J., & Resch, N. (1995). *Making A Difference: An Impact Study of Big Brothers/Big Sisters.* Philadelphia: Public/Private Ventures.

Vaillant, G. (2002). *Aging Well: Surprising Guideposts To A Happier Life from the Landmark Harvard Study of Adult Development.* Boston: Little, Brown, and Company.

Vigil, J. D. (1990). Cholos and gangs: Culture change and street youth in Los Angeles. In R. Huff (Ed.), *Gangs in America: Diffusion, Diversity, and Public Policy* (pp. 146–162). Beverly Hills, CA: Sage.

Wagner, M. & Golan, S. (1996). *California's Healthy Start School-Linked Services Initiative: Summary of Evaluation Findings.* Menlo Park, CA: SRI International.

Walker-Barnes, C. and Mason, C. (2001). Ethnic differences in the effect of parenting on gang involvement and gang delinquency: A longitudinal, hierarchical linear modeling perspective. *Child Development, 72,* 1814–1831.

Wallerstein, J., Blakeslee, S., & Lewis, J. (2000). *The Unexpected Legacy of Divorce: A 25 Year landmark Study.* New York: Hyperion.

Walsh, F. (1998). *Strengthening Family Resilience.* New York: Guilford Press.

Watt, N., Anthony, E., Wynne, L., & Rolf, J. (Eds.) (1984). *Children at Risk for Schizophrenia: A Longitudinal Perspective.* New York: Cambridge University Press.

Weitoft, G., Hjern, A., Haglund, B., & Rosen, M. (2003). Mortality, severe morbidity, and injury in children living with single parents in Sweden: A population-based study. *Lancet, 361* (9354). Retrieved from http://www.thelancet.com/journal/vol361/iss9354

Werner, E. (1986). Resilient offspring of alcoholics: A longitudinal study from birth to age 18. *Journal of Studies on Alcohol, 14,* 34–40.

Werner, E. & Smith, R. (1982). *Vulnerable But Invincible A Longitudinal Study of Resilient Children and Youth.* New York: McGraw Hill (paperback eds. 1989, 1998, New York: Adams, Bannister, Cox).

Werner, E. & Smith, R. (1992). *Overcoming the Odds: High-Risk Children from Birth to Adulthood.* New York: Cornell University Press.

Werner, E. & Smith, R. (2001). *Journeys from Childhood to the Midlife: Risk, Resilience, and Recovery.* New York: Cornell University Press.

Wilkes, G. (2002). Abused child to nonabusive parent: Resilience and conceptual change. *Journal of Clinical Psychology, 58,* 261–278.

Wolin, S. & Wolin, S. (1993). *The Resilient Self: How Survivors of Troubled Families Rise Above Adversity.* New York: Villard Books.

Zigler, E. & Hall, N. (1989). Physical child abuse in America: Past, present, and future. In D. Cicchetti and V. Carlson (Eds.), *Child Maltreatment: Theory and Research on the Causes and Consequences of Child Abuse and Neglect* (pp. 38–75). New York: Cambridge University Press.

CHAPTER TWELVE

"THAT HISTORY BECOMES YOU"

Slave Narratives and Today's Movement to End Poverty

WILLIE BAPTIST

MARY BRICKER-JENKINS

SARAH GENTRY

MARSHA JOHNSON

CORRINE NOVAK[1]

To maintain the economic institution of slavery, it served the interests of those who benefited from it to believe that those who lived in slavery were miscreants who required regulation to "produce," were somehow responsible for their misfortune, and sometimes, as the children of Hamm, were destined to their fate. Similarly, those who benefit from the economic institution of poverty today maintain and promote the fiction that people living in poverty are "lazy or crazy," are poor because they "made bad choices," or now, with a New Age turn of the Calvinist screw, are poor because they are "working out their karma."

Only with the lens of history do we see clearly the enormous strengths of the enslaved: They excavated from their experiences and aspirations new definitions of humanity and freedom that would inspire the abolitionist movement and, ultimately, the nation as a whole. Today there is a growing movement to end poverty that is based in the unity and leadership of the poor; informed by their analysis and inspired by their vision, many who are not now living in poverty are joining

---

[1]Authors are listed alphabetically; all are members of the Narratives Study Group of the Kensington Welfare Rights Union Education Committee. The research study on which this chapter is based was a project of that group. The authors were responsible for this study but wish to acknowledge the significant contributions of past members of the group, Jennifer Jones and Carrie Young, as well as all the participants in the study.

this movement for the abolition of poverty. They understand that their fate is inextricably linked to that of the poor.

Nobody is paid to build this movement. People do the work everywhere, often in uninviting, even hostile environments. They do the work "after hours" when others are enjoying "down time." Far from being lauded for their work, they are more often dismissed or even ridiculed by friends, families, and colleagues. Some of them believe that poverty cannot be ended in their lifetimes, but they do the work anyway. Why? How did these "ordinary people" develop a political consciousness that impels their work to end poverty in a world that says it can't be done? And what keeps them going?

These are the questions we pursue in this chapter. Informed by our reading of 19th century slave narratives, we sought the source of the strengths of leaders in the movement. Specifically, we conducted in-depth interviews with eight emerging leaders of the Kensington Welfare Rights Union (KWRU), exploring with them two primary questions concerning consciousness and commitment: 1.) how they developed a political consciousness that led them to become involved in the movement, and 2.) the organizational factors that sustain them in their work.[2]

We assumed that deepening our understanding in these two areas would help our organizing and retention efforts, but we also believed that the research act itself would consolidate the understanding and commitment of the participants. Beyond the considerable social science evidence to support this belief (see, for example, Cieri & Peeps, 2000; Couto, 1993; Passy & Giugni, 2000; Polletta, 1998; Polletta & Jasper, 2001), we had the evidence of the history of the abolition movement. Studying that movement, we learned of the power of the slave narrative in the development of collective consciousness and commitment. In his introduction to *The Classic Slave Narratives* (1983), historian Henry Louis Gates, Jr. tells us that "the slave narrative came to be a communal utterance, a collective tale, rather than merely an individual's autobiography. Each slave author, in writing about his or her personal life's experiences simultaneously wrote on behalf of the millions of silent slaves still held captive throughout the South" (p. 21). Further, a narrative was not considered complete until the slave had become free and was working towards the abolition of the institution of slavery. Individual liberation was a beginning, not the end (Baker, 1985; Gates, 1983; see also Foner, 1950).

Thus, for us, the abolition of slavery and the role of the narrative in that movement are more than a metaphor. They are models that inform our vision and our work. The study on which this chapter is based is part of a larger effort within KWRU to use people's narratives—or, as we often refer to them, documentation of violations of economic human rights—to consolidate the narrator's consciousness and commitment and to inform the public about the realities of poverty and the poor. Our participation in the Narratives Committee of KWRU is one part of our work in the movement and, in this instance, an opportunity for us to use our social work research skills to work toward the abolition of poverty.

---

[2]This chapter draws heavily from the Master's thesis of two of the authors, who conducted all of the interviews and initial coding of the data. See Gentry, Sarah M. & Johnson, Marsha L. (2003). *"We take a little power:" A study of political consciousness and sustained participation in narratives of members of the Kensington Welfare Rights Union*. Northampton, MA: Smith College School for Social Work.

We will begin this chapter with a brief description of organizational context for our work—KWRU, the Poor People's Economic Human Rights Campaign, and the movement to end poverty. Then, following an overview of the research we conducted to answer our questions, we will present our findings and thoughts about them. We do this—and all our work— with the hope that readers will have both a more finely textured view of the strengths of people living in poverty and a clearer vision of the possibilities of ending poverty.

THE ORGANIZATIONS AND THE MOVEMENT

The Kensington Welfare Rights Union (KWRU) is a membership organization of poor and homeless families and others who are not currently living in poverty but who know that it can and must be ended. Founded in the Kensington section of Philadelphia in 1991 by five "welfare moms," KWRU works from local to global levels to build a movement to end poverty based in the unity and leadership of the poor—that is, we consciously organize across color lines, focus heavily on leadership development, and pursue a program rooted in the analysis and vision of the organized poor.[3]

KWRU spearheaded the development of the Poor People's Economic Human Rights Campaign (PPEHRC), a national network of grassroots organizations. Each has its own program and organizing objectives, but they have come together with a particular mission—to end poverty in the United States and, in fact, in the world. The overarching strategy of the movement to end poverty is encapsulated in the mission statement of the PPEHRC:

> The Poor People's Economic Human Right's Campaign is committed to the unity of the poor across color lines as the leadership base for a broad movement to abolish poverty. We work to accomplish this through advancing economic human rights as named in the Universal Declaration of Human Rights—such as the rights to food, housing, health, education, communication and a living wage job.[4]

Parsing this statement reveals essentials of the campaign's analysis and methods. First, the *unity of the poor* is the *sine qua non* of the movement. This unity has at least two dimensions that challenge contemporary notions of organizing based on "identity" and "class." First, with regard to identity, there is no question that the instruments of racism, sexism, ableism, ageism, and other systems of targeted exploitation have resulted in disproportionate representation of members of these groups in poverty. However, those same instruments have been used to conceal the class nature of poverty and disunite the poor. Thus, organizing across color lines is essential to the building of the movement.

---

[3]See www.kwru.org for background and current activities of the organization.

[4]Adopted by the PPEHRC Steering Committee at its retreat, December 18–21, 2003, at The Highlander Center, New Market, Tennessee. The PPEHRC mission statement was fashioned from the KWRU mission statement and is nearly identical.

Our understanding of "class" also challenges contemporary notions of class as "culture" or "identity" or even income. As we scan the organizing terrain, we see the rise of a new class of economically vulnerable people, people who have followed all the rules—earned college degrees, dress and "look right," bought 401Ks, and so forth—who are one illness, layoff, or divorce away from foreclosure, unmanageable debt, or working three jobs to make it to the next day. We believe that these people can come to understand their economic vulnerability as the result of structural, not personal, characteristics and forces and, ultimately, grasp the inherent unity of interest between so-called poor, working class, and middle class people. They constitute, in fact, one class that can unite around common interests to claim their economic human rights.

We believe that the *leadership base* for the movement must be the program of the poor as a united and organized force. That is, the movement must be driven by a vision and a program fashioned from the experience of the poor—experience excavated and examined collectively to develop the kind of political consciousness that can inform action toward meeting everyone's basic needs.

The emphasis on *ending* poverty is important. For business and industry, poverty is raw material in the productive enterprise. The vision and program of most advocates and policymakers involve "reducing" poverty or "ameliorating" its effects while "managing" it through economic and social service instruments. But if you ask a poor mother which of her children she's going to leave in poverty when the policy goal of "50% reduction" is achieved, she will present a different analysis and vision. Only *ending* poverty is acceptable.

A primary organizing tool we have adopted is the Universal Declaration of Human Rights (UDHR) and, in particular, those articles that encompass economic human rights—Articles 23, 25, and 26 (United Nations, 1948)—the *concept* of economic human rights because they reflect, in their absence, the daily conditions of increasing numbers of people in the U.S. and, in their fulfillment, the perceived promise of the U.S. to its people since the inception of the nation. We were drawn to the *instruments* of the UDHR, especially the Covenant on Economic, Social, and Cultural Rights, because of their legitimacy in world opinion and the ways they speak starkly and simply to people, creating a potential basis for unity around a common vision.

In our estimation, we are at an early phase of movement-building; therefore, we must construct the scaffolding for the movement. Some of the required elements of that scaffolding are leadership, consciousness, relationships, and membership organizations (Baptist, 1996; Bricker-Jenkins, 2004). Leadership bolts together the other elements. Thus, we emphasize developing a core of *individual* leaders who can educate, organize, and consolidate the *class* leadership of the poor as a conscious social force. Not all of the individual leaders must come from the ranks of the poor, but they need to identify with and promote the program of the poor. Leadership development is the first—and necessary—stage of building a broad movement, and we recognize that it cannot be truncated.

This takes us full circle to the motivation for this study of consciousness and commitment. The study, we ventured, would not only generate knowledge about how leaders develop and what sustains them, but would also contribute to their development by helping them claim the legitimacy of their own narratives. Although our findings must be considered tentative and limited, we feel that both objectives were achieved. In the next section, we give an overview of the design and process of the study.

THE STUDY: NARRATIVES OF CONSCIOUSNESS AND COMMITMENT

Participating in study groups is integral to the organizational culture of KRWU. The Narratives Study group was formed in 1999 and began reading four bodies of literature: 19th century slave narratives and other works about the abolition movement; the history of poor people's movements in the United States and analyses of contemporary movements elsewhere in the world; research and theory on political consciousness, activism, and social movement participation; and participatory and interpretive traditions in research. This study has influenced our thinking and shaped several projects, including this study and an earlier study of the perceptions about social workers of people living in poverty and active in the movement (Jones, 2000; Jones & Bricker-Jenkins, 2002).

As noted above, the slave narratives inspired the study, and the research literature's support for the potential for enhancement of participants' consciousness and commitment further influenced our decision to use an interpretive approach (Padgett, 1998; Patton, 2001). Studies of poor people's movements in the United States were, of course, important reading, but limited in two ways: the common definition of what constitutes such a movement and the conceptualization of the movements. Piven and Cloward (1979), for example, analyze four 20th century "poor people's" movements, none of which challenged the fundamental structural arrangements that generate poverty as an economic institution. Further, their assessment of the Welfare Rights Movement of the 1960s and 70s concludes that people living in poverty can, for the most part, play only a limited role in leadership. As we have seen, KWRU operates from a fundamentally different position, one that is more akin to the landless workers' movement in Brazil (de Almeida & Sanchez, 2000).

We also read social movement and participation theories, including the early structural/grievance works, resources mobilization studies, the so-called "new social movement" literature, and the contemporary social constructionist approaches.[5] We found none of these adequate to encompass fully our understanding of participation in the contemporary movement to end poverty. However, it was not our intention to test theory, but to begin the process of understanding and ultimately theorizing our own experience, and all of the literature helped us define "lines of inquiry" that could be pursued in our semi-structures interview guide. Similarly, it seemed to us that no one theory could explain the emergence of consciousness and commitment as it would have to define the relationships among

---

[5]See Gentry & Johnson, 2003 for the literature review and details on study design.

(at least) contexts, demographics, relationships, interactions, "identities," and organizational factors as well as the array of subjective meanings individuals and groups develop for these. In this area as well we used the literature to develop lines of inquiry and "probes," leaving lots of room for the emergence of "indigenous categories" (Patton, 2001) in the analysis of the interview data.

The methods used in this study were informed by the work of phenomenologist Max Van Manen (1990). Van Manen's focus on illuminating meanings of lived experience was consistent with the purposes of our research. Phenomenology seeks to expose these meanings through analysis of text, or in the case of this project, the narrative. This research process is not a compilation of facts distilled into generalizations or theories; rather, it is a process of examining life experience and extracting or interpreting meanings that are often implicit.

Van Manen (1990) identifies six steps involved in phenomenological research: 1.) tuning into the phenomenon; 2.) investigating the experience as it is lived; 3.) reflecting on essential themes; 4.) describing the phenomenon through writing and re-writing; 5.) maintaining a pedagogical relation to the phenomenon (i.e., allowing the data to guide the evolving interview process and instrument); and, 6.) balancing the research context by considering parts and whole. These were the steps followed in data collection and analysis (which proceeded simultaneously), and the analyses (themes) were then presented to participants in a "member checking" group for interpretation, confirmation or not, and elaboration. Five of the eight participants attended this group, the transcript of which became part of the data and further augmented our understanding.

Participants were identified collectively by the Narratives Committee and approached initially by the KWRU Education Director (to assure potential participants that the Education Committee had approved the study).[6] Because we wanted to explore the effects of participation on leadership development, each was considered to be an "emerging" or potential leader in the organization. We sought—and achieved— gender and ethnic diversity as well as "sustained" participation—a minimum of six months active work in KWRU. We also wished to interview both people currently living in poverty and others active in the movement, and we were particularly interested in interviewing social workers. Half of those we hoped to interview had BSW or MSW degrees.

None of the twelve members approached declined to participate, but time allowed for only eight sets of interviews. Of the eight interviewed two of the eight identified as male and six identified as female. Six of the eight participants identified as white/Caucasian, one as multi-racial-African American, and one as Puerto Rican. Two of the eight participants were between 25–30 years of age, three between 30–35, and three between 40–50. All but two were married or in committed relationships at the time of the study. All but one were employed, and the unemployed person was in a "workfare" job. Three were currently living in

---

[6]This is standard protocol in the organization. It should also be noted that all of the members of the Narratives Committee were members of the organization and known to the participants.

poverty; of those who were not, three of the five had lived in poverty at some point in their lives.[7]

Each of two planned interview sessions with each participant was designed to last approximately one hour; however, we found that each interview lasted anywhere between 30 minutes and one and a half hours. As political consciousness and commitment are not static entities in the lives of human beings, we made a commitment to continue to revisit these questions on as many occasions as requested by our participants, so there was significant variability in the length of interviews, and third interviews were done at the request of the participant. All individual interviews were conducted face-to-face and were audiotaped. Each tape was transcribed and tentative themes in the data were identified prior to the member checking group.

In the next section, we present the findings organized around our two overarching research interests: the development of members' political consciousness, and the factors that sustain participation in the movement. This organization is somewhat arbitrary, however, as some contributing factors ("political education," for example) appear in both sections and, in reality, factors interact, ebb and flow in their significance, and may influence each other in different ways at different times. We will also discuss briefly the political impact of the study—its effects on participants, both those interviewed and the interviewers.

THE DEVELOPMENT OF POLITICAL CONSCIOUSNESS

We had hoped to find "common pathways" to political consciousness and activism but did not in this limited number of interviews. However, three interwoven themes emerged in the narratives of the participants: 1.) a *sense of injustice* in the world; 2.) *shifting the dominant narrative* (in this case, about poverty); and 3.) *hope* that change is possible.

Sensing Injustice

There are many people in the world who sense injustice who do not become activists, but this study and others (see, for example, Muller & Opp, 1986; Teske, 1997) suggest that it constitutes one of several essential ingredients in the alchemy of activism. All of the participants in this study identified a sense of something wrong in the world as an important part of their development. Most, but not all, spoke of early personal experiences of living in poverty, racial injustice, gender oppression, or a combination of these factors. Some came to KWRU to translate their sense of injustice into political action, and some came seeking help for individual concrete needs and found a nascent understanding of shared injustice awakened and channeled to participation in the organization.

---

[7]Although it was not a consideration in the construction of our sample, the demographics of those who had or were living in poverty roughly approximates the profile of poverty in the United States.

Heather's story typifies the latter process. Heather said, "Growing up there was always a sense of, like, I don't want to say conspiracy, but there was always a sense of like people don't care about us, they're just going to do whatever." She felt powerless in a system that had something wrong with it, but no sense of personal agency through collective action. That came later, beginning with her first contact with KWRU. She had a problem with being cut off from her welfare benefits. When she turned to KWRU for help, she was asked to share her personal narrative.

> [They] briefly explained to me that they were doing some kind of bus tour. I really didn't, to be honest, it kind of went over my head a little bit, like I didn't understand it. But they asked if I would come speak because they were having a send off rally. And I was like sure. I wasn't quite sure what a rally was because I don't think I'd ever seen a demonstration or rally or anything like that. So I did and I went and met them at Schmidt's Brewery. So the first time I actually met someone was at Schmidt's Brewery to speak at this rally and tell my story about the problem I was having with getting welfare at the moment, and I had lost my job because I couldn't afford to pay for childcare and I couldn't go back to school.

Heather initially contacted KWRU thinking they would help her get her benefits reinstated, which they did. They also, from the first contact, supported her budding understanding that hers was a systemic problem, not an individual one.

Similarly, Carmelo reported a situation faced by rapidly increasing numbers of workers in the United States:

> I had my job, but I don't got no benefits in my job . . . No health—no nothing. Then when I get sick, I went to the hospital—it was like three weeks. Then, after that when I came home, I had to be home like three weeks more . . . Then, I lost my apartment cause I don't have no-no-no income to pay my rent. I left my apartment.

He then came to KWRU, and was placed in a KWRU "Economic Human Rights House," a vacant property controlled by the Department of Housing and Urban Development which KWRU took over to house homeless people.

Through KWRU, Carmelo soon found other people who were experiencing similar problems. "And then because and between all the problems I have, I see how people go through it." Mere contact is not enough, however. As in Heather's situation, collective sharing and analysis of personal narratives supported the evolving awareness of systemic injustice: "We start telling our stories. You know, like, I tell my story, the other person is with me tell his story, you know. And we start like that."

In addition to collectivity, immediate and individualized response may be important in nurturing newcomers' sense of injustice as well as their loyalty to the organization. Elaine came to KWRU with a welfare and housing problem. When she called them on the phone the executive director told her to come in the next day, gave her a key to the office, and arranged for KWRU to become her community service work to keep her welfare benefits. Her work with KWRU is the first time that she has done political work. "I don't know what drew me here . . . I don't even vote." She had a lifelong sense that, "The people you stick in office are crooks, no matter who it is." Elaine is not comfortable with demonstrations and protesting but she is proud of the work she does answering the phones and helping people with their welfare problems. KWRU helped transform her manifestation of her sense of injustice from apathy to an individually comfortable form of activism.

Among these participants, the majority had been politically active prior to coming to KWRU in identity-based movements—the women's movement, those of people of color, the "LesBiGayTrans" movement and those of the constituent groups within it, and so forth. For them, the work of the movement to end poverty provided an opportunity to transcend identity-based work without losing sight of the ways that identity-based oppression might nuance the class dynamics that require and reproduce poverty. Laura, for example, had been involved in gender-based activism in college but, through working on a movement event, felt "this makes so much damn sense." Many, like Carrie, ultimately found identity-based activism alone to be "divisive," in that it can deflect attention from the roots of economic injustice. Ian's early work on the rights of young people engendered a crucial element in all political work: "That always made me look at power."

For some, formal education honed personal experiences into analytical instruments. Heather's first memory of political consciousness was as a 16-year-old single mother in a community college class. Her teacher "really had a way with describing how people's—bringing [out] people's individual struggles and situations and linking [them] to environmental conditions and what was really going on around people, and not so much of what was going on with the individual or how we fix that individual. And it really spoke to my own situation at the time . . ." Jennifer and Kristin's social work studies resonated with their personal experiences of injustice, leading them to want to act. Laura entered a graduate school for social work seeking opportunities for political work. Having worked in a social service agency, Laura realized, "something is really wrong about systems issues. So I had the analysis that we were working and aligned with a very messed up system and how damaging it was for people that we call our clients."

Whether they came seeking help with a concrete need or seeking a channel for activism, the stories of all the participants reflected the theme of sensing a systemic injustice in the world. This ingredient was necessary but not sufficient in the production of a political consciousness that led to activism. The deeply rooted dominant narratives about poverty and the poor had to change.

Shifting the Dominant Narrative

Dominant narratives serve not only to explain, but also to maintain social arrangements (Fulford, 1999). Whether it be patriarchy, heterosexism, feudalism, chattel slavery, or another dominant/subordinate form that furthers the interests of a dominant group, there will be a narrative that makes the arrangement seem appropriate, necessary, and even inevitable. Since the dominant group controls the institutions through which narratives are transmitted—government, media, religious and educational establishments, and the like—members of the exploited group usually believe the narrative that explains and justifies their subordination. For a movement to change such arrangements to take hold, an alternative explanation must take hold—one that is consonant with people's experiences and supports liberation rather than subordination. With regard to poverty, involvement in KWRU provided such an alternative narrative for these participants, one that "made sense" and was consonant with their experiences.

The uprooting of the dominant narrative did not come automatically, however, but evolved over time, supported by the organization's dialogical and didactic educational process. First, as Kristin said, she had to understand that "poverty isn't an accident."

Elaine illustrates the kind of personal experience that reveals the fiction in the dominant narrative (and policy) of ending poverty through employment of all welfare recipients:

> You have to have a high school diploma, GED, sometimes two years of college. They literally take you to these job interviews knowing you can't get the job, but you gotta have at least an interview . . . The usual answer you get with that is we still have a lot more applicants. We will contact you as soon as we're done. You never hear from them again. They're very polite about it.

Understanding that "the system" doesn't work, however, can co-exist with the dominant narrative's teaching that the individual is at fault. Heather experienced the strength of the dominant narrative even as she lived in poverty as she spoke of

> The images that are put out for people who might not be as educated, who might not have made it, or who have had kids young, or who have done this, that and the other . . . It's easy to say, oh that's why . . . Oh, she's got kids young, that's why she's poor.

Jennifer had been working with KWRU for some time before her narrative shifted:

> I was seeing poverty directly, but still had the mind frame that like . . . I think I was blaming the people. Like I thought the system was wrong that people should be living like that and that we should be doing something. Like there was all this wealth why aren't people living better? But, I . . . think there was a part of me still that saw it as, like, if these people did something different they could have been in a different place.

Another theme in the dominant narrative about poverty—that it is a "race problem"—was also dislodged for Jennifer. As a woman of color, the "race" explanation resonated, but it continued even after she had spent time volunteering in a poor white community in Appalachia. She illustrates the process of supplanting the dominant narrative:

> Suddenly I realized, like, OK, look how you had that experience and you just did not have an analysis to explain it. You just kind of somehow put it as OK this is that region of poor whites that are just out there.

The dominant "charity" approach to change is also refuted in the movement narrative. Laura said that she went through

> an educational process to really understand how [KWRU work] was different than some of the charity work . . . you know, how different than being in a women's

rights organization or that type of thing . . . learning more about really uniting the power to change our world basically. That's a much bigger type of work.

And Carmello spoke with passion about the marches and demonstrations in which he participates to make poverty visible, events in which the narrative of his life challenges the dominant narrative: "It's a lot of people they don't hear. Like those people, they got all those things. They don't see that because they all the way up there. We see that."

Hope

While participants differed in the scope and degree of structural change that might be achieved through their work—from Carmelo's hope for "a place to be warm and eat" for everyone to Carrie's "entire world that's just created around completely different priorities . . . other human beings and life over money"—their hope was grounded in a belief that the resources exist to actualize their visions. Laura hopes her work will help others replace the "scarcity" paradigm that serves the *status quo* with a perception of the abundance that exists in the world: "I hope that we really do come to see that we have the means to fulfill everyone's rights."

Most of the participants indicated that their hopes were nurtured by the study of history and social movements. Heather's comments about the goal of her work demonstrate an understanding of the phased nature of social transformation, an understanding that motivates action when personal gain seems unattainable:

> Initially I hope that there's going to be more of an appreciation for people who are poor and appreciation for what they actually are doing and trying to do with their lives, and the good things about those people, and not stigmatize them as much . . . I mean, eventually, yeah I hope poverty is eliminated. But I don't know if I'll see it in my lifetime. I'm hoping for my children's lifetime and I hope my children by seeing me involved in things like that, I hope that they can take in the values and understanding of what's going on in the larger society and how people are treating each other, and take that into their next generation.

SUSTAINING PARTICIPATION

Since the current stage of the movement requires leadership development, we must know what helps people sustain their participation and what organizational barriers they encounter. Social movement literature suggested several concepts that resonated with our participants' experiences.[8] Having an opportunity to choose among a *variety of roles,* each carrying *different levels of risk,* appears important (McAdam, 1982, 1986; Wiltfang & McAdam, 1991). Among our group, roles/risks ranged from helping those coming to the office with their concrete needs to going to jail for taking over government-owned abandoned housing. Paulsen (1991) and

---

[8]Naturally, there was much in the literature that was not reflected in these narratives. Since we were not testing hypotheses, the full literature review is beyond the scope of this chapter.

Ennis and Schreuer (1987) explore the significance of activists' sense of personal *efficacy*. Paulsen's finding that well educated, middle class students' sense of political efficacy stimulates activism is instructive, but leaves unresolved compelling questions about recognizing and nurturing efficacy among those whose participation carries higher risk, especially over the long haul.

Tarrow (1992), on the other hand, proposes the utilization of collective action frames that use *ideology and strategy* to create meaning and a sense of purpose and efficacy among participants in a given movement. As we shall see, our participants' narratives reflected Tarrow's analysis, as well as others that examine relationships among *collective action frames*, organizational *cultures*, the participants' making of *meaning* and *identity* (Hunt, Benford, & Snow, 1994; Klandermans, 1992, 1997). KWRU's educational programs and exchanges with movement organizations in other countries have been particularly valuable in the area of sustaining participation (de Almeida & Sanchez, 2000; Veltmeyer & Petras, 2002).

Since they study "identity" movements, so-called "new social movement" researchers have underscored the importance of *collective identity* in sustaining participation (see, for example, Johnston, Laraña, & Gusfield, 1994; Melucci, 1995; Poletta, 1998). As our participants noted, the movement to end poverty is decidedly not an identity movement. However, as Poletta and Jasper have noted, collective identity is also a factor in "interest-based" movements, in which "sustaining participants' commitment over time requires ritualized reassertions of collective identity and efforts to manage, without suppressing, difference" (2001, p. 292). Finally, both collective identity and the making of meaning are sustained when *life spheres* and *networks* reflect and reinforce activists' beliefs and actions (Passy & Giugni, 2000); our participants detailed the significance of these elements in sustaining their work and the ways they operate in the organizational context.

In the following sections, we will see these concepts reflected and illustrated in the themes that evolved in the participants' narratives: 1.) education, 2.) group identity, and 3.) meeting personal needs. Participants were also forthcoming about 4.) organizational and personal barriers to sustained participation.[9]

Education

As we have indicated, education is integral to the formal structure and culture of KWRU. Participants spoke of its importance in sustaining their work beyond the initial attraction to the movement; Laura provided an example as she reflected on her development: "I think there's some core values and beliefs that you have that attract you to a cause or a movement or a person who's about that cause or movement. And then it becomes more of who [you are] and, you know, not in a brainwashing cult type of way, but in a really empowering educational process."

Two overlapping types of education were cited: skill development and political education. *Skill development* was seen as a function of working in a group con-

---

[9]It is worth noting that, as of this writing, well over a year since the final interviews, all of the participants, including the authors, are active in the organization and the movement at large. Most have taken on additional responsibilities.

text. Specific skills included listening, mediating, learning to apologize for the sake of moving forward as a group, using better judgment about when to sit still and be quiet and when to move forward, maintaining hope in the face of adversity and hopelessness, skills in working with parents and children within the movement, public speaking, and working to maintain connections with fellow members of the organization. Underpinning these was the fact that work within the organization has required them to think and work collectively, an uncommon experience in the larger culture.

Political education occurred through self-study, dialog, and analysis—particularly of history and social forces. Some participants with higher education specifically contrasted self-study for edification with studying to pass a test or earn a degree. Study groups and buddy groups were particularly important. Heather talked extensively about how the dialogical educational process in the organization, particularly in the area of history, served to help her make sense of her current participation. She said,

> We would get together every week and we would study and we would read Martin Luther King and different movements and study early Christianity, study the slave movement, the abolition movement—to study different movements and to have a dialogue on that afterwards, and to take that to another level to help—it solidified my understanding of the movement, what it took to build a movement, what's involved in that, who's involved in that, and what needs to be done, and at what stage we were in in that.

The dialogical process also contrasts with and countervails the disbelief and erasure so often experienced by those living in poverty. Heather said "I learned to trust my instincts through being provided the environment to have these kinds of discussion and dialogue without being cut off or discredited."

Jennifer explained how the deepening of her understanding of social forces related both to the nature of her work and to sustaining it. Indeed, not acting was no longer an option:

> I always kind of saw injustice and wanted to end it and, you know, when I go and visit new places I always see homeless folks. I always see folks who look poorer than other people. I can't just not see it. And I know what's caused that. I know that there's, you know, a real fight for the minds of the people and it's, basically, the rich right now are winning. And until we really educate ourselves and get organized, they're gonna keep winning. So, it's hard to turn that off once you've opened it up and turned it on. I think that's one of the things that's kept me here.

Finally, the study of past social movements deepens both analysis and commitment as it locates the today's hard work in an unfolding process. Carrie said that one element sustaining her commitment and work in KWRU was "the belief and knowledge that people throughout history have done this kind of work. I feel connected with something. It's sort of like you become part of that history and that history becomes you."

Group Identity

The theme of group identity was strong and pervasive in the interviews. Participants talked about their relationship to each other and to the organization as an entity in itself, and three dimensions of group identity emerged clearly in their narratives: affective, instrumental, and intellectual. The *affective* dimension was reflected in the frequent references to the organization as a supportive network or "family." As Elaine said, "We're more like—the members, we're like family more than anything. But when one's in problems, they all get together and say, yeah we're gonna do this." The sense of familiarity, of "just knowing" from shared experience was noted. Heather described her first day with KWRU, "I didn't have to sit there and feel like an idiot explaining to them how I was treated when I went to the welfare office. They just shook their heads and agreed and totally understood, and it reminded me of a lot of the people I grew up with—the family." Carmelo also referred to the organization as a "growing family."

The *instrumental* dimension was reflected in the participants' understanding of collectivity as integral to the strategy of social change. Again noting the lessons of history, Jennifer said,

> I think it's possible to bring people together to change the way they think. I mean, there was a time when people didn't think like you know, slaves like, deserved certain human rights, like the idea to vote or the idea to choose a job that they wanted, to get married. And yet they changed the way people thought.

Heather described the tactical use of collectivity in the movement:

> And it really, really helps when you're standing out there doing something for what you believe in, but there's so many other people screaming at you and telling you the wrong thing. When you look at the other people [who] are committed in the same process and all, it just gives you the strength to understand so you know you're not just doing this alone. So it's a lot easier to be in that group than it is to say well I'm just going to tackle this world by myself, or put all the blame on myself.

The *intellectual* dimension of group identity was reflected in the participants' shared analysis and vision. All members referred to an economic human rights framework as they described their vision for a better world and explained how they were incorporating the framework into their various work activities. While differing in analytical details, all participants conveyed that poverty had structural roots. Building a movement based in the unity and leadership of the poor was at the core of the group's intellectual framework. Carmello explained the movement's foundation most succinctly: "We poor got together. It's good."

Meeting Personal Needs

Balancing employment, family, friendships, leisure time, with political work inevitably was a challenge, but having good friends and family in the movement provided ballast for many. Others mentioned the crucial support of family members not directly involved in the work. Laura, a social worker, particularly credited her employer for helping her integrate multiple spheres by providing resources and assistance in her political work. Since most of the organization's members live in poverty, having the information and advocacy resources available in times of crisis is invaluable. While overlapping and integrating life spheres can be counter-productive, it worked well for these participants.

BARRIERS TO SUSTAINED PARTICIPATION

The clearest *organizational* barrier cited was lack of resources. Working on the principle of "commitment, not compensation" (Baptist, 1996) KWRU is able to accomplish much with "person power," but programs and events do cost money. A national bus tour or march, for example, builds the movement at the grass roots, but costs many thousands of dollars. And leaders' daily struggle to survive is integral, not incidental, to the organization's operations. Kristin, a social work student at the time of the study, was working closely with one of the top leaders in KWRU. She said, "When you're trying to put together things [with a member] whose first priority is survival, it gets very frustrating and one thing can make it fall apart. I mean, obviously, what's going to take priority is that she's just lost her house and she's out on the street."

The collectivity that was cited as a strength in the movement could also pose a challenge. As Ian pointed out, when working in groups, particularly when resources are limited, "there's always going to be squabbling." The culture of the organization, however, provides a corrective in its "politics over personalities" dictum (Baptist, 1996). Jennifer referred to this as she spoke of organizational barriers:

> You know, I think that we do try to really push having politics over personalities because, you know, you're gonna fall out with people, and if you just walk away just because you're not getting along with somebody, then you must not really believe it's a right analysis. So, I think at those moments when I'm really angry at people, like, it's the politics that keeps me here. But, I know, on the other hand, part of what keeps me here is just they're really good people.

Organizational barriers sometimes spilled over into participants' *personal* lives. As mentioned above maintaining balance among multiple dimensions posed challenges, particularly since, like Carrie, all of the participants worked multiple jobs, either paid or unpaid:

> It's adjusting to the 14 to 18 hour work day, and that seven days a week as a matter of just routine. And that's been really hard. I mean, that was really hard because I'm someone who really values having free time to do stuff just by myself, not even with other people.

But Heather made reference to the therapeutic dimension of political work:

> I think sometimes being with KWRU can make it easier and make it harder. It's a two-way street. I think sometimes it helps me by not taking the stress out on my

family, but in another sense, it takes its toll sometimes as well. . . .It's less time that you can actually spend locating resources or working two jobs.

Several of the social workers in the group mentioned the actual and potential impact of the political work on their professional careers. After a civil disobedience arrest, one had received official "warning" that her professional license could be suspended. Another said he "backed off of doing some things because I didn't want to be on the news, and then trying to work connected to the state people." None of the participants was cavalier about the threat of losing a job; rather, they were measured, reflective, and committed to finding ways to continue their political work.

Indeed, members face the challenge of maintaining a sense of urgency when rewards are not immediately apparent, especially in a culture that promotes immediate gratification. Ian said, "I'm used to seeing some, you know, like, results right now. It's like what are we trying to do? Is this working? Is this going to be enough to really make things change?" And for those who have it, participants must remind themselves of the fragility of their economic stability. Jennifer faced the potential barrier of personal complacency by holding an economic analysis:

> And I think that I can really sometimes slip into denial of how easy it could be that, you know, [my husband] could lose his job and I could lose my job and we could lose the house that we have right now, and we could not have healthcare. So I think it's so easy for me to slip into that space of not really realizing how urgent of an issue this is because my immediate needs are taken care of today. And I think that's really dangerous.

IMPLICATIONS FOR PRACTICE

Like the 19th century slave narratives, these stories portray the consciousness and commitment of people determined to achieve economic justice. They are individual narratives whose full meaning cannot be understood or actualized apart from the collective experience. And, like the slave narratives, they can strengthen the skills and resolve of both narrator and listener. Considering each of these similarities points to some implications of this small but instructive study.

Working for economic justice is an ethical mandate for social workers (NASW, 1999), but we often seek individual solutions to the institutional problem of poverty. These narrators, several of whom were social workers, demonstrate that another way, a collective way, is possible and is happening. There is a movement to end poverty based in the unity and leadership of the poor, and social workers can and do unite with that movement.[10]

As others have noted (Rapp, 1998; Saleebey, 2002) focusing on strengths poses the risk of romanticizing oppression and pain. In an individualist culture, we

---

[10]The PPEHRC now has over 100 groups in the USA. For information, see www.poorpeopleseconomic humanrightscampaign.org or www.kwru.org for links.

tend to laud and elevate the stories of those who prevail despite the odds. In so doing, we can unwittingly oil the machinery of exploitation, which depends in part on advancing the myth of "personal responsibility" for one's poverty. These accounts reveal the greater strength achieved when the narrators weave their individual stories into the tapestry of a political movement—a process that begins with the simple act of telling the story to others who "just understand." There is much in the social work literature about "consciousness raising" groups, but few agencies make room for them in the current managed-care environment. This study compels us to help people connect with each other in such groups, and we can support their development outside the spectrum of formal services if necessary. Not only can participants experience the strengthening effect of affirmation and affinity, but those so inclined can gather strength from political activism. As Heather said,

> But as far as my sanity, I want to say . . . I think I could have become very depressed. I could be sitting in a counselor's office and talking about my problems very easily. I could be crying and saying this happened to me when I was younger, this happened, this happened, this happened . . . But I know I'm not alone and I know I'm one of the millions that are going through this same thing every single day.

Social workers have also discovered the therapeutic effects of the narrative for individuals and families. This study suggests that we should expand our understanding and use of narrative as a political tool. Our participants affirmed Couto's assertion that narratives can develop leadership and strengthen a movement organization (1993). Further, as others have found (see, for example, Polletta, 1998), our study consolidated individual participants' consciousness and commitment to the work of the collective. Kristin's reflection on her participation was typical:

> You know, it's like coming home when all your life you've felt or believed things and you find somewhere that gives you the outlet to, to really become who you are and to grow personally. So, you know, interviews like this, I just learn new things even talking about stuff in my own head. It clarifies and makes me stronger every time I talk about it. It makes me believe more and more and more in what I do.

Conducted in the tradition of participatory research, the study had a similar effect on the interviewers—the narrators' audience. As true partners in a social work research project, they too were strengthened. Halfway through the project, they reported, they realized that they were changing; not only were they learning from the participants, but

> each time we engaged this project, whether by conducting interviews, analyzing data, conducting the member checking group and reporting back to the Narratives Committee, we were "in community" with our political peers. Being in community with people who inspire, inform, and challenge us so frequently over the course of this project has ultimately served to deepen our commitment to the Kensington Welfare Rights Union. Throughout the project, we have witnessed economic injustice, engaged the questions of history and the value of social movements, deepened

our understanding of our peers and solidified our ties to the collective. Ultimately, we are moved and changed by the stories of the members as they have taken our thoughts and perspectives down new paths (Gentry & Johnson, 2003, p. 80).

We close with the hope that, like those who heard the narratives of the slaves and resolved to unite with them to end slavery, those who read this chapter will unite with us to end poverty.

DISCUSSION QUESTIONS

1. Do you think that poverty can be ended given the pervasive influence of capitalistic, marketplace thinking in our society? Why or why not?

2. How do the narratives of slaves inform the work of those individuals and groups who work to end poverty?

3. What does it mean to say that the unity of the poor is the essence and reason for being in these groups?

4. According to this research what were the steps in the development of political consciousness?

5. How important is it to be aware of the class nature of poverty?

6. As you read the report of this research what are the abiding strengths of those who live in poverty?

REFERENCES

Baker, H. A., Jr. (1985). "Autobiographical acts and the voice of the southern slave." *The Slave's Narrative.* Ed. Charles T. Davis & Henry L. Gates, Jr. NY: Oxford, 242–261.

Baptist, W. (1996). *On the poor organizing the poor.* Retrieved June 18, 2002 from University of the Poor, School for Social Workers Website: http://www.universityofthepoor.org/schools/social/articles/poororgpoor.html.

Bricker-Jenkins, M. (2004). Legislative tactics in a movement strategy: The Economic Human Rights—Pennsylvania Campaign. *Meridians, 4*(2), 108–113.

Cieri, M. & Peeps, C. (2000). *Activists Speak Out: Reflections on the Pursuit of Change in America.* New York: Palgrave.

Couto, R. A. (1993). Narrative, free space, and political leadership in social movements. *The Journal of Politics, 55*(1), 57–79.

de Almeida, L. F. & Sanchez, F. R. (2000). The landless workers' movement and social struggles against neoliberalism. *Latin American Perspectives, 27,* 11–22.

Ennis, J. G. & Schreuer, R. (1987). Mobilizing weak support for social movements: The role of grievance, efficacy, and cost. *Social Forces, 66*(2), 390–409.

Foner, P. S. (1950). *The life and writings of Frederick Douglas: Volume II pre-civil war decade 1850–1860.* New York: International Publishers.

Fulford, R. (1999). *The triumph of narrative: Storytelling in the age of mass culture.* New York: Broadway Books.

Gamson, W. (1975). *The strategy of social protest.* Homewood, IL: Dorsey.

Gamson, W. A. (1992). The social psychology of collective action. In A. D. Morris & C. McClurg Mueller (Eds.), *Frontiers in social movement theory* (pp. 53–76). New Haven, CT: Yale University Press.

Gamson, W. A. (1995). Constructing social protest. In B. Klandermans (Series Ed.) & H. Johnston & B. Klandermans (Vol. Eds.), *Social movements, protest, and contention: Vol. 4. Social movements and culture* (pp. 85–106). Minneapolis, MN: University of Minnesota Press.

Gamson, W. A., Fireman, B., & Rytina, S. (1982). *Encounters with unjust authority.* Homewood, IL: Dorsey.

Gates, Jr. H. L. (Ed.). (1983). *The Classic Slave Narratives.* New York: Mentor.

Gentry, S. M. & Johnson, M. L. (2003). *"We take a little power:" A study of political consciousness and sustained participation in narratives of members of the Kensington Welfare Rights Union.* Northampton, MA: Smith College School for Social Work.

Giugni, M. & Passy, F. (2001). *Political altruism? Solidarity movements in international perspective.* Lanham, MD: Rowman and Littlefield Publishers, Inc.

Hunt, S. A., Benford, R. D., & Snow, D. A. (1994). Identity fields: Framing processes and the social construction of movement identities. In H. Johnston, E. Laraña, Gusfield (Eds.), *New social movements* (pp. 185–208). Philadelphia: Temple University Press.

Johnston, H. (1995). A methodology for frame analysis: From discourse to cognitive schemata. In B. Klandermans (Series Ed.) & H. Johnston & B. Klandermans (Vol. Eds.), *Social movements, protest, and contention: Vol. 4. Social movements and culture* (pp. 217–246). Minneapolis, MN: University of Minnesota Press.

Johnston, H. & Klandermans, B. (1995). The cultural analysis of social movements. In B. Klandermans (Series Ed.) & H. Johnston & B. Klandermans (Vol. Eds.), *Social movements, protest, and contention: Vol. 4. Social movements and culture* (pp. 3–24). Minneapolis, MN: University of Minnesota Press.

Johnston, H., Laraña, E., & Gusfield, J. R. (1994). Identities, grievances and new social movements. In H. Johnston, E. Laraña, J. R. Gusfield (Eds.), *New social movements* (pp. 3–35). Philadelphia: Temple University Press.

Jones, J. (2000). *Doing the work: A Collaborative study conducted with members of the Kensington Welfare Rights Union, Philadelphia, PA.* Northampton, MA: Smith College School for Social Work.

Jones, Jennifer C. & Bricker-Jenkins, M. (2002). Creating strengths-based alliances to end poverty. In Saleebey, D. (Ed.), *The Strengths Perspective in Social Work,* 3rd ed. Boston: Allyn & Bacon.

Klandermans, B. (1992). The social construction of protest and multiorganizational fields. In Morris & McClurg Mueller (Eds.), *Frontiers in social movement theory* (pp. 77–103). New Haven, CT: Yale University Press.

Klandermans, B. (1997). *The social psychology of protest.* Oxford: Blackwell Publishers Ltd.

Klandermans, B., & Oegema, D. (1987). Potentials, networks, motivations and barriers: Steps towards participation in social movements. *American Sociological Review, 52,* 519–531.

Lo, C. Y. H. (1992). Communities of challengers in social movement theory. In Morris and McClurg Mueller (Eds.) *Frontiers in social movement theory* (pp. 224–247). New Haven, CT: Yale University Press.

Marx Ferree, M. (1992). The political context of rationality: Rational choice theory and resource mobilization. In Morris & McClurg Mueller (Eds.), *Frontiers in social movement theory* (pp. 29–52), New Haven, CT: Yale University Press.

McAdam, D. (1982). *Political process and the development of black insurgency, 1930–1970.* Chicago: University of Chicago Press.

McAdam, D. (1986). Recruitment to high risk activism: The case of freedom summer. *American Journal of Sociology, 92,* 64–90.

McCarthy, J. & Zald, M. N. (1977). Resource mobilization and social movements: A partial theory. *American Journal of Sociology, 82,* 1212–1240.

McClurg Mueller, C. (1992). Building social movement theory. In A. D. Morris & C. McClurg Mueller (Eds.), *Frontiers in social movement theory* (pp. 3–25). New Haven, CT: Yale University Press.

Melucci, A. (1995). The process of collective identity. In H. Johnston, & B. Klandermans (Eds.), *Social movements, protest, and contention: Vol. 4. Social movements and culture* (pp. 41–63), Minneapolis, MN: University of Minnesota Press.

Muller, E. N. & Opp, K. D. (1986). Rational Choice and Rebellious Collective Action. *The American Political Science Review 80,* 471–488.

National Association of Social Workers. (1999). *Code of Ethics of the National Association of Social Workers* (2nd ed.) [Brochure]. Washington, DC: Author.

Oberschall, A. (1973). *Social conflict and social movements.* Englewood, NJ: Prentice-Hall Press.

Olson, M. (1965). *The logic of collective action: Public goods and the theory of groups.* Cambridge, MA: Harvard University Press.

Opp, K. D., & Gern, C. (1993). Dissident groups, personal networks, and spontaneous cooperation: The East German revolution of 1989. *American Sociological Review, 58,* 659–680.

Padgett, D. K. (1998). *Qualitative methods in social work research: Challenges and rewards.* Thousand Oaks, CA: Sage.

Patton, M. Q. (2001). *Qualitative research and evaluation methods.* Thousand Oaks, CA: Sage.

Passy, F., & Giugni, M. (2000). Life-spheres, networks, and sustained participation in social movements: A phenomenological approach to political commitment. *Sociological Forum, 15,* 117–144.

Paulsen, R. (1991). Education, social class, and participation in collective action. *Sociology of Education, 64,* 96–110.

Peery, N. (1994). *Black fire: The making of an American revolutionary.* New York: The New Press.

Pfaff, S. (1996). Collective identity and informal groups in revolutionary mobilization: East Germany in 1989. *Social Forces, 75,* 91–117.

Piven, F. F., & Cloward R. A. (1979). *Poor people's movements: Why they succeed, how they fail.* New York: Vintage Books.

Polletta, F. (1998). "It was like a fever . . . " narrative and identity in social protest. *Social Problems, 45,* 137–159.

Polletta, F. & Jasper, J. M. (2001). Collective identity and social movements. *Annual Review of Sociology, 27,* 283–305.

Pope, J. (1990). Women in the welfare rights struggle: The Brooklyn Welfare Action Council. In G. West & R. L. Blumberg (Eds.), *Women and Social Protest* (pp. 57–74). New York: Oxford University Press, Inc.

Rapp, C. A. (1998). *The strengths model: Case management with people suffering from severe and persistent mental illness.* New York: Oxford University Press.

Sachs, J., & Newdom, F. (1999). *Clinical Work and Social Action: An Integrative Approach.* New York: The Haworth Press.

Saleebey, D. (Ed.) (2002). *The strengths perspective in social work practice.* Boston: Allyn & Bacon.

Sherkat, D. E., & Blocker, T. J. (1994). The political development of sixties' activists: Identifying the influence of class, gender, and socialization on protest participation. *Social Forces, 72,* 821–842.

Tappan, M. B. (1997). Interpretive psychology: Stories, circles, and understanding lived experience. *Journal of Social Issues, 53,* 645–656.

Tarrow, S. (1992). Mentalities, political cultures, and collective action frames. In Morris & McClurg Mueller (Eds.) *Frontiers in social movement theory* (pp. 174–202). New Haven, CT: Yale University Press.

Taylor, V. & Whittier, N. E. (1992). Collective identity in social movement communities: Lesbian feminist mobilization. In Morris & McClurg Mueller (Eds.), *Frontiers in social movement theory* (pp. 104–129). New Haven, CT: Yale University Press.

Teske, N. (1997). Beyond altruism: Identity-construction as moral motive in political explanation. *Political Psychology, 18,* 71–91.

Tilly, C. (1978). *From mobilization to revolution.* Boston: Addison-Wesley.

United Nations. (1948). Universal Declaration of Human Rights. Adopted December 10, 1948. GA Res. 217 AIII. United Nations Document a/810. New York: UN.

Van Manen, M. (1990). *Researching lived experience.* New York: Teachers College Press.

Veltmeyer, J. & Petras, J. (2002). The social dynamics of Brazil's rural landless workers movement: Ten hypothesis of successful leadership. *Canadian Review of Sociology and Anthropology, 39,* 79–96.

Wiltfang, G. L., & McAdam, D. (1991). The costs and risks of social activism: A study of sanctuary movement activism. *Social Forces, 69,* 987–1010.

Zinn, H. (1980). *A people's history of the United States.* New York: HarperCollins Publishers.

CHAPTER THIRTEEN

COMMUNITY DEVELOPMENT, NEIGHBORHOOD EMPOWERMENT, AND INDIVIDUAL RESILIENCE

DENNIS SALEEBEY

The profession of social work has gradually withdrawn much of its interest in, and emphasis on, community development and community organization as areas of practice, education, and inquiry. Some 30 years ago, nearly every school of social work had curricula, if not tracks, devoted to community organization. Today, few schools have a robust curriculum in any aspect of community, theory or practice. In this chapter, I would like to explore three interlocking, although rudimentary, developments that might have significant importance for the profession—in the restoration of theory and practice around community and the extension of the strengths perspective.

First, in a variety of fields outside of social work, there seems to be renewed interest in community phenomena, especially community development (Delgado, 2000; Hanna & Robinson, 1994; hooks, 2003; Kretzmann & McKnight, 1993; Mills, 1995; Pransky, 1998; Specht & Courtney, 1994). This rediscovery of community has brought refinements in thinking and action that have implications for the direction of the profession in the future. In addition, they provide some new language and perspectives with which to address the nettlesome problems of oppression, isolation, and marginalization that too many clients of social workers face.

Second, there has been a virtual explosion of knowledge in the field of individual, family, and community resilience (see, for example, Benson, 1997; McQuade & Ehrenreich, 1997; Walsh, 1998). Like the strengths perspective, these various literatures, developed somewhat independently, are founded on the idea that each individual, family, and community has capacities, knowledge, and means that enhance revitalization and these are usually interlocking and interdependent. Likewise there are factors, some operating, others immanent, that elicit and sustain resilient behavior, relationships, and institutions. Furthermore, there is thought to be a complex and abiding calculus of resilience—that community and individual or family resilience are inextricably bound together (Kretzmann & McKnight, 1993; McGoldrick & Carter, 1999; Mills, 1995; Schorr, 1997).

Finally, the notion of empowerment, favored these days by so many groups within the spectrum of political beliefs and by many professions, can be put into dramatic relief by some of the ideas we will discuss. A noble ambition or sentiment, empowerment as a practice sometimes falls far short of its intention. Nonetheless, the idea of empowerment as a framework for practice is regaining considerable ground in social work (Gutierrez & Nurius, 1994; Kondrat, 1995; Lee, 1994; Simon, 1994).

Some of the concepts of the emerging approaches to community development are discussed later in the chapter and then illustrated with reference to a number of current programs that operate from a strengths- and assets-based framework. But first, I would like to address an emerging sense of the notion of context—interpersonal, built, physical, and natural.

"THE POWER OF PLACE"[1]

The profession of social work has long maintained that where it does its work is in that space where the traffic between individuals, families, groups, and the environment flows. The code for this appreciation is person/environment or, more theoretically, the ecological/systems model. In the professional literature, pedagogy and inquiry, this transactional parcel is conceived of in fairly grand terms—including among others social institutions, organizations, service networks, and support systems. This is appropriate, but typically we ignore the immediate, proximal, ambient environments where people live out the rhythms and tempos of their daily lives—rooms, apartments, office cubicles, cars, atria, restaurants, bars, gardens, city blocks, hallways, neighborhood stores, waiting rooms, malls, cells, and the like. Social work has, to a large extent, ignored these smaller, more intimate milieus. It is important to pay attention to them for three reasons. First, whenever you talk of community, you are talking, in part, about these contexts. Second, small changes in these environments often bring big changes in behavior. The work of Roger Barker (1978) years ago on behavioral settings; and the more current work of William Bratton (1998) and others on making small changes in the immediate environments where crime takes place (dilapidated, poorly tended for neighborhoods, poorly tended public transportation) brings large dividends in reducing crime (this is the "Broken Windows" theory of crime—if a neighborhood or space looks like no one cares for or about it, then criminals are less likely to be restrained in their activities there). Third, these modest environments often profoundly affect our understanding and interpretation of people's behavior and our

---

[1]After working on a paper with this title, I came across a very helpful book by Winifred Gallagher with the same name.

own behavior. Judith Rich Harris (1998) makes a wry and telling point in her discussion of context and personality:

> Stability of personality across social contexts depends in part on how different or similar a person's contexts have been. Cinderella's two contexts (cottage and castle) were unusually divergent, so there was more than the usual amount of variation in her personality. But someone who met her after the prince carried her off to the castle wouldn't know that. They would only see her out-of-the-cottage personality. (p. 73)

The point? We often look inward or to the family to explain and understand behavior, but the immediate context—interpersonal, built, and physical—is a powerful influence on how we feel, think, and act. So the environment—be it school, neighborhood, or playground, and its people and structures—can be a major force in helping people to turn around their lives (see Chapter 12). And it may not take much to turn that environment from one in which deficits, disorganization, and destruction discourage and deflate everybody to one where people have hope and pride. Terry Woodberry, CEO of United Way in Kansas City, Kansas, said that he and a bunch of his colleagues tried to figure out what made a good neighborhood. After discussions with many neighborhood residents from different parts of the county (Wyandotte County), well-to-do and economically depressed alike, he and his group developed the following criteria: (1) Hopeful housing stock: A critical mass of apartments, houses, and grounds, whether in wealthy areas or poor, that show signs of being cared for, kept up, or refurbished.[2] (2) Symbols of community: These might be anything around which the community gathers, works, takes pride, or celebrates—sculptures, buildings, murals, community gardens, events. (3) Intergenerational relationships: These are a visible manifestation of the richness of the immediate interpersonal context, and of caring, connected relationships between older and younger residents. (4) Good neighbor stories: People tell and retell stories of good deeds, supportive acts, and acts of beneficence and the passing on of these stories is as important as the original event itself, providing a kind of poignant message about and narrative structure of the livability of the context.

So the context, however modest and small, can be a force for regeneration, healing, and transformation. And the good news is it may not take much to turn the context from despairing to hopeful. So it does seem clear that the fate of individuals and families is to an uncertain extent bound up with the character, resources, efficacy, myths, values, and relationships of the community. Many of the pressures that families and individuals face are intensified when they have been cut adrift from the safe moorings of a collective place to belong. Two of the factors that increase the assets, safety, and effectiveness of a community are civility and social capital. Civility is that set of expectations of and behaviors toward others that respects their feelings and ideas, cares about their condition, and honors their privacy. People who live in a hothouse or dissipating communal conditions need a

---

[2]HUD finally has this idea. They are tearing down high-rises and replacing them with more home-like structures and grounds, and people take some pride in their care.

generous fund of civility that they can bank on. Social capital refers to the human, economic, spiritual, and social stock of a community—those "funds" available for community development and action, and the confronting of conflict and trouble. Lisbeth Schorr (1997) says this about the relationship between social capital and families and individuals:

> The research makes it clear . . . that the capacity of families to do their child-rearing job is powerfully dependent on the health of their communities. A few children, blessed with extraordinary resiliency or unflagging adult support will be able to beat the odds, but most children growing up in severely depleted neighborhoods face a daunting array of risks that greatly diminish their chances of escaping poor economic, educational, social, and health outcomes. (p. 306)

I must point out here that the research suggests that far more than a few beat the odds—if we take the long view of their development. Nonetheless her point about the importance of social capital for individuals and families is well-taken.

COMMUNITY DEVELOPMENT: EMERGING IDEAS AND PRACTICES

Let us turn now to some of the emerging themes and practices around community development. A conviction that social workers have long prized but often forget in practice is that individual troubles and successes must be framed within the larger context of family, community, and society. To decontextualize individuals and groups as we attempt to help them is to strip away much of the essence of their identity. Community development harks us back to the time-honored belief in the importance of the person–environment interplay. Community work also has ties to social work's abiding interest in social justice as well as a recently diminished collectivist view of the world. In the collectivist view of human development, for example,

> development is perceived to be [a process] in which individuals learn to become participants in the organized social life around them—the family, neighborhood, school, work, voluntary associations, government, and so on. (Specht & Courtney, 1994, pp. 138–139)

Some Basic Ideas about Community Development

A few simple ideas bespeak the basics of community development in the 1990s and into this new century. One of the most basic of these ideas is that the community has the capacity to deal with many of the problems of individuals and families. Voluntary associations, clubs, leaders, institutions, all kinds of interest groups, and self-help groups are at the ready to help. Thus, many of the conceptions of community development focus interest on making an accounting of and using the assets, resources, and strengths available in the community. In this view, the beginning steps in community development involve assaying what resources exist in the community; what human and physical capital underwrite community life; what competencies and resources the people who live and work there possess; what organizations and associations having roles to play contribute to community wealth (Benson, 1997; McKnight, 1997). As in the strengths approach to practice with individuals, the first steps in the development process do not focus on the problems, deficits, and conflicts of the community. Rather, the emphasis is on first discovering the assets in the community.

Because practitioners are looking for and making an accounting of the resources, assets, and capacities of the community, they necessarily begin their work from within the community. External forces do exist and may even be crucial for community vitality. These factors ultimately will be addressed, but by searching for the assets, problem-solving capacities, and leadership in the community, practitioners stress the importance of locality, neighborhood, interdependence, and context, as discussed previously.

Being serious about appreciating and stimulating the resources, capacities, and assets that abound in the community requires that community development workers constantly be on the lookout to build or reconfigure relationships between themselves and residents and formal resident associations (Kretzmann & McKnight, 1993; Mills, 1995; Shaffer & Anundsen, 1993). As one volunteer community developer in an inner-city program for the community's youth said, "I love it when somebody tells me, 'You can't change those kids. Those kids are no good.' They're never *our* kids, it's *those* kids. And my philosophy is that they're *our* kids. They're *my* kids and they're *our* kids, as a community" (McLaughlin, Irby, & Langman, 1994, p. 97). The fundamental principle abides that the community and its surround may have the internal resources to propel the residents to a place of increasing energy, synergy, growth, prosperity, and progress, but the vehicle is often the development of trusting, caring, and responsible relationships.

For a variety of reasons, these ideas have been devastated in the 1980s and 1990s thanks, in part, to the forces of segregation, isolation and alienation, the separation of work and residence, and, importantly, the increasing inequity in the distribution of wealth and other social resources (McKnight, 1997). So "the sense of efficacy based on interdependence, the idea that people can count on their neighbors and neighborhood resources for support and strength has weakened. For community builders who are focused on assets, rebuilding [and building] . . . local relationships offers the most promising route toward successful community development" (Kretzmann & McKnight, 1993, p. 10). Regrettably, individuals and communities, especially those struggling against poverty, oppression, and isolation, often do not think of themselves as having an accessible fund of assets. Those outside the community, too often service providers as well as other institutions and individuals, act on stereotypes, myths, unquestioned assumptions about who people really are, and clearly do not regard them as having strengths and competencies. As Paula Wehmiller says, "When there are walls of ignorance between people [and communities], when we don't know each other's stories, we substitute our own myth about who that person or community is. When we operate with only a myth, none of that person's or people's truth will ever be known to us" (cited in Benard, 1994, p. 380). What assumptions, for example, do we make about the people who live in a given public housing complex and about the environment itself? And where did we acquire those suppositions? To operate as a professional seeking assets, searching out resilience is to turn your back on stereotypic, certainly class-based, and often media-induced, misunderstanding. In community development, a strengths- and assets-based orientation can induce optimism, hope, and motivation for both clients and workers.

From all this we may conclude the following about community and about community development: "A community is a dynamic whole that emerges when a group of people

- participate in common practices,
- depend on one another,
- make decisions together,
- identify themselves as part of something larger than the sum of their individual relationships,
- commit themselves for the long term to their own, one another's and the group's well-being" (Shaffer & Anundsen, 1993, p. 10).

In this somewhat idealized view (there *are* other views of community— especially from those who live in particular neighborhoods and communities), community development involves helping unleash the power, vision, capacities, and talents within a (self-defined) community so that the community can strengthen its internal relationships and move closer toward performing the important functions of solidarity and support, succor and identification, and instructing and socializing. The community must also be helped to strengthen its relationship to outside institutions, associations, and organizations. These can be the lifeblood that allows the community to find its heart, solve its problems, and reach its goals. But the primary resources to be found and employed are the strengths and resiliency, the skills and talents of the residents and members of the community.

COMING TOGETHER: COMMUNITY AND INDIVIDUAL RESILIENCE

Let us review here some of the ideas and conclusions from the varied fields of resilience research. We will see, as we do, that there is a growing sense that individual and familial resilience and the characteristics of the communities in which people live are inseparable.

A number of communal factors seem to be related to individual and familial resilience. The developmental infrastructure of communities, beyond caring and attentive families, is strengthened to the extent that it 1.) has caring adults or surrogate caregivers who provide safety, support, guidance, comfort, and mentorship; 2.) invites the gifts of, and supports youth involvement and participation in, community-building projects and in the moral and civic life of the community; and 3.) has high expectations of all youth with respect to their roles and responsibilities in community and family life (Benson, 1997; Benard, 2004). In this regard, decades of research continue to show that resilience is a process and an effect of *connection*. In Rutter's words, "Development is a question of linkages that happen within you as a person and also in the environment in which you live. . . . Our hope lies in doing something to alter these linkages, to see that kids who start in a [difficult] environment don't continue in such environments and develop a sense of impotency" (Benard, 1994, p. 8). To Emmy Werner and Ruth Smith, who have done the most ambitious longitudinal study of resilience and vulnerability, effective interventions (including natural ones) in every arena must reinforce the natural social bonds between young and old, between siblings, between friends, "that give meaning to one's life and a reason for commitment and caring" (1982, p. 163). Ernesto Cortes, an organizer for the Communities Organized for Public Service (C. O. P. S.), a community-organizing and community-building project in San Antonio for the last 20 years, emphasizes the importance of relationships and sharing stories in community projects of all kinds (Crimmins, 1995). John McKnight (1995) observes that a generative community relies on the gifts of everybody, not just the few. That includes groups seen as deviant. Melvin Delgado (2000) says that a strategy predicated on strengths and community capacity enhancement involves the following assumptions:

1. The community has the will and resources to help itself;
2. it knows what is best for itself;
3. ownership of the strategy rests within, rather than outside, the community;
4. partnerships involving organizations and communities are the preferred route for initiatives;
5. the use of strengths in one area will translate into strengths in other areas— in short, community capacity enhancement will have a ripple effect (p. 28).

The research on resilience challenges us to build this connectedness, this sense of belonging—by helping to transform families, schools, and communities to become "psychological homes" where people can find caring and support, respect, and opportunities for meaningful involvement, and, not insignificantly, where people can defend themselves against incursions and stresses of all kinds. Everyone has the potential for self-righting, the self-correction of life course, but it doesn't operate in a vacuum; it operates when environments challenge and support, and provide protective and generative factors. McLaughlin and colleagues (1994) after their research into the inner city and effective leaders and programs for youth, quote former gang-banger Tito as summing it up most aptly, "Kids can walk around trouble, if there is someplace to walk to, and someone to walk with" (1994, p. 219).

In a very important sense, then, fostering resilience and capitalizing on and extending strengths and capabilities is about building community and creating opportunities for belonging and participation. This is where the paths of community development and resilience cross. As social workers we know this and we certainly claim it: We work both sides of the psychosocial street, the individual and the environment, and the transactions between them. In fact, however, our recent history suggests that we have turned away—not completely, but too frequently—from our community obligations and the contextual side of practice. "Most important, social work's objective is to strengthen the community's capacity to solve problems through the development of groups and organizations, community education, and community systems of governance and control over systems of social care" (Specht & Courtney, 1994, p. 26).

According to Rapp (1998), strengths-based case management with individuals who have severe and persistent mental illness, depends mightily on the availability and use of supportive, instructive, and integrative natural resources within the community. The guiding presumption is that every community, no matter how burdened by economic dislocation or other social stresses, has an array of often untapped resources—people, institutions, and associations—that are potential collateral in insuring genuine integration into the community. These words bespeak the importance of caring and support across the life cycle and within the community.

Another important protective, maybe even generative, factor in a community—and this seems especially relevant for youth—is the existence of normatively high but not inappropriate expectations, seeing "potential not pathology" (McLaughlin et al., 1994, p. 96; see also Chapter 12, this volume). "Loving agendas [sic] and positive missions with productive and healthy purposes" for youth in trouble in communities are essential (McLaughlin et al., 1994, p. 97). Unfortunately, many communities see only gangs, drug abuse, delinquency, truancy, and violence, and shrink from providing youth the expectations of possibility and the connections to health-promoting people, places, and programs. The community and its membership, manifest in its face-to-face relationships, are powerful media for developing, sustaining, and enforcing expectations and norms. Those expectations that are communicated explicitly through the values, actions, and relationships within the community are the most durable and potent. Such expectations also encourage involvement in the community, imply membership, and foster the development and use of the capacities, strengths, and assets of individuals and families.

Related to the persistent communication of high expectations is the creation of *opportunities for people to be contributing members* of their community; opportunities for valued and consequential ways to be involved in family, work, school, associations, and the community at large. High expectations make no sense unless there is the prospect of becoming a collaborating community member, a real citizen with portfolio. A tragedy today in neighborhoods at all socioeconomic strata is that many people have little real chance for participation in the life of a given community whether we are talking of political concerns, economic development, social/associational relationships, or helping to confront the challenges that face a community. This is often true of elders and certainly of people who are viewed as deviant, but it is particularly true in the case of youth.

> The unique energy and creativity of youth is often denied to the community because the young people of the neighborhood are all too often viewed only in terms of their lack of maturity and practical life experience. Categorized as the product of "immature" minds, the legitimate dreams and desires of youth are frequently ignored by the older, more "responsible" members of the community. . . . Given the proper opportunities, however, youth can always make a significant contribution to the development of communities in which they live. What is needed for this to happen are specific projects that will connect youth with the

community in ways that will increase their own self-esteem and level of competency while at the same time improving the quality of life of the community as a whole. (Kretzmann & McKnight, 1993, p. 29)

EXEMPLARS OF COMMUNITY DEVELOPMENT PRACTICE

In this section we take a brief look at three community development programs and philosophies. Although the language is different in each of them, both are clearly assets and strengths based. Following presentation of these programs, we draw some lessons for social work community development practice.

Employing Individual Strengths to Vitalize Community

For a number of years the School of Social Welfare at the University of Kansas has developed and operated a number of modest community-building efforts in mostly economically distressed communities. These have included: 1.) an outreach and development program in two public housing communities in Kansas City, Missouri; 2.) a financial assets-building program (Individual Development Accounts) in an Hispanic community also in Kansas City, Missouri; 3.) a strengths-based program for helping to build community in an urban high school in Kansas City, Kansas; and 4.) working with a local community development agency in developing outreach programs especially to youth in the surrounding communities. Social work students, overseen by a faculty member, typically staff these programs. A professional social worker is responsible for the day-to-day coordination and operation of the program. Two programmatic ideas, not original with the School, have been particularly apt examples of strengths building within a community—the Saturday Academy and the Mini-Grant Program.

The Saturday Academy (the idea was originally developed by former Dean of the School of Social Work, Atlanta Clark University, Lou Beasley) provides youth with a number of opportunities to experience success, to learn a variety of life skills, develop new capacities and interests, to build on their existing strengths and aptitudes, and to expand their knowledge of and involvement in, the local community. The curriculum varies by each class of students who meet on Saturday mornings for three hours over a period of eight weeks. In the past, students have been instructed in and exposed to any number of skills and pursuits—photography, cooking, gardening, leadership, developing a web site, and contributing to the life of the community (a community garden, a neighborhood clean-up project, community mapping, for example). Each group of students is also encouraged to develop their own curriculum interests. A new element of this program is the development of the Community TREE (Teach Responsibility, Educate, Empower) in which graduates are encouraged to join and participate on an advisory board with select residents of the community. The purpose is to get together and to develop community projects, see them through and evaluate them. Underneath the TREE are the implicit ideas of intergenerational collaboration, and fortifying the tools of citizenship.

The minigrant program (recommended to us by Professor Steve Fawcett of the Human Development and Family Life Department of the University of Kansas) provides community residents or students (we have offered the program in communities and in a high school) with the opportunity to develop a proposal for a project that will benefit some part of the community or school. A panel of social work students and local residents (or students) reviews the proposal. If approved, the individual or group who applied is given anywhere from $50 to $200 to execute the project. The applicant(s) must submit an evaluation of the project upon its completion as well as updates as the project goes on. The program is meant to increase a variety of skills for applicants, to give them a stake and recognition in their community, to have a hand in building community efficacy, however modestly, and to create a more affirmative sense of self and of the community. The projects that applicants have proposed across different projects are a testament to the ingenuity and creativity that lies within the hearts and minds of all people.

Building Communities from within:
The Assets-Based Approach

Recognizing that many communities in the United States are either devastated physically and civically or deeply disturbed, John Kretzmann and John McKnight of the Center for Urban Affairs and Policy Research at Northwestern University have said this:

> In response to this desperate situation, well-intended people are seeking solutions by taking one of two divergent paths. The first, which begins by focusing on a community's needs, deficiencies and problems, is still by far the most traveled, and commands the vast majority of our financial and human resources. By comparison with the second path, which insists on beginning with a clear commitment to discovering a community's capacities and assets, and which is the direction [we] recommend, the first and foremost path is more like an eight-lane superhighway. (p. 1)

In the view of Kretzmann and McKnight (1993), each community has a surfeit of assets and resources, often unrecognized or underutilized. This is especially true of marginalized communities where individuals and groups have had to learn to survive under difficult and often rapidly changing conditions. These assets should be accounted for and mapped as a basis for working with and from within a community. The resources to be weighed are not just those of individuals but include local citizens' associations—those informal organizations in which citizens come together for the purpose of problem solving and/or building solidarity. More formal institutions—schools, government entities, businesses, churches, health and welfare organizations, colleges and universities—should likewise be included in the mapping of human and social capital within a community.

Three principles define this approach. First, it is *assets and strengths based.* Community workers start with the resources that are present in the community and not with what is missing, or what the community needs. Second, this approach to community development is *internally focused.* That is, it is very important to know what is going on within the community, what assets are available, and what individual and group capacities exist. The role of external factors and institutions is, for the time being, ignored. Rather the focus on the inner life of the community demonstrates the centrality of local control, local capital, local vision, and local ownership. Finally, if the first two elements of the assets-based scheme are to hold, then the process must clearly be *relationship driven.* If people are to be pulled into the life of the community and share their capacities, it will be done through the medium of relationship. A gift is given from hand to hand.

A significant part of assets-based community development occurs in the beginning with taking a capacity inventory, a strengths assessment, or a catalogue of community assets. The inventory is not a formal research tool. Its primary purpose is to gather information about, say, a specific person (it could also be family, organization, association, or institution) to see what they might give to a community resource bank and to help that person make a contribution to the community. But, this is a two-way street and that person should receive the gifts of resource and skill development, perhaps even education, income, and employment as well. What is actually done to help an individual contribute and receive the gifts of involvement, resource acquisition, and skill development? The practitioner must know how to

- assess the individual's skills and strengths, and then link them to the needs and aspirations of other residents or groups.
- add up the cumulative resources of individuals and groups in the community and, with the residents, combine them in the development of programs and resources the community genuinely wants and needs (for example, a food pantry, or a child care service).
- ensure that all those who make a contribution to the human and resource capital of the community have the opportunity, through connection with others, to move toward achieving personal and familial goals, to create or develop an enterprise, or to solve problems.
- help residents strengthen their sense of community through the development of activities that symbolically and practically cement ties between individuals and groups (for example, a street fair, a mini-grants program).
- help ensure that individual well-being and resilience are a part of all community activities; that there is real work, real responsibility, real opportunity to produce income, and genuinely positive expectations of success and accomplishment (Benard, 1991; Kretzmann & McKnight, 1993; McLaughlin et al., 1994; Mills, 1995; McLaughlin, 2000).

While the idea is to *connect* people as well as local associations and groups through the bartering of their capacities and resources, strengths, and competencies for mutual benefit, clearly none of this happens without the full involvement and direction of residents. Important, too, is the necessity to link residents with local businesses, local institutions and service providers, and other sources of capital and credit. Recognition of resident and community assets may be obscured by the shadow of labels such as "ex-con," "mentally retarded," "mentally ill," "dropout," or, in the case of associations and communities, "gang," "problem group," or "target population." But the root idea of community development is to identify local capacities and mobilize them, which involves *connecting people with capacities to other people, associations, institutions, and economic resources* (Kretzmann & McKnight, 1993): "[E]very living person has some gift or capacity of value to others. A strong community is a place that recognizes those gifts and ensures that they are given. A weak community is a place where lots of people can't give their gifts and express their capacities" (p. 27). A true community, then, invites and encourages participation. The Foundation for Community Encouragement puts it this way, "A true community is inclusive, and its greatest enemy is exclusivity. Groups who exclude others because of religious, ethnic, or more subtle differences are not communities" (Shaffer & Anundsen, 1993, p. 12).

In the case of older residents, for example, their potential is augmented by the fact that they may have time, they have history and experience and often economic resources, and they are very likely to be a part of a larger peer group that can be mobilized. To release seniors' capacities, making an account of the resources of elders in a given community or association is essential; but then an inventory of the resources of local individuals, associations, and institutions must be either completed or, if complete, consulted. Following that, the building of strong and mutually beneficial partnerships between local seniors and other individuals, associations, and institutions is requisite. Finally, having established strong connections, bonds, and alliances within the community, additional affiliations with resources outside the community may be built. Kretzmann and McKnight (1993) offer some examples:

- Seniors are involved in the Visiting Important Persons Program in which they visit less mobile elderly and try to assist with any practical problems. Seniors are trained to be able to provide CPR, to recognize drug abuse, to give bed baths and first aid, and to help with practical daily matters like budgeting and food selection and preparation. The oldest participant is an 82-year-old woman.
- Latch key kids who are feeling lonely, experiencing a crisis or just want to chat, can call on the telephone from their homes to senior citizens through the "Grandma Please" program.
- Seniors are recruited and trained to acquaint them with the local police station and other citywide departments. As a result, seniors visit other seniors in a door-to-door campaign in order to provide security evaluations and advice (pp. 59–60).

Assets-based community development work, although not always known by that name, is occurring around the country. The West Philadelphia Improvement Corps and Atlanta Clark University's Partners in a Planned Community program are just two examples of programs that have their focus, among other things, on the capacity of the community to invigorate itself.

Health Realization/Community Empowerment

The work of Roger Mills (1995) and the Health Realization Institute (2000) has led quickly to broad application in a number of fields including addictions, education, community policing, community development, and public housing, among others. Although the principles began evolving from work with individuals and groups, the first community demonstration project began in two Dade County, Florida, public housing communities (Modello and Homestead Gardens) in the 1980s, communities like many others beset with the results of poverty and racism—hopelessness, lack of opportunities and skills, high rates of violence, drug dealing, domestic violence, teen pregnancy, and school failure (even though these problems did not characterize many families and individuals in the community). The program began, as have subsequent ones, with community leadership training (normally 36 hours) and training for staff of agencies working with the residents. The training is oriented around Psychology of Mind (POM) principles that emphasize the power of creating life experience from thoughts; honoring and getting in touch with the health and wisdom within; learning how an external world of expectations and visions has obscured individuals' own inside world of possibility and calm. The essential feature of this is that those who have been taught now become teachers. Lest this all sound like some 1-900 nostrum, consider the following: After three years, comparative analysis of the results of pre- and post-tests of 142 families and 604 youths revealed improved parent–child relationships in 87 percent of the families; more than 60 percent of residents became employed from a baseline of 85 percent on public assistance; a 75 percent reduction in delinquency and school-related problem behaviors; a 65 percent decrease in drug trafficking; more than a 500 percent increase in parent involvement in schools; and only one student from these communities was failing from a baseline 64 percent failure rate (Mills, 1995, pp. 128–139; Health Realization Institute, 2000, pp. 9–10). These findings have been replicated in dramatic fashion in other community empowerment/health realization projects. Coliseum Gardens in Oakland, California, was beset not only by economic distress, but ethnic and racial divisions and hostility, crime, and gang-related violence. To cite just one of many amazing statistics, this community had the highest homicide rate of any in Oakland for a number of years. After 7 years, there has not been one homicide. Mills and his staff did all the "right stuff" at the outset: They fostered community ownership early on and developed collaborative relationships across many systems. The following quote gives some of the flavor of the program.

> We did everything we could to reduce sources of stress when we began our public housing programs in 1987. We helped our clients with emergency rental needs, paid utility bills, and provided supplementary food, clothing, and physical security. We offered job training and day care assistance. We worked hard to make circumstances easier for our clients. . . .
>
> At the same time, we never lost sight of the bottom line. . . . We wanted to see what could happen when people learned some practical ideas about how they could take charge of their own thinking. We hypothesized that they would begin to handle adversity with more hope and self-respect and find ways to improve their circumstances both as a community and on their own. We trusted that our clients' innate intelligence would surface as soon as they could drop their attachment to alienated or insecure patterns of thinking. We suspected and hoped that the buoyancy of the human spirit would deliver the resiliency they needed to frame their prospects and capabilities in a more hopeful light. (Mills, 1995, p. 128)

First, the principles that guided the program were consonant with some of the findings of the resilience research: the idea that resilience (the capacity to be relatively healthy despite exposure to a variety of severe risks and stresses) is *innate;* the idea that resilience is *directly accessible;* and that organismic wisdom, intelligence, and common sense inhere, to some degree, in all individuals even though buried by years of negative expectations, or the destructive and disheartening imagery and responses of others in one's life.

Second, the goal of "health realization," according to Mills, is to "reconnect people to the health in themselves and then direct them in ways to bring forth the health in others. The result is a change in people and communities which builds up from within rather than being imposed from without" (cited in Benard, 1994, p. 22). Again the importance of the idea of connection surfaces: For communities to make themselves more resilient, there has to be a critical mass of individuals and families who become attached to one another and committed to the community.

Third, the methods of health realization are based on the idea that people construct meaning in their lives. This meaning is expressed in thoughts, manifest in behavior, and fateful for the resilience and energy of the individual. Two sources of meaning (or thoughts) are 1.) those that are primal and indigenous— the immanent wisdom of the body/mind, the things that we appear, given a chance, to intuitively understand and know about ourselves and our world; and 2.) those that are socialized—thoughts that are engendered in us over time by others, by social institutions, by media, by the very culture itself. For too many people, these latter accretions of meaning add up to assumptions of fear, inadequacy, and discouragement. These conditioned networks of thoughts weave the imagery of victimization, a symbolism of blame, and an array of negative expectations (Mills, 1995). Feelings of anger, depression, and despair are the unfortunate progeny of these constructions. Such feelings often are expressed in victimizing or abusive behavior toward the self and others.

Fourth, health realization is based on teaching one to listen and hear the message of health, resilience, possibility, and hope. But this teaching (which will eventually be done by residents for each other) can only be done after creating a positive, caring, collaborative, egalitarian relationship. Mills puts it this way, "Perhaps the most vital ingredient is the establishing of empowering relationships" (1993, p. 29). He refers to "being in a state of service" in which "[w]e have no personal agenda other than what's in the client's best interest" (1993, p. 30).

Fifth, once you live the principles with your clients and in your professional life, then community organizing principles come to the fore, such as enlisting a core group of people, creating a forum for them to meet regularly in small groups, and facilitating the establishment of collaborative relationships with other residents, service providers, government agencies, and the marketplace.

Sixth, this model builds at the grass-roots level a critical mass in each community, and then between communities, that will help create change and put pressure in the right places to move toward policy changes that support human well-being and individual and collective efficacy.

The approach to members of the community occurs individually and in groups and is educative and informative as well as therapeutic, intending to help people discover the strength, capacity, and wisdom within. Establishing a respect-ful, collaborative, light-hearted relationship with residents—a relationship that sees clients as equals and as having the potential for insight, change, and growth—is essential. Furthermore, all individuals and groups are seen as potential teachers and therapists for other constituents of the community. Most important, it requires that helpers be in the real world of residents, in real time, and teach the power of hope. "When people think differently about their lives, their lives change" says Jack Pransky (1998, p. 259). Roger Mills (see page 253), an older man, white-haired, hardly charismatic, modest, honest but full of hope says this about his experience in Modello:

> The residents started to realize that what was keeping them down in life was their thoughts. See, they'd bought the con game. They'd bought the lie. They'd bought the rap that they're supposed to be poor and not be able to do any better—because they're Black, because they dropped out of school, because they started having chil-dren when they were thirteen, because they're in public housing and on welfare, because of whatever. They bought into that set of beliefs—but it's just a thought. *It's just a thought!* Everything is created and maintained via thought. That's the simplic-ity of it. And all they did was let go of that way of thinking, because they started to see it as beliefs programmed like a computer, as opposed to reality—not in a judg-mental or guilty way or with any kind of negativity—just as a fact . . . [And this capacity for thinking differently] is innate. Everybody has it. It's at the core of your psychological makeup. . . . It's the ability to see where everybody else is coming from, where they are getting stuck, and where you are. (p. 259)

NOTES ON COMMUNITY BUILDING
AND PROGRAMS THAT WORK

Community Building

Community building refers to the reality and possibility of restoring or refurbish-ing the sense and reality of community in neighborhoods. It involves among other things helping neighbors—individuals, families, and associations—in a commu-nity strengthen relationships with one another usually around mutually crafted projects. The idea is to replace the notion that they must be completely dependent on outside or professional organizations and institutions for help with the assump-tion that they have internal assets and capacities that can be developed and used in increasing the human and social capital of the community. The upshot of this is an increase in the sense of self-efficacy and power in the individuals, families, and associations of the community—they believe that they can make things happen!

Kingsley, McNeeley, and Gibson (1999) in their report on the growth of com-munity building initiatives outline several successful efforts in economically dis-tressed communities including the tenants of a Washington, DC, public housing community who assumed management of the project and, in the initial years, with the involvement of many residents and resident associations, set up its own educa-tional, social service, and economic development initiatives. As an example of their effectiveness, over the first few years they decreased the vacancy rate from 18 percent to 5 percent (vacancies are critical to these communities because the more vacancies there are, the more they are likely to be commandeered by drug dealers, etc. and/or the more likely the local housing authority may decide to cut back support or, in extreme cases, even close down the project). They also created more than 100 jobs for residents and helped 132 residents get off welfare. And, in 15 years of the program some 700 youths from the community have gone on to college and three-fourths of them have graduated. Stories like this are becoming more common. We can see several themes and appreciations that bind them together.

1.   They center interest on specific and doable community projects and initiatives that improve the community, invite participation, and increase the human and social assets (capital) of the community. Whether the project is a community mural, the development of a block watch, improving relationships with local schools, starting a parenting group, taking over maintenance of the grounds, or developing cooperative relationships with local police to confront the drug problem, the most important outcome is the building of connections between neighbors, developing capacities, trust, and the symbolic ownership of the community. These make future projects more likely and more likely to be successful.

2.   They are driven by communal interests, concerns, and hopes, and typically have extensive involvement of residents. Through these projects, members of the community discover that their interests, values, beliefs, and skills are tools to be used in making their neighborhood the kind of place they want to live in. This does not mean that they must foreswear help from outside agencies or the infusion of outside resources (such as funded local projects), but that the project and the encompassing community-building process are primarily an internal process involving as many residents as possible to avoid the development of a local "oligarchy."

3.   They are assets based. The shift is away from focusing on problem solving or even meeting needs to the development and employment of the residents' individual and collective strengths—knowledge, skills, tools, and resources—to evolve the kind of community that they want, and on their own terms. The basic idea here reflects one of the essential strengths principles: All communities, no matter how distressed, have an array, often untapped, of human, associational, natural, built, and institutional resources. These are to be used in the building of community—symbolically, practically, and experientially.

4.   They are comprehensive and vision based. These community-building efforts may begin with an accounting of the assets and resources of a community and then employing them on one or two doable but visible and important projects. But from there, as the vision of the community is articulated, more goals are enunciated and projects to meet those goals developed. More alliances within and without the community are nourished and the community is in motion. Part of the idea of comprehensiveness is to end the isolation from external institutions and organizations that these communities often suffer. Businesses, schools, social service and health agencies, law enforcement agencies, foundations, recreational institutions, etc. are seen as potential partners in helping the community achieve

their goals, but also in helping the institutions meet their needs. Businesses need customers and employees; law enforcement agencies need local help in fighting crime; schools need parental involvement. On the other hand, many residents need jobs, more avenues to opportunities, and more protections, and want to be players in the marketplace and local government.

5.   In keeping with the ideas about context and locality discussed earlier in the chapter, these initiatives are best tailored to discrete neighborhoods at the start where residents have some geographical proximity and identity, and daily face-to-face interactions. Thus the sinew of connection has already developed to some degree. However, it is conceivable that there may be umbrella institutions (also resident-driven) that bring together initiatives in various neighborhoods in terms of sharing ideas and resources.

6.   Finally, these community-building enterprises must be aware of the continuing racism and barriers to full citizenship that exist in many institutions and agencies. The idea of collaboration—bringing people and groups together—contains within it the dangers of racial, ethnic, class, and cultural conflict. But being mindful of these realities and always keeping the "eyes on the prize," the outcomes that may be mutually beneficial to all involved, may allow the parties to surmount those historic barriers and hoary conflicts. A part of this, too, is to recognize the strengths inherent in different cultures and groups—to celebrate those, to educate about them, to share differences, but most importantly to use them in moving toward the vision of community (Delgado, 2000; Kingsley et al., 1999; McKnight, 1995).

Programs That Work

Lisbeth Schorr (1997) in her continuing efforts to understand and detail the elements of programs for economically distressed individuals, families, and communities has gathered up what seem to be the characteristics of many programs that work. In particular, she has been interested in educational, family, and child welfare programs in communities where poverty, unemployment, and debilitating physical conditions abound.

Successful programs are almost always community based, nested in a neighborhood—of it, not just in it. They involve residents as well as professionals in common interests and pursuits, like helping our teenage mothers take care of their children or educating adolescents about sexuality and responsibility. Successful programs are adaptable, responsive to changing community conditions, and broadly conceived. They are in the game for the long haul, and will do what needs to be done—going way beyond professional and bureaucratic limitations. These are programs that think on their feet. Whatever needs to be done, they are willing to do it. While they acknowledge the real problems of individuals, families, and the whole community, they are as interested in, no, more interested in, the assets, strengths, and resources in the community. These are the tools for building programs that work. These programs thrive on the uncertainty but look to the possibility inherent in community-based work.

These programs think ecologically. They see children in the light of their families. But they see the families in the context of the community and the culture. Families that are sustained and supported in the raising of their children are essential to the developmental infrastructure of any community. And the reverse is true—strong communal ties and neighborhood institutions, and esprit, cultural tools, and rituals are the key to strong families. These programs involve the residents, young and old, the excluded and the influential, in significant, power-sharing ways. They are neither "rule-bound" nor "hidebound." "Successful programs are shaped to respond to the needs of local populations and to assure that local communities have a genuine sense of ownership. . . . These programs are both of the community and in the community" (Schorr, 1997, p. 7, 8).

The organizational culture (see the earlier discussion in this chapter of the health realization program) of these programs is one of health, energy, commitment, experimentation, innovation, collaboration, and excitement. Their mission is clear and based on a communal vision. The organization is committed to the vision, nurtured by common beliefs and values, but is flexible about the strategies that are required to achieve the mission. But the overriding value for the staff is competence, funded by the administrative assurance that they will have the tools, training, and resources to become competent and maintain that capacity.

Perhaps the most important aspect of successful programs is their dedication and ability to form trusting, mutual, credible, and respectful relationships with their clients and the community and its institutions. Staff will play many roles: confidant, advocate, counselor, partner, guide, and teacher. They will not be solely or even often guided by time-tested or shopworn theory, but are willing to act on their intuitions, their sense of what is needed, the urgency of the problem they face, and the clarity of their vision (Schön, 1987; Schorr, 1997).

CONCLUSION

I hope I have been able to convey the excitement of some of the developments in thinking about the relationship between community and individual resilience and putting them into practice. For our profession, these developments are affirmations of a noble and honorable legacy about which we may have become amnesic. The social work profession, over the years, has positioned itself to champion the cause of the underdog, the oppressed, and to envision and promote the idea of a world worth living in for all. We cannot do it alone, obviously, but we are becoming in danger of not doing it at all. The long traditions of community organizing and activism, of liberation theology, of radical confrontational politics, of Marxist transformation, have often looked askance at community development activities that do not address the sociopolitical sources of oppression. The approaches described here might seem to some to be engaged in selling out. But while we await the revelations of ultimate social metamorphosis, let us fortify ourselves and our communities to meet the daily struggles and challenges that life brings. John McKnight (1995) puts it this way:

Community is about the common life that is lived in such a way that the unique creativity of each person is a contribution to the other. . . . Our goal should be clear. We are seeking nothing less than a life surrounded by the richness and diversity of community. A collective life. A common life. An everyday life. A powerful life that gains its joy from the creativity and connectedness that come when we join in association to create an inclusive world. (p. 123)

When transformation comes, we will be ready to seize the moment. We would do well to be guided by the words of sixth-century Chinese philosopher Lao-tse.

If there is radiance in the soul, it will abound in the family.
If there is radiance in the family, it will be abundant in the community.
If there is radiance in the community, it will grow in the nation.
If there is radiance in the nation, the universe will flourish.

DISCUSSION QUESTIONS

1. How would you describe the relationship between the resilience of the individual and that of the community? Can you think of an example in which a community did or did not help promote the resilience or competence of an individual? What were the key factors?

2. Which of the exemplars of community development practice provides a model that you, as a social worker, would find most compatible with your values and methods? Why?

3. Even if you do not work in a community-building agency or organization, can you see how your agency might be able to employ some of these ideas or models to better serve the residents of the surrounding community?

4. To what extent do you think that social workers are obligated to understand the context of their clients' lives? What difference does that understanding make in your practice?

REFERENCES

Barker, R. G. (1978). *Habitats, environments, and human behavior.* San Francisco: Jossey-Bass.

Benard, B. (1991). *Fostering resiliency in kids: Protective factors in the family, school, and community.* San Francisco: Western Regional Center.

Benard, B. (1994, December). *Applications of resilience.* Paper presented at a National Institute on Drug Abuse conference on the role of resilience in drug abuse, alcohol abuse, and mental illness, Washington, DC.

Benard, B. (2004). *Resiliency: What We Have Learned.* San Francisco: WestEd.

Benson, P. (1997). *All kids are our kids.* San Francisco: Jossey-Bass.

Bratton, W. (with Knowlber, P.). (1998). *Turnaround: How America's top cop reversed the crime epidemic.* New York: Random House.

Crimmins, J. C. (1995). *The American promise: Adventures in grass-roots democracy.* San Francisco: KQED Publications.

Delgado, M. (2000). *Community social work practice in an urban context: The potential of a capacity-enhancement perspective.* New York: Oxford University Press.

Gladwell, M. (2000). *The tipping point. How little things can make a big difference.* Boston: Little, Brown.

Gutierrez, L., & Nurius, P. (Eds). (1994). *Education and research for empowerment practice.* Seattle: University of Washington School of Social Work: Center for Policy and Practice Research.

Hanna, M. G., & Robinson, B. (1994). *Strategies for community empowerment: Direct-action and transformative approaches to social change practice.* Lewiston, NY: EmText.

Harris, J. R. (1998). *The nurture assumption: Why children turn out the way they do.* New York: Free Press.

Health Realization Institute. (2000). *The understanding behind health realization: A principle based psychology.* Long Beach, CA: Author.

hooks, bell (2003). *Teaching community: A pedagogy of the oppressed.* New York: Routledge.

Kingsley, G. T., McNeeley, J. B., & Gibson, J. O. (1999). *Community building coming of age.* Baltimore: Development Training Institute

Kondrat, M. E. (1995). Concept, act, and interest in professional practice: Implications of an empowerment perspective. *Social Service Review, 69,* 405–428.

Kretzmann, J. P., & McKnight, J. L. (1993). *Building communities from the inside out.* Evanston, IL: Institute for Policy Research, Northwestern University.

Lee, J. A. B. (1994). *The empowerment approach to social work practice.* New York: Columbia University Press.

McGoldrick, M., & Carter, B. (1999). Self in context. In B. Carter & M. McGoldrick (Eds.). *The expanded family life cycle: Individual, family, and social perspectives.* (3rd ed.). Boston: Allyn & Bacon, pp. 27–46.

McKnight, J. L. (1995). *The careless society: Community and its counterfeits.* New York: Basic Books.

McKnight, J. L. (1997). A 21st-century map for healthy communities and families. *Families in Society, 78,* 117–127.

McLaughlin, M. (2000). *Community Counts.* New York: Public Education Network.

McLaughlin, M. W., Irby, M. A., & Langman, J. (1994). *Urban sanctuaries: Neighborhood organizations in the lives and futures of inner city youth.* San Francisco: Jossey-Bass.

McQuade, S., & Ehrenreich, J. H. (1997). Assessing clients strengths. *Families in Society, 78,* 201–212.

Mills, R. (1993). *The health realization model: A community empowerment primer.* Alhambra, CA: California School of Professional Psychology.

Mills, R. (1995). *Realizing mental health.* New York: Sulzburger & Graham.

Pransky, J. (1998). *Modello: A story of hope for the inner city and beyond.* Cabot, VT: NEHRI Publications.

Rapp, C. A. (1998). *The strengths model: Case management with people suffering from severe and persistent mental illness.* New York: Oxford University Press.

Saleebey, D. (2004). The power of place: Another look at the environment. *Families in Society, 85,* 1, 7–16.

Saleebey, D. (2001). *Human behavior and social environments: A biopsychosocial approach.* New York: Columbia University Press.

Schön, D. A. (1987). *Educating the reflective practitioner: Toward a new design for teaching and learning in the professions.* San Francisco: Jossey-Bass.

Schorr, L. B. (1997). *Common purpose: Strengthening families and neighborhoods to rebuild America.* New York: Anchor/Doubelday.

Shaffer, C. R., & Anundsen, K. (1993). *Creating community anywhere.* New York: Tarcher/Perigree.

Simon, B. (1994). *The empowerment tradition in American social work: A history.* New York: Columbia University Press.

Specht, H., & Courtney, M. (1994). *Unfaithful angels: How social work has abandoned its mission.* New York: Free Press.

Taylor, J. (1997). *Niches and practice: Extending the ecological perspective.* In D. Saleebey (Ed.). *The strengths perspective in social work practice* (pp. 217–227). New York: Longman.

Wakefield, J. C. (1996). Does social work need the eco-systems perspective? Parts I & II. *Social Service Review, 760,* 1–32, 183–213.

Walsh, F. (1998). *Strengthening family resilience.* New York: The Guilford Press.

Werner, E., & Smith, R. S. (1982). *Vulnerable but invincible.* New York: McGraw-Hill.

CHAPTER FOURTEEN

HONORING PHILOSOPHICAL TRADITIONS

The Strengths Model and the Social Environment

W. PATRICK SULLIVAN

CHARLES A. RAPP

It has been over fifteen years since the original statement on the strengths perspective appeared in the journal *Social Work*. Far from being warmly received, the article was originally rejected and finally appeared in the section "Briefly Stated" only due to ample amounts of persuasion and persistence shown by lead author Ann Weick. Since that time the strengths model has been implemented in a diverse array of practice arenas and has been the centerpiece of many books and articles. As would be expected, over time the original concepts inherent to the model have been modified or "reinvented" sometimes for the better, sometimes for the worse. It is our contention that one of the key principles of the strengths perspective, the pivotal role of the social environment in human and social development, is routinely abandoned in new iterations of the model and often ignored entirely in direct practice. This potential omission is of concern as a focus on the healthy and generative functions of the social environment and the importance of tapping such resources in the service of consumer goals has been historically viewed as a fundamental principle of the model and reflects important philosophical assumptions about human and social development.

To highlight the key role of the environment in human and social development is likely viewed by many social workers as self-evident. After all, as Saleebey (2004) notes, social work has "long claimed its niche as the space where traffic between the environment and individuals, families, and groups occurs" (p. 7). Accordingly, any reasonable model of human behavior must account for the influence of extra-individual forces on development. The reciprocal relationship between people and the environment, however construed, is a fundamental precept in social work and most professions concerned with the health and well-being of people. Yet, while general systems theory and ecological models may provide excellent templates for understanding human development and behavior, it is decidedly more difficult to use this knowledge to effect desired change (Thyer & Meyers, 1998; Wakefield, 1996).

Human development and growth is a transactional process that occurs within a social context. In the best of all circumstances young children are reared in environments where the meeting of basic needs is a guarantee, and families can secure the additional resources and supports necessary for a child to thrive. Successful adults are also adept in the art of acquiring and accessing resources central to improving their overall quality of life. However, each day social workers encounter individuals and families where this transactional process, this intersection if you will, is compromised. A wide range of converging forces seemingly conspire to restrict access to life-enhancing resources for those individuals Kretzmann and McKnight (1993) poignantly refer to as "strangers," those marginalized citizens who may be labeled, oppressed, segregated, or simply ignored. Sometimes the challenges people face *do* restrict their ability to interact effectively with the outside world. At the other end of the spectrum are cases where social resources are unjustly withheld from those facing unique challenges, the result of impulses as wide-ranging as fear and the desire to protect.

To deny access to genuine interaction and participation in community life, as well as the enriching resources the social environment can offer, thwarts both human and social development. In such cases individuals are sequestered in a world demarcated by physical and emotional barriers, both real and experienced, and have limited access to the tools necessary to escape their current predicaments. While we seem to be comfortable labeling and rejecting others who are different or require assistance, the net impact is a loss to society as a whole. As Kretzmann and McKnight (1993) have illustrated, the contributions of these very people, those viewed by some stakeholders as too damaged or too impaired to play a worthwhile role in the realization of the collective good, really do have talents and abilities that can be tapped to enhance community capacity.

In a similar vein, many of us have been trained to view the social environment with a jaundiced eye—yes, crime, drug abuse, domestic violence, and blight can be easily recognized. In some settings it is particularly difficult, and more time assuming to take another glance, to take an inventory of those aspects of the proximal social environment that promote growth, create opportunities, and offer basic building blocks for individuals and entire communities to reach their goals. Nonetheless, to be a successful strengths-based practitioner it is as important to complete an inventory of community assets as it is to engage in the strengths discovery process with individuals and families.

The strengths perspective offers a way to address, in a new and bold fashion the range of social issues and problems that currently vex us. In spite of our best efforts to date many of the most pressing problems faced by individuals, families, and the larger society appear to be intractable and this alone should implore us to strike out in new directions. This paper reaffirms a basic premise of the strengths model—that important gains are made in direct practice, community capacity, and public policy when efforts are extended to match and develop the inherent strengths of people *and* the social environment.

BASIC ASSUMPTIONS

The strengths perspective emerged from a series of case management pilot projects developed at the University of Kansas in the early 1980s all focused on people facing serious and persistent mental illnesses. Clearly what made these projects unique was the focus on consumer strengths, an unheard of proposition within the context of traditional mental healthcare at that point in history. In these early moments the term strengths-model had not yet been coined, indeed the name given to describe this effort was the Resource-Acquisition model—a designation that underscored the proposed centrality of community resources in the process of recovery from mental illness.

The Resource Acquisition model was predicated on two key assumptions that had guided innovative work in the field of child welfare. The first assumption asserts that behavior is a function, at least in part, of the resources available to people (Davidson & Rapp, 1976). While this may strike some as a peculiar notion, Saleebey (2002) observes:

> We often look inward or to the family to explain and understand behavior, but the immediate context—interpersonal, built, physical—is a powerful influence on how we feel, think, and act. So the environment—be it school, neighborhood, playground, and its people and structures—can be a powerful force in helping people to turn around their lives. (p. 230)

The second assumption, one that clearly links individual practice to social advocacy, is that our society values equal access to social resources (Davidson & Rapp, 1976). Here it is recognized that some families involved with the child welfare system, people facing serious mental illnesses, and others who can be deemed "strangers" often have difficulty accessing resources that should be available to them, and as a result professionals are often called upon to abet their efforts to obtain those social goods vital to their well-being.

Case management services cast in such terms had a familiar ring to veteran social workers regardless if they had served as front line caseworkers or in community organization roles. Here was an approach that honored time worn principles that evolved into more modern systems or ecological models of practice. However, in spite of the apparent similarities between existing practice theory and "good old-fashioned casework" it became apparent that an unbending focus on personal and environmental strengths required new methods and new tools to be sure, but also a new way of viewing problems and solutions.

The person-in-environment perspective, germane to social work practice recognizes the interdependence of people with the world around them. In daily life, contact with the environment nurtures, supports, protects, entertains, confuses and may threaten us. Accordingly, in direct practice it is essential for social workers to evaluate the impress of family, work, and the community at large on individual behavior and functioning. Yet, in conducting this assessment process there tends to be an overemphasis on the deficits or toxic elements in the social environment. While there are undoubtedly gaps and noxious elements present in the world around us, such a negative view of the social environment is not without its consequences. Kretzmann and McKnight (1993) have noted that the common analysis of community problems, often denoted as a needs assessment, can have an iatrogenic impact on community residents. While it cannot be disputed that neighborhoods and communities often face real concerns and real troubles, Kretzmann and McKnight (1993) remind us that this is only part of the total picture. The danger comes when residents begin to incorporate this negative view of their world, and draw inferences about themselves as a result:

> Once accepted as the whole truth about troubled neighborhoods, the "needs" map determines how problems are to be addressed, through deficiency-oriented policies and programs. Public, private and non-profit human services programs, often supported by university research and foundation funding, translate the programs into local activities that teach people the nature and extent of their problems, and the value of services as the answer to their problems. As a result, many lower income urban neighborhoods are now environments of service where behaviors are affected because residents come to believe that their well-being depends on being a client. They begin to see themselves as people with special needs that can only be met by outsiders. (p. 2)

By narrowing the focus to problems, threats, and gaps in the social environment our view of helping resources and the people we serve, as illustrated above, becomes unnecessarily constricted. The strengths model of social work practice offers an alternative conception of the people we often refer to as clients and their social environment. This perspective promotes matching the inherent strengths of individuals with naturally occurring resources in the social environment. Such naturally occurring resources are a source of strength in all social environments and available in all social environments. Recognizing, recruiting, and using these strengths can help maximize the potential of our clients and our community.

What is proposed here is a decidedly reciprocal process. Far too often the consumers social workers serve are viewed as burdens on the community—and it follows that when resources are made available to them this is viewed as a gift or charity. It is argued here that true social development occurs when those we serve are viewed as community assets, not as liabilities. Indeed recognizing the talents of those pushed to the margins is a vital first-step in the enhancement of community capacity.

> Each community boasts a unique combination of assets upon which to build its future. A thorough map of those assets would begin with an inventory of the gifts, skills, and capacities of the community's residents. Household by household, building by building, block by block, the capacity mapmakers will discover a vast and often surprising array of individual talents and productive skills, few of which are being mobilized for community-building purposes. This basic truth about the "gift-

edness" of every individual is particularly important to apply to people who find themselves marginalized by communities. It is essential to recognize the capacities, for example, of those who have been labeled mentally handicapped or disabled, or those who are marginalized because they are too old, or too young, or too poor. In a community whose assets are being fully recognized and mobilized, these people will be part of the action, not as clients or recipients of aid, but as full contributors to the community-building process. (Kretzmann & McKnight, 1993, p. 6)

ENVIRONMENT DEFINED

It is important to begin by considering the term environment, a concept that proves to be more elusive than it would appear. For some, the term quickly conjures up images of nature and the increasing concerns about the degradation and depletion of the earth's resources. For others, the built environment, particularly the condition of inner cities comes quickly to mind. Historically, social policies such as urban renewal were launched on an assumption that environmental conditions contributed to the pathological behavior of individuals and major social problems such as crime. In the area of mental health care, by illustration, there have been periods in the past and even today where environmental conditions have been seen to cause or provoke a persons' vulnerability for the expression of mental illness (Faris & Dunham, 1939; Torrey & Yolken, 1998). Furthermore, the potential power of environmental manipulation in treatment has influenced the physical design of psychiatric hospitals, and alterations in the treatment process inside the walls as reflected in past innovations such as the introduction of therapeutic communities and ward government.

Environment is defined in *Webster's New World Dictionary* (1979) as "all the conditions, circumstances, etc. surrounding, and affecting the development of, an organism." This definition indicates that environment cannot be understood monolithically—that in reality—all people function in a wide range of "environments" each day. Saleebey (2004) argues that "there is a sense of the environment that social work has, to a significant degree ignored—that is, the immediate, proximal, often small environment where people play out much of their lives" (p. 7). Consider those individuals considered socially adept. As a society we tend to admire people who can operate comfortably and with facility in a host of settings—from a rural bar to a boardroom of a Fortune 500 company. Some seem to have an almost innate knack to prosper socially, but it is more likely that they honed this skill through exposure and experience.

The developmental process described here is one that many people have experienced at various points in their life—and it is equally likely that most of us could find ourselves in social contexts for which we lack preparation. To illustrate, few of us have attended a State dinner, or visited the Pope or the Queen of England—hence, we would need instruction on proper protocols. However, despite the novelty of a given task, past experience and confidence can be drawn upon to navigate unfamiliar terrain. As we will explore later, many who seek social work services face isolation and social impoverishment, while others approach new situations with great anxiety and fear. Some may lack the basic experience that helps build the fund of knowledge that can be called upon to deal with novel situations and as a result a negative feedback cycle loop ensues that erodes a person's confidence, reinforces the disinclination to accept new challenges, and provides ammunition for others to shun them. In the final analysis people caught in this vicious cycle can slip into the world of "strangers" representing a personal and social loss.

The Social Niche

One useful framework that can be used to explore the transactional nature of human development is the concept of the social niche as devised by Taylor (1997). Taylor (1997), much like Thyer and associates (1998) argues that the ecological metaphors present in social work provide an important framework for thought and possibilities for action. Ecological models, Taylor (1997) observes, "draw attention to person-environment transactions . . . and it emphasizes holistic thinking and interactive process" (p.217). Human beings are social creatures, and as such the niche they occupy is a function of complex forces that go well beyond those needed for mere survival. Taylor's (1997) construct of "social niche" reflects this distinction and underscores the reality that humans:

> need social support, help in the construction of social norms and social skills, aid in setting socially meaningful goals, group feedback to establish and maintain consensus on social reality, and reciprocal ties of mutual aid. The variety and need for such social and intangible resources is uniquely human. (p.219)

If these social inputs are necessary for all humans to grow and develop they are critically important to many people who commonly use social work services. Consider those who face serious and persistent mental illness. Tragically, basic opportunities are lacking in the lives of many that face such daunting challenges. Social support networks shrink with each hospitalization leaving the individual and family to survive by their wits. Social rejection is omnipresent despite sustained efforts to enlighten the populace about the realities of mental illness and as a result many are relegated to special environments, notable in their differentiation from the world in which most adults reside, segregated spatially and emotionally from others. They suffer, in Taylor's (1997) words, from niche entrapment, becoming totally defined by their social category, in highly stigmatized environments with others of "their kind," and afforded few opportunities to obtain the feedback, skills, or opportunities to escape.

Figure 14.1 provides a theoretical representation of the factors that impact the nature of the social niche one occupies. While few people use the term niche in daily life, there are indications that we do think about our relationship with the surrounding environment with some regularity. For example, a job may be considered a "good fit," or a relationship gone astray is often deemed to be a poor "match." Similarly when we immediately feel comfortable in new surroundings it is deemed to "feel like home" or we simply note that we "feel at ease." Good fits or

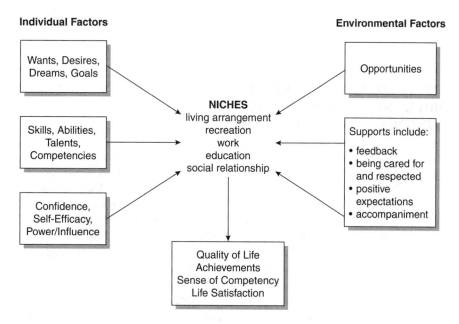

Individual Factors   **Environmental Factors**

Wants, Desires, Dreams, Goals

Opportunities

NICHES
living arrangement
recreation
work
education
social relationship

Skills, Abilities, Talents, Competencies

Supports include:
• feedback
• being cared for and respected
• positive expectations
• accompaniment

Confidence, Self-Efficacy, Power/Influence

Quality of Life
Achievements
Sense of Competency
Life Satisfaction

FIGURE 14.1   The Creation of Niches

matches require fewer emotional or physical adjustments, and when we land in an ideal setting or situation we tend to perform at our best, enjoy greater confidence, and feel protected and supported. When those blessed with resources and opportunities believe that key elements of their life are less than ideal they may, in everyday parlance, decide to "make a change." A new job may be secured, a better home purchased or the search may for a new mate initiated. Returning to Figure 14.1—the wants, confidence, skills, opportunities, resources, and social relations are all aligned for success.

Contrast this with the experience of many people who seek or are directed to seek social work services. In the worst scenario we find people who are homeless or live in settings that increase their chances of being victimized and exploited. Other consumers, like those who are violated physically and emotionally, may live in constant fear and even when helped they may be placed in unfamiliar surroundings that are frightening or isolating. The ability to make seemingly rational decisions and to plan for the future is compromised when faced with dire poverty. In the face of these troubling situations many consumers cannot "make a change." Not only are the resources needed to facilitate escape from entrapping niches lacking, but often others (e.g., professionals, families) assume they are helping by making choices for them. The desire of consumers to "feel at home" is not a criterion for placement in a congregate living facility, nor "a good match" the primary concern in the assignment of a roommate. It is suggested here that there are endemic aspects of the helping enterprise that impede recovery. Certainly, there are pragmatic considerations, primarily economic, that shape the structure and process of helping. However, there are also opportunities to forge new partnerships with the consumer and community that may prove to be both clinically and economically efficacious.

NICHE ENRICHMENT AND DEVELOPMENT: MOBILIZING PERSONAL AND ENVIRONMENTAL STRENGTHS

At the beginning of this essay it was noted that interest in the strengths model has exploded and this is particularly so in the area of clinical or therapeutic services. In the realm of direct practice there has been a great deal of work in such areas as designing assessment and interviewing tools, employing methods that enhance client motivation and interest in change, and in the process of goal and case planning that would be consistent with a strengths model. Returning to Figure 14.1, these efforts have largely focused on the left side of the equation—those attributes, attitudes, and behaviors on the part of individuals that can contribute to "niche" enrichment and personal development. It would stand to reason that competent professionals would be interested in discerning those attitudes and actions that can enhance the important work of consumers. In the immediate sections to follow some attention will be devoted to these concerns. However, to be true to the strengths model, attention must also be devoted to the right side of Figure 14.1, and here the attention shifts to methods and models concerned with the identification and acquisition of social resources consumers need to accomplish goals that they deem important to their life. Again examples from mental health practice will be used for illustration.

Professional-Consumer Relationships

We will begin this exploration with a discussion of one basic environmental interchange, but one vitally important to consumers—the helping relationship. When people are involved in professional services it is usually a difficult time in their life. Being under care reflects a sentiment held by self or others that, at the present, it is impossible for the individual to carry forth of their own volition. For many people the period is marked by one of the most profound of human emotions—despair. Despair is the feeling of being cast adrift in a world filled with the darkest of emotions and left without means of escape. A ubiquitous element in the recovery matrix is hope—a feeling at the polar opposite of despair. As an emotional state, hope reflects a bedrock belief in a better future and the inherent promise that cherished goals can be realized. First person accounts of the process of recovery confirm that hope is an indispensable ingredient for success:

> When one lives without hope, (when one has given up), the willingness to "do" is paralyzed as well (Deegan, 1988, p. 13).

> Hope is crucial to recovery, for our despair disables us more than our disease ever could (Leete, 1993, p. 122).

My mood changed—I was happy and hopeful once again (Fergeson, 1992, p. 29).

I find myself being a role model for other clients and am only a bit uncomfortable with this. For the first time, I begin to feel real hope (Grimmer, 1992, p. 28).

Success will never be realized if it cannot be imagined (Leete, 1993, p. 126).

Ideally, an encounter between a professional and a consumer should be hope provoking. So many consumers have faced a constant string of disappointments and have been dissuaded from goals that they have held dear. How might hope be re-activated? An exhaustive discussion of interpersonal practice will not be attempted instead a few basic themes will be introduced with the prospect that this short discussion will stimulate further inquiry into this essential phase of helping.

Virtually all methods of assessment in the helping professions focus on exploring the contours and textures of a person's problems, deficits, maladies, and pathology (Cowger, 1997). This process, in which client's have to recall their inadequacies, is far from hope-inducing and, worse still, can actually increase the sense of despair. In recent years, specialized assessments tools, geared to capture the competencies, goals, and dreams of consumers (Cowger, 1997; McQuaide & Ehrenreich, 1997; Rapp, 1998) have been developed to support strengths-based practice. Without question these assessments direct the attention of consumers (and practitioners) to different aspects of the consumer's life. It gives the consumer a chance to reveal what has gone well in their life, what they enjoy, and what they still hope to do. Much of the magic that can happen rests on the nature of the interaction between the client and professional, not the quality of the tool that is used.

Strengths assessments, or the process of strengths discovery, is an ongoing and fluid process that evolves as the relationship develops, more is learned, and comfort increases. The data that is gleaned is different from that generated from more traditional assessment processes—it involves an inventory of current and former activities, interests, goals, dreams, friends, favorite haunts and people, spiritual interests—all designed to paint a picture and tell a story—it is expansive not reductionist.

Facilitating Purpose

While hope may be the core ingredient to the helping process, the next step is perhaps the most crucial—translating this renewed optimism into action. Accordingly, a critical task for those in helping roles is to help facilitate the sense of purpose in the lives of consumers.

For those facing the most stringent of challenges, the intrinsic desire to attack each day has been vanquished. Consider this bleak portrait of mental illness: "I have nothing to live for, no drive but to just exist . . . Sometimes I sleep 12 to 14 hours because there's nothing else to do. No zest" (Stanley, 1992, p. 25). This respondents' observation is shared by many struggling through mental illnesses and other difficult life challenges, but the steps taken by many of these individuals to begin on the road back are particularly instructive.

And so I took my dreams off the back burner and claimed as my personal goals, understanding, writing and doing something to help others who were afflicted. Doing so was neither grandiose or magnanimous. It was survival (Keil, 1992, p. 6).

One short term goal was to further myself educationally, and I took buses to get to college (Reilly, 1992, p. 20).

You can live through any kind of a situation, if you find a reason for living through it. We survivors were daily living through impossible situations precisely by finding reasons for living (Fergerson, 1992, p. 30).

With Mark's death, I was snapped into a new awareness that resulted in my not only caring about others, but having a cause worth fighting for (Risser, 1992, p. 39).

Human services vary widely in the degree to which they facilitate or suppress purpose. In many environs, our programs and interventions are directed towards survival and maintenance. People are asked to adopt "client-hood" as their primary role, or passively except the recommendations of experts. Other programs create environments rich with opportunities to contribute and feel that there is purpose in what they do. Any review of the success of support groups, consumer directed programs, or vibrant community development activities underscores the importance of creating opportunities for people to serve in important and meaningful roles—oftentimes focused on helping others. In some situations, people are pressed into service because there are more important roles to be filled than people to fill them. Barker (1960) referred to such settings as undermanned, while more recently Rappaport, Reischl, and Zimmerman (1992), have used the gender neutral term underpopulated. Not surprisingly, good community developers are wise to harness the talents of residents and move them quickly to positions with significant responsibility and leadership functions.

Returning to Figure 14.1, a key force in niche enrichment comes from the expansion of individual talents and skills. Historically, the prime vehicles to help consumers in this life domain have been structured training programs or in treatment settings, skill building exercises, and groups. It is certain that these efforts have been helpful to many. On the downside, teaching people skills in a laboratory is similar to teaching history as a series of facts and dates without proper context. Education, strictly speaking, works better when there are chances to practice in real life. Here, people often must stretch, that is, assume unaccustomed responsibilities that force them to learn additional skills. In daily life, people often speak of "growing with the job." Such risk taking helps people gain a sense of mastery and prepares them to consider future challenges which will aid in their personal development.

This method of self-enrichment, and by extension, niche enlargement is only possible if people are afforded real opportunities and real-life settings. The deficit perspective, in contrast, pivots on the identification of the real or perceived inabilities of people. Once identified and labeled, these individual deficits can become insurmountable barriers to people prospering especially when coupled with an inflexible and inhospitable social milieu. Consider the central role of work—long noted as a key step in the recovery from mental illness. Traditional vocational programming found in many health programs, captured by the phrase "food, filth, and folding," does not mitigate this issue. For work to significantly contribute to recovery it must provide a connection to mainstream cultural activities and symbols. Traditional work programs, such as in-house services, or enclaves *may* be important steps towards recovery but to do so by building confidence and skills, and by providing structure and modeling opportunities. The argument here is that this should not routinely be considered an end or desired state.

Choose, get, and keep models of services, in the area or work, home, education, and leisure, are examples of strengths oriented models of service (Anthony & Blanch, 1988). By focusing on the necessary supports need for success, rather than the impediments to success created by mental illnesses or other disabilities, one by one, business by business, home by home, the niches of consumers are enlarged. Therefore, returning to Figure 14.1, key environmental factors, opportunities, and supports are linked.

THE MATCH GAME: ALIGNING INDIVIDUAL AND ENVIRONMENTAL STRENGTHS

Fostering a sense of hope and facilitating purpose are key ingredients in any successful professional helping relationship and should be desired outcomes at all phases of the process of care. It is vitally important that the early phases of helping, notably the assessment process stimulate this response in individuals and families. Faithfully executed, any strengths discovery process should meet this standard and there are several models of strengths-based assessment to chose from (see Cowger, 1997; Graybeal, 2001; McQuaide & Ehrenreich, 1997; Rapp, 1998).

Rapp (1998) has noted some key differences between strengths assessments and what might be tabbed the traditional or dominant model of assessment. One key difference is found in the end product. Where traditional assessments may help narrow down the specifics of a client's problem or malady—or even lead to a diagnosis—the strengths assessment is designed first and foremost to discover the client's wants, desires, dreams, and goals and does so from an ethnographic perspective. Hence, it is the consumer or family or community, not the professional who drives the process. Furthermore, the assessment considers a wide range of life domains, including work, leisure, social supports, health, and spirituality, and explores past, current, and aspirations specific to each area. The intent is to use this assessment, which is viewed as an ongoing process, to decipher a range of possible life goals that can be the focus of the helping relationship.

Intriguingly, the *process* of strengths discovery may be more valuable than the initial document that is generated. The ability of the practitioner to tease out the dreams, desires, and wishes of consumers is indispensable to success. From here the consumer/professional team explores past activities and interests in key life domains and begins an initial inventory of community resources that are essential for consumers to realize their goals and dreams.

As a dynamic tool, the strengths assessment should aid the delineation of consumer goals in key life domains (work, housing, health, leisure, etc.). These goals should be tailored to the specific needs of the clients ranging in degree of difficulty and level of specificity. At times additional supports are needed, like job coaches or mentors, but these services are still geared to buttress consumer strengths, and reflect an appreciation of the innate ability of all consumers to work.

Thus, by simple modifications in the environment a context is created for the individual to experience success. So at each successive step, beginning at the level of the one-to-one relationship, involvement with social agencies, to the first steps back into community, supports, feedback, and experience interact with the drive and will of consumers to succeed.

For those well versed in strengths-based helping the material above is familiar. For social workers, the humanistic aspect of strengths-based practice had immediate appeal. Shifting focus from the flawed to the healthy aspects of individuals and families also seemed to ring true with practice wisdom. However, truly operationalizing the key values of the strengths perspective is far more difficult than meets the eye. As Blundo (2001) has observed, staying true to the model requires "a real shift in orientation or basic viewpoint rather than merely adding a component" (p. 302). In terms of assessment, a component has been added when a section on clients strengths has been appended to the end of a traditional assessment form but little else changes, or when a practitioner devotes some attention to the goals and dreams of consumers but steadfastly believes that no progress can be made on such goals until the focal problem has been eradicated or reduced. This is traditional practice cloaked in strength's language. The pull to attend to problems and deficits is omnipresent and for many it is believed that more proactive work cannot proceed until such issues are dealt with. The strengths assessment represents an ongoing effort to build from a different base, and constantly searches for clues that can be used to tie a consumer's aspirations and goals to an environmental resource that can move the person towards greater health and satisfaction and to expand the avenue of available support that can be called upon in times of need.

There is little question that there are many facets of clinical social work practice that have been enhanced by the current interest in the strengths perspective. Nonetheless, the strengths model is also compromised, as a reviewing of the keystone assumptions would indicate, when practice focuses solely on the soul and psyche of the individual and ignores the resources and opportunities available in the social environment. Far too often social workers hold a narrow view of the range of resources available to people served—and in nearly any social agency anywhere in America and likely around the globe most lament the lack of such resources. The problem is that most practitioners, even those versed in the strengths model, engage in a deficits-based match game. Here the perceived problem or challenge a consumer faces is matched with the specialized resources designed to offset the identified condition. In simple terms, a client in need is routinely and automatically matched with a social service in spite of the reality that the demand for such services routinely outstrips the availability of these services. Some individuals clearly need these specialized services while others do not, but in essence social workers always face a log jam, one that can paralyze them and those they serve. Is there a way out?

The match game, played by strengths rules, is a far different process—one that may be more difficult and time consuming, but one that hopefully leads to better long term results. First, the strengths assessment, as noted above, should lead to a distinct and unique set of consumer goals, and to help realize these goals it is often necessary to access a wide range of normally occurring community resources. These resources are not specialized and designed to serve clients but rather the whole host of community offerings available to all citizens. Furthermore, these community resources may not be a business or an organization at all but a person or a park, a family or an Internet chat group. When resources are so conceived a world of possibilities is revealed—a world that expands well beyond a tattered and dog-eared resource book that rarely has time to rest on the bookshelf of a harried social worker. Helping clients gain access to community resources usually occurs on a case-by-case basis and that alone is why it is far easier to follow predictable routes and use tailor-made services. It is for this reason that the strengths discovery process should be broadened beyond the individual and family and must include an inventory of the possible resources in the immediate social environment with an emphasis on those that seem directly relevant to the clients' goals.

Mapping Community Assets

There was a time when there was a great debate about the role of social workers in clinical settings, but at this point in history there are far more professionals working directly with individuals and families than there are those serving as community organizers or in community development roles. When worlds are perceived to be distinct, there is little impetus to learn from the other, and opportunities to view problems and solutions from a different framework are lost. Classic community work is also undergoing a revolution of its own—one that involves moving away from a pervasive focus on community problems and pathology towards one that strives to build on community strengths and capacities. Naturally this movement requires a new set of conceptual tools and products. One shift involves a different manner of community assessment, from a traditional focus on community needs to a new perspective that is attentive to community assets.

Returning to Figure 14.1, it is illustrated that the ability to be successful involves the interaction of factors from both sides of the equation—the convergence of individual and environmental inputs. It is undeniably important to help clients rekindle interests and dreams, develop the skills and competencies that can help them realize their dreams, and in so doing increase their overall sense of competence and self-efficacy. While this is a good start, and it is the area where the most work has been done in strengths-based helping, more is needed. These same clients, in spite of the gains they make, still need, like all people, access to resources and opportunities to develop their skills, and along the way many need a full complement of formal and informal support to be successful. Behavior is contextual, and good strengths practice is concerned with the full continuum—from the heart, mind, and soul of the person to the world in which they live.

Kretzmann and McKnight's (1993) model of community development, particularly the method of identifying and mapping community assets, provides an important template for practitioners and programs who strive to assess strengths in the social environment. This process focuses on three key levels; the gifts of individuals, citizen's associations, and local institutions. As noted above, a central premise of this model is that those often overlooked—youth, older adults, and labeled people—should be viewed as assets to a community, not liabilities. Indeed, any strengths assessment should be designed to capture those abilities and interests that both serve the individual well in their future endeavors, and may prove to be a benefit to the community as well. Citizens' associations, the next level of community assets to inventory, certainly includes formal organizations and groups, but churches, various clubs, athletic programs, and cultural groups should not be ignored. Finally, local institutions, businesses, schools, and other education programs, as well as other social service programs located within the community must also be identified.

A review of the central tenants of assets-based community development mirrors, in a larger frame, guiding principles of strengths-based practice. First, community development "starts with what is present in the community, the capacities of its residents and workers, the associational and institutional base of the area—not what is absent or what is problematic, or what the community needs" (Kretzmann & McKnight, 1993, p.9). Second, the model is "internally focused" seeking solutions to problems first at the local level. Finally, the model is "relationship driven" and an important thrust of the work is to "build and rebuild the relationships between and among local residents, local associations and local institutions" (Kretzmann & McKnight, 1993, p. 9).

Strengths-based practice, like assets-based community development, focuses primarily on the strengths and abilities of people, not on their deficits or pathology. The relationship between professionals, clients, and the community is seen as an essential ingredient to success, and the importance of linking clients with natural community resources is also viewed as sound from both a clinical and fiscal perspective (Rapp, 1998).

The parallel between assets-based development and strengths-based practice underscores why these apparently disparate activities should be tightly coupled. Unfortunately, given the narrow manner in which some individual challenges are understood the relevance of any community level intervention is routinely overlooked. For example, it is undoubtedly true that serious and persistent mental illnesses are conditions impacted greatly by mysteries of the brain and body which we have yet to uncover. However, the process of recovery from these same illnesses cannot be left to science alone as the solutions to the real world problems people face as a result of illness—areas such as friendship, love, and meaningful work—are directly tied to the world around them. Homelessness, as another example, will not be solved solely by human service organizations and their staff but can only be impacted when bankers, business leaders, and real estate developers are sitting around the table as well.

To faithfully execute the strengths model means that social work practitioners and human service organizations cannot operate in an insular manner. If the problems and issues, goals, and dreams that consumers bring to a human service organization are directly impacted by the world that surrounds them helping strategies must be designed accordingly. It is here that Kretzmann and McKnight's (1993) work is relevant to the world of clinical practice. To conduct a community assets inventory involves the organization in community life, helps identify potential collaborators in their day-to-day business, and may create opportunities for the consumers they serve. When the barriers between the organization and the host community are seen as permeable both can prosper. A local family service agency can be seen as a vital source of support and information not just an enforcer of community standards. It can also prosper with residents taking key roles as outreach people, board members, etc. Community mental health centers can be viewed as a source of expertise that business and industry can depend on. Likewise, these same businesses can serve as a source of potential work opportunities for clients served by the agency.

In the best of all worlds human service organizations would join other interested parties in the process of mapping and exploiting community assets. This would underscore the fact that the organization is embedded and interested in community affairs and strives to learn from its constituents. The map itself becomes a dynamic resource guide of its own—a tool that practitioners can use to devise model interventions with consumers and be more receptive to the immediate needs of the community. In time, more work could even be devoted to health promotion and prevention.

Of course, there are a wide range of forces that tend to limit the proactive work that human service organizations can do—and get reimbursed for. So while the model offered above would be ideal, it is likely that the link between consumer and community will still be brokered case by case, situation by situation, by a social worker charged with assisting people in need. Regardless, almost all client goals involve finding and using a community resource. Everything from making friends, staying sober, to finding a job requires a fruitful exchange with the outside world. In some instances the barriers clients face either individually or collectively (i.e., those with mental illness, persons on parole) are robust—and it is here where practitioners are called upon to help.

Resource acquisition and advocacy have always been central themes in the strengths perspective. From the beginning these activities have been highlighted as important to bringing the model alive. For many of us taking advantage of the opportunities that surround us are second nature—sadly, for others the process is painfully difficult.

There are several key questions and activities that can guide the resource acquisition effort in a manner that addresses both individual and community need (Rapp, 1998). It is important to note that the process of matching consumer goals with resources is often a creative effort. Locating such resources is critical given the reality that most specialized helping resources are scarce, expensive, and in the final analysis may not forward the goals and dreams of consumers as adequately as those outside the human service world.

The first step is to consider what formal and informal resources exist to help a consumer to meet a stated goal. A simple goal, such as learning to cook nutritious meals could involve an in-house program, a community education course, formal university training, or finding a retired person in the community who would be willing to help. Some of these possible solutions will never be known if there hasn't been an effort to explore a wide range of nontraditional sources for the help people need.

Second it is crucial to consider how accessing a resource may benefit others, including those not affiliated with the program. Drawing from the example above it may be that some older adults would enjoy the companionship of others and offering assistance to a consumer who is learning to cook may also help fulfill their desire to continue to make a worthwhile contribution to the community. In this case the ability to cook is a talent or gift—one that could be shared with others. In this process the consumer is linked to the larger community, not a specialized world saturated with other clients and professionals. In specialized work programs for those with mental illness, notably supported employment, organizations often benefit by securing a cadre of eager, reliable, and committed workers and as a result it is a win-win situation for all parties concerned (Anthony & Blanch, 1988).

Hopefully, in this case-by-case work other stakeholders will begin to view marginalized citizens and the organizations that support them as true community assets. Getting to this point will likely take some time given the wide range of clientele social workers serve. Given this reality it is wise to assume that barriers will be encountered as consumers attempt to gain access to the resources they need. Here relationships must be established and maintained, staff must be seen as dependable and trustworthy, and necessary supports must be available to client's to help ensure their success. When working with consumers who are likely to raise community anxiety it is important to ascertain who the true gatekeepers to community resources are, and to work to develop a relationship with these same individuals, maintain the lines of communication, and seize every opportunity to recognize and reward those who have gone the extra mile accommodating the clients you serve. There are times when those we serve will be discriminated against on the basis of their challenge, and here a range of more active advocacy efforts, including invoking legal standards may be necessary (Rapp, 1998).

The quest is two-fold. First, social workers accept that their primary responsibility is to the consumer. With this in mind, social agencies must endeavor to put the consumer center stage and ensure that programs and policies are designed for the benefit of those they serve, not simply for their convenience. Here, consumer input is gathered on all fronts and this data is used to alter the day-by-day operations of the agency.

Social workers and human service agencies also have a responsibility to the communities that host them and an obligation to help shape those environments where people live, learn, work, and play, in a fashion that supports individual and collective welfare. Individual and social development is inextricably intertwined and when both are advanced individuals and communities prosper.

Community capacity has been defined as:

the interaction of human capital, organizational resources, and social capital exist-ing within a given community that can be leveraged to solve collective problems and improve or maintain the well-being of that community. It may operate through informal social processes and/or organized efforts by individuals, organi-zations, and social networks that exist among them and between them and the larger systems of which the community is a part. (Chaskin, Brown, Venkatesh, & Vidal, 2001, p. 7)

In essence, one of the impossible missions that social workers have accepted is to ensure that no one is ever left behind. At times it is seems like an isolated fight, one that is contested in a world of indifference. This work suggests that one fruitful strategy is to change the rule of engagement by linking the best of strengths-based practice with cutting edge models in community development with a single goal in mind—to enhance the capacity of individuals and society by recognizing and tapping the talents and gifts of marginalized citizens and to nour-ish the generative tendencies in the social environment.

DISCUSSION QUESTIONS

1. What does it mean to say that human development is a transactional process that occurs within a social context?

2. How would you describe a social niche?

3. What is the nature of the relationship between individuals and environments in the strengths perspective?

4. Part of a strengths approach to service is facilitating purpose in the lives of con-sumers. What does that mean? Can you give an example?

5. What is the match game?

REFERENCES

Anthony, W. & Blanch, A. (1988). Supported employment for persons who are psychiatrically disabled: An historical and conceptual perspective. *Psychosocial Rehabilitation Journal, 11*(2), 5–23.

Barker, R. G. (1960). Ecology and motivation. In M. R. Jones (Ed.), *Nebraska Symposium on Moti-vation*. Lincoln, NB: University of Nebraska Press.

Blundo, R. (2001). Learning strengths-based practice: Challenging our personal and professional frames. *Families in Society, 82*(3), 296–304.

Chaskin, R., Brown, P., Venkatesh, S., & Vidal, A. (2001). *Building community capacity*. New York: Aldine De Gruyter.

Cowger, C. (1997). Assessing client strengths: Assessing for client empowerment. In D. Saleebey (Ed.), *The strengths perspective in social work practice*, 2nd ed. (pp. 59–73). New York: Long-man.

Davidson, W. S., & Rapp, C. (1976). Child advocacy in the justice system. *Social Work, 21*(3), 225–232.

Deegan, P. E. (1988). Recovery: The lived experience of rehabilitation. *Psychosocial Rehabilitation Journal, 11*, 11–19.

Faris, R., & Dunham, H. W. (1939). *Mental Disorders in Urban Areas.* Chicago: University of Chicago Press.

Fergesen, D. (1992). In the company of heroes. *The Journal, 3*, 29.

Graybeal, C. (2001). Strengths-based social work assessment: Transforming the dominant paradigm. *Families in Society, 82*(3), 233–242.

Grimmer, D. (1992). The invisible illness. *The Journal, 3*, 27–28.

Keil, J. (1992). The mountain of my mental illness. *The Journal, 3* 5–6.

Kretzmann, J., & McKnight, J. (1993). *Building communities from the inside out: A path towards finding and mobilizing community assets.* Evanston, IL: Center for Urban Affairs and Policy Research. Neighborhood Innovations Network. Northwestern University.

Leete, E. (1993). The interpersonal environment: A consumer's personal recollection. In A. B. Hatfield & H. P. Lefley (Eds.), *Surviving mental illness.* New York: Guilford Press, (pp. 114–128).

McQuaide, S., & Ehrenreich, J. H. (1997). Assessing client strengths. *Families in Society, 78*(2), 201–212.

Rapp, C. (1998). *The strengths model.* New York: Oxford University Press.

Rappaport, J., Reischl, T., & Zimmerman, M. (1992). Mutual help mechanisms in the empowerment of former mental patients. In D. Saleebey (Ed.). *The strengths perspective in social work practice.* (pp. 84–97). New York: Longman.

Reilly, S. (1992). Breaking loose. *The Journal, 3*, 20.

Risser, P. A. (1992). An empowering journey. *The Journal, 3*, 38–39.

Roach, J. (1993). Clinical case management with severely mentally ill adults. In M. Harris, & H. Bergman (Eds.), *Case management for mentally ill patients.* (pp.17–40). Langhorne, PA.: Harwood Academic Publishers.

Saleebey, D. (2002). Community development, group empowerment, and individual resilience. In D. Saleebey (Ed.). *The strengths perspective in social work practice*, 3rd ed. (pp. 228–246). New York: Longman.

Saleebey, D. (2004). "The power of place": Another look at the environment. *Families in Society, 85*(1), 7–16.

Stanley, R. (1992). Welcome to reality—Not a facsimile. *The Journal, 3*, 25–26.

Taylor, J. (1997). Niches and practice: Extending the ecological perspective. In D. Saleebey (Ed.). *The strengths perspective in social work practice*, 2nd ed. (pp. 217–227). New York: Longman.

Thyer, B., & Myers, L. (1998). Social learning theory: An empirically-based approach to understanding human behavior in the social environment. *Journal of Human Behavior in the Social Environment, 1*(1), 23–32.

Torrey, E. F., & Yolken, R. (1998). Is household crowding a risk factor for schizophrenia and bipolar disorder? *Schizophrenia Bulletin, 24*(3), 321–324.

Wakefield, J. (1996). Does social work need the eco-systems perspective? Part 1. Is the perspective clinically useful? *Social Service Review, 70*(1), 1–32.

■ ■ ■ ■ ■

CHAPTER FIFTEEN

THE STRENGTHS PERSPECTIVE
Possibilities and Problems

DENNIS SALEEBEY

Focusing and building on client strengths is not simply a counterweight to the prevalence of the deficit model. It is an imperative of the several values that govern our work and the operations of a democratic, just, and pluralistic society including distributive justice, equality, respect for the dignity of the individual, inclusiveness and diversity, and the search for maximum autonomy within maximum community. There has been some criticism of the strengths perspective that turns on its blithe ignoring of the realities of structural poverty, institutional inequality, and the reality of oppression and discrimination.

John Longres (1997) makes the case that devotion to the strengths perspective may lead to the scrapping of those sociological and political ideas (e.g., Marxism, symbolic interactionism, and functionalism) that give an invaluable slant on the withering realities of oppression, alienation, and anomie. This is a serious criticism, if true. I do not think that there is anything in the strengths approach that requires ignoring the viewpoints and insights of any number of theories. I do think, however, that many of those theories have been misused to only illuminate the nether regions of the human condition, something that is not necessarily inherent in their character. Those theories are also formed around essential values. Some are founded on the belief in the altruistic and valorous core of the human condition and human nature. Others are funded by the belief that human nature is self-interested and acquisitive. Some are driven by the essential value of libertarianism (the highest value is individual rights), others by communitarian spirit (the highest value is interdependence). Some focus on human nature as basically economic, often political; others focus on human nature as grounded in the commons—the shared possibilities that only come forth in interaction, each person with the other (O'Toole, 1995). The point? That all theories have an inclination or two that prepares the ground for their evolution and that theories are often conflicted about the basic qualities of human nature and the human condition. The strengths perspective, not as grand as a theory, nor as evolved, by any means, recognizes the fallibilities of people and the grinding problems that they face, but it is an attempt to restore, beyond rhetoric, some balance to the understanding of the human condition such that we recognize and honor the strengths and capacities of people as well as their afflictions and agonies.

In a sense, everything depends on the vitality and fairness of the developmental and social infrastructures of the community and state. In Walzer's (1983) view, justice and equality do not call for the elimination of differences, but the elimination of certain kinds of differences—those defined or created by people in power that are the bedrock of their domination of fellow citizens, whether the differences are couched in the language of race, class, gender, sexual orientation, or religious belief. In his words:

> It's not the fact that there are rich and poor that generates egalitarian struggle but the fact that the rich grind the faces of the poor. It's always what one group with power does to another group—whether in the name of health, safety or security—it makes no difference. The aim, ultimately, of the fight for equality is always the elimination of subordination . . . no more toadying, scraping and bowing, fearful trembling. (p. xiii)

For us, the message is that some models and institutions of helping throughout the years have become pillars of this kind of inequality. They have evolved into means of domination through identity stripping, culture killing, status degradation, base rhetoric, and/or sequestering. We dominate, sometimes benignly with a velvet glove, and we may do it in the name of good, welfare, service, helping, or therapy. What we have finally done, *by emphasizing and assigning social status to a person's deficiencies, differences, and defects is to rob them of some of their inherent powers and motivations.* Or at the least we steal from them the opportunities, the courage, and the audacity to use those powers. In a sense, in the name of helping sometimes we have impoverished, not empowered. There have been times in the history of mental health, child welfare, poverty programs, practices, and policy when the focus has been almost exclusively on what's wrong with individuals who come under the glare of the profession and/or institution. Froma Walsh (1998) an experienced family practitioner, researcher, and educator, writes this about the mental health and, by implication, family fields of practice:

> In the field of mental health, most clinical theory, training, practice, and research have been overwhelmingly deficit-focused, implicating the family in the cause or maintenance of nearly all problems in individual functioning. Under early psychoanalytic assumptions of destructive maternal bonds, the family came to be seen as a noxious influence. Even the early family systems formulations focused on dysfunctional family processes well into the mid-1980s. More recently, popular movements for so-called "survivors" or "adult children of dysfunctional families" have spared almost no family from accusations of failure and blame . . . .With the clinical field so steeped in pathology, the intense scrutiny of family deficits and blindness to family strengths led me to suggest, only half-jokingly, that a "normal" family could be defined as one that has not yet been clinically assessed. (p. 15)

All of our knowledge (theories, principles) and all of our technical orientations must be examined, "critiqued, challenged, or corroborated in the light of their relationships to power and interest" (Kondrat, 1995, p. 417). Whether we discover that we are serving corporate interests, malign political claims, or benighted professional frameworks, if they, in any way, obfuscate or distort local knowledge, ignore and suppress personal and communal strengths and powers (cognitive, moral, behavioral, political), then we, too, have committed a root act of oppression.

Whatever else it is, social justice is understood only in terms of domination—domination of the distribution of social goods, those resources essential for survival, growth and development, transformation, simple security and safety. Welfare, communal support and connection, commodities, goods, health, education, recreation, shelter, all underwrite identity as well as personal resourcefulness and strength—the tools for becoming as human and competent as possible. A more just and equitable distribution system is at the heart of the development and expression of individual and collective powers and capacities. As social workers, we confront and promote the idea of strengths at two very different levels—policy (philosophy) and practice (principles)—but they always meet in the lives of our clients.

In the 1960s, we talked of "power to the people." That apothegm had many different meanings. Not the least of these was that a government or social movement must dedicate itself to returning social, economic, material, and political goods to the people who had been systematically denied them. The idea of returning power to ordinary and oppressed citizens alike raised nettlesome questions. What, in fact, do people need? What are citizens entitled to? Whose claims to scarce social goods shall prevail? How shall these goods be distributed? When the ardor of the 1960s was stanched in the mid-1970s, these questions had not been answered. Today, collectively, we seem no closer to answers.

In the 1980s, the New Federalism—Reaganomics, for some—made the idea that these social resources could be disbursed through the devices of the marketplace exceedingly attractive. But the marketplace, at best, can provide only limited resources, often on quite a selective and preemptive basis. And, it should be obvious to anyone who shops, trades, sells, or invests, that the marketplace is no venue for the pursuit of justice, equity, or recompense. Unless it might sell beans, philosophic assertions about fertilizing the roots of democracy seem frightfully out of place in the private, for-profit sector of the economy. One would think, however, judging by all the books, talk shows, workshops, infomercials available that the marketplace distribution of social and psychological capital has been a tremendous success. I think, rather, that this procession of pop-psych, pop-soc nostrums indicates that we have failed through conventional socializing institutions to help many individuals develop a sense of autonomy, personal mastery, or communal connection and failed to assist neighborhoods, communities, and cultures to retain their sense of value and distinctiveness.

As we lurched toward the millennium in the 1990s, the impetus for slicing the traditional ties between government and vulnerable people, between workers and corporations gained momentum. The welfare reforms of 1996 (the Personal Responsibility and Work Opportunity Act), all gussied up in the language of familial responsibility and participation in the workplace, still leave almost 14 million children poor. And while officials chortle at the success of getting people on welfare back to work, they ignore some obvious facts. First, most people (usually women and their children) used welfare as it was intended: as a temporary socioeconomic respite when work was not available. Roughly 70 percent of all AFDC recipients fell into this category. The other 30 percent had much more tenuous ties to the workplace because of lack of skills, personal difficulties, searing intergenerational poverty, mental and physical illness. Even given that, the total time spent on AFDC by all who ever received it is 6 years. Second, it is unlikely at this point that welfare reform will touch the dire circumstances, the problematic motivation, the dearth of ways into the opportunity structure of the latter group. The other 70 percent will do as they have done in the past (Albelda & Folbre, 1996; Edelman, 1997). This is not to say that AFDC was a smashing success. But it is to say that the values that originally inspired it were closer relatives of the considerations and necessities of social justice. Finally, the debate that led to these changes turned on old stereotypes of the poor; ignored many of the structural foundations of enduring poverty; smelled more than a little bit of racism; and ignored the fact that a dead-end job with few or no benefits, or a transient one, is worse in some ways than welfare, in that it does not assure, to as great a degree, the health and security of the children and other dependents involved. Since 2000 these trends have continued and widened.

We have argued in this book for a subtle change in the basic equation between equality, justice, community, and autonomy and asserted that there is power in the people and their environments. No matter how subordinated, marginalized, and oppressed individuals and communities may appear, people, individually and collectively, can find nourishment for their hopes and dreams, tools for their realization somewhere. These tools may be damaged, hidden, or out of circulation, but, whatever their condition, they are there awaiting discovery and/or expression. When we talk of building on client strengths, of respecting people's accounts of their lives, of regard and respect for a people's culture, we are, in a sense, giving testimony that, in spite of injustice and inequity, people do have prospects. People do show a kind of resilience and vitality that, even though it may lie dormant or assume other guises, is inward. In some ways, the work of the strengths perspective is a modest form of locality justice: aligning people with their own resources and the assets of the neighborhood or community. In the end, this work is about citizenship: helping individuals, families, and communities develop a portfolio of competencies and resources that more fully allow them to enact the duties and receive the rights of full citizenship. The quest for social resources and justice should never end, but we do not have to wait for the Godot of ultimate justice to do this work well.

QUESTIONS AND CAUTIONS ABOUT THE STRENGTHS PERSPECTIVE

Those of us who have been involved in practice, education, research, and training using the strengths perspective have encountered a number of concerns expressed by practitioners and students. I will present these in the form of questions.

Isn't the strengths perspective just positive thinking in another guise? The United States has a long and honored tradition of positive thinking that even today is alive and well. From Mary Baker Eddy to Norman Vincent Peale to Anthony Robbins, our society has enjoyed an array of positive thinkers purveying their own nostrums and panaceas on television, in books, in workshops, from the pulpit, and through other media. My view is that the strengths perspective is not the mindless recitation of uplifting mantras or the idea that relief and surcease from pain and trauma is just a meditation or glib reframing away. Rather, it is the hard work of helping clients and communities build something of lasting value from the social wealth and human capital within and around them. There is little else from which to create possibility and prospects where none may have existed before.

Your expertise as a professional social worker is obviously one of the resources to be used, but by itself professional cunning and craft is not enough; social services are not enough. We must help find, summon, and employ the resources of the client or community. But people, especially people living against the persistent rush of dire circumstance, are not prone to think of themselves and their world in terms of strengths or as having emerged from scarring events with something useful or redeeming. In addition, if they also happen to be or have been clients of the health, mental health, or welfare systems, they may have been indoctrinated in the ideology of weakness, problems, and deficiencies. They are not easily dissuaded from using these ritual symbols to understand themselves and their situation. The strengths perspective requires us, as well, to fashion collaborative, appreciative client relationships that we have been taught are the basis for effective, principled work with clients. Establishing such relationships obliges us to a strict and accurate accounting of client assets. Finding these and utilizing them compels arduous and careful work.

Aren't you ignoring the real problems and difficulties that people have especially when they are at the point of seeking help? In a recent sly polemic about the strengths perspective, an approach suspect because it pays no attention to problems and is ignorant of the capacity-building history of social work, McMillen, Morris, and Sherraden (2004)[1] write:

> In one corner, in black spandex, we can find the social worker therapist with a keen focus on his client's psychopathology, waving above him a copy of the American Psychiatric Associations, *Diagnostic and Statistical Manual of Mental Disorders*. In the other corner, with her white flowing robes, open arms, and olive branch in her teeth, stands the social work partner ready to work as an equal with her disempowered neighbors to create sustainable change. (p. 1)

Pretty funny stuff, the insinuation of sexism aside. What we seek is a balance, a balance that is hard to come by, given the realities of contemporary practice heavily influenced as it is by diagnostic injunctions of medicine and psychiatry (the National Institute of Mental Health has virtually assured that it will only fund research and projects that use the DSM as the standard for defining disorders to be

---

[1]This is from the prepublication galley proofs.

treated and investigated (outcome research)) (Duncan & Miller, 2000), the reimbursement styles of insurance companies and the sway of the pharmaceutical industry (see Chapter 1 for some of the problems of medication as treatment). We want to assure that the often overlooked capacities and resources, and resourcefulness of individuals, families, and communities are not disregarded but are part of a serious assessment and a vital framework for understanding and helping. In the recovery (from serious and debilitating mental illness) movement, you will hear narratives from all kinds of people from all walks of life that tell the story of having one's identity consumed by the label, schizophrenic, for example (Ridgeway, 1999). How, for many, maybe most people who suffer from this most serious mental disorder the possibility of recovery rides on the wings of hope for a better day—even if only better because one now has her own apartment, or has a real job.

Case management with people who have serious and persistent mental illness begins with these assertions: that these individuals have had and do suffer from a serious human condition that has biopsychosocial and spiritual components; that they have had or do have hallucinations or delusions; that they have probably experienced serious ruptures in the tempo and pace of their lives; that they may need medication and support for a lengthy period of time. But the strengths perspective is driven by the idea that each of these individuals has prospects and possibilities. The essential presumption is that they will recover and that there are a variety of internal and external resources still available to them. In a pilot study of the recovery of people with serious mental disorders, the 71 consumers who were interviewed identified several factors critical to recovery. The most important elements, in order, were the ability to have hope; developing trust in one's own thoughts and judgments; and enjoying the environment—basking in the warmth of the sun, listening to the sounds of the ocean, sitting in the shade of a tree. Simple pleasures and ready possibilities (Ralph, Lambric, & Steele, 1996).

If practitioners using a strengths framework do disregard the real problems that afflict clients and those around them and, thus, end up contributing to the damage done to people's lives, that is capricious, perhaps even reckless. There is nothing, however, in the strengths approach that mandates the discounting of the problems of life that people bring to us. In each of the chapters of this book, authors call for a responsible, balanced assessment and treatment plan, seeking to undo the too-often imbalanced deficit or problem assessments. All helpers should evaluate and come to a reckoning of the sources and remnants of individual and family troubles, pains, difficulties, and disorders. Often, this is where people begin, this is what they are compelled to relate, these are matters of the greatest urgency. There may well be the need for catharsis, for grieving and mourning, for the expression of rage or anxiety. We may also need to understand the barriers, both presumed and real, to the realization of hopes, dreams, and expectations. As Norman Cousins (1989) suggested, we shouldn't "deny the verdict" (diagnosis/assessment) but "defy the sentence" (prognosis/outcome).

Once having assessed the damage and the disappointment, we must ensure that the diagnosis—the assessment—does not become the cornerstone of an emergent identity. To avoid that possibility, we want to calculate how people have managed to survive in spite of their troubles, what they have drawn on in the face of misfortune or their own mistakes. We want to understand what part of their struggle has been useful to them. We want to know what they know, what they can do, and where they now want to go. Whatever else the symptoms that so bemuse us are, they are also a sign of the soul, of the struggle to be more fully alive, responsible, and involved (Moore, 1992). For social workers, the goal may not be the heroic cure, but the constancy of caring and connection and working collaboratively toward the improvement of day-to-day living, in spite of, or because of, symptoms. So what is of interest to us is how people have taken steps, summoned up resources, and coped. People are always working on their situations, even if just deciding for the moment to be resigned. As helpers, we must tap into that work, elucidate it, find and build on its promise. In some contexts, even resignation about or acceptance of one's condition may be a sign of strength.

It is well, too, to keep in mind that labels always bespeak the reality of an outsider, they collectivize and abstract real experience, and make the client's own experience and stories seem alien and contrived. We must use labels judiciously if at all, and with a profound respect for their distortions and limitations, and also with an equally profound respect for their potential to "mortify" individuals (Goffman, 1961), stripping them of their distinctive identity, and overwhelming them, through a variety of rituals and social processes, with their new and exotic identity. It may be useful, however, to think of a label as a designation given too quickly, without sufficient biopsychosocial assessment, and delivered through the efficacies and efficiencies of the power inequality between professional (and institution) and client.

Why is it that people do not look as though they have strengths? Why do they seem beaten, angry, depressed, and rebellious? Dominated people are often alienated people; they are separated from their inner resources, external supports, their own history and traditions. People struggling with cruel circumstance, the betrayal of their bodies in disease, or foundering in the larger social and economic world also find themselves isolated, alienated from their own resources and sense of self and place. One of the key effects of alienation is identification with the oppressor. Such identification may assume many forms but it is, regrettably, common. One of its forms is the assumption of the self-identifying terms of a diagnostic label: Or, in other words, to be what the oppressor says I am (Freire, 1973). Herb Kutchins and Stuart Kirk (1997) remind us that the mental health enterprise turns on the administration of people's minds and the bureaucratization of their health. Both depend on the power to define. The more specific the definition, as in DSM IV, now the DSM IV TR (Text Revision) (American Psychiatric Association, 2000), the more the authenticity of inner experience and perception, the more the availability of capacities becomes lost. Consider, Joel Kovel (1981) says, ADHD (Attention Deficit Hyperactivity Disorder)—a disorder manifested by the fact that some kids, usually male, move around too much, that is, at least too much for school authorities (this is not to deny that there is a *much smaller* group of youth who do seem to have complex neurobiological abnormalities underlying what some would label their hyperactivity). The child occupies the wrong kind of space in too little time and is thus considered to have a disease. Once the child is so defined, the system can control and administer. Once defined, the child also has the beginnings of a new identity so that some years down the road, he might define himself as a hyperactive adult.

Isn't it true that the strengths perspective simply reframes deficit and misery? Some people have claimed that what proponents of a strengths-based approach really do is simply reconceptualize the difficulties that clients have so that they are sanitized and less threatening to self and others. In this way, someone with paranoid schizophrenia is regarded as having an extraordinary and acute sensitivity to other's meanings and motives. Or a person gripped by addiction is attempting to rediscover that lost creativity within. Thus, clients and workers do not do the hard work of transformation, normalization, and amelioration, risking action and building bridges to a larger world. But, again, the strengths approach does honor the pains of what has been called schizophrenia. The approach's tenets, principles, and methods were forged in intense work with people thought to have severe and persistent mental illness. In every case, to the extent that they apply, the authenticity of symptoms, delusions and hallucinations, the neurochemical and structural abnormalities and the necessity of medication are acknowledged and become part of the work of constructing a world of possibility and opportunity for the individual and family. We are not in the business of talking people out of painful realities. Remember, *it is as wrong to deny the problem as it is to deny the possible!* But there is a kind of reframing to be done—to fashion an attitude, a vocabulary, a story about prospects and expectation, and a four-color glossy picture of the genuine individual lurking beneath the diagnostic label. This is work—creating access to communal resources so that they become the ticket to expanded choices and routes to change.

How does practice from a strengths perspective change what social workers do? If we are to believe advertisements for ourselves, maybe not much. But both loudly and implicitly, the chapters herein have decried the hegemony of the medical model, the caricature of the helper as sly and artful expert, as applied technologist, the idea that the world of the professional social worker travels a different orbit than the clients'. So, must we surrender our status as experts, our esoteric and practical knowledge and lore? While we might want to reexamine the notion of expert, especially the implicit paternalism nestled within it, we do have special knowledge and would be foolish to deny that. But, it might be very important to critically analyze and rethink the assumptions and the consequences of the use of our knowledge, as well as their cultural, racial, class, and gender distortions and biases. Many have commented on the attractive alternative to the usual construction of professional intervention developed by Donald Schön and Chris Argyris (Schön, 1983)—reflective practice (see discussion in Chapter 1). Opting for relevance rather than rigor, Schön's description of the reflective practitioner not only highlights the considerable artistry, intuition, and extemporaneousness of practice, but also a radically different contract between client and professional, very much in keeping with the strengths perspective.

A reflective contract finds the practitioner with obvious knowledge and skills to offer for service but also recognizes that the professional is not the only one in the contractual relationship with the capacity for enlightenment. The professional defines the work as a mutual quest in which the client is joined in a search for solutions, surcease, and success. Both parties to the contract have control: In a sense, they are independent but bound together. The professional asks the client to continually judge the work that is done and to revise its content and course as necessary. In any case, the core of the contract is in the establishment of an authentic connection to the client. In Schön's (1983) words,

> the reflective practitioner's relation with his [sic] client takes the form of a literally reflective conversation. Here the professional recognizes that his technical expertise is embedded in a context of meanings. He attributes to clients, as well as to himself, a capacity to mean, know, and plan. . . .He recognizes the obligation to make his own understandings accessible to his clients, which means he often needs to reflect anew on what he knows. (p. 295)

The nature of the contractual relationship changes in the direction of power equalization, mutual assessment, and evolving agreements. In a sense, the worker is the agent of the individual, family, or community. This may put the social worker in direct conflict with the agency, as discussed further in this section.

Perhaps the biggest change in practice will be a change in vision, the way in which we see and experience clients, even the most disreputable and frightening clients. Suspending skepticism, disbelief, and even our cynicism about clients and client groups will probably not be difficult for many social workers. We are of good heart, after all. But beyond that, to see in the internal and external environments of misery, pain, self-delusion, even self-destruction, the glimmer of potential, the glint of capacity, virtue, and hope asks of us a significant deepening of our consciousness of, and openness to, clients' worlds.

How can I work from a strengths orientation if my agency is riddled with the deficit model? We can hardly be about the business of empowering clients if we feel weak, powerless, defenseless, and alienated from our own work because of agency policies, philosophies, and attitudes toward clients. There is little doubt that in agencies where social control trumps the socialization of clients, deep pessimism about client motives exists. Negative expectations of clients hold thrall, work is defined in terms of controlling damage, and clients are defined in terms of degrees of manipulation and resistance, and the health of workers is compromised (Benard, 1994; Duncan, Hubble, & Miller, 1997). Burnout, turnover, dissatisfaction, and fatigue are too often the fruits of work conducted under these conditions. In my own experience, these conditions exist far more commonly than we think. They create an atmosphere polluted with negative or shrunken expectations of clients, and shrouded in a fog of anger, disappointment, and cynicism on the part of professionals.

If you work in such an agency, must you succumb to the blandishments and protective seductions of such a view of clients? We think not. There is always choice. For example, you can choose how you will regard your clients. You can take the time and make the effort to discover the resources within the client and in the environment. You can choose how you will interpret and use information about the client as well as deciding what information you will seek. Over the years, in a class on the biopsychosocial understanding of mental health and mental disorder, two suggestions from students stand out. In our state, as in many others, to be licensed as a social worker at the highest level, you must have had a course in psychopathology (understanding and making diagnoses using the DSM IV). The document itself is unremittingly negative and, as was observed before, turns each individual into a case. A student suggested that the five axes of assessment should be expanded to six. Axis VI would be a detailed accounting of the resources and strengths of the individual. She added that in every staffing you would be obligated to declare and demonstrate the positive attributes and environmental resources of the client—no matter how modest.

A second student once asked why there wasn't a diagnostic strengths manual—an attention-grabbing suggestion to say the least. With the suggestions of students, I embarked—somewhat tongue in cheek—on such an endeavor (Saleebey, 2001). This comes from the observation that it is difficult to employ a strengths perspective if you do not have a language or lexicon for doing so. One example: Under the section, 300.00 Estimable Personal Traits, we find 301.00 *Trustworthiness.*

> Criterion A.   For at least 6 months, nearly every day, the individual has exhibited at least three of the following:
>   1. Did what he or she promised
>   2. Kept at a task that had many snares and difficulties
>   3. Did not reveal a confidence
>   4. Stuck by a relative, friend, or colleague during a rough time
>   5. Did more than expected
>
> B.   This is not better explained by codependency or a pathological desire to please.
>
> C.   Such behavior must have improved the lives of other people.
>
> D.   Rule out the possibility of a self-seeking desire to cash in on these loyalties later.

How can I and why should I give up the disease or deficit model of the human condition when it is so acceptable and widespread in our culture, generally, and the culture of helping, in particular? Even though the devolution of health and mental health care toward managed care, the rise of third-party payments and vendorship, licensing, and the spread of private practice all play a part in the amplification of the disease model, it is, ultimately, an act of individual intention and purpose to put it in proper perspective. To do so you must examine it critically, examine the consequences of its exclusive employment in your work, and consider the advantages that the addition of a strengths-based approach would confer on your professional work and on the welfare of your clients. The disease model has reigned in many fields, in some since the 19th century (psychiatry, for example), but it has produced very little in the way of positive results. By almost any measure, the problems we oppose with the tools and dispositions of the disease/medical model remain rampant and poorly understood, except at the most general level (Peele, 1995). As Hillman and Ventura (1992) claim, in a different arena, "We've had one hundred years of psychotherapy and the world is getting worse!"

The disease framework has reproduced itself over and over again in many different contexts. In spite of notable failures in treating common human frailties and conditions, more and more behavior patterns, habits, life transitions, life dilemmas, and personal traits—from excessive shopping to extremist thought, from persistent sexual activity to adolescent turmoil—are regarded as illnesses. This is not to ignore some successes. The neurobiological understanding (and psychopharmacological treatment) of some major mental disorders; the gradual unraveling of the mystery of the genetic components (and their interactions with the environment) of temperament; and the neuropsychological bases of emotions, memory, cognitive states of all kinds, as well as those of mental disorders, all have been remarkable. It is also instructive to note that many interpersonal psychotherapies work. (Assay & Lambert, 1999; Strupp, 1999). Many of them are successful to the extent that they capitalize on the assets and resources of clients and their environments, and have the prospect of hope embedded in their philosophies and practices. It was Jerome Frank (1973) who first pointed out that people usually come to psychotherapists because they are demoralized. Often they are demoralized because they cannot get what they want or get to where they want to go. Restoring hope by dismantling the blockage to hope is a central part of effective psychotherapy and healing. But the impudence and truculence of the human condition, in all its astonishing variety, still remains.

The disease framework, whatever else it is, is a kind of cultural discourse or conversation. It is a vocabulary that has consequences for those who are designated or defined under its lexicon or those who employ it. Kenneth Gergen (1994), taking a social constructionist[2] view of the situation, comments on the power of the deficit discourse promoted in the mental health field: to encourage social hierarchies (doctor/expert knows best and has the power to act on that knowledge) heightens the erosion of community (we focus almost always on individuals and ignore the context of their suffering or struggles), and fosters what he calls "self-enfeeblement."

> Mental deficit terms . . . inform the recipient that the "problem" is not circumscribed or limited in time and space or to a particular domain of his or her life; it is fully general. He or she carries the deficit from one situation to another, and like a

[2]Roughly, social constructionism is an emerging point of view that emphasizes the role of interpretation, discourse, relationships, and language in understanding and making sense of human experience.

birthmark or a fingerprint, as the textbooks say, the deficit will inevitably manifest itself. In effect, once people understand their actions in terms of mental deficits, they are sensitized to the problematic potential of all their activities, and how they are infected or diminished. The weight of the "problem" now expands manyfold; it is as inescapable as their own shadow. (pp. 150–151)

Yes, but . . . many social workers and agencies claim that they already abide by a strengths regimen. A review of what their practices actually involve often reveals applications that stray from an orientation to client strengths. The question is, "How would you know if you or your agency was practicing from a strengths perspective?" To be able to answer this, as Charlie Rapp has commented, would move everyone along in the articulation and use of this perspective. Let us give it a try. First, the emotional atmosphere in the agency and your own emotional state would be more passionate and buoyant. The expectations of both clients and staff would be more heartening and hopeful, creating a more uplifting ambience in the agency. Second, clients and their families would be more actively involved in their own journey to a better life, but also in the agency, participating as real partners and collaborators in program, policy, and helping (e.g., mentorship) to the extent that they wished. Third, the language and ethos of the agency (and the records and archives) and everyone in it—clients included—would be abundant with terms, phrases, metaphors, and categories that directly refer to the resources and capacities of clients and communities, the range of possibilities in people's lives, individually and collectively, and the shades and facets of enriched and collaborative helping relationships. It would also reflect clients' native languages and discourse metiers. Fourth, the realization and expression of health and hopefulness would be intense and embracing. Finally, the level of expertise of social workers would be expansive and balanced as they work to understand the continuing interplay of problems and possibilities in people's lives. This is a minimal list but perhaps a beginning. So, look around the agency or organization where you work or have a field placement. What do you see? Feel?

Get real! There is evil in the world; people can do horrible things to each other and to innocent victims. Isn't that true? It would be naive and disingenuous to deny the reality of evil. Apart from any philosophical efforts to define what it is, there is little doubt that there are individuals (and groups) who commit acts that are beyond our capacity to understand, let alone accept (see Chapter 1). But writing off such individuals and to circumscribe certain behaviors as irredeemable is an individual moral decision that you must make. Such a decision is not always rendered with clarity or certainty. For example, would you agree with George Bernard Shaw that "[t]he greatest of our evils and the worst of our crimes is poverty"? Or would Sophocles' cry, "Anarchy, anarchy! Show me a greater evil!" be more compelling? Certainly the world has endured, on both small and large scales, horrendous destruction of both spirit and life itself. Everyday brings with it another disclosure of tyranny of the soul and body—the capture of the minds and bodies of others. But in terms of our work, there are at least three things to consider in answering this difficult question:

1. There may be genuinely evil people, beyond grace or redemption, but it is best not to make that assumption about any individual first, even if the person has beaten his spouse or if he has sold crack to school-age kids.
2. Even if we are to work with people whose actions are beyond our capacity to understand or accept, we must ask ourselves if they have useful skills and behaviors, even motivations and aspirations that can be tapped in the service of change to a less destructive way of life.
3. We also must ask if there are other more salutary and humane ways for these individuals to meet their needs or resolve their conflicts. We cannot automatically discount people without making a serious professional and moral accounting of the possibility for change and redemption.

Finally, in my experience when the judgment of clients as being beyond hope is made, it often relates more to the rendering of them as manipulative, threatening, or resistant within the treatment process.

In Erich Fromm's view, there is an uncanny commonality underneath those behaviors that destroy and demolish human spirit and those that uplift and assert it. Each individual or group bent on either the destruction or the affirmation of humankind does so from the requisite meeting of basic existential needs—for something to be devoted to, for roots, a place, and affective ties to others, and for a sense of coherence and integration, among others. These essential and compelling needs can be met through the blandishing of weapons, or the extension of the hand of friendship and care (1973).

Does the strengths model work? We can argue about what constitutes evidence but given our usual methodological appetites, both quantitative and qualitative research shows that the strengths perspective has a degree of power that would suggest its use with a variety of clients. The most current research summary compiled by Rapp (1998) does imply that the strengths model, when evaluated on its own or compared to other approaches, is efficacious in working with people with severe and persistent mental illness. If we examine various outcome measures—hospitalization rates, independence, health, symptoms, family burdens, achievement of goals, degree of social support among others—between and within studies, the strengths model consistently shows that it delivers results with populations that typically, over time, helped with more conventional methods, do not do as well on these measures.

It must be stated that modesty is appropriate here. Weick, Chamberlain, and Kreider reported in Chapter 6 the results of some of the earlier, nonexperimental studies of strengths-based case management. In another four experimental or quasi-experimental studies, statistically significant results were found for positive changes in independent living, symptoms, a variety of quality of life/social functioning outcomes when compared to standard practices (Macias, Farley, Jackson, & Kinney, 1997; Macias, Kinney, Farley, Jackson & Vos; Modricin, Rapp & Poertner, 1988; Stanard, 1999). A recent non-experimental study (Barry, Zeba, Blow & Valenstein, 2003) compared the outcome of veterans who received assertive community treatment (ACT) versus strengths-based models. Both groups reduced inpatient days and were "clinically improved" but people getting strengths-based case management (SBCM) services were significantly better in terms of symptoms. Rapp and Goscha (2004) compared the structural principles or active ingredients that make SBCM and ACT more effective than standard services. Twenty-two quasi- or experimental studies were reviewed and some of the ten structural principles that make ACT and SBCM more effective than standard services include: case managers delivering as much of the services as possible; natural community resources being the primary partners; and the combining of both individual and team case management as helpful. These results, however, do not include any of the studies reported in this volume. Likewise, it does not include the substantial research done from other but related vantage points, such as the health realization work reported in Chapter 13. Nor does it include the research done on the factors that make helping, regardless of school, theory, or perspective, efficacious. (See Chapter 5.) It does not include the newly emergent studies of the recovery process for people with serious mental illness. Much remains to be done. But if we add to these studies the reports of practitioners around the country, the testimony of clients, and the witness of our own experience (these are data, too), there is no compelling reason to shrink from the strengths approach to practice.

Whatever else it might be, however else it might be construed, the strengths perspective, like other perspectives, is a manner of thinking about the work you do. The test of it is between you and those with whom you work. Do they think the work has been relevant to their lives? Do they feel more adept and capable? Have they moved closer to the hopes, goals, and objectives that they set before you? Do they have more connections with people and organizations, formal and informal, where they find succor, a place, occupation, project, time well spent, or fun? Do they have more awareness and respect of the energy and aptitude that they have forged in the fires of anguish and trauma? Do they have the sense that you will be with them and for them as they try to construct a better life for themselves? Do they know that you trust them eventually to continue on a path without your help, guidance, and good will?

In the end, the superordinance of the disease model should be foresworn because it discourages two facets of good social work practice:

- searching the environment for forces that enhance or suppress human possibilities and life chances
- emphasizing client self-determination, responsibility, and possibility so cherished in the rhetoric of social work practice

An unthinking and monolithic devotion to the disease model undercuts, in the broadest and deepest way, the possibility of personal autonomy and community responsibility by sparing no human behavior from the intimation of disease. Even when we acknowledge the reality of an illness, we are not absolved from finding resources within that person, her environment, and her relationships, and assisting her in capitalizing on those in living beyond or even with the disease and improving the quality of her life.

OF PARADIGMS AND PROSPECTS:
CONVERGING LINES OF THOUGHT

In many different places and through many different means, it is claimed that Western culture, perhaps the world, is undergoing a fundamental paradigm shift. If we define a paradigm as a framework crafted of symbols, concepts, beliefs, cognitive structures, and cultural ethos so deeply embedded in our psyches that we hardly know of its presence, the crumbling of an existing paradigm and the rise of another can be a deeply disturbing phenomenon. While there is profound disagreement and even conflict about what the old paradigm is, and what it is being replaced with, some have seen the hegemony of the rational, linear, scientific worldview challenged by the rise of a perspective that is more interpretive—a paradigm that claims that, when it comes to the human condition and human nature, there are no singular, objectively wrought truths to be had. No perspective is final and maybe even no perspective is superior to another. All are deeply rooted in a particular social context, linguistic and discourse traditions (psychiatrists talk differently than car salespeople or nuclear physicists who talk differently and see a different world than school teachers, and so forth) and, thus, make sense therein, but might appear as sheer lunacy in another time and place.

There is comfort here for voices that have struggled too long to be heard, for cultures and peoples whose understanding of the world has been thrust aside or debased, for all those who have something to bring to the intellectual, moral, and spiritual marketplace. There is also encouragement here for other paths of knowing and being in the world. Others disagree with this perspectivalism. But, it does seem to many that "for better or worse, the world is in the midst of the torturous birth throes of a collective emergence of an entirely new structure of consciousness" (Wilber, 1995, p. 188). It may be that we are moving in the direction of some sort of integration of the spheres of life, seeing and expressing the intricate and still-evolving connections between the body, mind, and environment; the earth, cosmos, and spirit. None of this will occur without tremendous upheaval and resistance, and no one can be certain, if the older paradigm is shattering, what will appear in its place.

What has all this to do with the strengths perspective? In a modern way, the strengths perspective moves away from the disease paradigm that has dominated much of the professional world, the scientific and technological realms. That model, described in various ways throughout these chapters, assumes a different viewpoint on clients and our work with them than the strengths model does. So to begin to surrender it can be a wrenching experience—in a moderate fashion, as disruptive as larger, more cosmic shifts in consciousness. But it is nonetheless a shift in consciousness, a change in the way that we see our clients and regard our work. Fortunately, we are not alone in this transformation of our professional consciousness. In other disciplines and professions, fault lines have appeared, and new conceptual and practical structures are becoming visible. Some of these have been alluded to in the previous chapters. There are four that I want to briefly emphasize in this concluding chapter.

Resilience

In the fields of developmental psychology and developmental psychopathology in particular, it has become clear that children exposed to risk in their early years do not inevitably consummate their adult lives with psychopathology or sink into a morass of failure and disappointment. The field is not of one mind here, but after arising out of the presumption that there are specific and well-defined risks that children will face, and these will always end in some sort of developmental disaster, it now seems clear that most do not; most children surmount adversity and, while bearing scars, do better as adults than we might have predicted. Yes, some children do face trauma, institutional and interpersonal, so toxic that to emerge unscathed or relatively functional would be miraculous. But even here, there are miracles. We need to understand better what makes them happen. Consider alcoholism and children growing up in homes where alcohol abuse and its attendant profligacy on the part of one or both parents is a frequent phenomenon. The literature has it that these children are at serious and elevated risk for alcohol abuse as adults as well as other assorted personal struggles and failings. But most children of parents who have serious alcohol problems do not become alcoholic drinkers; many deliberately structure and restructure their lives to avoid such an eventuality. Identical twins show a discordance rate for alcoholic drinking of 40–50% (meaning that about half the time, when one twin has clearly documented drinking problems, the other twin *does not*). Many people who end up struggling with alcoholism have no family history of it at all. And our common assumption that *all* families where there is alcoholism are disorganized and dysfunctional could stand closer scrutiny.

So it is a mixed and sometimes bewildering picture that we have. There are reports of people who have recovered from alcoholism on their own. Not really on their own, as George Vaillant (1993) points out, but with some mix of the following: social supports, hope (again) and faith, luck, timing, social context, temperament, the incidence of protective factors in the environment (often the most important, as others have pointed out, is the presence of one person—a friend, spouse, peer, coach, etc., who cares and is steadfast in that attention). Scott Miller and Insoo Kim Berg (1995):

> However, surprising finding from our own work is that the solution to a person's alcohol problem need not look like or even be related to the problem. Indeed we have personally worked with and met hundreds of clients who solved their alcohol problems by doing things that are not related to in any direct fashion. These have included spending more time with the family, developing an exercise regimen finding a satisfying hobby, joining a social or religious group, changing friends, eating three good meals a day, and getting a job. (p. 19)

Vaillant (1993) reports a similar scenario for one of the subjects of the decades long Harvard Study of Adult Development, Robert Hope (a pseudonym). Unemployed and in the grip of alcoholism in his 20s, by the time he was in his 30s, he had stopped drinking. He attributed that to marriage to a strong and sympathetic spouse. But after their divorce some ten years later he continued, with difficulty, on his path to recovery. Those things that seemed to make a difference? Learning to more productively express his anger, developing the ability to elicit social supports, and becoming more honest and open about himself.

But one thing is clear from the research, not just on children growing up under these circumstances but other stressful and challenging ones as well: These children, when they become adults, most of the time ($\frac{1}{2}$–$\frac{2}{3}$) do not succumb to the particular risks and vulnerabilities that supposedly inhered in their childhood experience. That they suffered is clear, but it is not the issue here (Wolin & Wolin, 1995).

Any environment is a welter of demands, stresses, challenges, and opportunities, and these become fateful, given a complex array of other factors—genetic, constitutional, neurobiological, familial, spiritual, communal—for the development of strength, resilience, hardiness, or diminution of capacity. We are only now learning what factors lead to more hopeful outcomes. Clearly in almost every environment, no matter how trying, there lurk not only elements of risk, but protective and generative factors as well. These are people, resources, institutions, and contingencies that enhance the likelihood of rebound and recovery, or may even exponentially accelerate learning, development, and capacity. To learn what these elements of the body/mind/environment equation are, we have to go to the community, the family, and the individual and learn from them how transformation or resilience developed.

One of the more celebrated studies, mentioned previously, of the development of resilience in children as they grow into adulthood was the longitudinal research begun in Kaua'i, Hawaii, in 1955 by Emmy Werner and Ruth Smith (1992). In their earlier report (1982), they reported that 1 out of every 3 children who were evaluated by several measures to be at risk for adolescent and adult problems developed, as it turned out, into competent and confident youths at age 18. In their follow up, Werner and Smith (1992) found that a surprising number of the remaining two-thirds had become caring and efficacious adults at ages 32 and 40. A more specific and telling example: Only one-third of the children who had developed serious emotional and behavioral problems in adolescence had some continuing midlife problems. More surprising yet, by age 40 only 4 percent of the delinquent youths in the study had committed additional crimes (Werner, 1998). One of their central conclusions is that most human beings have self-righting tendencies and are able to effect a change in life trajectory over time, but this tendency must be supported by internal and external factors. One of the many factors that contributes to that is the presence of a steadfast, caring adult (or peer in a few cases). It need not be a parent nor need the relationship be an everyday affair. Other factors included a sense of faith and coherence of meaning, even during times of turmoil and trouble; schools that fostered and encouraged learning and the development of capacities and that had a buoyant, optimistic spirit in the classroom; teachers and mentors who instructed, guided, supported, and acted as protective buffers to the incredible stresses that some of these children faced. The children themselves often showed problem-solving abilities and a persistent curiosity.

But as discovered in Werner and Smith's study, over the past few years, elements of communities and neighborhoods have emerged as important in the balance among risk, protective, and generative factors. In those communities that seem to amplify individual and familial resilience, there is awareness, recognition, and use of the assets of most of the members of the community, through informal networks of individuals, families, and groups. Social networks of peers and intergenerational mentoring relationships provide succor, instruction, support, and engagement (Benson, 1997). These are "enabling niches" (Taylor, 1997), places where individuals become known for what they can do; where they are supported in becoming more adept and knowledgeable; where they can establish solid relationships within and outside the community; where they are, in fact, members and citizens in good standing. In communities that provide protection, generate growth, and minimize risk, there are many opportunities for participation in the moral and civic life of the community. In this way, the most abundant resources for the promotion of resilience, health, and self-righting are natural and available in most every community, to one degree or another. But if we do have programs designed to enhance capacities and the rebound from adversity, Lisbeth Schorr (1997) in her review of programs that work (see Chapter 13) to prevent poor or "rotten" developmental outcomes for children found they typically had seven qualities: 1.) they were comprehensive, flexible, and responsive to local needs and interests; 2.) they crossed traditional professional and bureaucratic boundaries; 3.) they saw the child in the context of the family; 4.) they saw the family in the context of the community; 5.) they had a long-term commitment to prevention; 6.) they were managed by competent and caring individuals; 7.) their services were coherent and easy to use.

There is also a relationship between health, adversity, and resilience. In a comprehensive review of studies that have documented how people may benefit from adversity, McMillen (1999) culled out and fashioned from the data the following factors. First, a difficult, even traumatic event, once faced, may lead to greater confidence that another challenge can be met, bringing with it an increase in the perceived efficacy of one's ability to handle adversity, making future stressful events seem less toxic. Second, as many people have discovered, a seriously adverse event may encourage a deep review of one's values, beliefs, priorities, commitments, relationships, and pastimes. Such changes may really enhance one's health and lifestyle. Third, when trouble surfaces, a person may discover unrealized sources of support from other people, as well as realizing their own vulnerability. Both of these may, in turn, lead to a revised and more positive, balanced view of other people. Finally, in the struggle to cope with an aversive and forbidding event, a person may find the seeds of a new or revised meaning. The questions, "Why me? Why now?" may lead to an authentic existential shift of gears.

So resilience is dependent on the interaction of factors at all levels, from biological to personal, to interpersonal, and environmental. Not only do children and adults learn about themselves and develop strengths as they confront challenge and adversity, if they are lucky they find and make connection with compatriots in the making of a better life, and they find themselves in a community where natural resources are available, no matter how sparse they might seem.

According to many resilience researchers, it turns out that resilience is a common facet of the human condition. Ann Masten (2001) argues that:

> What began as a quest to understand the extraordinary has revealed the power of the ordinary. Resilience does not come from rare and special qualities, but from the everyday magic of ordinary, normative human resources in the minds, brains, and bodies of children, in their families and relationships, and in their communities. (p. 9)

Health and Wellness

Health and wellness are artifacts of a complex, reticulate relationship between body, mind, and environment. Generally speaking, the body is built for health maintenance. Much of Western medicine is predicated on fighting illness when it occurs, often with substances that are, even when carefully employed, toxic (for example, cortisone). Natural or spontaneous healing, on the other hand, depends on the resources that lie immanent in the body, as well as psychological readiness and environmental encouragement. To realize health, to experience regeneration after trauma or disease, to achieve levels of functioning unimagined earlier, some of the following factors are essential and understood.

- People do have the innate capacity and wisdom for health and healthy living. The possibility of soundness and wholeness lie within (Mills, 1995; Pelletier, 2000; Weil, 1995).
- Positive beliefs about oneself and one's condition—hopefulness—seem indispensable for recovery and regeneration (Synder, 2000).
- Health-promoting positive emotions probably support, or elevate, the functioning of elements of the immune system because whatever else they are, they are hormonal events (Restak, 1995).
- The community plays an important role in health sustenance. The connections between people, important mutual projects, the mentoring and support, the common visions and hopes that occur in vibrant and vital communities are important to health and recovery. Hope always has a collective element (Snyder & Feldman, 2000).

The resilience and health and wellness literature run parallel in many regards. Both assert that individuals and communities have native capacities for restoration, rebound, and the maintenance of a high level of functioning. Both suggest that individuals are best served, from a health and competence standpoint, by creating belief and thinking around possibility and values, around accomplishment and renewal, rather than focusing on risk and disease processes. Both indicate that health and resilience are, in the end, communal projects—an effect of social connection, the pooling of collective vision, the provision of guidance, and the joy of belonging to an organic whole, no matter how small.

Story and Narrative/The Therapies of Meaning Creation

The constructionist view, in its many guises (see the discussion of perspectivalism earlier in this section), urges us to respect the importance of making meaning in all human affairs. Human beings build themselves into the world, not with their meager supply of instinct, but with the capacity to construct and construe a world from symbols, images, icons, language, and ultimately stories and narratives. While culture provides these building blocks, we impart, receive, and revise meanings largely through the telling of stories, the fashioning of narratives, and the creation of myths. Many are given by culture, some are authored by families, individuals, and subcultures. And there is always some tension between the culture and the self in this regard. But individuals and groups do tell their own stories. Stories serve many purposes. They are about dreams, discovery, redemption, trouble, courage, love, loss—every element of the human experience and condition. They instruct, chasten, guide, comfort, and surprise. They provide a sinew of connection between those who share them. They survive because they have human value and humane consequences. We are prepared by our own history as a species and as individuals to respond to the medium of stories. Good stories grounded in our experience can elevate us or put us firmly in the bed of familial, intimate, and cultural relationships in ways of our own making, not somebody else's. Children are socialized in large part by stories and narratives. For children today, however, the stories are not so much rooted in family and culture, neighborhood and community, but in the media and the marketplace. Mary Pipher (1996) says this:

> Now the adults who are telling stories [read: the media] do not know the kids who are listening, do not love them and will not be there to comfort them if they are confused and upset by their stories. Another problem is that the stories that are told are designed to raise profits, not children. Most of the stories children hear are mass-produced to induce them to want good things instead of good lives. . . . We need stories to connect us with each other, stories to heal the polarization that can overwhelm us all and stories to calm those who are frightened and who hate. These stories would offer us the possibility of reconciliation. (pp. 270–271)

Some single mothers in a public housing community were encouraged to relate their stories of survival under what were often siege conditions (O'Brien, 1995). Reluctant at first, they often reiterated the public's and media stories about people like themselves, and their initial attempts were not very flattering. But once they got into it, they all had distinctive, sometimes buried, stories to tell about survival. These stories were often about courage, wiles, faith, relationship, struggle, and uniqueness. These women were not saints; they were simply human beings who, facing the enormous difficulties of being poor, isolated, often unemployed, and raising children alone, had somehow managed to make it. If there was a persistent theme in these stories, it was resilience. And it was important for these women to share their stories. Most times, no one cared how they happened to see their worlds. Without encouragement to tell, some of their world was unconstructed, or not of their making. It was, they said, important for their children to hear these stories. These were in some ways cautionary tales admonishing the listener—children, too—on the dangers out there and how to avoid them. They were ennobling as well. Listeners were instructed on the managing of hardship and ordeals, and the mounting of internal and external resources in its face.

Groups who suffer under the domination of the larger culture and social institutions frequently do not have their stories told or heard in the wider world nor, regrettably, sometimes in their own world (Rosaldo, 1989). One of the human costs of being oppressed is having one's stories buried beneath the landslide of stereotype and ignorance. This means, then, that one of the genuine strengths of people(s) lies in the fabric of narrative and story in the culture and in the family. These are generative themes (Friere, 1996), and they capture the hopes and visions, the trials and tribulations, the strengths and virtues of a people, of a family. It is part of the work of liberation, renewal, and rebuilding to collaborate in the discovery, projection, and elaboration of these stories and accounts. A story told and appreciated is a person, family, or culture affirmed. While we understand that there is an innate capacity or urge toward health in the human body, we may not understand as well that in a story or narrative may be the health of a culture.

Solution-Focused Approaches

Coming from the work and philosophy of Steve de Shazer, the clinical work and writing of Insoo Kim Berg and Peter De Jong, and the recent work of Scott Miller, Mark Hubble, and Barry Duncan, the solution-focused approach to helping has gained ground, both in terms of its clinical use, but also in terms of increasing empirical support. Although it does not attend pointedly to strengths, it does have an implicit and abiding interest in the strengths of individuals and families (De Jong & Miller, 1995). And, as yet it has not, in my view, really concentrated on the resources and solutions in the environment. John Walter and Jane Peller (1992) say the basic question asked by this approach is "How do we construct solutions?" And such a question, they argue, harbors certain assumptions: there are solutions; there is more than one solution; solutions can be constructed; that therapists and clients do the constructing; that constructing means the solutions are invented or made up not discovered; and how this is done can be said and shown (Walter & Peller, 1992). From the outset, in solution-focused work, the eye is always on the goal, the end, and the solution and the thinking, imagining, motivating, and relating that takes place around solution development is independent of the processes that sustain problems. Furthermore, the emergence of solutions obscures and trumps the further development of problems.

Of great importance to the practitioners of this approach is this question: How do theories, methods, and practitioners actually contribute to the elaboration and intensification of the problems presented to them by clients? Duncan and others (1997) suggest the following: 1.) Certain conditions invite the expectancy of difficulty or impossibility (think of borderline personality disorder or urban ghetto youth) and "attribution creep"—the expansion of negative impressions based on the expectancy that things will not get better, probably worse. These impressions are hardy blooms and difficult to prune. 2.) Theories often have within them negative countertransference. That means that they create word pictures of groups of clients that are often pessimistic or invalidating (the psychodynamic view of schizophrenia, for example, or the at-risk view of certain groups of children and their neighborhoods). Likewise, they mute the theories and language of the individual and culture. 3.) Often, when solutions of one kind or another do not work or the problem turns out to be refractory, practitioners (parents, teachers, all of us sometimes) do more of the same. And as more of the same produces a hardening of the problem, we do even more of the same. Think of parents and their adolescent children. A midnight curfew on the weekend doesn't do it? How about an 11:00 P.M. curfew? Not effective? How about a 10:00 P.M curfew for the whole week? Or consider a psychiatrist with little time to see each patient. One antidepressant doesn't do it? How about another? And another? 4.) It is common to think of many individuals or families as unmotivated or treatment resistant if they do not respond to our blandishments. Sometimes we make things worse by overlooking or misunderstanding the client's motivation. The fact is that every client has some range of motivations. They just may be out of the purview of our approach and intent. It is also true that clients have their own theories about what is wrong. Duncan, Hubble, and Miller (1997) recount the work they did with 10-year-old Molly. Suffering from debilitating nightmares, sleeplessness, night terrors of various kinds, she was unable to sleep in her own room. Part of the work of solution-focused therapists is to find out what the individual thinks is the problem and how she or he would propose to fix it. What Molly offered was a way to rearrange her room so it was more defensible and comfortable. She barricaded her bed with pillows and stuffed animals against unwanted nightly visitors. This was a young girl who had been seen by four different professionals, was on imipramine for depression and anxiety, and was thought to be in the midst of a dysfunctional family. But the effecting of her solution brought immediate relief. This is also what Malcolm Gladwell (2000) calls a Band-Aid solution. These are ways out of predicaments and they are "inexpensive, convenient, and remarkably versatile solution[s] to an astonishing array of problems" (p. 256).

Positive Psychology

In recent years, some psychologists have been looking at the detrimental effects of always emphasizing what is wrong, what is missing, what is pathological, and the like and have begun to turn their gaze to the strengths and virtues of people. I must say here that psychology seems oblivious to the strengths approach in social work practice which has predated many of the "new" ideas of positive psychology. Martin E. P. Seligman, the putative founder of positive psychology has this to say, "I believe it is a common strategy among all competent psychologists to first identify and then help their patients build a large variety of strengths, rather than just deliver specific damage-healing substances" (pp. 6–7). Among the strengths he speaks of are: courage, rationality, optimism, honesty, perseverance, realism, capacity for pleasure, and others. Three of the major differences between this budding approach to psychological understanding and practice and the strengths approach in social work is that our profession recognizes that: 1.) almost anything, given circumstances and context can be a strength or asset; 2.) many strengths and resources are to be found in relationships, and in environments—social, physical and built, large, and intimate; and 3.) that strengths practice often involves helping people put together their personal assets and their environmental resources toward the building of a better life. One without the other makes for very difficult practice.

Clearly there is a convergence in these approaches of appreciations, perspectives, and points of view. While differences remain, the union of certain assumptions and standpoints is heartening to say the least.

CONCLUSION

The contributors to this volume—most of whom are practitioners as well as scholars and educators—hope that you find something of real value here that can be translated for use with the individuals, families, and communities that you serve. We all believe that the initiatory act in employing a strengths perspective is a commitment to its principles and underlying philosophy—a credo that, in many regards, is at serious odds with the approach we have variously labeled the deficit, problem, or pathology orientation. We firmly believe that once committed you will be surprised, even amazed, at the array of talents, skills, knowledge, and resources that you discover in your clients—even those whose prospects seem bleak. In a nutshell, that is, for us, the most convincing rationale for embracing a point of view that appreciates and fosters the powers within and around the individual. The authors also hope that you have found some tools to assist you in the promotion of the health, resilience, and narrative integrity of your clients. But, in the end, what will convince you to stay with this perspective is the spark that you see in people when they begin to discover, rediscover, and embellish their native endowments. That spark fuels the flame of hopeful and energetic, committed and competent social work.

DISCUSSION QUESTIONS

1. You have finished the book. Where do you stand now on the utility and relevance of the strengths perspective? How will you understand problems that people bring to you now?

2. Do you think that you can practice from a strengths perspective no matter what sort of organization or agency you work at?

3. If you do assume a strengths perspective what will you say to people who think you are being Pollyannaish?

4. What are the limits and weaknesses of the strengths perspective?

REFERENCES

Albelda, R., & Folbre, N. (1996). *The war on the poor: A defense manual.* New York: New Press.

American Psychiatric Association (2000). *Diagnostic and statistical manual of mental disorders IV TR.* Washington, DC: American Psychiatric Association.

Assay, T. P. & Lambert, M. J. (1999). The empirical case for the common factors in therapy: Quantitative findings. In M. A. Hubble, B. L. Duncan, & S. D. Miller (Eds.), *The heart and soul of change: What works in therapy.* Washington, DC: APA Press.

Barry, K. L., Zeber, J. E., Blow, F. C., & Valenstein, M. (2003). Effect of strengths model versus assertive community treatment model on participant outcomes and utilization: Two-year follow-up. *Psychiatric Rehabilitation Journal, 26,* 268–277.

Benard, B. (1994, December). *Applications of resilience.* Paper presented at a National Institute on Drug Abuse conference on the role of resilience in drug abuse, alcohol abuse, and mental illness, Washington, DC.

Benson, P. L. (1997). *All kids are our kids: What communities must do to raise caring and responsible children and adolescents.* San Francisco: Jossey-Bass.

Cousins, N. (1989). *Head first: The biology of hope.* New York: Dutton.

De Jong, P., & Miller, S. D. (1995). How to interview for client strengths. *Social Work, 40,* 729–736.

Duncan, B. L., Hubble, M. A., & Miller, S. D. (1997). *Psychotherapy with 'impossible' cases: The efficient treatment of psychotherapy veterans.* New York: Norton.

Duncan, B. L., & Miller, S. D. (2000). *The heroic client: Doing client-directed, outcome-informed therapy.* San Francisco: Jossey-Bass.

Edelman, P. (1997, January). The worst thing President Clinton has done. *Atlantic Monthly, 282,* 43–58.

Frank, J. D. (1973). *Persuasion and healing.* Baltimore: Johns Hopkins University Press.

Friere, P. (1973). *Pedagogy of the oppressed.* New York: Seabury.

Freire, P. (1996). *Pedagogy of hope.* New York: Seabury.

Fromm, E. (1973). *The anatomy of human destructiveness.* New York: Holt, Rinehart, & Winston.

Gergen, K. J. (1994). *Realities and relationships: Soundings in social construction.* Cambridge: Harvard University Press.

Gladwell, M. (2000). *The tipping point: How little things can make a big difference.* Boston: Little, Brown & Company.

Goffman, E. (1961). *Asylums.* New York: Doubleday/Anchor.

Hillman, J., & Ventura, M. (1992). *We've had one hundred years of psychotherapy and the world is getting worse.* San Francisco: HarperSanFrancisco.

Kondrat, M. E. (1995). Concept, act, and interest in professional practice: Implications of an empowerment perspective. *Social Service Review, 69,* 405–428.

Kovel, J. (1981). *The age of desire: Reflections of a radical psychoanalyst.* New York: Pantheon.

Kutchins, H., & Kirk, S. A. (1997). *Making us crazy: DSM: The psychiatric bible and the creation of mental disorders.* New York: Free Press.

Longres, J. (1997). Is it feasible to teach H2SE from a strengths perspective? No! In M. Bloom & W. C. Klein (Eds.), *Controversial issues in human behavior and the social environment.* Boston: Allyn & Bacon.

Macias, C., Farley, O. W., Jackson, R., & Kinney, R. (1997). Case management in the context of capitation financing: An evaluation of the strengths model. *Administration and Policy in Mental Health, 24,* 535–543.

Macias, C., Kinney, R., Farley, O. W., Jackson, R., & Vos, B. (1994). The role of case management within a community support system: Partnership with psychosocial rehabilitation. *Community Mental Health Journal, 30,* 323–339.

Masten A. (2001). Ordinary magic: Resilience processes in development. *American Psychologist, 56,* 227–238.

McMillen, J. C. (1999). Better for it: How people benefit from adversity. *Social Work, 44,* 455–468.

McMillen, J. C., Morris, L., & Sherraden, M. (2004). Ending social work's grudge match: Problems versus strengths. *Families in Society, 85,* 317–325.

Miller, S. D., & Berg, I. K. (1995). *The miracle method: A radically new approach to problem drinking.* New York: W. W. Norton & Co.

Mills, R. (1995). *Realizing mental health.* New York: Sulzburger & Graham.

Modricin, M., Rapp, C. A., & Poertner, J. (1988). The evaluation of case management services with the chronically mentally ill. *Evaluation and Program Planning,* 307–314.

Moore, T. (1992). *Care of the soul.* New York: HarperCollins.

Ornstein, R., & Sobel, D. (1989). *Healthy pleasures.* Reading, MA: Addison-Wesley.

O'Toole, J. (1995). Goods in common: Efficiency and community. In M. Adler (Ed.), *The great ideas today: 1995.* Chicago: Encyclopedia Britannica.

Pelletier, K. R. (2000). *The best alternative medicine: What works? What does not?* New York: Simon & Schuster.

Pipher, M. (1996). *The shelter of each other: Rebuilding our families.* New York: Ballantine Books.

Ralph, R. O., Lambric, T. M., & Steele, R. B. (1996, February). *Recovery issues in a consumer developed evaluation of the mental health system* (pp. 1–13). Paper presented at the 6th annual conference of *Mental Health Services Research and Evaluation Conference.* Arlington, VA.

Rapp, C. A. (1998). *The strengths model: Case management with people suffering from severe and persistent mental illness.* New York: Oxford University Press.

Rapp, C. A., & Goscha, R. (2004). The principles of effective case management of mental health services. *Psychiatric Rehabilitation Journal, 27,* 319–333.

Restak, R. M. (1995). *Brainscapes.* New York: Hyperion.

Ridgeway, P. (1999). Recovery. Lawrence, KS: School of Social Welfare, University of Kansas.

Rosaldo, R. (1989). *Culture and truth: The remaking of social analysis.* Boston: Beacon Press.

Schön, D. A. (1983). *The reflective practitioner.* New York: Basic Books.

Schorr, L. B. (1997). *Common purpose: Strengthening families and neighborhoods to rebuild America.* New York: Anchor/Doubleday.

Seligman, M. E. P. (2002). Positive psychology, positive prevention, and positive therapy. In C. R. Snyder & S. J. Lopez (Eds.), *Handbook of positive psychology.* New York: Oxford University Press.

Snyder, C. R. (2000). Hypothesis: There is hope. In C. R. Snyder (Ed.), *Handbook of hope: Theory, measures, and applications.* San Diego: Academic Press.

Snyder, C. R., & Feldman, D. B. (2000). Hope for the many: An empowering social agenda. In C. R. Snyder (Ed.), *Handbook of hope: Theory, measures, and applications.* San Diego: Academic Press.

Stanard, R. P. (1999). The effect of training in a Strengths model of case management on outcomes in a community mental health center. *Community Mental Health Journal, 35,* 169–179.

Strupp, H. H. (1999). Essential characteristics of helpful therapists. *Psychotherapy, 36,* 141–142.

Taylor, J. (1997). Poverty and niches: A systems view. In D. Saleebey (Ed.), *The strengths perspective in social work practice* (2nd. ed.). New York: Longman.

Vaillant, G. E. (1993). *The wisdom of the ego.* Cambridge, MA: Harvard University Press.

Walter, J. L., & Peller, J. E. (1992). *Becoming solution-focused in brief therapy.* New York: Brunner/Mazel.

Walzer, M. (1983). *Spheres of justice.* New York: Basic Books.

Walsh, F. (1998). *Strengthening family resilience.* New York: Guilford.

Weil, A. (1995). *Spontaneous healing.* New York: Knopf.

Werner, E. E. (1998). Resilience and the life-span perspective: What we have learned—so far. *Resiliency in Action, 3,* 1–8.

Werner, E. E., & Smith, R. S. (1982). *Vulnerable but invincible.* New York: McGraw-Hill.

Werner, E. E., & Smith, R. S. (1992). *Overcoming the odds.* Ithaca, NY: Cornell University Press.

Wilber, K. (1995). *Sex, ecology, and spirituality: The spirit of evolution.* Boston: Shambhala.

Wright, B., & Fletcher, B. (1982). Uncovering hidden resources: A challenge in assessment. *Professional Psychology, 13,* 229–235.

INDEX